William Smythe Babcock Mathews

How to understand music: a concise course in musical intelligence and taste

To which is added a Pronouncing dictionary and condensed encyclopedia of musical terms and information

William Smythe Babcock Mathews

How to understand music: a concise course in musical intelligence and taste

To which is added a Pronouncing dictionary and condensed encyclopedia of musical terms and information

ISBN/EAN: 9783337220501

Printed in Europe, USA, Canada, Australia, Japan

Cover: Foto ©Thomas Meinert / pixelio.de

More available books at **www.hansebooks.com**

OBJECT-LESSONS AND ESSAYS.

How to Understand Music:

A CONCISE COURSE IN

MUSICAL INTELLIGENCE AND TASTE.

TO WHICH IS ADDED A PRONOUNCING DICTIONARY AND CONDENSED ENCYCLOPEDIA OF MUSICAL TERMS AND INFORMATION.

By W. S. B. MATHEWS.

CHICAGO:
LYON & HEALY, PUBLISHERS.
1881.

COPYRIGHT, 1880, BY W. S. B. MATHEWS.

TO MY MOTHER,

WHOSE UNWEARYING CARE, INEXHAUSTIBLE PATIENCE, AND NEVER-FAILING
ENCOURAGEMENT, HOPE AND LOVE, HAVE MANY TIMES ENABLED
HER SON TO OVERCOME DIFFICULTIES OTHERWISE
INSURMOUNTABLE, THIS WORK IS DEDI-
CATED AS A FEEBLE TOKEN
OF GRATITUDE AND
AFFECTION,
BY
THE AUTHOR.

PREFACE.

As a text book, the present work covers a new ground. Its prime object is to lead the student to a consciousness of music as MUSIC, and not merely as playing, singing, or theory. It begins at the foundation of the matter; namely, with the observation of musical phraseology, *the art of hearing and following coherent musical discourse*. This occupies the first two parts, and covers a wide range of topics, as will be seen by reference to the table of contents, or the chapters themselves.

From that point the studies take a different turn, and lead to the perception of the inner something which gives music its life. That inner life of music is IMAGINATION and FEELING, and almost the entire remainder of the work is taken up with the study of music in relation to these, its Content. These studies, like those in the externals of music, begin simply, at the very line where form and content touch. In their progress they take in review the principal works of the classical and modern schools, as will be seen by reference to Parts III, V, VI, VII, and VIII. The object of all this study is two-fold; first, to develop in the pupil a consciousness of the inherent relation between music and feeling; and, second, to do this by means of master-works, which, of course, form the only complete and authoritative illustrations of this relation. In this way the musical perceptions are sharpened, the student is introduced to the best parts of musical literature, and thereby his taste and musical feeling are cultivated. It is easy to see, therefore, that this book occupies a ground not previously covered by a text book.

In *form*, the chapters are object-lessons. Such and such works, or parts of works, are supposed to be played or sung to the pupils, who observe in them such and such peculiarities. This form was selected because it is the true way of communicating this instruction, which can not be taken into the mind through the reason, but must be called up within the mind through a comparison of sense-impressions with each other, and these, again, with the feelings which they awaken. Music is one thing, and ideas about music another. It is the design of this study to *bring the pupils to music*; for doing this, the book marks out a plan, and furnishes along with it such ideas about music as will aid the process.

The *Illustrations*, or pieces to be played, cover a wide range, especially in the higher departments, and the objection has been made that they are too difficult. To this it can only be answered that the very essence and pith of music is here in consideration, and that the points in discussion could be adequately understood only by the help of these great works, wherein they are fully illustrated. It will be found possible, generally, to omit the most difficult works in cases where there is no one to play the parts of them here wanted. In other cases, where an entire lesson turns on difficult works, it is safe to conclude that if there is no one to play any part of them, there will be no one to understand them, and the lesson may be postponed.

In Part Fourth we have, in effect, an outline of *Esthetics*. The Author believes that the time has come when Art-appreciation, and especially Music, has much to gain by such an orientation of itself with reference to cardinal principles. These four chapters, naturally, address themselves to th mature and serious. They are not written for children, nor even for youth. A work like this addresses many adults, experienced teachers, and friends of music, on whom a discussion of this kind will not be lost. Doubtless the execution is crude, and in a subsequent edition will be improved; it is hoped that the expectation of this may serve to draw a veil of charity over any present imperfection.

The *Historical* sketches are merely sketches, and are in part reprinted by permission of Messrs. Biglow and Main, from the New York *Musical Gazette*. They may be made the basis of lectures or schoolroom talks, in connection with their Illustrations.

The *Dictionary*, at the close, affords a mass of readily accessible information, such as is in constant demand among students and teachers, but is not elsewhere to be found except in large Encyclopedias of many volumes. The preparation of it has involved much more labor and expense than was anticipated· but its value for ready reference is unmistakable.

CONTENTS.

PART FIRST.

LESSONS IN MUSICAL PHRASEOLOGY.

I. Thematic and Lyric.—II. Phrases and Periods.—III. Cadence.—IV. Modulation.—V. Counterpoint and the Contrapuntal Spirit.—VI. Variations.—VII. Rhythmic Pulsation and Measure.—VIII. Measure and Rhythmic Motion.—IX. Rhythm and Motivization.

PART SECOND.

LESSONS IN MUSICAL FORM.

X. Elementary Forms. — Phrases and Periods. — XI. Open and Closed Forms. — XII. Irregular Period Forms. — Unitary Forms. — XIII. Binary Forms. — XIV. Ternary Forms. — The Rondo. — XV. The Sonata Piece. — XVI. The Sonata as a Whole.

PART THIRD.

PRELIMINARY STUDIES IN THE CONTENT OF MUSIC.

XVII. Content Defined.—XVIII. The Intellectual and the Emotional.—XIX. Passages, Cadenzas and Effects.—XX. The Sensuous and the Idealized.—XXI. Descriptive and Suggestive Music.

PART FOURTH.

STUDIES IN ART.

XXII. The Ideal and the Object of Art.—XXIII. The Nature and Meaning of the Beautiful.—XIV. The Symbolic, the Classic, and the Romantic in Art. XXV. The Content and Meaning of the Different Arts.

PART FIFTH.

STUDIES IN CLASSICAL MUSIC.

XXVI. The Playful.—XXVII. The Tender and Soulful.—XXVIII. The Contented and Jovial.—XXIX. The Earnest.—The Sonata as a Whole.—XXX. The Beautiful in Classic Music, and the Transition Towards the Romantic.

PART SIXTH.

STUDIES IN THE ROMANTIC.

XXXI. The Chivalrous.—XXXII. The Gentle and Sentimental.—XXXIII. The Humoristic and Passionate.—XXXIV. The Fanciful and the Pleasing.—XXXV. The Sensational and the Astonishing.

PART SEVENTH.

STUDIES IN SONG.

XXXVI.—The Formative Influences in Music Generally.—The Influence of Poetry Upon Music, and the Conditions of Their Successful Union.—XXXVII. Simple Ballads.—XXXVIII. Recitative.—XXXIX. The Aria.—XL. The Thoroughly Composed Song (*Durchcomponirte Lied*), and the Arioso.—XLI. The Opera and Oratorio.

PART EIGHTH.

BIOGRAPHICAL AND MISCELLANEOUS SKETCHES.

XLII. Bach.—XLIII. Handel.—XLIV. Haydn.—XLV. Mozart.—XLVI. Beethoven.—XLVII. Mendelssohn.—XLVIII. Schumann.—XLIX. Chopin.—L. The Piano-Forte Virtuosi and Liszt.—LI. Wagner, and the Music of the Future.—LII. Of Programmes.—LIII. A Study in the Psychology of Music.

PART NINTH.

PRONOUNCING DICTIONARY AND CONDENSED ENCYCLOPEDIA OF MUSICAL TERMS, INSTRUMENTS, COMPOSERS AND IMPORTANT WORKS.

APPENDIX

MUSICAL NOTATION, AND THE PRINCIPAL MELODIC EMBELLISHMENTS, WITH THE PROPER MANNER OF PERFORMING THEM.

Part First.

LESSONS IN MUSICAL PHRASEOLOGY.

Lesson First.

MOTIVES, PHRASES AND PERIODS.

It is the object of this lesson to lead the pupil to observe the division of the music into periods and phrases; and subsequently to develop a perception of the different modes of period structure here distinguished as thematic and lyric. As it is the sole design of this course of lessons *to facilitate intelligent hearing*, the pupils' powers of observation are to be appealed to from the start. He is to be clearly informed of what he is expected to hear; the proper selections are then to be played over as many times as necessary until he does observe. Each stage of the lesson is to begin with a definition, or explanation of the phenomenon or peculiarity of music it is desired to observe. Inasmuch as these earliest lessons represent only the beginnings of musical discrimination, the definitions in them will possess somewhat of the character of off-hand approximations to the truth, leaving exact statements to come later, when the pupils are better prepared to appreciate them. The definitions here given represent so much of the truth as the pupil at this stage is ready to receive. As thus:

1. A passage of melody that makes complete sense is called a *Period*.

Play the first three or four of the Schubert danses twice through, and more, if necessary. Instruct the class to say "Period" aloud at the close of every period. Do not let the playing stop for them to speak, but the feeling of repose may be intensified by slightly emphasizing the cadence, and perhaps retarding a little, if found necessary. As the period forms in these danses are clearly defined, it will be found easy to observe them.

Let this be followed by No. 2 of the list of illustrations, repeating it as often as necessary, the pupils signifying every period-close by the word "Period," as before.

No. 3, treated in the same manner, will conclude this stage of the lesson.

2. A passage of melody that makes sense, but not complete sense, is called a *Phrase*.

This topic is to be treated in the same way as the previous, the pupils announcing the completion of every phrase by the word "Phrase." Begin with No. 3, for in this the phrases are clearly defined. Follow this by the next illustration, which may need to be repeated several times. Then go back to No. 2 again, for its phrases. This may be followed, if convenient, by No. 5 of the illustrations, treated separately for periods and phrases. Then take up No. 6, going over this also for both periods and phrases.

3. A fragment of melody that is reiterated over and over, or transformed and developed into a period, is called a *Motive*. (A motive is a musical *text*.)

Begin by playing several times over the first six notes of No. 6, which form a melodic figure. Then play the various transformations of this figure which occur during the piece, omitting the accompaniment. Then play the entire first part of the Novellette (preceding the slow melody), and let the pupils observe how many times the melodic figure is repeated. It will be seen that this motive is the germ of the entire movement.

Then take up No. 7, where will be found a period composed from one motive—that contained in the first four notes.

Play again No. 3, and cause it to be observed that the melody there is not developed out of a single motive, nor predominantly out of any one motive. Thus we come to recognize two different forms of period-structure. In one of them the periods are developed mainly from a single motive; in the other there is a flowing melody.

4. Music developed out of a single motive, or a small number of motives, is called *Thematic*, or motivized.

Examples of this mode are found in Nos. 6, 7, 8, 9, and 10.

5. Music not developed motivewise, but having a flowing melody, is called *Lyric*.

Examples of this kind are Nos. 1, 2, 3, 4, and the slow melodies in Nos. 5, 6, and 9.

Several lyric and thematic examples should be played one after the other in irregular order, until the pupils readily distinguish between them.

MUSICAL ILLUSTRATIONS.

1. Schubert Danses (Peters' Ed.)
2. Schubert Menuetto in B min., op. 78 (Peters' Ed. "Schubert Pieces).
3. Adagio, from Beethoven's Sonata in F min., op. 2, No. 1 (16 measures.)
4. No. 1 of Mendelssohn's "Songs Without Words" (Peters' Ed. "Kullak").
5. Allegro from Beethoven's Sonata in E♭, op. 7.
6. Schumann Novellette in E, op. 21, No. 7.
7. Thirty-two measures of Finale of Beethoven's Sonata in D min., op. 31, No. 3.
8. Bach, Two-Part Inventions, No. 1, in C (Peters' Ed.)
9. Schumann Novellette in B min., op. 99.
10. First movement of Sonata in F min., op. 2, No. 1, Beethoven.

LESSON SECOND.

THEMATIC AND LYRIC. CLOSER OBSERVATION OF MOTIVES.

This lesson pursues the same line as the first, in order to bring the point out more clearly in the pupils' minds. Begin by a recapitulation of that lesson. Play again the Schumann Novellettes and Beethoven Adagio for periods and phrases.

Then play the Novellette in E clear through, in order to call attention to the lyric middle part. Play then the *Adagio* from Sonata Pathetique, of Beethoven, first for them to determine whether it is thematic or lyric; then for phrases and periods.

The second part of the lesson is to be devoted to a Bach Prelude; the one in B min. in the second book of the Well-tempered Clavier suits well for this purpose, especially as there is a copy to be had (Root & Sons Music Co., Chicago), in which the motives are numbered. The immediate purpose is to recognize the different motives. This prelude, *e. g.*, contains seventeen or eighteen different motives. Probably the best way of securing sharp listening will be by first playing over a single motive several times, in order to fix it securely in the minds of the listeners. Then play the entire prelude, requiring each listener to observe how many times that motive occurs in the course of the piece. When the playing is done, ask each one in turn to state how many times the motive was repeated in the course of the work. It will be found that a majority of the class will have succeeded in recognizing the motive at most of its repetitions. It will then be well to play another motive, and then go through the work again, in order to see how many times that one occurs.

Take next, *e. g.*, the Bach Two-part Invention in F, No. 8, and play it first for "Thematic or Lyric?" Then define clearly the first motive, and go through the piece, the pupils meanwhile listening to discover how many times that motive occurs *in the right hand alone;* then go through it again, to see how many times the same motive occurs in the *left hand alone*. The object of this exercise is to lead the pupils to attend to the left-hand part, as well as the treble. If there is time, it will be well to play through the Schumann Novellette in B min., for the pupils to count the number of times the leading motive occurs in it.

Play again eight measures of the *Adagio* from Sonata Pathetique, in order to show that in lyric music there is generally a flowing melody and accompaniment, and that the leading melody is not to be found in the bass or intermediate parts, as in most of the examples of thematic music thus far introduced.

6. **Lyric music is founded on the people's song. It is simple, natural music. Thematic music represents a more active musical life, and was primarily derived from the dance. Excitement finds expression mainly through thematic music; repose through lyric.**

MUSICAL ILLUSTRATIONS OF SECOND LESSON.

1. The Schumann Novellettes in E (op. 21, No. 1) and B min. (op. 99).
2. Adagio from Beethoven's Sonata Pathetique.
3. Bach's Prelude in B min., No. 24 in Vol. II of "Clavier."
4. Bach's Two-part Invention, No. 8.

LESSON THIRD.

ON CADENCE.

7. A cadence is a formula of chords leading to a close. Thus, *e. g.*, in the key of C:

Ex. 1.

So in the key of E♭:

Ex. 2.

(Play also in several other keys.)

Besides this, which is called a *Complete* cadence, there are other cadences, the most common varieties of which are the Half Cadence and Plagal Cadence. The latter is the well known "Amen" cadence of church music. For example, play No. 1, above, and conclude with the following two chords, added:

Ex. 3.

This is also called the *Church* Cadence.

8. The complete cadence is used to mark the close of periods and important divisions in musical compositions.

Listen now to the *Adagio* from the first Beethoven Sonata, and when I play a cadence, say "cadence." At the end of the first phrase there is a "half-cadence." (Play it.) Those who are able may also point out the half-cadences.

Play also *Adagio* from Sonata Pathetique; also, Schubert Menuetto in B min., and, finally, the *Adagio* in E from Beethoven's Sonata in E min., op. 90.

If there is any difficulty in the pupils recognizing the cadences in these works, it will be well to introduce two or three pieces of church music, for further practice in recognizing cadences.

Point out, also, the cadences in the Bach Invention in F, No. 8, the Invention in C, No. 1, and the Fugue in G min., first volume of "Clavier."

MUSICAL ILLUSTRATIONS OF THIRD LESSON.

1. Adagios from Beethoven's Sonatas, No. 1 in F, op. 2, and op. 13 in C min.
2. Adagio from Beethoven Sonata in E, op. 90.
3. Schubert Menuetto in B, op. 78.
4. Bach's Inventions in F (No. 8), and C (No. 1).
5. Bach's Fugue in G min. (No. 16), from "Clavier," vol. 1.

LESSON FOURTH.

IMITATIVE AND FUGUE FORMS.

9. Imitation in music takes place when a second voice exactly repeats a melody or phrase already heard in another voice.

The term "voice" here means voice-part. Observe, *e. g.*, the Bach Invention presently to follow, and you will perceive that it has only two voices, a bass and soprano. It is in strict style, to the extent that each part or voice contains no chords. Each part might be sung by a single voice; and two singers, a bass and soprano, could sing the whole piece.

Listen now to the right hand alone, and point out the end of the first phrase. It is:

Ex. 4.

The first eight notes form the subject for imitation. Throughout the first period the treble leads, and the bass afterwards imitates. In the seventh measure the second period begins, and the left hand leads. (Plays.) Listen and see how many times the bass imitates the treble throughout this piece. (Seven times, viz.: in measures 1, 2, 15, 16, 17,

18, and 20.) Listen again and see how many times the treble imitates the bass. (Four times.)

Listen now to the Eighth Invention, and see how many times the treble imitates; also how many times the bass.

The subject of the Fourth Invention is this:

Ex. 5.

Listen as it is played through, and tell me how many times this subject is repeated. (Plays.)

10. A fugue is a composition in which one voice announces a subject or theme, which is taken up in turn by the other voices, each one entering after the previous has completed the subject.

In fugues the imitating voice does not enter upon the same degree as the antecedent, nor on the octave of it, as in most of the examples so far given; but replies in a different key, according to certain rules characteristic of this form of composition. The voices not performing the subject play complemental parts, called counter-subjects. As a first example, listen to the following fugue in G minor, from Bach's "Well-tempered Clavier." The subject is:

Ex. 6.

How many times is this melodic figure repeated in the course of the fugue? (Plays.)

Are fugues thematic or lyric?

Listen now to the Menuetto from Beethoven's Sonata in E♭, op. 31. Is it thematic or lyric? Observe the imitation at the beginning of the second period.

Hear also the Scherzo from Beethoven's Sonata in C, op. 2. Is this lyric or thematic? Is it imitative or not?

Hear also Schumann's Spring Song. Observe the imitation in measure 18, where the alto imitates the soprano motive in the seventeenth measure; also in measures 23 and 24, where the tenor imitates the soprano phrase of the previous two measures. (In playing, bring out these imitations by sufficient accentuation.)

MUSICAL ILLUSTRATIONS.

1. Bach's First, Fourth, and Eighth Inventions.
2. Bach's Fugue in G min., Clavier.
3. Menuetto from Beethoven Sonata in E♭, op. 31.
4. Scherzo from Beethoven's Sonata in C, op. 2, No. 3.
5. Schumann's Spring Song, from "Album for the Young." (No. 15).

LESSON FIFTH.

OF COUNTERPOINT AND THE CONTRAPUNTAL SPIRIT.

11. **The term "counterpoint" means, in general, any new voice-part added to one already existing.**
In a very rudimentary use of the term, it would be permissible to describe the bass of an ordinary people's song, like "Hold the Fort," as a counterpoint, though, to be sure, it is a very poor one. The idea of counterpoint carries with it not only the construction of an additional voice to one already existing, but of an *independent* and *individually distinct* voice, and not of a mere natural bass. Thus, *e. g.*, observe the bass of "Hold the Fort." (Plays.) You perceive that the bass has properly no melody or movement of its own, but is all the time concerned with furnishing a proper foundation to the chords. Take now, on the other hand, Ewing's air, "Jerusalem the Golden." (Plays.) Observe the bass, how freely and independently it moves, and to what interesting harmonies it gives rise. How much more inspiring than the monotony of "Hold the Fort!" The bass of Ewing's "Jerusalem the Golden" is contrapuntally conceived.

Observe, again, this Gavotte of Bach's; it is in D (from a violin sonata). In this, properly speaking, we have little counterpoint.

Listen now to the following: It is Bach's Gavotte in D min. from one of his *suites*. Notice the bass, and you will find that it has a steady rhythmic motion of eighth notes. This bass has what is called "a contrapuntal motion," and of that variety called "two against one," that is, every melody note has two notes in the counterpoint.

Again, observe this Invention of Bach's, in E minor. In the first part there is no contrapuntal motion; but with the second period it begins. Observe. (Also referred to in the next lesson.)

Listen now to this church tune, "Dennis." Is it contrapuntal or not?

Listen to this Chorale. Is this contrapuntal or not? If contrapuntal, in which part does the counterpoint lie? (It may be proper to say that the counterpoint in this piece is of the kind called "note against note," with occasional "passing" notes; and that the principal counterpoint is the bass.)

Observe, again, the Bach Invention in E min., No. 7, in the Three-part Inventions. In the first thirteen measures there is not what is called a "contrapuntal motion." In the fourteenth measure such a "motion" begins in the bass, and from that point onwards for twenty-three measures there is a contrapuntal motion of sixteenth notes, interrupted only by the omission of a single sixteenth note at the beginning of its twelfth measure. The motive is transferred from one part to another; for four measures it runs in the bass, then for five measures it alternates between the soprano and alto; it is then transferred to the bass for four measures; the soprano retains it during the remaining ten measures. In listening to this, one should also observe that the leading motive of the piece is constantly transferred from one key to another, and one voice to another.

Counterpoint gives dignity to a music-piece. It does this because it displays *intelligence*, and that in such a way as to heighten the musical quality of the piece.

Musical Illustrations.

1. Hold the Fort. (Any other popular song will do as well, *e. g.*, Dr. Lowell Mason's "Work, for the Night is Coming.")
2. Ewing's "Jerusalem the Golden."
3. Gavotte in D, Bach. (Arranged by Dr. Wm. Mason.)
4. Gavotte in D min., Bach. (Pieces Favoris, Bach. Edition Peters.)
5. Bach's Three-part Invention in E min., No. 7. (Peters.)
6. Church Tune, "Dennis."
7. Chorale, "St. Paul," "Sleepers, Wake."

LESSON SIXTH.

VARIATIONS.

The lesson to-day begins with the following air from the Andante of Beethoven's Sonata in G, op. 14. This will be played twice in order to fix it in your memory. (Plays twenty measures.)

Observe now the following strain and see if it has any resemblance to the previous. (Plays the next ensuing twenty measures.)

In what respect is this like the air at beginning? Listen now to the harmony of the first eight measures. (Plays as before.)

Hear also this, the harmony of the first eight of the sixteen measures last played.

Ex. 7.

It will be seen that they are exactly the same, except that the melody is now in a middle voice.

Observe now the melody of the first eight measures. (Plays again eight meas. of air.) And the melody of the eight measures played afterwards. You perceive that the melody is the same, although in the latter case it is assigned to the tenor. The accompaniment, however, is considerably elaborated, and comes above the melody; the time also is cut up into half and quarter beats. We have here a *variation in the form* of the air. The melody and harmony are the same; merely the form of them is changed without imparting any essentially new meaning to the air. Observe now the second variation of the same air. (Plays.) In this you hear the melody in the soprano, but entering always on the half-beat. When it is played on the beat you at once recognize it. (Plays air in simple form.) This, also, as you see is merely a variation *in the form*. The harmony and melody are the same as before, and there is therefore no new meaning except such as is derived from or denoted by the increasing animation and complexity of rhythmic motion.

The next variation is a little more elusive in character. It begins:
Ex. 8.

When played softly the melody is not distinctly perceived, but seems to be looking out at us through a veil. If the upper notes of the right hand part are played alone (as indicated by the accent marks.) it is at once perceived that we have here the melody in its original form. Here also the melody and harmony are unchanged, and here again, consequently, we have no essentially new meaning.

Consider now the following air from Beethoven's Sonata in A flat, op. 26. (Plays air.) Observe now the first variation. (Plays.) Here we have a more decided departure from the original. The harmony remains the same; enough of the melody remains unchanged to enable the listener to refer it to the air just heard as its source. Still it is in several respects a new air.

The second variation makes a still wider departure. (Plays.) Here you observe that the melody is cut up into repeating notes, and placed in the bass. In the third variation the key is changed to the minor of the same name, and the original harmonic figure is carried out in syncopation, producing a distortive effect, not unlike that of viewing your face in a bad mirror. In the fourth variation we have the air transformed into a *scherzo*, a playful movement, as different as possible from the repose of the original air. The fifth variation, again, brings back the original air, but much ornamented.

In both these sets of variations is to be observed the same law of progression, namely, *from the simple towards greater variety and diversification.* The coda at the end of the last set was for the purpose of conducting the movement back again to a natural repose.

These variations in the last set (A flat, op. 26) are of a different kind from those first examined. In these not only is the form of the original air diversified, and in that way varied, but the variations are of such a nature that they have the effect of imparting or bringing out a new meaning in each variation. Beethoven was the great composer of this form of variation.

Let us examine another set of variations by Beethoven, his Eight

Variations on the theme "Une Fièbre brûlante," by Gretry, found in the volume of "Beethoven's Variations." Each one of these is to be compared with the theme until its construction is obvious, and its relation to the theme plainly understood. Another example of formal variations is to be found in the Andante and variations of Beethoven's Sonata Appassionata, op. 57. (Bülow's edition.) See also Mozart's variations in A, in one of his sonatas (No. 12, Peters' edition).

12. A variation of an air is an amplification of it, or unfolding, by means of auxiliary notes, rhythmic devices, changes of movement, etc., yet in such a way as to leave resemblance enough between the theme and variation to indicate their relation.

In order to do this and yet allow the varying to be carried to the full extent of the composer's genius, it is usual to arrange the series of variations progressively according to their elaboration, the simplest first.

13. Variations are of two kinds, *Formal* and *Character*. In the former the air or theme is elaborated without changing its original meaning or expression. Of this kind are the Beethoven variations in C and D♭ (Nos. 1 and 5, below). Character variations change the original *character* or expression of the melody, as was seen in the Beethoven variations in A♭.

LIST OF ILLUSTRATIONS.

1. Andante from Beethoven's Sonata in G, op. 14, No. 2.
2. Air and Variations in A♭, from Sonata, op. 26.
3. Variations on Gretry's "Une Fièbre brûlante," Beethoven.
4. Air and Variations in A, No. 12 of Peters' ed. of Mozart's Sonatas.
5. Andante and Variations from Beethoven's Sonata Appassionata.

LESSON SEVENTH.

RHYTHMIC PULSATION AND MEASURE

14. Rhythm means "measured flow."

Music is measured by a pulsation which goes entirely through the movement at the same rate of speed, like the human pulse. This fundamental rhythmic pulsation is commonly expressed by the accompaniment. Observe now the accompaniment of this little waltz. (Plays left-hand part of the first Schubert waltz.) Beat with your hands on the table before you, the same pulsation while I play.

Mark the pulsation in the example I now play. (Plays No. 2, in the list.)

In the same manner mark the pulsation in the example, I now play. (Plays a polka, No. 3, or any other convenient one; but not too fast. Be sure that it sounds here like four beats in the measure.)

These pulsations are grouped by means of accents into groups called *measures*.

There may be two, three, four, six, nine or twelve pulsations in a measure. Observe now the following, mark the pulsations and the accents, and tell me how many pulsations there are in a measure. (Plays No. 1, again. Be sure that every measure has a decided accent.)

Observe the following: (Plays No. 4.)

How many pulsations are there in a measure in this example? (Plays No. 5.)

Mark the pulsation in No. 6. (Plays.)

Observe now the measures in the same. (Plays again.) How many pulsations were there in a measure? (If not correctly answered, repeat the example and accent a little more.)

Observe the pulsation in this example. (Plays No. 7.) This admits of being understood in two ways: If played slowly it sounds like six pulsations in a measure. (Plays.) If played more rapidly and accented a little differently, it sounds like two triplets in the measure, and you naturally beat it as if there were two pulsations in a measure. (Plays.)

Observe the pulsation in this example. (Plays No. 8.)

Observe now the measures and tell me how many pulsations in a measure. (Plays again.)
Mark the pulsation in this example. (Plays No. 9).
How many pulsations in a measure? (Plays again if necessary.)
Observe the pulsation and the measures in this example. (Plays No. 10.)
Observe further that the same pulsation runs through an entire movement. (Plays No. 11, the class marking the pulsation by a motion of the hand for each pulse, paying no attention to the measures.)

NOTE:—There are two opinions in regard to the ultimate nature of measure, one holding it to be "a portion of time," the other "a group of pulses." The true conclusion would seem to be that measure in music is "portion of time" manifested by means of pulses and accents. Measure is the precise analogue of *foot* in poetry. Poetic quantity is also related to time. We ourselves, and every thing that we know by our senses or think of under sense-forms of thought, are related to time or space. Music is related to time, and so is meter. The time of music is in the rhythmic pulsation, measure, and rate of movement. And so measure in its ultimate nature is certainly *time;* but time is not measure until it becomes recognized as such through the rhythmic pulsation and accent; and therefore it is sufficiently correct for musical purposes to think of measure as pulse-grouping, as is here done.

LIST OF ILLUSTRATIONS.

1. The First of the Schubert Waltzes.
2. Schumann's Nachtstücke in F, op. 24, No. 4.
3. A Polka, *e.g.* Karl Merz's "Leonore Polka."
4. The Waltz from Weber's "Der Freyschütz." (Any other quick waltz will do as well.)
5. Schubert's Menuetto in B minor.
6. Two strains from the Schumann Nachtstücke in C, op. 24, No. 1.
7. "The Carnival of Venice."
8. Chopin Polonaise in A.
9. Sixteen measures of the Adagio in Sonata Pathetique.
10. Thirty-two measures of Rondo in same sonata.
11. Allegro from Sonata in F, op. 2, No. 1, Beethoven.

LESSON EIGHTH.

MEASURES AND RHYTHMIC MOTION.

Begin this lesson by recapitulating enough of the previous one to refresh the memories of the class concerning measures. Use, if convenient, other examples, only be sure to select at least two, each, in double, triple and common time.

15. A rhythmic pulsation may be called a *rhythmic motion*, and, when satisfactorily completed by an accent, is called a *Rhythm*.

(Plays here a scale in common time, like that in "table A," in Mason's Pianoforte Technics.)

The rhythmic motion may be twice as fast as the pulsation. Thus, *e.g.*, the *Adagio* in Beethoven's Sonata Pathetique is written in 2-4 time with a pulsation of sixteenth notes. The effect is as if you were to count four in a measure and each pulse had two notes. (Plays.) Counting four in a measure, the motion here is a half-pulse motion.

Example nine of the previous chapter had the same kind of motion. Observe the bass, and at the same time count the time aloud while I play. (Plays.)

Observe now the first nineteen measures of Beethoven's first sonata, example eleven of the previous chapter. Mark the pulsations and measures, and tell me whether it is a pulse-motion or a half-pulse motion. (Plays. This must be repeated until the pupils are conscious of the quarter-note motion which is unmistakable in the first nine measures, and strongly implied in the first nineteen.)

Observe again how the motion changes in the twentieth measure. (Plays again from the beginning through to the double bar.) From the twentieth to the forty-first measure there is what sort of a motion? ("Half-pulse." But play it until they observe it.) What kind of a motion begins at the forty-first measure? (Quarter-pulse. Plays it.)

Observe now example five, especially in regard to the change of motion. What sort of a motion has it at beginning? (Plays, "Pulse-motion.") Where the motion changes, raise your hands. (Plays again. "Half-pulse" motion begins in tenth measure of the second period.)

Observe the trio of the same. What sort of a motion has it? (Plays.)

LIST OF ILLUSTRATIONS.

1. Scale of C or G in 4s (rhythm completed).
2. Adagio from Sonata Pathetique.
3. Rondo of same Sonata.
4. Allegro from first Sonata.
5. Menuetto from Beethoven's Sonata in F min. (op. 2, No. 1).

LESSON NINTH.

MEASURES, RHYTHMIC MOTION AND MOTIVIZATION.

In the examples of the previous lessons we have observed in every piece a rhythmic pulsation carried through the piece at a uniform rate; and in connection with this a full-pulse, half-pulse or other rhythmic motion, which changes several times in the course of a piece, being generally quicker towards the last.

Thus, *e. g.* observe the first eight measures of Pauer's "Cascade." What is the pulsation? What the motion? (Observe the half-pulse motion in the bass.) (Plays.)

Observe now that the melody has a certain definite motivization of its own. Its rhythm is

Ex. 9.

This rhythmic figure is repeated over and over. Observe now the rapid motion that begins after the theme is completed. Here we have an eighth-pulse motion in the fine work, a half-pulse motion in the bass, and a full-pulse motion in the melody. (Plays.)

Observe the combination of measure-pulses, rhythmic motions and motivization in the Bach Invention in E min. In the first thirteen measures there is a half-pulse motion, except the fifth measure, which has a quarter-pulse motion. (Plays, the pupils marking the measure-pulses by motions of the hand.)

Along with this is the melodic subject which runs through the piece. Its rhythm is

Ex. 10.

At the fourteenth measure a quarter-pulse motion begins in the counterpoint and continues for twenty-three measures. (Plays.)

MEASURES, RHYTHMIC MOTION AND MOTIVIZATION. 25

Again, take the Allegro of the sonata (No. 3, on the list of this chapter). This is in 6-8 time and has the effect of two pulses in a measure. Throughout the first twenty-four measures there is a triplet (or "third-pulse") motion transferred from bass to treble, and back again, but not interrupted. (Plays twenty-five measures.) From there to the thirty-ninth measure there is no uniform motion, but two different rhythms alternately appear. (Plays.) From the thirty-ninth to the fifty-ninth the triplet motion appears again. At this point the triplets disappear and we have a full-pulse motion for eight measures.

Observe, again, the rhythm of this polonaise. (Plays the Chopin Polonaise in A, No. 4, of the list.) Here we have a three-pulse measure, with half and quarter-pulse motion.

Ex. 11.

At the entrance of the second subject (in D maj.), the rhythm of the melody changes to this figure.

Ex. 12.

Rhythm is the primary element in a motive, and is in fact that to which it owes its name of motive, or mover.

A conspicuous example of rhythmic uniformity carried through almost an entire long movement is afforded by Beethoven's *Allegretto* in the Seventh Symphony, which moves in this figure.

Ex. 13.

It will also be useful to study the manner in which rhythmic characterization of subjects is managed in long movements generally; as *e. g.* in any of the binary and ternary forms analyzed in the second part of this work. (See Lessons Thirteenth and Fourteenth.)

LIST OF ILLUSTRATIONS.

1. Pauer's Cascade.
2. Bach's Invention in E min. (Three-part, No. 7.)
3. Allegro of Sonata in E flat op. 7, Beethoven.
4. Chopin's Polonaise in A.

Part Second.

LESSONS IN MUSICAL FORM.

Lesson Tenth.

THE ELEMENTARY FORMS. CLOSED FORMS. VAGUE PERIOD-GROUPS.

16. A Form in music is a period, or group of periods belonging together; or possibly belonging together only to the extent of being connected with each other, and more or less contrasted with a following homogenous and well-closed period group.

By "well-closed" is meant "fully and decidedly closed." Thus for example, observe the following three waltzes of Schubert. (Plays the first three numbers in Schubert's Danses.) The first has for its leading motive this:

Ex. 14.

This motive occurs six times in the first two periods. The second has for leading motive this:

Ex. 15.

This occurs five times in two periods. Analyze the third in the same way.

Observe, again, that the first waltz begins and ends in the key of A flat. So also the second and third. The cadences are complete and satisfactory. This will be better observed by playing the accompaniment alone.

Observe, further, that the first two periods are intimately connected by reason of the predominance of the same leading motive in both. So also are the two periods of the second waltz. Two of these periods together, make "a form." The two periods in each form are homogenous, because in the same key and having the same ruling motive. Each form is a "closed form" because it concludes in its own principal key and is shut off from the following periods by the entrance of new motives and a new movement.

Again, listen to the first twenty measures of Beethoven's first sonata, in F min. op. 2. (Plays.) Mention the periods. There are two of them. The first ends in the dominant of the principal key, in the eighth measure. The second begins with the same leading motive, but immediately forsakes it, and builds with the second motive of the first period. The first period begins in F minor, and ends with the dominant of it. This is a half-cadence, and denotes incompleteness. The second begins in C minor, and finally ends in E flat, as the dominant of A flat, the key of the next-following period. The first period is the principal subject of this sonata, and is not a "closed form." The second period is modulatory or transitional, and is designed to lead across to the introduction of the second principal subject, which enters at the last beat of the twentieth measure.

Take, again, the Adagio of this same sonata. Observe the periods of the first sixteen measures. (Plays.) Here, again, we have two periods. They are homogenous, because the second period concludes with the principal motive of the first, and in the same key. Both periods begin and end in F major. They are sharply cut off from the next following periods, because these latter begin in a new key and with new motives. These first sixteen measures, therefore, form a homogenous period-group of two periods, which unite to make "a closed form." The next following fifteen measures also contain two periods. The first one has eleven measures. It begins in D minor. It ends in C major. It is followed by an abridged period of four measures, or perhaps better, an independent section of a transitional character. These two periods are not homogenous, their modulatory structure is vague, and therefore they do not unite to make a form.

Observe now the Menuetto of the same sonata. (Plays.) How many Periods have we? (Plays.) The first subject has this motive. (Plays motive of Menuetto.) When the form is complete and a new one enters, say "Form." (Plays.) Class listens and says "form" as the forty-first or forty-second measure is begun. The three periods in these forty-one measures should then be examined again in order to discover whether they unite to make a homogenous period-group, and a closed form. The *trio* may then be examined in the same way.

Examine in the same way the first sixteen measures of the *Adagio* of Sonata Pathetique. Then the next following twelve measures. Then the eight measures following this (the repetition of the theme.) And the fourteen measures following this. All these are period-groups, more or less homogenous.

Take next the first seventeen measures of the Finale of the same sonata. This also is a closed form.

It would be well to introduce also a *salon* piece, as, *e. g.*, Wollenhaupt's Whispering Winds, the pupils watching for new subjects, and pointing out the ends of the closed forms. Mason's Danse Rustique is another good example.

MUSICAL ILLUSTRATIONS.

1. The first three of Schubert's Danses   (Peters' Ed., No. 150.)
2. Part of first movement of Beethoven Sonata, op. 2, No. 1.
3. Part of the Adagio of the same.
4. Menuetto of the same.
5. Part of the Adagio of Sonata Pathetique.
6. Part of Finale of the same.
7. Salon Pieces, such as Wollenhaupt's " Whispering Winds," and Mason's " Danse Rustique."

LESSON ELEVENTH.

FURTHER EXAMINATION OF OPEN AND CLOSED FORMS.

In the previous lesson Closed Forms were the subject of our examination. In opposition to the term "closed," we might apply to imperfectly closed period-groups the term "open," although the expression "open form" is to a certain extent a solecism. If, now, we listen attentively to the period-group immediately following the double-bar in the principal movement of a sonata, we shall find it to consist of from two to four or five imperfectly closed periods, freely modulating. (Plays fifty-seven measures in E minor, *Allegro molto e con brio*, of first movement of Sonata Pathetique.) Now observe the first part of the same movement. (Plays.) We see that this contains two distinctly marked forms; and that the part following the double-bar is in reality a free-fantasy on certain leading motives out of the first part.

Again, observe the Impromptu in A flat, (op. 29,) of Chopin. (Plays.) Of how many closed forms does this consist? Analyze the first form into its periods. (Plays again, and again until successfully analyzed.)

Observe the Schumann Novellette in E, No. 7, op. 21. (Plays.) Of how many closed forms does this consist? (Plays again.)

NOTE.—It may be well to remark that this work consists of three forms, the melody in the middle (in A maj.) being the second, and standing between the other two.

Examine now the Bach Gavotte in D minor, No. 3 in Bach's "Pieces Favoris." (Plays.) Listen again and point out the periods. (Plays.) Does this consist of one form or more than one? (One, since the same motive prevails throughout the movement.)

Observe now the Gavotte in D, immediately following the previous. (Plays.)

This, as you perceive, is composed on the same motive as the previous, but in a major key, whereas that was in minor. This also constitutes a single "closed form."

Observe now the first Mendelssohn Song without Words. (Plays.) Define the periods as I play. (Plays again.) How many forms have we in this? (Ans. One form, of three periods.)

We have thus discovered that a long piece of music may consist of several shorter forms.

17. A piece consisting of a single form is said to be in "Unitary Form," whether of one, two, three, or four periods.

Generally a unitary form will contain not more than three periods, the first and last of which at least must be homogenous with each other.

Examples of unitary forms are numerous and owing to their brevity easily recognized.

Single church-tunes are one-period unitary forms.

Examine Schumann's "Traumerei; Also the "Entrance" and "Wayside Inn" of the Forest Scenes, op. 82, Nos. 1 and 4. Also Mendelssohn's "Hunting Song." Test them separately and repeatedly for (1) periods, (2) homogeneity of periods, and (3) for close of forms.

MUSICAL ILLUSTRATIONS.

1. Extract from Allegro of Sonata Pathetique.
2. Impromptu in A flat, op. 29, Chopin.
3. Schumann Novellette in E, No. 7, op. 21.
4. Gavotte in D min. from Bach's "Pieces Favoris." (Peters' Edit., No. 221.)
5. First Song without Words. Mendelssohn.
6. "Traumerei " Schumann.
7. "Hunting Song." Mendelssohn.

LESSON TWELFTH.*

IRREGULAR PERIOD-FORMS AND PERIOD GROUPS.

The natural length of the simple period is eight measures in slow or moderate time, and sixteen in quick time. But in good writing these lengths are constantly varied by shortening, extending, etc., to such a degree that period-lengths of forty or fifty measures are sometimes found.

The true way to distinguish periods from each other is by their *motives* and the relation of Antecedent and Consequent.

The simple period consists of two similar sections (or halves) standing in the relation of antecedent and consequent.

Each of these sections, again, consists in general of two phrases, making four phrases in the period. As a rule two of these phrases are entirely or very nearly alike, and the other two correspond or answer to each other, having a similar rhythm, but different harmony and melody.

Thus, (Beethoven),

In the same manner analyze the first eight measures of the *Adagio* in the Beethoven sonata in F, op. 2, No. 1. Also the first eight measures of the Adagio of Sonata Pathetique. This is the simplest form of period. The first eight measures of the Beethoven sonata in G, op. 14, No. 2, afford an example of a period in which the antecedent contains the same phrase twice repeated; and a consequent entirely different.

* This Lesson may be omitted at the dictation of the teacher.

IRREGULAR PERIOD-FORMS AND PERIOD GROUPS.

The *Antecedent* in the period is the part that asks a question; it presents the subject in an incomplete form. The *Consequent* completes the form, answers the question, and so forms an equipoise to the antecedent. It does this by (1) completing the rhythm (*i. e.*, by filling up the natural number of eight or sixteen measures,) and (2) by returning to the tonic. Thus in the example above, No. 16, the first section leads to the dominant; the second returns to the tonic.

Sometimes the period does not return to the tonic, but leads off to some foreign key. In that case the period is incomplete, and is either of a transitional or a modulating character, or else is intended to be properly finished at some subsequent appearance of the same subject. An example of this kind is found in the first eight measures of Schumann's *Aufschwung*, where the antecedent is in F minor, and the consequent concludes in A flat.

Periods are extended to nine, ten or twelve measures, by prolonging the cadence, or by inserting matter just before the point where the cadence was expected.

A complex period is one in which the antecedent is repeated, usually in a higher pitch, thus intensifying the feeling of expectation and making the consequent more satisfactory when it does come. An example of this is found in Schubert's Sonata in C. Thus:

Ex. 17.

One of the most remarkable examples of this kind is a period in Chopin's Scherzo in B flat minor, op. 31, (beginning with the sixty-fourth measure) which extends to fifty-three measures, the antecedent being repeated four times: viz., in G flat, A flat, D flat, and in D flat in octaves. It may be proper to add, however, that many would regard this passage as in reality consisting of two periods, the first ending with the first consequent. It is a question of names merely, the last antecedent and consequent having precisely the same content as the first, additionally emphasized by means of the octaves.

A period-group is a succession of periods on the same motives (as in unitary forms) or on different motives, as in transitional periods and the "elaboration" of sonatas. (See Chap. VI.) These parts of composition may be easily studied by the student privately, using the Ditson reprint of the Bülow (Stuttgart) edition of the Beethoven Sonatas.

For our present purposes it is enough to be able to recognize the principal subjects in extended movements. Ability to follow the treatment of transitional passages and elaborations is a more mature accomplishment.

LESSON THIRTEENTH.

BINARY FORMS.

18. A Binary Form is a form composed of two unitary forms, which may or may not be connected by means of intervening passages or transitional periods. The two forms uniting to compose a binary form, stand in the relation of Principal and Second. The Principal stands at the beginning, and is repeated after the Second. Thus the Principal occurs twice; the Second once. This is for the sake of unity.

This is one form, e. g., of the Menuetto of the Beethoven Sonata in F min., op. 2, No. 1. (Plays until the class clearly perceive the construction.)

In the older forms of this kind we sometimes find the Second composed from the same motives as the Principal, but changed from minor to major, or *vice versa*. Bach's Gavotte in D minor is an example of this kind. (Plays as many times as necessary.)

Observe also the Menuetto by Schubert, in B minor, op. 78. (Plays, as before.)

In both these cases the Second comes in what is sometimes called a milder form than the Principal, and is of a softer and less pronounced character. In this form it is called a *trio*, probably because in the olden time these parts were performed by a smaller number of instruments.

Observe also, the Chopin Polonaise, in A, op. 40. (Plays until the class perceive this form.)

In other cases, again, the Second is of a more animated character. Observe the Adagio from Beethoven's first sonata. (Plays.)

Sometimes the Second is not so distinctly a unit as the Principal. This is the case, *e. g.*, in the Largo of Beethoven's second sonata. (Sonata in A, op. 2, No. 2.) (Plays.)

Binary forms are frequently extended by a Coda composed of new material, put in after the repetition of the Principal in order to lead more satisfactorily to a close. Such an example we have already in the Largo last played. Observe again, the Scherzo from Beethoven's Sonata in C, op. 2. No. 3. (Plays, and repeats, until the class successfully analyzes it.)

Very many popular pieces are in this form. For example, Wollenhaupt's "Whispering Winds." (Plays.) The first page is introduction. The next four constitute the first form, the Principal. The part in six flats is the Second. Then the Principal occurs again, but in an abridged form. This is followed by a new strain serving as Coda, or conclusion.

Observe also Chopin's little waltz in D flat, op. 64. (Plays.)

Also the Chopin Impromptu in A flat, op. 29. (Plays.)

The Chopin Scherzo in B flat min., op. 31, is another example of this form.

LIST OF ILLUSTRATIONS.

1. Menuetto, Beethoven's Sonata in F, op. 2.
2. Bach's Gavotte in D min. (Peters' Ed. Bach's Favorite Pieces, No. 221.)
3. Menuetto in B min. Schubert, op. 78.
4. Chopin Polonaise in A, op. 40.
5. Adagio from Beethoven's Sonata in F, op. 2.
6. Largo, from Beethoven's Sonata in A, op. 2, No. 2.
7. Scherzo, from Beethoven's Sonata in C, op. 2, No. 3.
8. Wollenhaupt's "Whispering Winds."
9. Chopin's Valse in D flat, op. 64.
10. Chopin's Impromptu in A flat, op. 29.
11. Chopin's Scherzo in B flat min., op. 31.

LESSON FOURTEENTH.

TERNARY FORMS.

19. Any musical form consisting of three distinct unitary forms, is called *Ternary*.

Observe, *e.g.*, the following: (Plays Adagio of Sonata Pathetique.) The first subject is this: (Plays eight measures.) The second is this: (Begins in seventeenth measure and plays seven measures.) The third subject is this: (Plays fourteen measures in A flat minor, beginning after the repetition of the Principal, which ends in the thirty-sixth measure.)

These subjects we will designate as Principal, Second and Third. Observe now when I play the movement through, and as I begin each subject, say "Principal," "Second" or "Third," as the case may be. (Plays.) Observe again the character of the different movements. The Principal is a pure lyric; the Second is much less reposeful; the Third, again, is lyric, but the triplet motion in the accompaniment evinces an excitement such as we do not find in the Principal. Observe again while the movement is played through from beginning to end, and see how many times each subject occurs. (Plays. The Principal occurs three times, the Second and Third once each.)

This movement is type of a rare class, namely, of a slow movement in ternary order.

Another example of ternary form is to be found in No. 2 of Schumann's Kreisleriana. This work consists of a Principal, the first thirty-seven measures. First Intermezzo, or "Second," twenty-six measures; Principal, thirty-seven measures. Second Intermezzo, or "Third," fifty-four measures; Transitional matter bringing back the Principal, and the conclusion of the whole, forty-seven measures.

20. The most common form of this order is the Rondo, or round, a form deriving its name from its returning to the same theme, circularwise, after every digression.

Observe, *e. g.*, the following. (Plays two periods, seventeen measures of the Beethoven Rondo in C, op. 51.) This is the Principal.

Then follows a transition of seven measures, leading to the key of G. (Plays.) Then the Second in G, ten measures. (Plays.)

This is followed by the "return," a series of passages leading back to the Principal. (Plays nine measures.) Then follows the Principal shortened to eight measures. (Plays.) Here enters the Third subject in C minor. It consists of three periods: First, eight measures; Second, seven, and Third, six. Twenty-one in all. (Plays.)

This is followed by a transition of three measures, the Principal in A flat, thirteen meas., and passage of three meas. leading back to the Principal in C, shortened to thirteen measures, followed by the conclusion, thirty-one measures. (Plays.)

Thus we see that the primary elements of this Rondo are three. The Principal, (Plays eight meas.,) the Second, (Plays ten meas.,) and the Third, (Plays eight meas.) Everything else in the Rondo is subordinate to these three leading ideas. These, again, are subjected to the Principal, which by its four recurrences impresses itself upon the attention as the principal idea of the work.

Observe again these three ideas. (Plays them again.) Now let us see if you know them when you hear them. (Plays the first three or four measures of each several times in various orders until the class easily recognize them.)

Observe now while I play the entire work through and designate the leading ideas as "Principal," "Second" and "Third" as they appear. (Plays, the class responding.)

Still further exercise in this form may be had by treating other pieces in the same way. In order to save space, the work is not given here entire, but only the analysis.

Thus, another example is the Rondo from Beethoven's sonata in C, op. 2, No. 3. Its plan is: Principal and transition twenty-nine measures; Second and transition thirty-eight; Principal and transition thirty-four; Third, in F, much elaborated, seventy-eight; Principal thirty-seven; Second and transition thirty-five; Conclusion sixty.

(NOTE.—In treating a work so large as this, it is better to begin by playing separately the three principal ideas, and afterwards going through the entire work in the same manner as the preceding.)

The Rondo in Beethoven's sonata in A flat, op. 26, is another example.

Still another is the Rondo in Beethoven's sonata in B flat, op. 22. This work consists of Principal, (two periods, 9 and 9) 18 measures; transition 4; Second 9; transition (two periods, 9 and 9) 18; Principal 18; transition 5; Third, (four periods, 6, 17, 6, 10), 39; Principal 18;

transition 6; second abridged, and transition 29; Principal 18; Coda (12 and 5) 17.

In the Rondo of Sonata Pathetique the Principal occurs *four* times.

The Rondo is founded on the people's song, and in its essential spirit is easy and rather cheerful.

LIST OF ILLUSTRATIONS.

1. Adagio of Sonata Pathetique.
2. No. 2 of Schumann's Kreisleriana, op. 16.
3. Rondo in C, Beethoven, op. 51. (Peters' No. 297.)
4. Rondo from Sonata in C, Beethoven, op. 2, No. 2.
5. Rondo in A♭, op. 26, Beethoven.
6. Rondo in B♭, op. 22, Beethoven.

LESSON FIFTEENTH.

THE SONATA PIECE.

We begin in this lesson the examination of the most important form known to instrumental music;—so important, indeed, that many theorists designate it the "principal form," and say unqualifiedly that it is the type of all serious forms. This, as we shall see, is claiming too much for it, for there are in fact two primitive types, the people's song the type of the *lyric*, and the ancient binary form the type of the *thematic*.

The form we now take up is called the "Sonata-Piece," or simply the Sonata-form, because it is this form which gives name to the three or four separate forms combined in the sonata.

Observe now this piece. It consists of three large divisions. The first part contains several distinct ideas, as thus: (Plays the following motives:)

Ex. 18.

(1.)

(2.)

(3.)

(Plays then the first page of Beethoven's Sonata in F. op. 2, as far as the double bar.)
Observe again this entire page. (Plays again.)
Now listen to the following while I play, and tell me if your hear any motives you have heard before. (Plays fifty-two measures beginning at the double bar.)
Let us familiarize ourselves with the original motives. (Plays the motives Nos. 1, 2 and 3 in different orders until the class is able to name each one as heard "one" "two" or "three.") Now listen to these fifty-two measures again, and when either of these original motives occurs, name it "one," "two" or "three," according to which it is. (Plays then the part again, and very clearly, the class naming each motive as it occurs.)
Observe now the continuation of this movement. (Plays the remainder of the movement, from the re-entrance of the theme.) Does this resemble either of the two parts previously played? (Play again until the class discover that it is precisely similar to the first part.)

21. Thus we find our sonata-piece to consist of three parts, the third of which is like the first, and the second is a fantasia on the leading motives of the first. The fantasia is called the "Elaboration."

The first subject is called *Principal;* the next the *Second* (or by the Germans the *Song-group* or "lyric period"); the third, the *Close.*

Again observe this. (Plays the first part of Beethoven's Sonata in C minor, op. 10 No. 1, as far as the double bar.)
Listen again and designate the Principal, Second and Close. (This will prove a matter of some difficulty. The Principal ends in the thirty-first measure. The Second begins in measure fifty-six. The melodious passage beginning in measure thirty-two is really of a transitional nature. This will become plain by hearing several times the two passages; the transition, measure thirty-two to forty-eight, and the Second, fifty-six to eighty-six; it will then appear that the latter is a completely organized period, a consistent melody, whereas the former is merely a series of melodic and harmonic sequences. The part from forty-eight to fifty-five inclusive is a pedal-point. Measures seventy-six to ninety-four a continuation of the cadence of the Second. In measures eighty-six, etc., the motives of the Principal are recalled.)

The Elaboration should then be studied until its motives can be referred to their origin in the first part of the work. The Elaboration ends at the fifty-third measure after the double bar; at that place a pedal point begins, lasting until the re-entrance of the theme in the sixty-third measure.

The Sonata-piece is of so important a character, including, as it does, the genius of all seriously composed music, that it will be well to return to the subject several times, at considerable intervals. On these occasions new examples should be taken up, for which purpose the following analyses are appended. The early sonatas in the Stuttgart edition (Ditson's reprint) as far as op. 53, are analyzed in respect to their form, and will be found very convenient for studies of this character.

The first movement in Beethoven's sonata in G, op. 31, has this plan: Principal in G, thirty measures; Passage fifteen; Transition proper twenty; Second, in B maj. and B min. (twenty-three and ten) thirty-three; partial conclusion thirteen. The Elaboration begins at the double bar, and for twenty measures handles the second motive of the Principal. It then takes up the "passage" figure out of the first part and carries that through to the forty-eighth measure, where the harmony remains stationary on the dominant seventh of the principal key. This is continued as a sort of pedal-point to the seventy-ninth measure, where the Principal is resumed.

The first movement of Beethoven's Sonata Appassionata contains four important ideas. The analysis of the whole movement is as follows:

Principal, F min. (sixteen and eight), twenty-four measures; Transition eleven; Second, and passage, in Ab, fifteen; partial conclusion (ten and five) fifteen. The Elaboration contains six periods. The first from the Principal, little changed, in E min., thirteen measures; then, the same motive capriciously handled, passing through E min., C min., Ab to Db, fifteen measures; third, transition, as before, little changed, sixteen measures; fourth, leading idea of the Second, capriciously evading a cadence and passing through Db, Bb min., Gb, B min., G, F min., fourteen measures; fifth, passage work on diminished seventh of E, seven measures; sixth, pedal-point on C, dominant of F min., the principal key of the work, thus leading back to the Principal which then follows, five measures. The Recapitulation closes with the conclusion very much extended. For whereas in the first part the partial conclusion had only two periods, fifteen measures in all, the full conclusion has no less than nine periods, and seventy-four measures, as thus: I. Same as in partial conclusion, ten. II. Partial conclusion extended, eleven. III. Motives from Second, seven. IV. Cadence work, nine. V. Passage, nine. VI. From transition in first part, four. VII. From Second, nine. VIII. New matter, eight. IX. Pedal point to close, seven measures.

The Sonata-piece is sometimes used for slow movements, in which case the elaboration is less extended. An example of this is furnished by the *Adagio* of the sprightly Sonata in B flat, op. 22 of Beethoven. Its plan is this. FIRST DIVISION, not repeated: Principal, E flat, twelve meas.; transition, six; Second, B flat, nine; partial conclusion, three. ELABORATION: I, motive from principal, nine; II. seven. REPETITION: Principal, E flat, eleven; transition, eight; Second nine; conclusion, three.

Quite a number of the last movements in the Beethoven Sonatas are designated *Finale*. These are generally not Rondos, but precisely like the Sonata-piece, except that directly after the double bar there follows a third melody, called a Middle-piece (*Mittelsatz*) which takes the place of the Elaboration. An example of this is furnished by the Finale of the first Sonata of Beethoven, F min., op. 2. These movements may be distinguished from Rondos even by inexperienced students, by means of the double bar, which does not occur in Rondos.

The Sonata-piece is derived from the "Ancient Binary Form," which is the form of the Bach gavottes, courantes, etc. It consists of two parts, the first of which is repeated. In Courantes the first part is generally about three periods long, on the same or very slightly different motives. In the Sonata-piece these three periods have been expanded into separate subjects. After the double bar the original motives were worked up in the dominant of the principal key. This part has become the elaboration. A return to the subject in the principal key completed the movement, as in the Sonata-piece.

ILLUSTRATIONS.

1. First movement of Sonata in F, op. 2. No. 1. Beethoven.
2. First movement of Sonata in C minor, op. 10, No. 1. Beethoven.
3. First movement Sonata in G, op. 31, No. 1. Beethoven.
4. First movement Sonata Appassionata, op. 57, Beethoven.
5. *Adagio* from Sonata in B flat, op. 22. Beethoven.

LESSON SIXTEENTH.

THE SONATA AS A WHOLE.

The name "Sonata," as we have already seen, properly belongs to a certain form, or single movement; but in process of time it has come to be applied to an entire work, consisting of three or four movements, only one of which is properly a sonata. In this larger sense all trios, quartetts and chamber music generally, as well as all symphonies are sonatas, having the same form as pianoforte sonatas, only somewhat longer.

The sonata as a whole consists of three or four movements, or forms, of which at least one is a sonata-piece. In general the sonata-piece is the first form. The second is an *Adagio* or other slow movement. The third either a Rondo or a Finale.

When the sonata has four movements, a Minuet, Allegretto, or Scherzo, intervenes between the slow movement and the Rondo. In a few cases this short movement precedes the slow movement. The general plan of the sonata, therefore, is this:

SONATA-PIECE; SLOW MOVEMENT; RONDO (OR FINALE).

Or this:

SONATA-PIECE; SLOW MOVEMENT; SCHERZO; FINALE.

Let us begin with an easy example. Observe the Beethoven Sonata in F, op. 2, No. 1. (Plays the entire sonata.) You recognize the separate movements, having already heard three of them in the previous lessons. What we wish to observe now is that the movements thus associated into a single work have no motives in common, are in different keys, and generally contrasted with each other; yet that they go together to make up a sort of story, a musical cycle, which seems more and more satisfactory as we become better acquainted with it. Listen again to the whole work. (Plays again.)

Sonata Pathetique is an example of a sonata in three movements, unless we count the *Grave* introduction for an independent form. In this work the contrasts are extremely strong, not only between the leading ideas of each movement but between the different movements.

The Introduction opens as follows: (Plays eight measures.) This very slow movement is followed by a very tumultuous one. (Plays the first period of *Allegro*.) And this, again, by a wonderfully deep and reposeful Adagio. (Plays eight measures.) After this comes the Rondo, a cheerful yet plaintive movement. (Plays first period.)

These different movements are not without certain bonds of union. These are, first, the *Sequence of Keys*. The Introduction and Allegro are in C minor; the Adagio in A flat, a nearly related key; and the Rondo, again, in C minor. Besides this there is a certain *Rhythmic Pulsation* common to all the movements. Thus a sixteenth-note in the *Grave* is nearly of the same length as the half-note in the Allegro, a sixteenth in the Adagio, and a half-note in the Rondo.

NOTE.—The contrasts in this sonata are intensified by the usual, and probably correct, tempos, which make the half-note of the Allegro considerably quicker than the sixteenth in the Introduction, recovering the movement again in the Adagio where the sixteenth corresponds to the sixteenth in the Introduction. The Rondo goes slightly faster, but not quite so fast as the Allegro, (the half-note of the Allegro being at the metronome rate of 144, and of the Rondo about 126.)

The principal point to observe in hearing a sonata is the progress of the emotion, the cycle of feeling. In the first movement we have generally the trouble, the conflict; in the second repose; and in the closing movement the return to the world again.

In the same manner should be examined Mozart's Sonata in F, (No. 6, Peters' edition,) Beethoven's Pastoral Sonata, op. 28, the Sonata in G, op. 31, that in C minor, op. 10, etc.

This exercise should be distributed over a considerable lapse of time; it occurs again in a later chapter. (Lesson XXIX.)

Part Third.

THE CONTENT OF MUSIC.

LESSON SEVENTEENTH.

CONTENT DEFINED.

We have here three small pieces of music, all well made, and in fact works of genius.

The first is the Bach Invention in F, (No. 8 of the two-part Invention) already known to us. The second is the first two strains of the *Andante* in Beethoven's Sonata in F minor, op. 57. The third, the Schubert Menuetto in B minor, op. 78. Observe them. (Plays.)

Let us consider the impression they leave upon our consciousness. The first has the spirit of a bright, rather talkative, but decidedly talented person, who is not wanting in a certain mild self-conceit. The second is full of repose and deep feeling. As we hear it over again a seriousness comes over us, as when one enters a forest in an autumn day. The third has a spice of the heroic in it, as well as a vein of tenderness; the latter especially in the second part (the trio).

2. Or take, again, two other pieces. The first is the Adagio of Sonata Pathetique; the second Chopin's Polonaise in A. (Plays.) The first has a deeply tender spirit, sad yet comforted. In the second we have the soul of a hero and patriot who hears his country's call.

3. Or take again two pieces by a single author, and for our first trial let them be by Bach. They are the Inventions in F, (No. 8, as before,) and the three-part Invention in E minor, No. 14. (Plays.) The first has the character already assigned to it. The second is full of repose and quiet meditation.

4. Or take, again, two pieces by Chopin. Let them be the Nocturne in E flat, op. 9, and the Polonaise in A, already heard. (Plays.)

In the nocturne we have a soft and tender musing, as when at twilight one sinks into a tender day-dream.

From these and multitudes of other examples that might be adduced it will be seen that there is in music something beyond a pleasant turning of words and phrases, something more than a symmetrical succession of well-contrasted periods. Every piece leaves a greater or less effect upon the feelings. It has its own spirit of grave or gay, heroic or tender. This inner something, this *soul of the music* we call Content.

22. The whole Content of a piece is the total impression it leaves upon the most congenial hearer. Or, as another has said, "The whole Content of a piece is all that the author put into it, technical knowledge and skill, imagination and feeling."*

The Content is to be found out by hearing the piece a sufficient number of times for its meaning to be ascertained. The Content is not some peculiarity of the piece that can be pointed out, but the final impression it leaves after repeated hearings. It is for that reason that the examples thus far referred to have been such as were already familiar through previous citation.

Pieces lacking Content are merely empty forms—bodies without souls. There are many such to be met with.

A piece may be of considerable length and elegantly written and yet contain but a small Content. Compare, *e. g.* these two pieces. The first is Fields' nocturne in B flat, one of his cleverest works. The second, Schumann's Romance in F sharp, op. 28. (Plays.) The first is an elegant piece of verse, but it says very little. The second is extremely earnest and heartfelt; yet even this is not of such deep meaning as, *e. g.*, the Largo of Beethoven's second sonata. (Plays.)

(These works should be repeated until the pupils or the greater part of them perceive the differences of which mention is made. It is a mistake to tell them beforehand the qualities they are to find. Let them learn to *feel them* for themselves.)

As music is a much more complete emotional expression than speech, it will be found impossible to fitly describe in words the general impression musical master-works make upon the feelings of congenial listeners. "*Congenial* listeners," is said, because when one lacks a

*J. C. Fillmore.

musical soul, or is out of the mood for it, a piece makes no impression upon him.

The principal difference between the creations of genius and those of an inferior order is one of Content. Any student who will study the best models, and follow the directions of competent teachers, may master the technical art of the musical composer, so as to satisfy a technical criticism in all respects. But unless he happens also to have musical feeling of a high order, his works will be nearly or quite wanting in Content. Even among the greatest composers there are some (Francis Joseph Haydn, *e. g.*,) whose works are masterly in form and taste, but as a rule elegant rather than deep.

In general every piece falls into one of two categories. Either it is *stimulative* or *restful*. All well-written thematic works belong to the former category; lyric movements to the latter.

The stimulative effect resides in the quick movement, and a vigorous harmonic and melodic movement. The restful, in a quiet movement, generally slow or at least moderate, and a lyric structure.

List of Illustrations.

1. Bach Invention in F. (No. 8.)
2. Andante from Beethoven's Sonata in F min., op. 57. (sixteen meas.)
3. Schubert Menuetto in B min.
4. Adagio of Sonata Pathetique. (sixteen meas.)
5. Chopin's Polonaise Militaire in A.
6. Bach's three-part Invention in E min. No. 14.
7. Chopin Nocturne in E flat, op. 9.
8. Field's Nocturne in B flat.
9. Schumann's Romance in F sharp.
10. Largo of Beethoven's Sonata in A, op. 2, No. 2.

LESSON EIGHTEENTH.

THE INTELLECTUAL AND EMOTIONAL.

Let us observe again two of the pieces out of the last lesson. They are the Bach Invention in F, No. 8, and the theme of the Andante in the Beethoven Sonata appassionata, op. 57. (Plays.)
Which of these seems to mean the most? Which one has the more feeling in it? (This point must be dwelt upon and the pieces played repeatedly until the pupils perceive that there is more feeling in the Andante.) Let us analyze the phraseology of the Andante. Its interest is chiefly harmonic. Its peculiarly serious expression is due to the alternation of the tonic and subdominant chords, thus:

Ex. 19.

The effect of gravity is also partly due to the low position of the chords in absolute pitch, especially of the seventh-chord which opens the second period. To the same impression the slow movement conduces. The passage presents nothing of outward sensuous melody for the ear to seize upon.

On the other hand, observe again the phraseology of the Bach Invention. (See Chap. IV, where it is analyzed.) It consists almost wholly of two motives which are repeated many times in different keys and in both voices. The first is the bold arpeggio figure, the first six notes of the treble. The last tone of this motive is also the first of the second figure, the descending run in sixteenths. These two motives together make a phrase and form the principal idea of the piece.

This phrase occurs entire ten times in the Invention; besides these the first motive occurs six times, and an inverted imitation of it (see measure 21, in the bass) several times more.

Thus it would hardly be too much to say that the entire Invention consists of nothing more than this single idea, and that the two speakers, or rather singers (the treble and bass) arrive at nothing new after all their prolonged discussion.

In the harmonic structure of this piece we find a decided plan. It begins in F major. At the seventh measure it goes into C major, and makes a cadence in this key in the eleventh measure, closing with the accent of the twelfth measure. Then ensues the middle part which begins in C, passes into G minor, D minor, B flat and so back to F. The climax occurs in the nineteenth or twenty-first measures.

The construction of so elaborate a piece from so few materials is an evidence of intellectual activity on the part of the composer.

2. Another example of a similar mode of construction is afforded by the Bach Invention in C, No. 1, analyzed in Chap. IV. This work also consists of a single phrase imitated, transformed, transposed, carried through C, G, D minor, A minor, F, and so back to C, and all this within a compass of twenty-two measures.

3. Yet another example of this mode of construction is afforded by the Bach Fugue in C minor. (Clavier, No. 2, Plays.)

In all these a leading subject is taken as a text, not to come back to and repeat entire as in the Rondo and other binary and ternary forms, but to *work with*, to transpose and transform, to elaborate by means of harmonic treatment until an entire movement is built up out of it. This is the type of musical composition as it existed in Bach's time. Some pieces are more emotional than others, but all of them are built up on this plan. They contain *Musical Thought*. These transformations of motive are equivalent to reasoning in language. To appreciate them properly one needs to follow the idea through all its modifications and modulations.

The opposite of this mode of structure, as we have long ago seen, is the lyric, the natural type of the emotional. Observe now, for the sake of the contrast, the first sixteen measures of the Beethoven Adagio from the Sonata in F, op. 2, No. 1. (Plays.)

In general the following may be advanced as a sound doctrine regarding the Intellectual in Music.

All thematic music is of an intellectual character. In order to fully appreciate it, the hearer needs to firmly seize the leading motive, so as to be able to follow it through its various transformations. Such a following out and participating in the author's musical thought, implies an unconscious comparison of the motive with its various transformations. All thematic music is characterized by more varied modulations and a more artificially contrived, or at least a freer, harmonic structure than is found in lyric. Here, again, in this elaborate harmonic setting, we have the trace of mastership on the part of the composer; a token of his musical *thinking*, as distinguished from merely meditating.

Yet this kind of music is not unemotional. On the contrary, it is sometimes intensely exciting. When this is the case the effect is due to a fitly chosen harmonic progression by means of which a climax is attained, and the intensification of the effect through the reiteration of the leading motives.

The leading motive is repeated many times in all music, for in this way only can unity be attained in a music-piece. There is this difference, however, between the repetitions in thematic and lyric pieces, viz., that in lyric pieces the motive is repeated unchanged, but in thematic pieces with manifold changes.

Thematic music is at first unattractive to hearers in general, because they do not know how to hear it properly. When they hear the same piece many times they become reconciled to it, and in the end enjoy it and even prefer it to lyric pieces they at first thought more beautiful.

One of the most decided examples of the intellectual in music is afforded by counterpoint. (See Lesson V.) The simplest theme treated contrapuntally acquires a dignity which was before wanting. In double counterpoint the intellectual is even more strongly marked.

The strictest type of musical composition is the Fugue. In this a single subject forms the substance of it. This subject can not be transformed with absolute freedom, but each imitation must take place on a particular degree of the scale. Thus, *e. g.*, if the antecedent is in the tonic, the imitation or answer ("consequent") must be on the dominant, and *vice versa*. When a modulation takes place and the subject appears in a foreign key, the imitation takes place in the dominant of that.

Besides these restrictions there is also the "counter-subject" which every voice must take up immediately after finishing the subject. Thus the counter-subject forms almost an invariable accompaniment to the subject throughout the Fugue. In spite of these limitations Bach was able to use this form with such freedom as to leave us a very great number of Fugues which are not only masterly in their construction but emotional and thoroughly free and musical, and among the most cherished treasures of the musician's repertory.

NOTE.—Students desiring to study Fugue analytically can do so in Mr. James Higgs' "Fugue" (in Novello's "Music Primers," price one dollar.) Those able to read German will find a very interesting treatment of the subject in the third vol. of J. C. Lobe's *Kompositionslehre*, in which he bases his theories on Bach's remarkable work "*Die Kunst der Fugue*" (Peters' Ed.) a series of twenty-four Fugues on a single subject.

The subject of this lesson may be continued through another one,

48   HOW TO UNDERSTAND MUSIC.

in which case the "list of additional illustrations" will be found useful.

LIST OF ILLUSTRATIONS.

1. Bach's Invention in F.
2. Andante from Beethoven's op. 57. (sixteen meas.)
3. Bach's Invention in C. No. 1.
4. Allegro from Beethoven's Sonata in F, op. 2 No. 1.

ADDITIONAL ILLUSTRATIONS, NOT ANALYZED ABOVE.

1. Bach's Fugue in C minor, Clavier, No. 2.
2. Schubert Impromptu in C minor, op. 90, No. 1.
3. Bach's Fugue in G minor, Clavier, No. 16.
4. Schubert Impromptu in E flat, op. 90, No. 2.
5. Lefebre-Wely's "Titania."
6. First movement of piano solo in Chopin's Concerto in E minor, op. 11.
7. Handel Chaconne and variations in G. No. 3 of Köhler's Handel's "Lessons, Pieces, and Fugues." (Peters' Ed. No. 40.)
8. Handel's Capriccio in G minor, No. 2 of "Seven Pieces" in same volume.

LESSON NINETEENTH.

PASSAGES, CADENZAS AND EFFECTS.

Sequence is the general name given to the immediate repetition of a phrase or motive whether in unchanged or modified form.

In thematically composed periods the motive is followed by several repetitions of it in a somewhat changed form. The Sequence thus formed proceeds no farther than compatible with a graceful return to the key in which the period is intended to conclude. A Sequence not thus returning and completing itself into a period, becomes either an independent section, or a *passage*, which is the general name given to such parts of a music-piece as do not fall into periods. The following, *e. g.*, is a very simple passage.

Ex. 20.

Here is one slightly more complex.

Ex. 21.

PASSAGES, CADENZAS AND EFFECTS.

Observe the following two passages from Cramer's First study. (Plays as far as the middle of the eighth measure.) Observe also the passage descending from the second beat of the tenth measure to the first note of the thirteenth. (Plays.) Also the ascending and descending passages following. (Plays the whole study.) Explain the construction of these passages. Thus, e. g., the right hand ascends in the thirteenth measure and three measures after by sequencing on the figure at a Ex. 22.

Later it descends by sequencing on figure b, Ex. 22.

Ex. 22.

Such passages as these differ from regularly constructed phrases in this, that being composed of a merely artificial sequencing on a single motive, whatever sensible or definite may come of it must be owing to the harmonic treatment and progressions.

Passages in musical composition serve the purpose of gracefully connecting one part of a work with another, and of relieving the attention from the strain of the thoughtful or deeply expressive periods between which they intervene. In this use we find them in Bach, Handel, Haydn, Mozart, Beethoven, and in fact all good composers. In modern writers, however, they have been very much developed and have been made the vehicle for the display of bravoura effect, especially on the pianoforte. The effectiveness of a passage is in proportion to its apparent difficulty, which impression, again, is derived either from the visible labor of the player, or from the inability of the hearer to understand the construction of it. Any such Sequence as those in Exs. 20 and 21 is easily comprehended by even an inexperienced ear. But we find in various modern works passages not susceptible of ready analysis by the ear, especially when played rapidly. Thus, e. g., observe this cadenza from Liszt's Rigoletto. (Plays Chromatic Cadenza on p. 4 of that piece.) When played rapidly it produces an immense effect. It is derived from the chromatic scale. Let us build it. Suppose we take a descending chromatic scale of one octave.

Ex. 23.

Instead of descending simply, in this way, let us go down by sequences of a motive ascending one degree, played with both hands.

Ex. 24.  etc.

Now let the little finger play a chromatic scale a sixth above the treble and a sixth below the alto. Then the right hand will play this:

Ex. 25.

And the left hand this:

Ex. 26.

And both hands this:

Ex. 27.

In Chopin's works we find a great variety of passages consisting generally of a combination of sequences of diminished sevenths resolved chromatically. Of such a kind are, *e. g.*, the following from the Concerto in E minor. Here (p. 165 of the Augener edition of Klindworth's Chopin) are two ascending sequences of diminished chords, differently treated (second and third lines).*

On p. 168 of the same edition we have a different passage constructed on the same general plan. (See in general, the chain of passages following the soft melody in C, middle part of the first movement of the Chopin Concerto.)

Reference may also be made if convenient to the Cadenza in the Rivé-King edition of Liszt's Second Rhapsody.

*Reference is here made to the sequences immediately preceding the close of the solo part in E major, first movement of Concerto in E minor.

LIST OF ILLUSTRATIONS.

1. Cramer's First Study.
2. Cadenza from Liszt's "Rigoletto."
3. Passages from Chopin Concerto in E minor.

LESSON TWENTIETH.

THE SENSUOUS AND THE IDEALIZED.

In dance music all its good harmony and melody, and graceful treatment generally, are made subservient to the sense of physical motion. Thus, e. g., observe the following. (Plays a part of Strauss' "Blue Danube Waltzes.") This music unquestionably is genuine and valid, but it appeals mainly to the dancing instinct. As played by the the orchestra it is much more voluptuous than it appears on the pianoforte.

Observe now another waltz. (Plays Karl Merz's "Pearl of the Sea.") In this we have the dance-instinct also addressed, but not in so enticing and voluptuous forms as in the Strauss music. This belongs to the class of "drawing-room waltzes," and partakes of the naïveté of the People's Song.

Again, take a still less pronounced type. (Plays the Chopin Waltz in E flat, op. 18.) Here we have also a waltz; the same rhythm and the same form. Yet in this piece the sensuous element has retired. It is not now an actual flesh-and-blood dance to which the composer invites us, but to a poetically conceived meditation upon a waltz. Here the fancy runs wild. This we see in the extremely rapid tempo, which is more than three times as rapid as a waltz could be danced.

The Strauss "Blue Danube" reminds us of the whirling ballroom, the thickly perfumed air, the blazing lights, and all the sensuous intoxication that goes with it. The Merz waltz is still a dance, a flesh-and-blood dance, but no longer so exciting. It is a nice, hearty family dance under the trees in open sky. The Chopin waltz leaves the physical scene entirely. This is the idealized dance.

Observe again the following. (Plays the waltz from Gounod's "Faust.") And then this. (Plays the Chopin Waltz in A flat, op. 42.)

Here again we have the same contrast. One of the pieces invites us to a real waltz; the other to an idealized revery. Which is the material? And which the poetic?

If convenient it will be well to show here how the physical "Faust" waltz is itself idealized, although in a sensational direction, in Liszt's arrangement of Gounod's "Faust." Here we have the dreamy melody in the middle of the waltz dwelt upon and idealized, and the slow movement interposed, recalling the first meeting of Faust and Marguerita.

The same distinction between dance music proper, and parlor music in dance forms, prevails throughout all the movements originally designed to control the physical motions, such as the March, Waltz, Polka, Mazurka, Minuet, etc. It will be felt by the observant that those pieces which most strongly suggest and invite to physical motions (as the Strauss waltzes, for example) stop there, and do not possess a poetic Content.

LIST OF ILLUSTRATIONS.

1. Strauss' Blue Danube Waltz. (Any other *superior* dancing waltz will do.)
2. Karl Merz's " Pearl of the Sea."
3. Chopin Waltz in E flat, op. 18.
4. Waltz from Gounod's " Faust." (Sydney Smith, perhaps.)
5. Chopin Waltz in A flat, op. 42.
6. Liszt's Gounod's " Faust."

LESSON TWENTY-FIRST.

DESCRIPTIVE, SUGGESTIVE AND POETIC MUSIC.

Quite in line with the previous lesson, we have here to do with music in which certain external events or objects are referred to by means of music.

Observe the following. (Plays Henry Weber's "The Storm," but without naming it.) Ask the question: "Do any of the class know this piece?" If none of them know it, ask them to tell what it means. It will prove a very amusing experiment, the accounts will be so different. If any of the class already know it, ask them to remain quiet, and allow the others to give their explanation of it. When this has been done, read aloud the author's prefatory note as follows:

"The Storm. An Imitation of Nature(!) The following is the idea conveyed by this composition. A shepherd is going home with his flock—while he is playing an air on his flute a storm approaches. The thunder, the roaring of the water, the crash of trees and the fire-bells are to be heard in succession." (Plays again.) As an "imitation of nature" this pretty little piece is scarcely successful. For although the flute and the muffled thunder are tolerably suggested, the crash of trees and roaring of the waters do not appear. The fire-bells also would scarcely be heard in a pastoral neighborhood. However, this is a point relating to the poetic conception, with which we have really nothing to do. Our question is, Do these musical figures really represent or remind us of the natural objects to which the author refers them? To this question we must return a decided negative. Even with all the resources of the modern orchestra in the hands of such a master as Wagner, a storm is very imperfectly represented.

Again, observe this. (Plays Mr. G. D. Wilson's "Shepherd Boy.") This pretty little piece has no imitation of nature as such. A name is given it which serves as a starting point. But the music gives us neither the rocks, the grass, the sheep, the sheep-bells, the boy, his crook, or the bright sky over head, but only the peaceful and monotonous spirit of such a scene. This is an Idyll and not a description.

For a still more fortunate example observe this. (Plays Schumann's "The Hobby Horse" No. 8, out of the Album for the Young, without naming it. When the piece is concluded, ask the class their impression of it, as to what it means or represents.) In such a piece as this it is not possible to infer the meaning of the author from simply hearing the piece. But when the clue is afforded, the suitability of the music becomes apparent.

Observe also "The Jolly Farmer" No. 10 in the Album for the Young. (Plays.) This piece might be called by any other name that would be sufficient to account for its simplicity, heartiness and satisfaction. Schumann's title is on the whole the easiest hypothesis by which to account for it.

Plays also "Santa Claus" No. 12 in the Album, the Spring song No. 15, the little Romance No. 19, and the Sailor's song No. 37.

It will also be advantageous to study in this connection, as time serves, Schumann's "Scenes from Childhood" op. 15. These thirteen little pieces are extremely varied and clever, and belong rather to *poetic* music, than to descriptive music proper.

The difference here implied is this: — In descriptive music it is attempted to represent the external traits of objects by means of music, in such a way that a person hearing the music will recall the object, which is practically impossible. In poetic music it is attempted *to represent the spirit* of such and such natural objects or experiences. The title serves to connect the two. Whoever hears the music without knowing the title, hears only some very animated and widely different pieces of music, interesting and fresh considered simply as music. When he knows the title he has in that a clue to the composer's intention or desire of representing something beyond the actual content of the music as such. Such pieces, therefore, form useful study for pupils not yet thoroughly musical.

Of the same class but in a lower grade are the fanciful titles so common in parlor pieces, such as "Warblings at Eve," "Monastery Bells," "Maiden's Prayer," etc., in all of which the title was an afterthought, put on to sell the piece, frequently, indeed, assigned by some other than the composer, and often with very little reference to the actual Content of the music.

Observe again this. (Plays the "Battle of Prague," without announcing title.) This, again, is an independent and fairly well made piece of music, a Sonata, indeed. That the low tones represent cannon no one would know except he knew the intention.

If convenient it will prove very interesting in this connection to observe a four-hand performance of Wagner's "Ride of the Valkyrie," one of the most singular compositions before the public.

There are also at least two of the Beethoven Sonatas which are of especial interest in this connection. They are "The Pastorale" op. 28, and "The Adieux, the Absence and the Return," op. 84.

List of Illustrations.

1. "The Storm" by Henry Weber.
2. "The Shepherd Boy," G. D. Wilson.
3. "The Hobby Horse," etc. from Schumann's "Album for the Young," op. 68.
4. "The Battle of Prague," by Kotzwara.
5. "Scenes from Childhood," op. 15. Schumann.
6. "Sonata Pastorale," op. 28. Beethoven.
7. "The Adieux, the Absence, and the Return." Sonata op. 81. Beethoven.

Part Fourth.

STUDIES IN ART AND THE BEAUTIFUL.

CHAPTER TWENTY-SECOND.

SECTION FIRST. THE IDEAL AND ITS PHASES.

Every thing that *is*, stone, plant, tree, landscape, building, animal and man himself, presents itself to the mind in two aspects. First as an actual appearance, an established and ordered existence, proceeding according to its own laws and expressing its own nature. Man at first accepts it in unquestioning simplicity. Presently, however, this unquestioning acceptance of whatever *is* because it *is*, gives place to a spirit of inquiry which seeks to know *why* it is. The answer to this gives the second aspect of things: namely, that every thing that is is the representation or embodiment of some particular *idea*, which existed before the appearance of it, either in the present individual or any of its predecessors.

Thus if we attentively consider a piece of crystalline rock, as of granite, we find it first a merely natural appearance, an inanimate substance, a piece of matter. But when we meditate upon it more deeply, we perceive that its particles are organized into crystals, determinate forms, in the construction of which the particles of matter have followed certain laws. Thus, beyond all we can learn of the piece of granite by mere inspection, there lies back of this its *law*, the ruling principle of its *type*; the *idea*, of which granite is the expression. So every piece of inorganic nature manifests laws, ideas, which are back of the natural appearance.

In an organized existence, as, *e. g.*, a plant, we recognize the *idea* much more clearly. For, whereas in the crystal the impelling force acted in the original formation once for all, in the plant we have before us a continual creation. With its leaves open to the sunshine and showers, and its rootlets groping in the soil for moisture and other elements of its being, it gathers to itself from the world about it whatever is most necessary for its growth, and shapes and fashions it according to the organic law of its species. Here, then, we come upon certain rudimental appearances of self-determination; or, as we might otherwise say, upon a higher step in the representation of idea.

How much stronger is the expression of idea in a tree! Take the oak. The acorn is a little fruit, scarcely larger than the end of your finger. Planted, it yields but a tender shoot. But when a hundred suns of summer have shone upon it, and a century's winds and storms beat upon it, how sturdy and grand it stands! There is in the oak an *idea*, the law of its being; and sunshine, rain, storm and passing years, but afford it opportunity to bring this idea to expression—to work out its own *ideal*.

Again, consider the animal, more highly organized, gifted with self-movement, and with a certain amount of mind and intelligence; nay, even with the more precious qualities of friendship and affection. Yet each kind is true to its type. Individuals differ, but there is behind all these variations the idea of the species, the type of the kind, the *ideal*, from which no one varies in any radical degree.

Thus we come to the still higher expression of idea in man, whose glory is his mind; his complex and wonderful intellectual and emotional nature, the image of God. This it is which investigates the outer world, arranges her phenomena into orderly sequence of cause and effect, and classifies her appearances according to their essential character. It is the mind of man which multiplies the wants and capacities of life, as well as the means of gratifying them. Still more the mind shows itself in literature, and here in such true sense as to make all these other achievements seem of no meaning and significance as if they were indeed only the very "small dust of the balance." Thus we have in the lower department of mental effort, what we might call the "matter-of-fact" part of literature, the newspapers and magazines through which man learns of the doings and ideas of his fellow men throughout the world, and the histories in which he learns of the rise and fall of nations, and reads the lessons of the past. How wonderful is the evidence these give of far-reaching human thought and sympathy! But above this great practical department of literature which relates itself to material success, we find Poetry, and Imaginative Composition of every kind, in which the human spirit soars into higher regions of fancy and feeling. Here the soul is represented as unhampered by accidents of fortune, or as triumphing over them in the exuberant force of its own individuality. Nay! the spirit searches into the eternal principles of good and evil, and sets them in order before us. This progress goes yet further in Art. Temple, Statue, Picture, Symphony and Psalm, all unite in giving evidence of a spiritual activity in man which rises above the routine of everyday life and its necessities, into the clear and more enduring radiance of the ideal.

Thus, whether we consider the progress of creation, from the rudimental forms of the earliest geological periods to the highly organized beings which occupy the earth at the present time; or if we study one natural appearance after another and see how plainly each bears witness to the existence of a higher law, an eternal idea which determines its appearance, and then again combine these into an ascending system of excellence:—in either case we have to do with ideas and the Ideal; and so with everlasting truth, the inner nature of things, the soul, and immortal interests; for the ideal is the abiding, the eternal. As Schopenhauer says:

"For thousands of years a chemical force slumbered in matter until the touch of re-agents set it free; then it appeared, but *time* is only for the appearance not for the force itself. For thousands of years galvanism slept in copper and zinc, and they both lay resting over against silver, which as soon as all three are combined under proper conditions must burst out in flames. Even in a dry seed-corn for three thousand years the slumbering force lay hidden which in the final appearance of suitable circumstances bursts out as plant. But, as before, *time* is not for the idea itself, but only for its appearance."

Again, let us observe further that in no single individual is its own ideal fully realized. Even in the lowest types, as crystals, it is rare to find fully formed specimens, but rather they mostly appear with a corner broken here, a line or proportion distorted there, and so on. On the higher plane of plant-life the difficulty of discovering a perfect specimen is much greater. In one the branches are not symmetrical; in another the stem is distorted; even a single perfect leaf is rarely seen. A perfectly formed animal is equally rare. Whether belonging to the lowest grades of animal life or the highest, or at any intermediate place in the scale, in almost every individual we find some imperfection or other; a hard winter, a season of famine, an untimely and unsuccessful struggle for supremacy;—some one or all of these have interfered with the development of the animal, and have left their mark of imperfection upon him. In man is this much more the case. A form perfect in all its proportions we never see. It is even difficult to discover perfectly proportioned single members. In his mental disposition, likewise, the same imperfect results are observed. For wherever we search we discover no complete man; but on the contrary unbalanced faculties, contradictory impulses, imperfectly developed reasoning powers, undisciplined affections, and in short a general want of harmony and coherence in the manifold capacities of the soul.

Nevertheless, in all these innumerable degrees of manifestation, the Ideal itself remains steadfast and eternal. For although we may not be able to discover a single individual but lacks some element of perfection or grace, yet we have at least our idea of the *average* excellence of many individuals of the same class, and in this an imperfect ideal. Beyond and above this, again, is the much higher ideal arrived at by collecting all the most eminent perfections ever known in individuals of a given class, and combining these together into the conception of a more perfect crystal, plant, animal, or character than any one has even seen realized.

In like manner, there is no delicacy or splendor of color, nor any sweetness and harmony of tone, no pleasant savor or odor, no symmetry or grace of form, nor any magnificence of mental endowment or genius of any kind, but that beyond it one immediately imagines something more satisfactory and complete. Thus in all these, the sensuous and the purely spiritual as well, we have our human ideals which we form by collecting and combining separate perfections. These remain steadfast, or become constantly more complete in spite of the counteracting influence of the discovery of imperfections in individuals. Beyond these, again, exists the true ideal, perfectly known only to God, but in some feeble degree imaginable to the specially gifted or inspired; and these are the naturalists, statesmen, prophets, seers, artists and poets of the world, who all find their true distinction in their successful divination and communication of the ideal.

Under the term *Ideal*, therefore, we properly include every thing that is eternal and true. Any object in nature or art is ideal according as it manifests in outward form the inner nature of the Ideal.

There are three great phases of the ideal which include within themselves all possible grades of goodness and excellence; and imply as opposites all grades of imperfection and wrong. These all inclusive phases are the TRUE, the BEAUTIFUL, and the GOOD.

Under the name True we include not only all truthfulness of statement and teaching, whether relating to material objects, to history, or to speculation, but also all genuineness and consistency, or the quality of agreement between the *appearance* and the *real nature* in any material thing or person.

The conception we call Goodness relates to the moral nature, and involves in it the idea of the exercise of benevolence and love as the habitual motive of action. This form of the ideal is that habitually appealed to in religion. In its lower applications it involves the idea of fitness, suitability, adaptation to a proposed end.

The ideal we call the Beautiful involves in it predominantly the quality of *perfection of appearance*, and is expressed in forms addressed to sense-perception, or to the inner senses. Truth is primarily addressed to the intellect; Goodness to the moral nature; Beauty to the senses.

All these, the True, the Beautiful and the Good, unite in the One Ideal, GOD.

All qualities of the ideal whether in material things, animals, or personal character, are but reflections, imperfect appearances, or intimations of the Divine.

SECTION SECOND. THE DESIGN AND SCOPE OF ART.

Art has for its object the expression of the Ideal in sense-form; or, which means the same thing, the expression of the Beautiful.

"The sole principle of Art is cognition of the ideal; its sole design the communication of this knowledge. While *Science*, tracing the restless and inconstant stream of manifold principles and sequences, in each point reached finds always something further, and never a last limit, nor yet ever can find complete satisfaction (just as little as one by running can reach the point where clouds touch the horizon): *Art*, on the other hand, is already at the limit. She arrests the object of her contemplation out of the stream of the world-course, and holds it isolated. And this Single, which in the stream was but a little vanishing part, becomes for her a *representative of the whole*, an Equivalent of the endless Many in space and time. She remains fast, therefore, by this separate. She stops the wheel of time; relations vanish for her; only the *essential*, the Idea, is the object.

"We can, therefore, straightway designate Art as *the examination of things in their eternal nature and meaning*, in contrast to the examination of things in their temporal aspects, which is the way of sense-perception and knowledge. This latter mode is an endless, like a horizontal line; the former is a perpendicular cutting the horizontal line at a chosen point. The usual mode of examining things is the reasonable one, which in practical life, as in science, is alone valid and profitable. The other is in Art the only valid and profitable. The scientific is the mode of Aristotle; the artistic, in the main, that of Plato. The first is like the furious storm, which hurries along without beginning or limit, bends, moves, and carries every thing along with it; the second like the quiet sunbeam which cuts its way through the storm entirely unmoved by it. The first like the innumerable, tempestuously-moving drops of the water-fall, which, constantly changing, suffer no glance to linger upon them; the second like the rainbow resting in stillness upon this tumultuous crowd."*

The Powers of Art are thus broadly defined by Hegel: "It is the task and scope of art to bring to our perception and spiritual realization all that in our thought has a place in the human spirit. That well-known sentence, *Nihil humani a me alienum puto*, Art shall realize in us."

Its design is, therefore : To awaken and to animate the slumbering feelings, desires and passions of all kinds ; to fill the heart and to permit to be conscious in man everything developed and undeveloped which human feeling can carry, experience, and bring forth, in its innermost and most secret parts; whatever the human heart in its manifold possibilities and moods desires to move and excite; and especially whatever the spirit has in its thought and in the Idea of the most Essential and High; the glory of the Honored, Eternal, and True.

"It may also express unhappiness and misery, in order thus to make wickedness and criminality conceivable, and to permit the human heart to share every thing horrible and dreadful, as well as all joy and happiness. Then fancy may at last indulge herself in vain sport of the imagination, and run riot in the ensnaring magic of sensuously entrancing contemplation."

That is to say : It is within the power of Art to portray the entire content of the human spirit; its evil no less than its good. Nevertheless the proper mission of Art, as the expression of Beauty, forbids

*Schopenhauer.

the representation of the evil except in so far as it can be used for contrast in order thereby to reveal a deeper beauty. Any use of evil in art other than in this subjection to good, makes false art.

SECTION THIRD. CONDITIONS OF ART AND OF ITS ENJOYMENT.

The effectiveness of Art rests primarily upon the fact that our knowledge of the outer world comes in through sensation and sense-perception, and thus first reaches the feelings and will. Therefore, whether it is the external reality itself which occupies the attention, or only the appearance of it (as in pictures, drawings, or representations) "by means of which a scene, or relation, or life-moment of any kind is brought to us,— it remains for our soul the same, in order to depress or rejoice us according to the nature of such an idea, to stir and excite and to thrill us with the feelings and passions of anger, hatred, and sympathy; of anxiety, fear, love, esteem, and wonder; of Honor and of Glory.

"This waking up of all sensations in us, the education of our feelings through each life-picture; to set in operation all these inner movements through a merely deceptive external presence—it is which is especially seen as the peculiar, unexcelled power of art.

"Nevertheless, Art in this manner, impresses good and bad upon the feelings and ideas; and the design should be to strengthen it to the noblest, so as to nerve it up to the most thoughtful and useful inspirations." (Hegel.)

In all art-work we have to do with two elements, "first a content, design, meaning; then the expression, representation and realization of this content; and both sides so brought together that the *outer* and material is presented only as the representation of the *inner*, and not otherwise: as that which the *covering* has received and expressed out of the *content*."*

The Fine Arts are Architecture, Sculpture, Painting, Music, and Poetry (including all imaginative composition). Each one of these

*Hegel.

seeks to express the beautiful in its own way, according to the nature and capacity of the material through which it works.

In order to thoroughly appreciate and justly estimate any masterwork of art, therefore, we need to consider its conception or intention, and the technical merits of its execution. Hence, the intention of the previous parts of the present work has been to lead to an intelligent observation of the more external qualities of music as a form of art. This having been measurably accomplished, we here enter upon a consideration of the content or meaning of music, in doing which we find it most convenient and helpful to inquire also concerning the scope and meaning of all the arts, as well as the leading characteristics of the beautiful itself which they all have for their ideal.

All forms of the Beautiful as we saw in the beginning, are to be enjoyed through *contemplation* rather than *thought*. A beautiful sunset, a grand mountain view, a great moment in history, lose their charm of beauty or grandeur when we reason about them and occupy ourselves with an inquiry into the scientific principles underlying them. The drops of water in the rainbow are but ordinary examples of the substance chemically known as H_2O. It is only our own accidental position with regard to them and the sun, which enables us to perceive in them the beautiful token of God's remembrance. We look, and behold! it is there! We approach to analyze it, and lo! it is gone.

All art and all perception and enjoyment of the beautiful, come through childlike faith and openness of spirit.

And whenever for the sake of study and knowledge we analyze an art-work in order to surprise the secret of its construction, we need to re-create it again, according to the simple directness of its meaning as art, in order to recover its charm and inspiration.

CHAPTER TWENTY-THIRD.

OF THE NATURE AND MEANING OF THE BEAUTIFUL.

Under the term "Beautiful" are included an innumerable manifold of meanings, so great and in their higher reaches so glorious, that language fails in power to express them, and even the mind is lost amid the bewildering splendor. For in this term we reckon together all that is pleasing in sensation, contentful and satisfactory in contemplation, or kindling and inspiring in spiritual perception. It embraces within itself every graceful and lovely existence in created things, all that artists have represented, poets dreamed, or seer and revelator made known, and every possibility of splendor, glory, and excellence, which the longest ages of eternity shall make real to the blessed.

Since, then, the Beautiful itself is not yet fully revealed, it is no wonder that a complete and satisfactory discussion of the subject has never been made, for such an achievement is in its nature impossible.

Nevertheless, every act of æsthetic judgment involves within it the determination of "beautiful" or "un-beautiful," and hence the soundness of our subsequent progress in the present studies requires of us here such preliminary consideration of this wonderful ideal as we may be able to attain to. Of all writers on this subject Ruskin is the most eloquent and suggestive, though perhaps not the most complete in scientific form. The liberty is taken, therefore, of availing ourselves of his words, to piece out the more systematic, rational, and practical classification we find ready to our hand in Lotze's work on "Æsthetics in Germany" ("*Aesthetik in Deutschland*" by Hermann Lotze, Munich, 1868).

"By the term beauty," says Ruskin,* "properly are signified two things. First, that external quality of bodies, which, whether it occurs in a stone, flower, beast, or in man, is absolutely identical, which, as I have already asserted, may be shown to be in some sort typical of the Divine attributes, and which, therefore, I shall, for distinction's sake, call typical beauty; and, secondarily, the appearance of felicitous fulfilment of function in living things, more especially of the joyful and right exercise of perfect life in man. And this kind of beauty I shall call vital beauty.

*"Modern Painters," Vol. II., p. 27.

"Any application of the word beautiful to other appearances or qualities than these, is either false or metaphorical, as, for instance to the splendor of a discovery, the fitness of a proportion, the coherence of a chain of reasoning, or the power of bestowing pleasure which objects receive from association, a power confessedly great, and interfering, as we shall presently find, in a most embarrassing way with the attractiveness of real beauty."

All modes or degrees of the Beautiful may be counted in three categories. These are: (1.) The Pleasing in Sensation. (2.) The Satisfactory in Contemplation, and (3.) Beauty of Reflection.

SECTION FIRST. THE PLEASING IN SENSATION.

All the faculties of sense-perception and sensation are susceptible of pleasurable exercise, but none of them awaken in us sensations of a distinctly elevated character save only the two ideal senses of sight and hearing.

These are the two avenues along which most of the ideas come which relate us to the kingdom of spiritual existence. In the pleasurable exercise of these senses there is not only the vision of intelligence and the voice of wisdom, but a manifold and entirely pure and proper pleasure of sensation as such.

This we have in the purity, contrasts, harmonies, and sequences of color, such as form a material foundation for our enjoyment of beauty or gorgeousness in nature or art.

So, also, in tone, we have the various grades of consonance, and especially the contrasts and agreeable combinations and gradations of tone-color as in orchestral works, and in human voices. Of this kind, also, is the pleasure derivable from chromatically modulating chords, such as we find in the works of Spohr and Gounod, and very often in Italian opera; where no idea is suggested or intended, but only the sweet, the pretty, the well-sounding.

All these are unmistakably pleasurable, and at the same time allied to the perception of the beautiful. They all have implications which suggest higher qualities of the beautiful, as one may see below in Ruskin's words on Purity.

"PURITY, *the Type of the Divine Energy.*—The only idea which I think can be legitimately connected with purity of matter, is this of vital and energetic connection among its particles, and that the idea of foulness is essentially connected with dissolution and death. Thus the purity of the rock, contrasted with the foulness of dust or mould, is expressed by the epithet 'living,' very singularly given in the rock, in almost all languages; singularly I say, because life is almost the last attribute one would ascribe to stone, but for this visible energy and connection of its particles; and so of water as opposed to stagnancy. And I do not think that, however pure a powder or dust may be, the idea of beauty is ever connected with it, for it is not the mere purity, but the *active* condition of the substance which is desired, so that as soon as it shoot into crystals, or gathers into efflorescence, a sensation of active or real purity is received which was not felt in the calcined *caput mortuum*.

"And again in color. I imagine that the quality of it which we term purity is dependent on the full energizing of the rays that compose it, whereof if in compound hues any are overpowered and killed by the rest, so as to be of no value nor operation, foulness is the consequence; while so long as all act together, whether side by side, or from pigments seen one through the other, so that all the coloring matter employed comes into play in the harmony desired, and none be quenched nor killed, purity results. And so in all cases I suppose that pureness is made to us desirable, because expressive of the constant presence and energizing of the Deity in matter, through which all things live and move, and have their being, and that foulness is painful as the accompaniment of disorder and decay, and always indicative of the withdrawal of Divine support. And the practical analogies of life, the invariable connection of outward foulness with mental sloth and degradation as well as with bodily lethargy and disease, together with the contrary indications of freshness and purity belonging to every healthy and active organic frame, (singularly seen in the effort of the young leaves when first their inward energy prevails over the earth, pierces its corruption, and shakes its dust away from their own white purity of life,) all these circumstances strengthen the instinct by associations countless and irresistible.

"And then, finally, with the idea of purity comes that of spirituality, for the essential characteristic of matter is its inertia, whence, by adding to it purity or energy, we may in some measure spiritualize even matter itself. Thus in the descriptions of the Apocalypse it is its purity that fits it for its place in heaven; the river of the water of life that proceeds out of the throne of the Lamb, is clear as crystal, and the pavement of the city is pure gold, like unto clear glass."

SECTION SECOND. THE SATISFACTORY IN CONTEMPLATION.

But above pleasures of mere sense-perception as such, mere ebb and flow of sensation, we must reckon the quiet pleasures one has in merely contemplating a beautiful object. One of the most obvious examples of this is the satisfaction universally experienced in looking at a beautiful face. Such is the gratification one involuntarily feels in its symmetry, its pleasantness and justice of proportion, that for a long time one overlooks whatever of emptiness or shallowness of spiritual expression it may betray. Nay, with some observers this pleasure is so strong that it suffices to overcome the strongest and best grounded elements of dissatisfaction one may have in the personal character of the owner of the face.

The foundation of this satisfaction lies in Symmetry ("the type of the Divine justice") of which Ruskin speaks thus:

"We shall not be long detained by the consideration of this constituent of beauty, as its nature is universally felt and understood. In all perfectly beautiful objects, there is found the opposition of one part to another and a reciprocal balance obtained; in animals the balance being commonly between opposite sides, (note the disagreeableness occasioned by the exception in flat fish, having the eyes on one side of the head,) but in vegetables the opposition is less distinct, as in the boughs on opposite sides of trees, and the leaves and sprays on each side of the boughs, and in dead matter less perfect still, often amounting only to a certain tendency towards a balance, as in the opposite sides of valleys and alternate windings of streams. In things in which perfect symmetry is, from their nature, impossible or improbable, a balance must be at least in some measure expressed before they can be beheld with pleasure. Hence the necessity of what artists require as opposing lines or masses in composition, the propriety of which, as well as their value, depends chiefly on their inartificial and natural invention. Absolute equality is not required, still less absolute similarity.

"A mass of subdued color may be balanced by a point of a powerful one, and a long and latent line overpowered by a short and conspicuous one. The only error against which it is necessary to guard the reader with respect to symmetry, is the confounding it with proportion, though it seems strange that the two terms could ever have been used as synonymous. Symmetry is the *opposition* of *equal* quantities to each other. Proportion the *connection* of *unequal* quantities with each other. The property of a tree in sending out equal boughs on opposite sides is symmetrical. Its sending out shorter and smaller towards the top, proportional. In the human face its balance of opposite sides is symmetry, its division upwards, proportion.

"Whether the agreeableness of symmetry be in any way referable to its expression of the Aristotilian *Ισότης*, that is to say of abstract justice, I leave the reader to determine; I only assert respecting it, that it is necessary to the dignity of every form, and that by the removal of it we shall render the other elements of beauty comparatively ineffectual; though on the other hand, it is so to be observed that it is rather a mode of arrangement of qualities than a quality itself; and hence symmetry has little power over the mind, unless all the other constituents of beauty be found together with it."

All degrees of the satisfactory in contemplation depend chiefly upon the qualities which naturally appertain to and cluster around symmetry. They are Regularity, Moderation according to law, Harmony, and Proportion, all of which are the qualities we discover first in the beautiful things of nature.

All of these, again, show themselves equally in *space-relations*, and in *time-relations*. Those of space, or of visible forms, are already referred to in the extract from Ruskin, above.

The element of *time* properly includes every thing in music; not only its measure and rhythm, but even its harmony and melodic organization, since tone itself finds its power in regularly determined vibrations, which although physically taking place in space, enter the soul only in the forms of time. In this respect they ally themselves to a deeper department of the soul; for Schopenhauer very cleverly points out that space-relations as such are not received into abstract thought, but transformed into those of *time*, as all the equations and computations of planetary spaces are carried on in mathematical formulæ. In other words, space itself is nothing more than *time made visible*. Time and Eternity are the symbols of immortality.

Now in the element of time we have in music innumerable relations and cunningly intermingled gradations of harmony, proportion, order, symmetry, and the like, as we have already seen in our studies in phraseology and form; and as we shall see yet more plainly in our studies in classical music particularly.

Moreover, these elements of beauty imply also *unity*, else there would be no *Single* in which the beauty inheres. And so it follows by implication that in *order*, *proportion*, and *harmony*, we have the "unity in variety" so often quoted and so little understood. But this element of Unity has a yet higher reach, therefore its particular discussion is reserved for the next section.

In all these together we have Formal Beauty, the outward conditions of beauty; or purely physical beauty, the *form* in which the higher spiritual beauty may inhere. And formal beauty, again, implies as its check or safe-guard yet another quality, of which Ruskin shall tell us.

MODERATION:
The Type of the Divine Government by Law.

" I have put this attribute of beauty last, because I consider it the girdle and safeguard of all the rest, and in this respect the most essential of all, for it is possible that a certain degree of beauty may be attained even in the absence of one of its other constituents, as sometimes in some measure without symmetry or without unity. But the least appearance of violence or extravagance, of the want of moderation and restraint, is, I think, destructive of all beauty whatsoever in every thing, color, form, motion, language, or thought, giving rise to that which in color we call glaring, in form inelegant, in motion ungraceful, in language coarse, in thought undisciplined, in all unchastened; which qualities are in every thing most painful, because the signs of disobedient and irregular operation.

"And therefore as that virtue in which men last, and with most difficulty attain unto, and which many attain not at all, and yet that which is essential to the conduct and almost to the being of all other virtues, since neither imagination, nor invention, nor industry, nor sensibility, nor energy, nor any other good having, is of full avail without this of self-command, whereby works truly masculine and mighty are produced, and by the signs of which they are separated from that lower host of things brilliant, magnificent and redundant, and further yet from that of the loose, the lawless, the exaggerated, the insolent, and the profane, I would have the necessity of it foremost among all our inculcating, and the name of it largest among all our inscribing, in so far that, over the doors of every school of Art, I would have this one word, relieved out in deep letters of pure gold — *Moderation.*"

SECTION THIRD. THE BEAUTIFUL IN SPIRITUAL PERCEPTION.

We now reach the degree where the beautiful fully becomes what in the original conception it was defined to be, namely, the expression of the ideal in sense-forms (or in outward appearance). When we contemplate a gorgeous sunset, we experience much more than a merely contentful satisfaction in splendid masses of crimson and gold lying above the western horizon. It is not the magnificent and incredible purity of the colors, nor the pleasing evanescence of the silently changing cloud-masses, nor yet any sensuous gratification in the brilliant lights reflected from the mountains in the east, or the passing sails on the ocean, but rather an inspiration and kindling of spirit such as all sensitive and highly organized natures well know, and which all recognize as among the most spiritual moments of their lives. Or when one looks off from a mountain top, how grand and exhilarating the experience. So, again, as one listens to a great symphony, how it thrills and overpowers with its exquisite expression. In all these experiences, and in an endless number of similar ones left unmentioned here because so universally recognized, we have always two elements: some object or combination of objects presented to sense-perception, and as such satisfying at least the chief demands of formal beauty; and, second, a kindling of emotion in the soul, a suggestion of the unutterable and the ineffable, which for the moment makes even common natures poetic and appreciative.

This play of the imagination, this unconscious kindling of soul, ranges through all grades, from the merely pleasing to the most overpowering sense of the Infinite, as in the sublime. But it is in some degree inseparable from the highest perception of beauty, and depends more upon sensitiveness and fineness of organization in the beholder, than on any definable physical properties of the object awakening it. We call it, therefore, the beautiful in spiritual perception; or, with Kant and Lotze, the "beautiful in reflection," as if in contemplating these objects something of the radiance of the spiritual world was reflected upon the beholder, or called up from the depths of his own soul. This emotion is what Richard Wagner calls "the sense of the illimitable;" and what Ruskin eloquently describes as intimations or suggestions of Unity, Repose and Infinity:—

UNITY:—*The Type of the Divine Comprehensiveness.* "All things," says Hooker, " (God only excepted,) besides the nature which they have in themselves, receive externally some perfection from other things." Hence the appearance of separation or isolation in any thing, and of self-dependence, is an appearance of imperfection; and all appearances of connection and brotherhood are pleasant and right, both as significative of perfection in the things united, and as typical of that Unity which we attribute to God, and of which our true conception is rightly explained and limited by Dr. Brown, in his XCII lecture; that Unity which consists not in his own singleness or separation, but in the necessity of his inherence in all things that be, without which no creature of any kind could hold existence for a moment, which necessity of Divine essence I think it better to speak of as comprehensiveness, than as unity, because unity is often understood in the sense of oneness or singleness, instead of universality, whereas the only Unity which by any means can become grateful or an object of hope to men, and whose types therefore in material things can be beautiful, is that on which turned the last words and prayer of Christ before his crossing of the Kedron brook. "Neither pray I for these alone, but for them also which shall believe on me through their word. That they all may be one, as thou, Father, art in me, and I in thee."

" And so there is not any matter, nor any spirit, nor any creature, but it is capable of an unity of some kind with other creatures, and in that unity is its perfection and theirs, and a pleasure also for the beholding of all other creatures that can behold. So the unity of spirits is partly in their sympathy, and partly in their giving and taking, and always in their love; and these are their delight and their strength, for their strength is in their co-working and army fellowship, and their delight is in the giving and receiving of alternate and perpetual currents of good, their inseparable dependence on each other's being, and their essential and perfect depending on their Creator; and so the unity of earthly creatures is their power and their peace, not like the dead and cold peace of undisturbed stones and solitary mountains, but the living peace of trust, and the living power of support, of hands that hold each other and are still; and so the unity of matter is, in its noblest form, the organization of it which builds it up into temples for the spirit, and in its lower forms, the sweet and strange affinity, which gives to it the glory of its orderly elements, and the fair variety of change and assimilation that turns the dust into the crystal, and separates the waters that be above the firmament from the waters that be beneath; and in its lowest form, it is the working and walking and clinging together that gives their power to the winds, and its syllables and soundings to the air, and their weight to the waves, and their burning to the sunbeams, and their stability to the mountains, and to every creature whatsoever operation is for its glory and for its good.

Now of that which is thus necessary to the perfection of all things, all appearance, sign, type, or suggestion must be beautiful, in whatever matter it may appear. And so to the perfection of beauty in lines, or colors, or forms, or masses, or multitudes, the appearance of some species of unity is in the most determined sense of the word essential.

But of the appearances of unity, as of unity itself, there are several kinds which it will be found hereafter convenient to consider separately. Thus there is the unity of different and separate things, subjected to one and the same influence, which may be called subjectional unity, and this is the unity of the clouds, as they are driven by parallel winds, or as they are ordered by the electric currents, and this is the unity of the sea waves, and this of the bending and undulation of the forest masses, and in creatures capable of will, it is the unity of will or of inspiration.

And there is unity of origin, which we may call original unity, which is of things arising from one spring and source, and speaking always of this their brotherhood, and this in matter is the unity of the branches of the trees, and of the petals and starry rays of flowers, and of the beams of light, and in spiritual creatures it is their filial relation to Him from whom they have their being. And there is unity of sequence, which is that of things that form links in chains, and steps in ascent, and stages in journeys, and this, in matter, is the unity of communicable forces in their continuance from one thing to another, and it is the passing upwards and downwards of beneficent effects among all things, and it is the melody of sounds, and the beauty of continuous lines, and the orderly successions of motion and times. And in spiritual creatures it is their own constant building up by true knowledge and continuous reasoning to higher perfection, and the singleness and straight-forwardness of their tendencies to more complete communion with God.

And there is the unity of membership, which we may call essential unity, which is the unity of things separately imperfect into a perfect whole, and this is the great unity of which other unities are but parts and means, it is in matter the harmony of sounds and consistency of bodies, and among spiritual creatures, their love and happiness and very life in God.

REPOSE:—*The Type of the Divine Permanence.* Repose, as it is expressed in material things, is either a simple appearance of permanence and quietness, as in the massy forms of a mountain or rock, accompanied by the lulling effect of all mighty sight and sound, which all feel and none define, (it would be less sacred if more explicable,) ἔνδοσιν δ'ὁρέων κορυφαί τε καὶ φάραγγες, or else it is repose proper, the rest of things in which there is vitality or capability of motion actual or imagined; and with respect to these the expression of repose is greater in proportion to the amount and sublimity of the action which is not taking place, as well as to the intensity of the negation of it. Thus we speak not of repose in a stone, because the motion of a stone has nothing in it of energy nor vitality, neither its repose of stability. But having once seen a great rock come down a mountain side, we have a noble sensation of its rest, now bedded immovably among the under fern, because the power and fearfulness of its motion were great, and its stability and negation of motion are now great in proportion. Hence the imagination, which delights in nothing more than the enhancing of the characters of repose, effects this usually by either attributing to things visibly energetic an ideal stability, or to things visibly stable an ideal activity or vitality. Hence Wordsworth, of the cloud, which in itself having too much of changefulness for his purpose, is spoken of as one "that heareth not the loud winds when they call, and moveth altogether, if it move at all." And again of children, which, that it may remove from them the child restlessness, the imagination conceives as rooted flowers " Beneath an old gray oak, as violets, lie." On the other hand, the scattered rocks, which have not, as such, vitality enough for rest, are gifted with it by the living image; they "lie crouched around us like a flock of sheep."

Thus, as we saw that unity demanded for its expression what at first sight might have seemed its contrary (variety), so repose demands for its expression the implied capability of its opposite, energy, and this even in its lower manifestations, in rocks and stones and trees. By comparing the modes in which the mind is disposed to regard the boughs of a fair and vigorous tree, motionless in the summer air, with the effect produced by one of these same boughs hewn square and used for threshold or lintel, the reader will at once perceive the connection of vitality with repose, and the part they both bear in beauty.

Hence I think that there is no desire more intense or more exalted than that which exists in all rightly disciplined minds for the evidences of repose in external signs, and what I cautiously said respecting infinity, I say fearlessly respecting repose, that no work of art can be great without it, and that all art is great in proportion to the appearance of it. It is the most unfailing test of beauty, whether of matter or motion, nothing can be ignoble that possesses it, nothing right that has it not, and in strict proportion to its appearance in the work is the majesty of the mind to be inferred in the artificer. Without regard to other qualities, we may look to this for our evidence, and by the search for this alone we may be led to the rejection of all that is base, and the accepting of all that is good and great, for the paths of wisdom are all peace. We shall see by this light three colossal images standing up side by side, looming in their great rest of spirituality above the whole world horizon, Phidias, Michael Angelo, and Dante (and Beethoven—ED.); and then, separated from their great religious thrones only by less fullness and earnestness of faith, Homer, and Shakspeare; and from those we may go down step by step among the mighty men of every age, securely and certainly observant of diminished lustre in every appearance of restlessness and effort, until the last trace of true inspiration vanishes in the tottering affectations or the tortured insanities of modern times.

There is no art, no pursuit, whatsoever, but its results may be classed by this test alone; every thing of evil is betrayed and winnowed away by it, glitter and confusion and glare of color, inconsistency or absence of thought, forced expression, evil choice of subject, over accumulation of materials, whether in painting or literature, the shallow and unreflecting nothingness of the English schools of art, the strained and disgusting horrors of the French, the distorted feverishness of the German;—pretence, over decoration, over divisions of parts in architecture, and again in music, in acting, in dancing, in whatsoever art, great or mean, there are yet degrees of greatness or meanness entirely dependent on this single quality of repose.

INFINITY:—*The Type of the Divine Incomprehensibility.* "Whatever beauty there may result from the dew of the grass, the flash of the cascade, the glitter of the birch trunk, or the fair daylight hues of darker things, (and joyfulness there is in all of these,) there is yet a light which the eye invariably seeks with a deeper feeling of the beautiful, the light of the declining or breaking day, and the flakes of scarlet cloud burning like watch-fires in the green sky of the horizon, a deeper feeling, I say, not perhaps more acute, but having more of spiritual hope and longing, less of animal and present life, more manifest, invariably, in those of more serious and determined mind, (I use the word serious, not as being opposed to cheerful but to trivial and volatile;) but, I think, marked and unfailing even in those of the least thoughtful dispositions. I am willing to let it rest on the determination of every reader whether the pleasure he has received from these effects of calm and luminous distance be not the most singular and memorable of which he has been conscious, whether all that is dazzling in color, perfect in form, gladdening in expression, be not of evanescent and shallow appealing, when compared with the still small voice of the level twilight behind the purple hills, or the scarlet arch of dawn over the dark troublous-edged sea." . . . . . .

"It is not then by nobler form, it is not by positiveness of hue, it is not by intensity of light (for the sun itself at noonday is effectless upon the feelings), that this strange distant space possesses its attractive power. But there is one thing it has, or suggests, which no other object of sight suggests in equal degree, and that is,—Infinity. It is of all material things the least material, the least finite, the farthest withdrawn from the earth prison-house, the most typical of the nature of God, the most suggestive of the glory of His dwelling-place. For the sky of night, though we may know it boundless, is dark, it is a studded vault, a roof that seems to shut us in and down, but the bright distance has no limit, we feel its infinity, as we rejoice in the purity of its light."

SECTION FOURTH. THE PERCEPTION OF THE BEAUTIFUL ONE OF THE HIGHEST FACULTIES OF THE SOUL.

Thus it plainly appears that in its ultimate relations the perception of the Beautiful is one of the highest faculties of the soul. For as Hegel points out, there are three kingdoms of absolutely spiritual activity, having the same content, namely knowledge of God; and differing from each other only in the form in which they bring the ideal to consciousness. These three kingdoms of spirit are *Art*, *Religion* and *Philosophy*.

Art communicates its content through sense-forms; Religion through the "representing consciousness"; and Philosophy through free thought addressed to the pure reason. Art is most nearly related to Religion, "because both have to do with heart and feeling" (Hegel).

Still in the very nature of the medium through which it communicates, namely *sense-forms*, Art has great temptation to remain with and of the senses exclusively. And this we find plainly illustrated in all periods of its development. Even in the times when there was *high* art in the world, there has always been along with it a *low* or debased art, appealing to the senses as such, and remaining there. The department of Painting has been perhaps the most exposed to this debasement, from which, indeed, it has never been able entirely to free itself.

Music and Poetry also have at times fallen under the same temptations, as we see in the music of Strauss and Gounod, and some of the poetry of Byron and Swinburne. We need to be on our guard, therefore, against all forms and degrees of this low art, which may always be known by its peculiarly sensuous charm, and its lack of higher and deeper suggestion.

In this light also we discover the moral relations between the practical pursuit of Art, Religion and Philosophy. The latter, indeed, has to do with pure reason, and is rarely found conjoined with an active condition of the artistic faculties. Between Art and Religion, however, (as between Science and Religion,) there has long been a misunderstanding, having its origin in the one-sidedness of their respective votaries. The pursuit of Art in the highest sense necessarily relates one to Religion, because it not only exercises his heart and feelings, but calls out his highest spiritual intuitions as such. Artists in whom the religious sense is wanting, will be discovered on careful consideration to be concerned with low forms of art, either resting in the sensuous as such, or at the most not rising above the enjoyment of formal beauty. Art in the lowest stage is intoxicating in its effect upon the mind, and debilitating; in the second stage it is absorbing and contentful to those in whom the sense of formal beauty is acute, and if they yield themselves to this purely external charm, it has the effect of filling up the attention to the exclusion of the higher activities of the soul. Still, between Art in this second stage and Religion there is no contradiction nor incompatibilty. On the contrary, the influence of Art is useful provided that merely formal beauty be not made an end.

Art also exercises great influence upon Religion, and has the tendency to soften the rigor of its dogmas and practices, and encourages in it a broader humanity, as we may see plainly enough by comparing Puritanism with later forms of vital religion. Besides, Art aids Religion in a very important way by furnishing it with its revelations of beauty and truth in sense-forms, in availing itself of which Religion becomes intelligible and attractive to the common mind.

On the other hand, Religion exercises important influence upon Art, especially by elevating the thoughts of the artist, and purifying his soul, thereby permitting truth to shine into it with greater lustre. And so we may conclude on *a priori* grounds that the exercise of religion is helpful to the artist, and that we have a right to expect from him in such case a higher and more inspiring revelation of beauty, than would otherwise be possible. And this, also, experience confirms, as we see plainly in such men as Dante, Michael Angelo, Bach, Handel and Beethoven, who are of the very highest type.

CHAPTER TWENTY-FOURTH.

THE SYMBOLICAL, THE CLASSICAL, AND THE ROMANTIC IN ART.

The progress of Art has been gradual, from the imperfection and crudity of early attempts, to a well-nigh perfect beauty in the time of its full development. Thus it may be said in general that "the oldest works in all forms of art yield in themselves vague contents: in poetry, simple history, Theogenies fermenting with abstract ideas and their incomplete expression; separate saints in stone and wood, etc. The representation remains unpliant, monotonous or confused, stiff, broken. Especially in the pictorial arts is the visible expression dull; in repose not that of the spiritually deep in itself, but mere animal emptiness; or else sharply distorted and immoderate in characteristic expression.

"So likewise are the forms of the human body and their movements dead; the arms hung on the body, the bones not articulated, or else awkward, angular, sharply moved; so likewise the figure untempered, dumpy, or immoderately meagre and extended. Upon the externals, on the contrary, garments, hair, weapons and other adornments much more love and care are bestowed; but the folds of the garments, e. g., remain wooden and independent, without fitting themselves to the form of the body (as we can see often enough in the old-time pictures of the Virgin Mary, and the saints).

"Even so are the earliest poems incomplete, disconnected, monotonous, only ruled remotely by one idea or sensation; or else wild, vehement, the different ideas confusedly entangled, and the whole not yet brought together into a firm organization."*

Nevertheless these early monuments have a certain rude impressiveness and grandeur which has been felt by many generations of the human race who have appeared, admired, and passed away in the presence of these imposing memorials of the thoughts and aspirations of the earlier times.

Progress in art has arisen mainly from a clearer perception of the ideal. It may be divided into three stages, called by Hegel the Sym-

*Hegel's *Aesthetik*, II, p. 246.

bolical, the Classical, and the Romantic. These differ from each other, not only in a progressive elevation of the faculties addressed by Art, as suggested by the classification of the previous chapter, but also in the mode of conceiving the ideal itself. The complete discussion of these ideas and their illustration in the various arts would take us far beyond present limits. The barest outline will suffice.

SECTION FIRST. SYMBOLIC ART.

The Symbol is a natural object, having a plain relation to the idea it represents; thus, the lion is the symbol of courage; the fox, of cunning; the ox, of patience; the sheep of simplicity; the elephant of docility and power; etc. Besides these natural symbols derived from the animal kingdom, there are also abstract symbols, whose meaning is almost universal; such as the triangle, symbol of the trinity; the circle, of eternity; etc. Yet each one of these natural objects has in it something more than the limited meaning it affords as a symbol. Thus the lion is not only courageous, but fierce and treacherous; the ox is patient, but also slow and stupid; the fox is cunning, but in his own degree is fierce and blood-thirsty also. And in this we find a natural limitation or inherent ambiguity in symbolical art.

Symbolical art is in general the entire art of the Oriental nations. To this class belong the towers of Babel, Pyramids, Pagodas and Temples of China and India, the sculpture and temples of Assyria and Egypt; Myths, the Niebelungen lied, etc; as well as much of the poetry of the Old Testament, as, *e. g.*, parts of Ezekiel, etc. In all these the meaning is unclear; each work of this period is a sphynx, an enigma.

The sculpture of the symbolical period is mighty and vast. One thinks of the colossal Memnon, the statues at Karnac, the figures of gods in China and India, monstrous figures outraging all principles of natural form, yet strangely impressive to so many millions of the human race, who have found in these their clearest emblem of the Divine. In all these symbolical productions the beautiful, as such, is not sought. It is the mighty, the grand, the eternal, the everlasting, the all-creating;—these are the vague forms in which the Eternal and Absolute suggests itself first to the human race.

We find that in every nation, whenever movement takes place, the symbolical in art gradually merges into the beautiful. Temples lose something of their massiveness in favor of lightness and symmetry. The gigantic structures of Egypt give place to the delicate proportions of the Parthenon and Acropolis. The many-armed gods yield precedence to the scarcely super-human forms of Jupiter, Minerva, Venus and Apollo. The eyes of Zeuxis and Apelles discover for mankind the beauty everywhere veiled in nature. Thus Art comes to the classical period, when beauty has become complete, in so far as it resides in form.

SECTION SECOND. CLASSICAL ART.

Classical art is above all unconscious of any want of harmony between the ideal and the means by which it must be expressed. The human form, that temple of in-dwelling spirit, is especially the chosen type of this period, and sculpture, therefore, its distinctive expression. Of the content and meaning of this form of utterance there will be occasion to speak in the next chapter. For the present let it be observed that sculpture shows a progress towards the spiritual in art. The Greek artist, in forsaking the vast masses of architecture in favor of the comparatively insignificant bit of marble only so large as the human form, was beginning to learn the same lesson that was taught to one of old, hid in the cleft of the rock, that not in the lightning, the earthquake, nor in the thunder could one find God, but in the "still small voice." Yet here we anticipate, for the voice, as a token of soul, was the peculiar ideal of the Romantic.

At present the artist advances only so far as to discover in the human form the most complete expression of the beautiful. Thus Hegel says (Bryant's translation):

"The Greek ideal has for its basis an unchangeable harmony between spirit and sensuous form — the unalterable serenity of the immortal gods; but this calm has about it something cold and inanimate. Classic art has not comprehended the true essence of the divine nature, nor penetrated to the depths of the soul. It has not known how to develop its inmost powers in their opposition, and again to re-establish their harmony. All this phase of existence, the evil, the sinful, the unhappy, moral suffering, the revolt of the will, remorse, and the agonies of the soul, are unknown to it. Classic art does not pass beyond the proper domain of the veritable ideal.

"As to its realization in history, it is scarcely necessary to say that we must seek it among the Greeks. Classic beauty, with the infinite wealth of ideas and forms which compose its domain, has been allotted to the Greek people, and we ought to render homage to them for having raised art to its highest vitality."

This was the perfect completion of formal beauty. All the qualities of symmetry, proportion, harmony, unity, and the like that enter into and constitute perfection of form, are here manifested in exquisite loveliness. As Hegel says: "There neither is nor ever can be anything more beautiful."

Greek plastic art attained its highest achievements in the time of Phidias. Immediately after this Socrates, Plato and Aristotle, successively, "effected for man, once for all, the perfect distinction between idea and sensuous image — between content and form — the indissoluble union of which, it can not be too much insisted upon, constitutes the central characteristic in classic art. Thus had the human mind passed beyond the limits of the classic ideal, and henceforth the history of classic art is but a history of its decline and fall." *

SECTION THIRD. ROMANTIC ART.

The key of romantic art is "internal beauty of spirit" as distinguished from outward beauty of form. This ideal began to appear in later sculpture. We have a token of it in the well-known Venus de Medici, where the effort is made to represent the modesty of a delicate woman appearing unclad in public. The conception is just, but untrue to the spirit of the classical ideal; for in this nothing is represented but the eternal, the enduring. This conflict between womanly delicacy and the public gaze, creates shame, an unbeautiful and temporary affection.

Collision is the principal means of the romantic. By collision is meant a conflict between opposing principles, in the out-come of which the superiority of the nobler principle is made to appear. Collision is totally foreign to architecture, and almost so to sculpture. Later sculpture, as the well-known Laocoön, introduces this element, but to the destruction of absolute formal beauty. The work of art is no longer *beautiful* out-right and in itself, but beautiful on the whole, and considering what it means.

In romantic art it is not the human form, the outward covering which furnishes the artist his ideal of beauty, but the *inner*, the soul, the disposition, the *life*. Hence sculpture which has to do mainly with form, gives place to painting, which affords perspective, places its heroes in suitable scenes, and contrasts one personage with another; painting in turn gives place to music and poetry. The meaning of these various changes will appear in the next chapter where we have to examine each art in its turn.

In all this later cycle of art the key-tone is unmistakeable; it is beauty of spirit rather than of the form.

* Bryant.

"The material of romantic art, at least with reference to the divine, is extremely limited. For, in the first place, as we have already pointed out, nature is deprived of its divine attributes; sea, mountain, and valley, streams, springs, time and night, as well as the universal process of nature, have all lost their value with respect to the representation and content of the absolute. The images of nature are no longer set forth symbolically. They are stripped of the characteristic which rendered their forms and activities appropriate as traits of a divinity. For all the great questions concerning the origin of the world — concerning the whence, the whither, the wherefore of created nature and humanity, together with all the symbolic and plastic attempts to solve and represent these problems — have vanished in consequence of the revelation of God in the spirit; and even the gay, thousand-hued earth, with all its classically-figured characters, deeds, and events, is swallowed up in spirit, condensed in the single luminous point of the absolute and its eternal process of redemption (*Erlosungsgeschichte*). The entire content, therefore, is thus concentrated upon the internality of the spirit — upon the perception, the imagination, the soul — which strives after unity with the truth, and seeks and struggles to produce and to retain the divine in the individual (*Subjekt*). Thus, though the soul is still destined to pass through the world, it no longer pursues merely worldly aims and undertakings. Rather, it has for its essential purpose and endeavor the inner struggle of man within himself, and his reconciliation with God, and brings into representation only personality and its conservation, together with appliances for the accomplishment of this end. The heroism which can here make its appearance is by no means a heroism which makes its own law, establishes regulations, creates and transforms conditions, but a heroism of submission, for which everything is settled and determined beforehand, and to which there thenceforth remains only the task of regulating temporal affairs according to it, of applying to the existing world that higher principle which has validity in and for itself, and, finally, of rendering it practically valuable in the affairs of every-day life. We may now comprise in a single word this relation between content and form as it appears in the romantic — for here it is that this relation attains to its complete characterization. It is this: just because the ever-increasing universality and restless working depth of the soul constitute the fundamental principle of the romantic, the key-note thereof is *musical*, and, in connection with the particularized content of the imagination, *lyrical*. For romantic art the lyrical is, as it were, the elementary characteristic — a tone which the epic and the drama also strike, and which breathes about the works of the arts of visible representation themselves, like a universal, fragrant odor of the soul; for here spirit and soul will speak to spirit and soul through all their images."*

CHAPTER TWENTY-FIFTH.

THE IDEAL AS MANIFESTED IN THE DIFFERENT FORMS OF ART.

In each one of the different arts we are able to trace the progress of the human mind through the various stages of art-conception described in the previous chapters, although the complete progress is not fully illustrated in any one of them.

SECTION FIRST. ARCHITECTURE.

The oldest of the arts is architecture. Hegel enumerates three general classes of structure which are essentially symbolical in character. These are: (1) Works built for a union of people; such were the great works of the Assyrians, Egyptians, etc., all of which were in effect religious works. So Goethe says, "What is holy? That which binds many souls together."

(2) Works intermediate between buildings and sculpture. Such are the Indian Pagodas, the Obelisks, the Memnon, Sphynx, and Labyrinth, expressive of vague ideas or mystical conceptions.

(3) The transition to the classical, as in the Egyptian tombs, Pyramids, etc.

Classical architecture we find in the Greek temples. Romantic architecture finds its expression in the Gothic Cathedrals of the middle ages.

Architecture in general is related to the Ideal as the expression of the symmetrical, the regular, the united, the grand; — the utterance of spirit which has seized the material from without and formed it, but which is neither represented nor conceived as residing in it. So, *e. g.*, the Memnon had no voice of its own, but was played on from without by the rising sun.

*Hegel, Bryant's translation.

SECTION SECOND.   SCULPTURE.

Sculpture has for its central idea "the wonder that soul should dwell in body."* Again: "Sculpture, in general, perceives the wonder that spirit imagines itself in the wholly material, and so forms this externality that it becomes actually present in it, and acknowledges therein the suitable look of itself."

"Sculpture is the peculiar art of the classical ideal as such."† Thus it belongs properly to the classical epoch, and the few works of the symbolic period are to be regarded rather as apprentice works in which the artist is acquiring the plastic control over his material, than as independent and significant expressions of the ideal.

Hegel speaks of three styles in classical sculpture: 1. The *Hard, Austere, Strong*, characterized by great masses and simple content.

2. The *Purely Beautiful*, characterized by a more living beauty, and represented in the works of Phidias.

3. The *Pleasing* style, where beauty gives up something of its eternal repose for the sake of gaining a greater appearance of human interest. The Apollo Belvidere if not properly to be reckoned in this category, is at least transitional between the style next preceding and this.

The Content and meaning of this form of art is already fully expressed in the previous chapter on "Classic Art," to which reference is again made. The pith of it all is in the following sentence in the third volume of the *Aesthetik:* "Sculpture has for its principle and content, *Spiritual Individuality* as the classical ideal, so that the Inner and Spiritual finds expression to the spirit in the immediate bodily appearance, which art has here to represent in actual art-existence." Or, again, as Bénard phrases it, "The Content of sculpture is the essence, the substantial, true, invariable part of character," as distinguished from what is accidental and transient.

So, also, Mr. Wm. M. Bryant: "Sculpture constitutes the first step in advance beyond Architecture, and it *pauses with this first step*. It takes as its object the simple form of the human body, and by this form it expresses spirit, because spirit does not yet know itself apart from this form."

Doubtless the artist turned himself to the human form as the most suitable expression of the ideal in consequence of living in Greece, a land so mild of climate and so simple in mode of life as to afford on every side attractive examples of fully developed, healthful, beautiful

*Hegel.   †Bryant's Hegel's Philosophy of Art, "Introductory Essay."

men and women. This outer manifestation of vital beauty was encouraged by the influence of the games and gymnastic training, so that taking one reason with another it may be doubted whether any part of the world at any period of its history ever afforded a sculptor so satisfactory a surrounding as Greece in its prime. At the same time intellectual life had become more vigorous. The imagination had long been kindled by the Homeric poems, recited universally by the strolling minstrels. The constant wars between the different States, and the varying fortunes of defense against the Persians did much to stimulate the mind and bring out the force of individual character. Thus it happened that the works of Phidias were produced soon after the times of Pythagorus, and shortly before the days of Socrates. This was the moment when the classical idea reached an equilibrium between form and content.

As already pointed out, Socrates, and after him Plato and Aristotle, accomplished once for all the separation between *form* and *content* in art. The human spirit went forward to a higher development; it turned inward to deeper and more immortal thoughts. It was then that Romantic Art became inevitable, and therein a revelation of the ideal in living, self-determined beauty, for which sculpture was inadequate.

SECTION THIRD. PAINTING.

When we think seriously upon the art of painting and remember its list of triumphs from the days of Appelles and Praxiteles to Raphael, Correggio, and Angelo, and even to our own times, we cannot wonder that so many writers upon art have taken this as the type and complete expression of the artistic faculty.

Painting represents the dawn and progress of a deeper perception of the beauty of the visible world. Evidently it began in *color*, the effort to represent the evanescent glories of the heavens at sunrise or evening, the exquisite tints of flowers, masses of foliage, etc.

At first painting was merely decorative, and was employed to beautify the walls of the more precious shrines, the best rooms in the homes of the wealthy, etc.

Afterwards it became *imitative*. The forms and tints of flowers and fruits were its subjects. We trace this very distinctly in the well-known anecdote of the two great Greek painters who had a trial of skill. One of them painted a plate of cherries so naturally that the birds came and pecked at them; the other represented a fly on the nose of a portrait so naturally that the other artist attempted to brush it off in order to examine the picture better. Therein he acknowledged his superior; for he himself had deceived only the unreasoning birds, while the other had deceived an artist.

Painting in any large sense involves at least three arts: Drawing (the art of representing outlines as they really appear), Color and Perspective. The appearance of solid projection, that is to say, the appearance of *reality*, depends upon the latter. There is reason to suppose that color and drawing were brought to a high degree of excellence by the Greeks and Romans, as indicated by the anecdote given above, and by the Pompeian discoveries, where in some of the rooms the colors remain to the present day as clear as when first put upon the walls, nearly two thousand years ago.

The subjects of painting in that olden time, as we have said, were flowers, fruits and other natural objects not requiring difficult perspective for their intelligible representation, and the gods and goddesses of the popular mythology, episodes from Homer, and the poets, etc.

To the painters (and their brethren the poets) mankind owes its perception of the beautiful in nature. The plowman, wearily treading in the furrow the livelong day, sees not the fleecy clouds above him, nor is he inspired by the mighty pinnacles and peaks of the mountain horizon towering so grandly, as if matter herself were striving upward toward her God. Nay, he overlooks even the delicate perfection of the daisies and buttercups whose sunshine his furrow so relentlessly ends. Yet in the water he drinks to quench his thirst he might, if he would, see all these distant glories repeated; as if, out of this pure fountain of refreshing, the voice of God called to man to look upward for the secret of the beautiful and the holy. But it is only once in a thousand years that a Burns rises above the depressing influence of a plowman's environment. It is the idle painter, or his brother, the poet, lolling at ease under the shading oak to whom this deeper vision of beauty is revealed.

When we speak of painting as a form of high art, representative of the spiritual meanings of nature and life, we immediately think of that glorious company of great Italian masters of the fifteenth century, chief among whom were Raphael (1483–1520), Leonardo da Vinci (1452–1519), Titian (1477–1576), Michael Angelo (1474–1563), Tintoret (1512–1594), Paul Veronese (1532–1588). Nor can we forget their eminent successors in the next century, Claude Lorraine (1600–1682), and Rembrandt (1606–1669).

In the productions of these great artists we find the art of Painting unfolded in all its capacities except that of strict, literal *realism*—

imitation of nature as such; this was left for later masters. Every production of these old masters has its mannerisms. Natural forms are conventionalized, or at times distorted, with unhesitating boldness. Historical anachronisms are common in the historical pieces. But they show, nevertheless, a life, a meaning, an expression of spirit, such as nowhere existed in this art before.

Were we to analyze the impressions they severally produce upon us, we should find certain marked differences in the faculties to which they appeal, as pointed out in Chapter XXIII. Thus, *e. g.*, the works of Titian and Paul Veronese are noted for their magnificent and exquisite coloring. In this quality they appeal to the "pleasing of sensation," and less decidedly to the spiritual as such. Raphael is noted for the *expression* of his works. They are characterized by a serene and matchless grace, such as one seeks in vain elsewhere. Michael Angelo, on the contrary, is neither a great colorist, nor a composer of graceful forms. But he conceives with such superhuman boldness, and pierces so deeply into the very pith and marrow of the world about him, that he stands recognized on all hands as one of the very greatest minds who have made human nature illustrious by their participation in it.

The art of Painting also shows a progress beyond sculpture, in the direction of the spiritual. The massive matter of architecture, and the solid dimensions of sculpture, have here given place to merely the *appearance* of matter. But this diminution of material is accompanied by a most important increase in power of expression, and this especially in the direction of a more complete mastery of the scale of beauty. For here at the basis of it we have the wonderful delights of color and "tone," an entire new kingdom of sense-gratification. Every facility for representing human relations and deeds, which sculpture or *basso-relievo* could furnish, here exists entire, and in the far greater perfection of natural perspective. Only in a single direction is there a loss, namely in the direction of the sublime, in which architecture certainly has greater power. Yet this concession is immeasurably atoned for by the wonderful increase in power to represent the feelings of the soul. For while Architecture gave us the mighty enigmas of Egypt, and the everlasting beauty of the Parthenon; and Sculpture revealed to man the beauty and dignity of his own form when permeated by a noble soul, and thus by images of Mercury and Jupiter led his mind toward the true God; Painting has given to mankind not only the beauties of field and flower, and preserved for him a life-like semblance of the living faces of its heroes, but has portrayed in bodily form the incarnate sufferings of his Redeemer.

SECTION FOURTH.   MUSIC.

The three forms of art previously examined have this in common, that they address the observer by means of *forms* permanently existing in *space*. Architecture deals in matter in vast masses, only a small proportion of which in any single form comes into actual contact with spirit. The exterior, the form, is shaped and fashioned by spirit according to its own ideal. In a pyramid, for example, how slight a proportion of the whole is the surface. The inner part does indeed bear the impress of spirit in the fact of its location so as to maintain the integrity of the form; yet this relation to spirit is faint at most. In a temple the mass of matter is greatly reduced and the interior parts are, distinctly subservient to the mechanical necessities of structure. Here therefore, soul has left its impress upon a much greater proportion by the whole mass than in the pyramid.

Sculpture again greatly reduces the quantity of matter, and is much more particular about the quality of it. Only the finest marble will answer to the artist's demands. But here art has to do with the *form* and with the *surface*, which practically is the form. The inner is inert, dead. Yet sculpture conceives of this inner part as having been alive, as is indicated by the care with which muscles and joints and all particulars which indicate internal organization are represented. The spirit does not reside even in the most speaking statue; yet one thinks it a suitable residence of soul, and scarcely wonders at the miracle of Psyche.

In painting, the quantity of matter is still further reduced, and art has to do with forms, and the *appearances of matter*, by means of which, as we saw, relations of soul are manifested.

Yet all these forms of art deal with forms permanently existing in space, outside of and entirely separate from the most appreciative observer. As Hegel well says, "Painting, as we saw, may likewise give expression in physiognomy and shape, to the inner life and energy, the determinations and passions of the heart, the situations, conflicts and fate of the soul; but what we have always before us in painting, are objective appearances, from which the observing *I*, as inner self, remains entirely separate. One may never so completely absorb and sink himself in the subject, the situation, the character, the form, of a statue or painting, admire the art work, gush over it, nay, may completely fill himself therewith;—it matters not, these works of art are and remain independent objects, in review of which we come not beyond the position of an observer."

Music, on the contrary, builds no permanent fabric in space. It has no *form* which can be seen. It is a voice. Out of the unseen, in cunningly modulated tones, it speaks to the heart of the hearer. Like the voice itself it no sooner utters its word than it is silent. Whenever we would recall its message we must recreate the informing word.

In this way music approaches the observer as none of the previous arts can. When it is perceived it is no longer something outside of and separate from the observer; it is within him; it has penetrated into the very center of the soul. Hence its power to absorb the observer, to carry him along with it, so that men everywhere "delight to sing with the melody, to strike with the measure, and in dance music it comes into the very bones."

This remarkable power of music lies fundamentally in the sense of hearing to which it appeals, and in *time*, which is the material of its form. For by the sense of hearing we are brought into our nearest relations to other souls. It is with the *ear* that man receives the word of reproof, the approval of his fellow, and the commandment of his God. This wonderful mechanism of hearing is particularly the sympathetic channel of feeling. Many shades of emotion may be conveyed by modulations of the speaking voice, without use of words. All this material of inflection and pitch relation, carried to an almost infinitely greater perfection of delicate organization than in speech, Music employs with such cunning mastership as to indicate very plainly that *this* was one of the ends intended in all the delicate organization of the inner ear.

But music rests its greatest power in its modulation in *time*. The beat, the measure, chimes in with the human pulse, hurries it or retards it; the motive brightens up the rhythm, modifies it, characterizes and individualizes the different moments in a piece; and measure, motivization, and rate of movement, all combine with the melodic and harmonic filling up, to complete a form of utterance in which soul speaks to soul not of its ideas and notions, but of its *feelings*, its general *states*. Thus the content of music, in general, is *Emotion*. "It extends itself in every direction for the expression of all distinct sensations and shades of joyousness, serenity, jokes, humor, shoutings and rejoicings of soul : as well as the graduations of anguish, sorrow, grief, lamentation, distress, pain, regret, etc.; and, finally, aspiration, worship, love, etc., belong to the proper sphere of musical expression." (Hegel's *Aesthetik*, III. 144.)

Of the material of music we have already learned in the earlier lessons of this course. Its form is a symmetrically co-ordinated succession of movements, expressive of a sequence or cycle of feelings.

Thus music in its very nature expresses spiritual relations. True the material of hearing may lend itself to play. Mere jingle is not without charm. Agreeable, piquant, or bizarre combinations of tone-color may tickle or delight the sense of hearing without uttering a message to the soul. But properly conceived all these are part of the vocabulary of this voice ; part of its material for spiritual communication. Therefore music is in itself a romantic art. And it quite agrees with this idea that its systematic and artistic development is the very latest of all the arts.

Hence the terms symbolical and classical have only a modified application in it, as we shall hereafter see. The earliest attempts at music, such as the Gregorian or Ambrosian hymns, the oldest songs of the church, we may well enough style symbolical. They fully agree with the peculiarities of this epoch in all the other arts. The true handling of the material, the value of tone as tone, and the significance of time and melodic modulation they have not yet fathomed. And yet their quaint cadences have a strange power, and are the source of all the distinctly "ecclesiastical" conventionalities of music.

The classic in music exists in all those works which afford a content entirely harmonious and commensurate with their form. Such works are those of Bach, Haydn, Mozart, and part of those of Beethoven and Schubert.

In many works of the latter two composers, form and content do not coincide ; the beauty of the form as form is sacrificed to the expressiveness and meaning of the work. Here, therefore, form is less than content; and we have the romantic moment in art. To this category belong many of the Beethoven works, notably such as the "moonlight" sonata, and the last two or three, almost everything of Chopin's and Schumann's, etc. The true relation of all this, we shall learn later. (See Parts V. and VI.)

SECTION FIFTH. POETRY.

We have seen from the beginning of this discussion that the beautiful is the expression of the ideal by means of forms directly addressed to the senses and intuitions, rather than to the reason. In architecture the ideal merely begins to appear; in sculpture it shines out more plainly, though even in this form the spirit is not living; in painting are represented transition movements of human life, the very point of spiritual defeat or triumph, and thus we go deeper than the merely outward form, and become conscious of the inner life of spirit as represented in the appearance before us. In music we go still further in the same direction. For here we have not a representation which stands outside of us and over against us, independent, to appreciate which requires that the beholder should at least yield himself to it; but instead of it a finely organized and infinitely complex *voice*, which tells its story directly to the soul, and as already pointed out moves and excites the hearer, " carries him along with it, quite otherwise than the way" in which other arts affect him. Music represents the self-moved activity of the soul. In no other art is the difference so great between the inspired and the merely mechanically-put-together.

Yet music also has its limitations. As already pointed out in the passages on Romantic art, the true meaning of this stage of development is the final beauty of spirit attained through conflict and suffering. The ideal of the romantic is none other than that of the Christian religion itself; the attainment of complete repose, and blessedness of spirit, in which bodily sense and appetite and all the negative or sinful elements of the moral nature are finally subjected to the reason, itself illumined by clear vision of the truth, and the whole spirit glorified into the image of the Divine. This state is attainable only through conflicts, in which one after another the evils of the nature are met and overcome; nor yet by conflict only, but by conflict sustained in faith and love. This is the Christian ideal. Nor is it the mission of art to instruct or definitely or directly aid the individual in this work. Yet in an indirect way it does do this and always will. For it is the artist who earliest sees the beauty of every natural appearance, the deeper meaning of the lake, and ocean; and it is the artist, the poet, who sees deepest into the depths of the soul. Hence in art-works one finds represented the moments of this redemption conflict, through which every individual must pass; seeing which the tempted soul takes heart again, knowing that some one has already passed by the same path to victory.

Now these conflicts of the spirit are not representable in architecture or sculpture. Later sculpture tried this; but it is a work foreign to the proper genius of that art. In painting they may come to a limited extent. But a painting is necessarily but a single moment of life; it gives us only a position, a relation, a contrast. Whereas no account of a soul-conflict is intelligible which does not give us the opposing principles, and also their collision and final resolution in the triumph of the good; and this is a story too long for painting.

Music can give us a prolonged action of the soul, a life-history, and in this is its great superiority in spirituality to the other forms of art. Nevertheless we come here to its limitations. A collision is an opposition of evil and good. The good, in music, is the consonant, the well-sounding, the melodious, the pleasing; the evil is the dissonant, the discordant, the dis-united, the heterogenous. Now music itself as music has properly and chiefly to do with the consonant, or with the dissonant introduced in strict subjection to the consonant. Just as soon as the dissonant forms any considerable proportion of the musical artwork, it ceases to be music and becomes unmusical, tiresome, as we see in long passages of Wagner's later operas. The proper sphere of music is to portray the progress of the soul from grief or sadness to comfort, joy, and blessedness; it can do this with an intelligibility entirely its own. It is, so to say, the art of the ideal sphere of the soul, the sphere into which sin and its consequent suffering has never entered. Whatever is bright, tender, joyful, resolved, or noble, music expresses with peculiar power. But evil lies outside its pure province. This, then is one of its limitations.

Music suffers a second limitation in its entire want of relation to reason. It is the office of reason to receive from the senses and the understanding the apparent facts of the outer world, to compare them, discern their essential nature, and especially the deeper laws that regulate their co-ordination and succession. It is also its office to determine concerning any particular piece of conduct that in view of its real nature and its relation to other parts of the same life, it does or does not conduce to virtue; that such and such things are related to the lower parts of the nature, and such and such others to the higher. Reason is the faculty of man by means of which he generalizes and so arrives at a distinct conception of the truth. This faculty is, therefore, the ruling intelligence of the entire man with power to co-ordinate his movements and conduct as well as his thought so as to bring him more rapidly and surely along the road to goodness and God. Now music is outside of reason. Reason begins to act only when it is furnished with distinctly formulated conceptions or thoughts, and these are not found in music. Music and reason, therefore, have nothing in common with each other, but belong to different departments of the soul. Music goes in through sense-perception and addresses the feelings directly as such. Reason operates in the range of thought, and by comparisons between the information it receives from sense-perception and its own *a priori* conceptions (time, space, and causality) is able to arrive at certain forms of truth; which may or may not afterward be applied to the feelings and motives of conduct.

Thus as soon as art contemplates conflicts of soul and a blessedness of victory residing in a complete union of all the powers of the spirit, including the reason, some higher and more universal form of art becomes inevitable. Such a form we have in poetry, which expresses itself not in shapes and forms outwardly visible as such, but through words, which reason understands.

Because it finds its expression in words and through ideas and conceptions properly belonging to reason, poetry comes into near proximity to prose, to ordinary discourse. Poetry is distinguishable from prose in its *form* as well as its *content*.

The poetic form or mode of expression is imaginative and picturesque. However intensified by thought, the mode of expression must be such as to create in the inner sense *pictures of the outer world*, or of such and such living beings in such and such conflicts and relations. Thus poetry in its picturesque modes of embodying thought addresses the inner sense exactly as an external reality resembling it would address the same feelings going in through the ordinary gates of sense-perception. This is the distinctive trait of poetic expression. Verse is an added grace, which is useful in so far as it lends smoothness and musical quality to the discourse, and is a token of the complete control which the creative artist exercises over his material. Verse also serves a purpose in idealizing the style and so setting it apart to nobler uses than those of common every-day life.

The *content* of poetry is spiritual existence and eternal truth, as illustrated in the lives and conduct of men. " The entire circle of the outer world enters poetry only in so far as the spirit finds its activity in ruling over the material ; as the environment of man, also, his outer world, which has its essential value only in reference to the inner of consciousness, but dares not make claim to the honor of being itself the exclusive subject of poetry. Then the word, this most plastic material, which belongs immediately to the spirit, and is the most capable of all of seizing the interests and movements of things in their inner life, must here be applied to the highest meaning of which it is capable.

" Thus it becomes the chief task of poetry to bring to consciousness the power of spiritual life, and especially whatever swells and sinks in human passion and feeling, or passes quietly before the attention; the all-embracing kingdom of human idea, activity, work, fate, the machinery of this world and the divine government. So has it been and still is the most general and broadest teacher of human kind. Its teaching and learning are knowledge and experience of this which is. Star, beast, and plant neither know nor experience their law; but man exists in the suitable law of his actual life only when he knows what he himself is and what is about him; he must know the power which drives and manages him;—and such a knowledge it is which Poetry gives in it's first substantial form." (Hegel.)

The superior power of poetry lies equally in its mode of expression and in its content. In the former because all men comprehend and are moved by picture-building discourse. This mode of expression also lends itself most easily to the artist's way of conceiving truth, which is by direct intuition and not by reason. Hence in the earliest time the deepest eternal truths were perceived, not clearly, but as if through a veil; in epic, ode, psalm, prophecy, and drama they found clearer and clearer expression. And thus long before the philosopher had discovered that man had a soul, Poets and seers had shown to the spirit of man the love and providence of his God.

The principal kinds of poetry are three: *The Epic*, which treats of the deeds of heroes, and the fortunes of a people; the *Lyric*, in which the human heart sings its own sorrow, hope, joy, or love; and the *Drama*, in which men live and act before us, and so by collisions and conflicts the lesson of motive and consequence is read.

In its very nature, therefore, the art of Poetry is universal. It belongs to every age, and to every grade of intelligence. And in all it elevates, refines, and educates.

Yet in its very definiteness and the completeness with which the artist may work out his full meaning in it, it leaves less room for the imagination of the reader. And in this respect Music possesses a certain advantage over it. We have thus completed the circle of the arts, and have seen in all, and more and more plainly as we have advanced, that the ideal of them all is the expression of the *True* in sense-forms —in other words, the expression of the beautiful.

Art is a sort of Jacob's ladder on which from the days of Adam until now the angels of God have descended to man, and up which man has gone to seek his God.

Part Fifth.

STUDIES IN CLASSICAL MUSIC.

LESSON TWENTY-SIXTH.

THE PLAYFUL MOMENT IN THE CLASSIC.

We find the starting point of the playful in the classic in such productions of Bach, as the little fugue in C minor, No. 2 in the "Clavier." (Plays.) Here the playful spirit is unmistakable. It is shown in the rhythm, the quick movement, and especially in the way in which one part catches up another. These, again, are to be referred to the Gigue of Bach, Mozart and other composers of that day, which were an idealized form of an old Italian dance in triplet rhythm.

Observe now the following: (Plays the Scherzo from the Beethoven Sonata in C, op. 2.) This charming little piece deserves to be heard twice. It is one of the most complete little bits of imitative writing to be found in Beethoven. This is in thematic style.

Observe now this: (Plays the Allegro in E flat, ¾ time, third movement of the Sonata in E flat, op. 7.) This is the lyric style at first, but in the second period falls into the imitative forms for a while. The charming feature in this work is its delicacy. Observe that the "trio" refrains from definitely enunciated melody, although a melody is suggested by the progression of its harmonies.

Again, observe this: (Plays the Menuetto from Sonata in D, op. 10.) In point of structure, this little piece very much resembles the Allegro last played. The impressive feature in it as one knows it better, is the peculiarly graceful turn of the melody, in which it is not surpassed by any of the Beethoven short movements.

Observe again this, which is in the form of a Rondo: (Plays Finale of Sonata in G, op. 14.) Here we have a similar spirit, and the agreeable contrast of the singing melody in C which begins in the seventy-third measure.

Still more unmistakable in its form, and very beautiful in its way, is the Scherzo from the "Pastoral" sonata of Beethoven, op. 28. This movement goes very fast. It is relieved by a trio which contains a lovely melodic phrase, repeated several times with different harmonies. (Plays.)

Of the same general character are the other playful movements in the Beethoven Sonatas. Those in the sonatas for piano and violin, as well as the trios for violin, 'cello and piano, afford yet more decided humoristic traits. They are full of quirks and catches of time, caprices of motives — in short, they are frolicsome.

Movements of this kind were introduced into the sonata by Beethoven, as a compensation for the greater length and seriousness he imparted to the other movements as compared with those of Haydn and Mozart. Independent movements of this kind are, however, numerous in the Bach, Haydn and Mozart works. See, *e. g.*, the Mozart "Pieces," (Peters' ed.) and similar collections of other composers. All of these movements are idealized dance-forms.

LIST OF ILLUSTRATIONS.

1. Bach Invention in C, No. 1.
2. Scherzo from Beethoven Sonata in C, op. 2.
3. Allegro (3d mov't) of Sonata in E flat, op. 7, Beethoven.
4. Menuetto from Sonata in D, op. 10, Beethoven.
5. Finale of Sonata in G, op. 14, Beethoven.
6. Scherzo from Pastoral Sonata, Beethoven.

LESSON TWENTY-SEVENTH.

THE TENDER AND SOULFUL IN THE CLASSIC.

In order rightly to comprehend the works of the greatest composers we need to give especial attention to their deepest and tenderest moments. These, of course, are to be found in the slow movements of the sonatas and symphonies. These movements are founded upon the people's song; they are in lyric forms, in slow and sustained melodies, which in the longer movements are contrasted with second and third subjects of a different character, as we already saw in our studies in form.

The general type of these movements is the *Cantabile*. They are not to be found in Bach, nor yet in Handel. Haydn gives us the form but not the deep spirit we now look for in a movement of this kind. A pleasing example is found in one of his symphonies. (Plays *Largo Cantabile* from Haydn's symphony in D, No. 5 in Wittman's arrangements for piano solo, Ed. Peters, No. 197.) The second subject is in the principal key of the movement, G, beginning in the thirty-first measure.

The slow movements in the pianoforte works are not so serious or well-sustained, because the pianoforte of that day had not the "singing tone" necessary for properly rendering movements of this kind. For the same reason such movements can not be met with in the Mozart pianoforte sonatas. In these the ideas lack breadth and depth. In Mozart's string quartettes and symphonies, however, we find movements of this kind beautifully sustained, but not characterized by the depth we find in Beethoven. Such a movement is the Andante from the 5th Quintette. (Plays.) Another example is the Larghetto in D from the Clarinet concerts. ("Mozart Album," Ed. Peters, No. 1823, p. 36.)

Beethoven, however, is the great master of this type of composition. We find traces of it even in his earliest works, as in the *Adagio* of the first sonata, op. 2 in F minor. This movement was originally written by him when he was fifteen years old; it formed part of the first quartette for piano, violin, viola and 'cello. The quartettes were not published until after his death. The principal subject is extremely tender and fine. (Plays the entire movement.)

The *Largo appassionata* of the second sonata, op. 2 in A, is a still more notable example. The principal idea of this movement is extremely large, and full of feeling. The second idea, beginning with the last three notes of the eighth measure, is rather insignificant, and indeed is used merely as an interlude. The second subject, proper, begins with the last three notes of the nineteenth measure. The depth and seriousness of this movement are due to its slow pace, the long tones in the melody, and the low staccato notes in the bass, which give an impression of repressed passion.

The beautiful *Adagio grazioso* of the sonata in G, op. 31, No. 1, is perhaps a better example of a purely classical movement of this kind, since it has all the classic peculiarities in a high degree; such as repose, symmetry, moderation, purity, and an exquisite grace such as one may search through many volumes elsewhere without finding. (Plays.) This piece, as indeed the whole sonata, seems a purely classical work. It means absolutely nothing more than it says. It is a beautiful example of Beethoven's most cheerful work when he was at the very prime of his health and powers. Many other works of his mean more than they say and so belong to the romantic. This one is the full expression of its own idea, and for that very reason requires a certain maturity and refinement of taste to properly appreciate it.

A short movement in dance form, but in very much the same serious vein, is found in the Menuetto in E flat, out of the third sonata of this opus 31. (Plays.)

A very long but beautiful movement in similar spirit is furnished by the second part of the sonata in F, op. 90. This is one of the most refined and satisfactory cantabile pieces of Beethoven. It has in it an exquisite air of tenderness and nobility, like that of a refined and noble woman. (Plays.)

Yet another movement of the same kind is found in the *Tempo di Menuetto* of the sonata in G, op. 30, for piano and violin, one of the three great ones dedicated to the Emperor Alexander II. (Let this be heard if convenient.) Nor ought we to overlook the exquisite *Andante* and variations of the *Sonata appassionata*, op. 57, which are also characterized by the same repose and elevated beauty. (Plays.)

In all these movements the predominant impressions are of repose, and depth of soul. As Hegel says of Greek sculpture, "this is the unalterable permanence of the immortal gods."

LIST OF ILLUSTRATIONS.

1. Largo Cantabile from Haydn's 5th Symphony, in D, No. 5, in Wittmann's arr. for piano solo, Ed. Peters, No. 197.
2. Andante from Quintette, Mozart.
3. Adagio from Sonata in F, op. 2, No. 1, Beethoven.
4. Largo Appassionata from Sonata in A, op. 2, No. 2, Beethoven.
5. Adagio Grazioso from Sonata in G, op. 31, No. 1, Beethoven.
6. Menuetto from Sonata in C minor, op. 31, No. 3, Beethoven.
7. Tempo di Menuetto from Sonata in G, op. 30, Beethoven.
8. Andante and Variations from Sonata, op. 57, Beethoven.
9. Larghetto in D, from Clarinet Concerto, Mozart (p. 36 in "Mozart Album," No. 1823 Peters.)

LESSON TWENTY-EIGHTH.

THE CONTENTED, THE JOVIAL, THE COMFORTABLE, AS EXPRESSED IN THE RONDO.

As to its form the rondo consists of a principal subject three or four times repeated, with second and third subjects intervening between these repetitions. As already appeared in the second part of this work, the rondo differs from the sonata-piece in having less thematic work, and less seriousness. The rondo is derived from the people's song, and represents a spirit of cheerfulness, of burgher-like satisfaction; a comfortable contentment in life which is too lively for repose, and too cheerful for work or striving. Thus, *e. g.*, observe the following: (Plays Rondo in E flat from Beethoven's op. 7.)

In the very first idea we have this feeling of rather satisfied comfort, and the secondary matter only serves to bring this spirit out more plainly.

For another example take the rondo out of the little sonata in G, op. 14, No. 2. This is still more playful. (Plays.)

Even in the serious and deeply moved sonatas, the rondo is in a spirit which indicates that conflict has had its victory in happiness or something approaching it. (Plays rondo of sonata *pathetique*.)

One of the most interesting of the Beethoven rondos is the extremely bright and clever Rondo Capriccioso, op. 129, one of his very latest compositions. The theme of this might have been written by Haydn, it is so clear and sunny, but Haydn could never have indulged himself in the endless caprices of the elaboration. (Plays Rondo Capriccioso of Beethoven.)

If further examples are desired, let them be found in the two rondos of Beethoven, op. 51 in C and G, and Mendelssohn's well-known Rondo Capriccioso.

In several of the Beethoven sonatas we find in place of the rondo a movement called "Finale," which is in the same form as the sonata-piece except that a third subject (or middle-piece) takes the place of the Elaboration. An example of this is found in the first sonata in F, op. 2. In other instances the Finale is a sonata-piece, but conceived in a lighter spirit. Such are found in the Sonata op. 10 in C minor, op. 31 No. 2 in D minor, op. 31 No. 3 in E flat, etc.

LIST OF ILLUSTRATIONS.

1. Rondo of Sonata in E♭, op. 7, Beethoven.
2. Rondo of Sonata in G, op. 14, No. 2, Beethoven,
3. Rondo of Sonata Pathetique, op. 13, Beethoven.
4. Rondo Capriccioso, op. 129, Beethoven.
5. Two Rondos, op. 51, Beethoven.
6. Rondo Capriccioso, Mendelssohn.

LESSON TWENTY-NINTH.

THE CYCLE OF THE SONATA.

The form of the sonata-piece and the composition to which it has given its name we have already considered in Lessons XV. and XVI. The emotional characteristics of its component parts have now been considered in detail. We are ready, therefore, to enter upon the study of the work as a whole. This cannot be done profitably otherwise than by repeatedly hearing an entire sonata until one knows it in its separate movements and parts, and again in the unity of the complete work, so that one thinks of the different movements as chapters in the same life-history, or as successive and logically-related states of the same person. This unity of the sonata as a whole is one of the peculiar excellencies of Beethoven's works. We do not find the same comprehensive grasp on the part of any other composer in this form of composition.

The first movement represents the earnest and intellectually determined part of the work. The second, the reposeful and deep moments. The third, the out-come into healthful, every-day activity. If there are four movements, a playful moment intervenes between the second and third or the third and fourth, as a sort of interlude. The first movement, therefore, strikes the key-note of the whole work. If its subjects are trivial and scantily handled, no great depth of sentiment in the following part, the slow movement, can reasonably be expected. We already know that the different movements in the same sonata have no motives in common; they are not even in the same key. They are not composed at the same time. Generally we may conceive of a sonata-piece as having first occurred to the composer merely as a single motive, with certain dimly-perceived possibilities of elaboration. Possibly a second motive, that of the lyric digression, was thought of at the same time. Perhaps the entire Principal was written out immediately; by chance the Second also, though this is not common. The intervening passage work and the elaboration may have occupied the leisure moments of several days. Thus after considerable delay the composer is in possession of the entire first movement. It may be a week later before he composes the slow movement, and a month before the sonata is finished. Yet this does not go to deny the unity of the sonata as a whole. For do not novelists write the most absorbing tales in precisely similar piecemeal way? These delays represent the time of meditation, during which the author decides what the natural out-come of his characters shall be, taking into account all the circumstances of their history as represented.

In some cases the motives of a work were thought of several years before they were finally worked up. In Beethoven's "note-books" (rude memorandum books of music paper, on which he wrote down at the moment any good idea that struck him) we find the motives of his symphonies sometimes for several years before the symphony was composed. Some of these motives undergo remarkable changes before they come into a form satisfactory to the great master. When the sonata is done it is not always satisfactory. Thus, the well-known "*Andante Favoris* in F" of Beethoven was written to go in the Waldstein sonata in C, op. 53. But on trial it did not suit him; perhaps because of its length. So it was taken out and published separately, and the short "Introduction" which now stands there, put in its place. Yet it would be wrong to conclude from this that the association of pieces in the sonata was a matter of experiment, instead of insight and logical development. It is rather as if an author had concluded on reflection that in a certain chapter he had allowed an unsuitable weight to certain tendencies in some one of his principal characters.

A few general traits of these sonatas we may easily observe. Thus, if the first movement is vigorous and strongly marked, the ensuing movements partake of the same decision. To take a very strong example, consider Sonata *Pathétique*. Here the Introduction (*Grave*) opens very broadly and passionately. (Plays.) Then follows an equally forcible Allegro which goes at an extremely rapid pace, and is strongly accented and marked by wide transitions of power. (Plays.) The Elaboration in this is equally forcible, and includes motives from the Introduction as well as from the Allegro proper. (Plays.) Then after the completion of this movement, there follows an Adagio of the most deep and spiritual expression. (Plays.) On this follows a Rondo, which manifests the habitual carelessness of the rondo, as through a veil of tears. The third subject in it is perfectly dry and unemotional, only to give place for an unusual and unprecedented recapitulation of the principal subject of the rondo. It may be confessed that this rondo, fine as it is, sometimes seems inadequate to the sonata it concludes; and yet Beethoven put it there, and the world generally accepts this as one of his most satisfactory.

Again in the sonata in F, op. 2 No. 1, we have an extremely fortunate example of association. The Allegro is founded on one of Friedmann Bach's. It has no properly developed lyric digression. The Adagio is one of the loveliest, and as we know, taken out of a youthful work. The Menuet is pretty, and the Finale charming and impetuous, and saved from a flavor of the morbid only by the exquisite melody in A flat (third subject).

It is unnecessary to multiply examples. To properly comprehend the sonata in all its possibilities is to comprehend everything in instrumental music. All that can here be done to assist the student is to suggest the unity of the sonata as a whole. More must come by study and experience. It will be found a profitable experience in every way to resume this study from time to time, using the four-hand arrangements of the symphonies of Haydn, Mozart and Beethoven. Some one work is to be taken and each separate movement studied until it becomes familiar; afterwards the entire symphony, and this, also, several times in succession. It is an excellent thing in a boarding school, for example, when an eight-hand arrangement of one of these works is undertaken; we have there immediately four pupils practically interested in one work. The length of time necessary to bring such a performance to a satisfactory state, suffices to thoroughly familiarize the entire school with the motives and leading features of the work. In this way very much genuine musical cultivation can be had in places where orchestral music is never heard. For such a purpose a list is added, below.

List of Illustrations.

1. Sonata Pathetique, op. 13, Beethoven.
2. Sonata in F minor, op. 2, Beethoven.
3. Four-hand arrangement of Beethoven's Septette, op. 20.
4. Beethoven's 2d, 5th and 7th Symphonies, for four hands. (Peters' ed.)
5. Beethoven Sonatas for Piano and Violin, arranged for four hands. In particular Nos. 5 in F, 7 in C minor, and 8 in G.

LESSON THIRTIETH.

THE BEAUTIFUL IN CLASSIC MUSIC, AND THE TRANSITION TOWARD THE ROMANTIC.

As compared with sensational modern works, classical music seems cold, impassive. Much of this impression depends on one's musical habits of thought. A student who spends a large part of his practice on finger exercises and studies, will find almost any classical sonata musical and grateful to him; but one who idles away his prescribed "hours" on pleasing and capriciously chosen pieces, and never practices exercises or studies, will find a sonata tiresome—at least, until it is heard often enough for its real character to impress itself upon an inattentive player. Still it is by no means necessary for a student to avoid modern works in order to enjoy a sonata. It will be enough if he is willing to decide for himself that he prefers *music* as such, to the strained and forced or empty in expression.

When we take up a piece of Bach's, as, for example, the first movement of the Italian Concerto, it at first seems tame. When heard many times, however, a certain fluency and genuine melodiousness appear in it, which betray the touch of genius. (Plays.) The piece seems to our ears somewhat too long. This impression is not due to its absolute length, but to its want of contrast. If we take up a larger piece of Bach's, such as the Passacaglia in C min. (organ works arranged for four hands), we find in it a certain monotony, yet a decided progress toward a climax. The piece is a set of variations on a "ground bass," or *cantus fermus* which goes through all the variations unchanged. It ends with a splendid fugue. When we compare these variations with each other we observe that each is more complex than the preceding. (Plays theme and variations, remarking the commencement of each. Afterwards it would be well to examine the variations in detail, pointing out the motives of each. Then play the whole again.) In all this we have no new disposition or emotional contrasts represented, but only an unfolding of what was already possible in the theme. As the rose in full bloom displays no petals which were not enrolled in the bud, so these latest and most luxuriant blos-

soms give us nothing that was not already implied in the theme.
Nevertheless it was only Aaron's rod that budded, and it is only a
theme of such a man as Bach that blossoms out like this.

Here we come upon one of the characteristic moments of classical
music. It is that in which music itself is trying its wings for itself.
Nothing here seeks expression save only the musical ideas themselves,
nay, the single idea of the theme, and its logical implications.
In order to appreciate it, therefore, one needs to hear it many times,
and especially to have within himself a really musical nature. All the
greatest masters since Bach have admired, wondered at, and enjoyed
these works of his, the greatness of which lies in the lengths they go
as music, and their entire freedom from anything like *emotional* effort.
They are not without emotional expression; they could not be, with a
rhythmic pulsation so thoroughly established and so long maintained,
for the heart falls in with it and retards or accelerates in sympathy.
Add to this the constantly augmenting energy of the motivization, and
we have a certain amount of emotional expression in spite of the monotony of the harmonic foundation. Yet with all its energy and
strength, and its climax, it remains in some way cold. It is like a wonderful statue in music.

Let us examine it in the light of our studies in the beautiful.
Beginning on the lowest plane, we ask what has it for the pleasure of
hearing? In answer it must be at once admitted that merely sensuous
charm is not here sought. It sounds well; all its dissonances are properly prepared and resolved, and the finest of all harmonic instincts pre-
sided over the arrangement of its chord-sequences. Here, therefore,
it yields only negative results. We ask again, what has it for satisfaction in contemplation? And in this direction it has much to say
for itself. Each period is symmetrical and well concluded. The
strictest unity prevails throughout. The work as a whole does not
manifest symmetry, since it does not consist of two, three, or any number of sections or members standing over against each other. This
element of form is wanting. The Passacaglia is merely the life-history of a single idea from its first simple form through its development
to its return again into repose, the *Nirvana* of music. Yet this development itself is traced with such skill, each step follows so naturally on the preceding and the whole is managed without any overdoing
or forceful effort, that in the unity and movement of the work we have
one of the earliest forms in which the beautiful, as such, found expression in music. Nor is the work without a decided outlook in the direction of the higher perception and spiritual realization of beauty.

Perhaps this is shown in the persistence of the theme; and its final conflict and victory in the fugue. All that goes before is to interest us in the theme. We must not forget that in Bach's day, lovers of music generally were familiar with fugal phraseology and followed with readiness and interest all the vicissitudes of the subject as only musicians now do, so that intricacies of treatment which sound to us somewhat far-fetched and difficult, sounded to them natural and right. On the other hand, the extreme modulations common in modern works, and the brilliancy and comparative looseness of treatment in modern pieces, would have occasioned them a genuine shock of surprise and disapproval.

Again, let us observe the Andante from Mozart's fifth quintette for strings (No. 3 on the list below). It is in the form of a rondo. The principal subject is this. (Plays first subject, 16 measures.) The second subject is in E flat. (Plays.)

Now when we attentively consider the impression this work makes upon us, we immediately perceive that it manifests the elements of formal beauty in a much more complete degree than the Bach works just mentioned. Considered merely as music it is less serious than the Bach pieces. For this reason it bestows less attention upon developing a single subject. The world goes more easily here than there. Life has certain ameliorations. The episode comes not in the form of additional trouble for the theme, but in a complete digression from it, like a visit to a new world. (Plays entire movement again.) Such an introduction of a complete digression within a movement is very rare in Bach. Mozart's appreciation of its restfulness marks his deeper comprehension of the emotional nature of music. Examined with reference to its degree of beauty this piece does not manifest important difference from that of Bach. Thus in the merely well-sounding the Mozart Andante is stronger. It has more symmetry and sweetness; a more evident harmony and proportion of parts; the complete digression into another key relieves the ear. Still this last comparison is hardly fair, for the Passacaglia has its modulatory structure determined by its ground bass. On the other hand the Bach piece is very much more earnest and vigorous. The intellectual element preponderates in it. As already pointed out, it is a monologue, a discussion of a single theme carried out thoroughly in all its parts, with no regard for the hearer. The Mozart Andante, on the contrary, is distinctly lyric. It is a song. And so in all its parts it is simpler, more easily comprehended, more pleasing. Yet both pieces are so masterly in their way that neither can be accredited with a general superiority over the other. The latter marks a progress in the direction of the secular, and the softer and less divine sides of beauty.

Or take, again, the Beethoven "Moonlight" sonata. Its first movement is also a monody on a single theme. (Plays the first strain of melody of Adagio in sonata.) It is of the most plaintive character. The same spirit pervades the entire movement. (Plays the entire movement.) This sonata has always been regarded as a cry of the heart. The beautiful as such, the symmetrical, reposeful, the well-proportioned and sweet, are not here the objects of expression. But instead of them we have the very heart of the composer; its sorrow, its grief, its desire. (Plays again.)

This wonderfully sad movement is followed by a Scherzo which to some extent relieves the tension. The afflicted mourner takes up again the sympathies and associations of life; not with undisciplined buoyancy, but with a sad and tender resignation. Is this all fancy? (Plays Allegretto.) On this, again, follows the Finale, which is in fact a regularly constructed sonata-piece with all its appurtenances. In this we have the soul in its hours of solitude, when, no longer distracted by the world about it, all the waves of its grief come over it. At times hope springs up, but only to be immediately overwhelmed. (Plays the entire Finale.)

Thus in the whole sonata as well as the movements separately, we have a life history, not of a single musical theme and its implications (as in the Passacaglia), but a story of the human heart, a voice from the soul. However fine we may find this sonata in point of construction, we do not listen to it for its music merely. It is distinctly a poem, carrying a meaning which is not in any sensuous charm of pleasantly chosen harmonies or agreeable sequences of melody, nor yet in any formal beauty. Indeed, the beautiful, as such, is not the impression this work leaves upon us, but its *expression*, its *sorrow*. In this, then, we come upon the romantic moment of music, when art becomes the expression of the joys and sorrows of the soul.

Yet another example. Let us take the Beethoven Sonata in E flat, op. 31 No. 3. This belongs to the more pleasing moments of experience. The Allegro opens with a motive that sounds like a question, an impression having its source partly in the motive itself but more in the harmony which supports it. The entire movement is short and not seriously intended. (Plays entire movement.) This is followed by a Scherzo which has something song-like in it, although it is in the same form as the preceding, a sonata-piece. (Plays.) This is followed by a Menuetto, a genuine *cantabile* movement (one of the loveliest, by the way), which is a simple binary form. (Plays.) This, again, is followed by the Finale, which also is a sonata-piece, perhaps the only example in the Beethoven sonatas where three of the forms of the same sonata are of this kind. This movement is extremely jolly and pretty. (Plays.) Listen now to the entire sonata. (Plays entire sonata.) Here, as you perceive, we have not a moment of grief or any deep sorrow, nor yet any great moral earnestness. But instead of it the musical, the symmetrical, the pleasing, the beautiful. If now we would be fully conscious of the musical distance we have passed over we should hear again the Bach Passacaglia. (If agreeable the Passacaglia may here be heard again.)

When we thus bring these two extremes, or at least widely separated points, of the musical scale into juxtaposition, we are able to realize that the beautiful itself is not the principal subject of the Bach piece; and that from Bach to Beethoven a great progress has been made in the direction of the lovely and the expressive.

Yet one more example. Let us observe carefully the Air and Variations in B flat by Schubert. (Plays Schubert's air from the Impromptu in B flat, op. 142. Then play the beginning of each variation, calling attention to the motivization of each, and afterward the entire piece.) In this lovely work we have something very different from any thing we find in the Passacaglia, or even in the Mozart Andante. Yet its prevailing expression is one of beauty and grace. A careful examination of it will indicate considerable attention to the well-sounding, a strict but purely unconscious observance of formal beauty, and beyond this a perceptible flavor of more inward and exquisite movement of spirit. Yet this without at all going into the depths of the soul. Like a pleasant sunset, one regards it with delight, but composure. As when the duties of the day are done, its pleasant experiences remembered, all its annoyances and cares forgotten, in peaceful contemplation one awaits the hour of sleep.

In all these examples we have had to do chiefly with formal beauty, save where the "Moonlight" sonata brought us to a still more inward exercise of spirit. The progress thus traced, from the strict musical logic and elevated formal beauty of Bach, through the pleasing and enchanting in Mozart, Beethoven and Schubert, and the deeply heartfelt in Beethoven's latest works, goes yet further in the romantic school, as we shall hereafter see. This same progress is traced from the vocal side in Part VII., on Songs, where new conditions lead to new and important results. The smaller classical composers, such as Clementi and Dussek, display in the main the same general characteristics as we have observed in Beethoven, yet with less unity and imaginative power. Indeed we must think of Dussek as an imitator, or at least follower of Mozart, and as breaking no new paths. Bach, Haydn, Mozart and Beethoven comprehend everything that properly belongs to the classic in music.

LIST OF ILLUSTRATIONS.

1. Allegro from Bach's Italian Concerto.
2. Passacaglia in C minor for the organ. Bach. (Arranged for 4 hands on the piano. Peters' Ed. No. 224.)
3. Andante from 5th Quintette, Mozart. (4 hands. Peters' Ed. No. 997.)
4. The "Moonlight" Sonata of Beethoven, op. 27 No. 2.
5. Sonata in E flat, op. 31 No. 3, Beethoven.
6. Impromptu in B flat, op. 142, Schubert.

Part Sixth.

STUDIES IN THE ROMANTIC.

LESSON THIRTY-FIRST.

THE CHIVALROUS.

"The chief content of Chivalry," says Hegel, "may be expressed as *Honor, Love*, and *Fidelity*." The idea of chivalry carries with it the heroic, the tender, the graceful and considerate, and above all the noble and dignified, or, as Southerners say, "the high-toned." This phase of musical expression finds its most congenial expression in the works of Chopin, especially in the Polonaises. Yet the polonaise expresses these graces in many instances with a certain qualification. The Chopin polonaise not only represents the phases of chivalry, but there runs through it the sad and almost morbid element of Polish character, as if the unfortunate history of this country had imparted a tinge of sadness even to its moments of victory. Of the polonaise in general, Liszt writes:

"While listening to some of the *polonaises* of Chopin, we can almost catch the firm, nay, the more than firm, the heavy, resolute tread of men bravely facing all the bitter injustice which the most cruel and relentless destiny can offer, with the manly pride of unblenching courage.

"The progress of the music suggests to our imagination such magnificent groups as were designed by Paul Veronese, robed in the rich costume of days long past; we see passing at intervals before us, brocades of gold, velvets, damasked satins, silvery, soft and flexible sables, hanging sleeves gracefully thrown back upon the shoulders, embossed sabres, boots yellow as gold or red with trampled blood, sashes with long and undulating fringes, close chemisettes, rustling trains, stomachers embroidered with pearls, head-dresses glittering with rubies or leafy with emeralds, light slippers rich with amber, gloves perfumed with the luxurious att͟ar from the harems.

"From the faded background of times long past these vivid groups start forth; gorgeous carpets from Persia lie at their feet, filagreed furniture from Constantinople stands around; all is marked by the sumptuous prodigality of the magnates who drew, in ruby goblets embossed with medallions, wine from the fountains of Tokay, and shod their fleet Arabian steeds with silver ; who surmounted all their escutcheons with the same crown which the fate of an election might render a royal one, and which, causing them to despise all other titles, was alone worn as *insigne* of their glorious equality."

Thus in the Military Polonaise of Chopin, already heard several times in the course of these studies, we have the martial element strongly brought out. This runs through the whole piece. In form this polonaise is of the simple binary order. The second leading subject beginning:

Ex. 28.

is of the nature of a "trio." Yet in this, where if anywhere we would look for the expression of tenderness, the military ardor glows still unquenched. After one strain of this we encounter a different spirit. What is it? (Plays the middle strain of trio beginning with the trill on C sharp in the bass.) This is in effect a salute. It is as if we had been witnessing a grand review. Here the general and his staff ride down the line, and we hear the salute of honor, the roll of musketry, the blare of the trumpets, and see the waving of the colors.

On the other hand let us examine a work in which there is much greater diversity of momentary expression, and consequently much less coherence.

Observe, now, the following: (Plays the first twelve measures of Polonaise in C sharp minor, op. 26.) Here the first four measures have the force of a full period; they start off splendidly, with the greatest determination and courage. In the next eight measures this courage still exists, it is true, but with it a vein of weakness becomes apparent. (Plays this phrase; and then repeats the entire period.)

At the twenty-fifth measure a new figure meets us, not referable to any warlike spirit as such. It more reminds one of Liszt's description of the complicated figures and constantly fresh inventions introduced into the Polish dance. (Plays seven measures.) At the tenth measure of this part the chivalrous spirit reappears. (Plays to the end of this part; *i. e.*, to the signature of five flats.)

Here enters an entirely new spirit. Our valiant soldier has become entangled in the snares of love. Yet note how tender his devotion. With what subtle nobility of tenderness he breathes his love. (Plays sixteen measures of this part.) Here at the seventeenth measure a different spirit enters. It seems a conflict, a dialogue. Above we hear the woman's voice, gentle, persistent, tender; below the man's, more importunate, not so reserved and regular. The *denouement* each hearer may imagine for himself. When this little conflict is over we have again the gentle song of love which opened this part. And thus the piece ends. (Plays.)

Observe again the entire piece. (Plays the whole piece.) It consists, as you perceive, of two equal parts or pictures, different sides of the same nature. The first martial and ardent; the second tender and pleading. The work has no unity except in so far as the uniform rhythmic pulsation throughout the piece enables us to recognize, underneath all those moods, the beatings of the same hearts.

Here, again, and in order to study the polonaise from a different stand-point, observe the following: (Plays Polacca Brilliant in E, op. 72, Von Weber.) This, as you perceive, is a melodious and poetic piece, but it lacks the nameless grace and charm of the Chopin works, though to very many, and perhaps to all, there is something extremely pleasing in its freshness, which has nothing in it of a morbid character.

Again, observe this little polonaise of Schumann's: (Plays the polonaise in D, out of the papillons, op. 2.)

In order to understand this phase of music fully we need to examine three more works. The first is the Chopin polonaise in A flat, op. 53. This is in the grand style. Observe the Introduction. (Plays sixteen measures.) See how strong and resistless the impulse! Then enters the theme. (Plays from seventeenth measure to the end of this part, through forty-eighth measure.) Here at the forty-ninth measure there enters one of those capricious figures referred to by Liszt. Evidently it is of a grandiose and somewhat startling character; it is repeated with emphasis (represented by the transposition to a higher degree). At the fifty-seventh measure a grand and dignified melody begins, which presently brings us again to the theme. (Plays four measures and four measures; and then this melody; then the theme and so on through the Principal to the change of signature.)

Here at the change of key a new caprice presents itself. In the treble we have a very quiet melody; under it in the bass a monotonous octave figure repeated over and over many times, at first very softly, then by degrees louder. It expands and expands until it fills the whole field of observation; then it subsides only to mount up once more. (Plays through the passage containing bass running passage in octaves.) At the end of the octaves there enters a gentle figure in G major, afterwards transposed to A flat, and this, after some time, leads again to the principal, and so to the close. (Plays last part of piece.) Observe now the whole work. (Plays the entire polonaise.) This piece, in spite of a considerable degree of contrast between the various strains, is essentially of one spirit, and that of an extremely heroic, dignified, and noble character.

Another work of this class and remarkable for still greater contrasts, though, as a whole pervaded by a more refined (and possibly effeminate) spirit, is the Chopin polonaise in E flat, op. 22. This work is preceded by a charming *Andante Spianato*, which belongs to the tender side of emotion. The polonaise enters thus: (Plays.) In the sixtieth measure of the polonaise proper (not counting the orchestral *tutti* intervening between the andante and the polonaise) a series of strong contrasts begins. Here we have two lines of extremely bold octaves in both hands. (Plays.) In the sixty-seventh measure a soft and delicate melody enters, concluding with some delicate cadencing, in the sixty-ninth, etc. (Plays.) In the seventy-third measure a bold and fiery passage bursts in, closing with an octave passage. (Plays.) In the eighty-third measure a lovely melody in C minor begins. (Plays.) But enough. Suffice it to say that in this piece we have almost every phase of the Chopin nature represented, and it is rightly counted for one of his most exquisite works.

Still another and more sensational work of this school is Liszt's Polonaise in E. This great work (one of the best of Liszt's) contains very few of the refinements we have seen so abundant in the work last considered. Nay, it is even less so than the heroic polonaise in A flat. Yet it is a concert-piece of the same general type, and as such deserves to be carefully heard. The finest work in it is in the Cadenza. (Plays.)

LIST OF ILLUSTRATIONS.

1. Chopin's Polonaise Militaire, op. 40, No. 1.
2. Chopin's Polonaise in C sharp minor, op. 26, No. 1.
3. Polacca Brilliante in E, Weber, op. 72.
4. Schumann's Polonaise in D (out of Papillons, op. 2).
5. Chopin Polonaise in A flat, op. 53.
6. Chopin's Andante and Polonaise in E flat, op. 22.
7. Liszt's Polonaise Heroique in E.

LESSON THIRTY-SECOND.

THE GENTLE AND SENTIMENTAL; THE DEEPLY TENDER.

The earliest consistent examples of this kind of spirit worked out in pianoforte music in simple forms, are to be found in some of the Haydn adagios and andantes, and the Field nocturnes, the latter most particularly. Field very probably derived more or less suggestion from the slow movements in Beethoven sonatas, all of which, as far as the "Waldstein," appassionata and "Kreutzer" sonatas, were published before the Field nocturnes. In many of the earlier sonatas of Beethoven we find short passages in the genuine nocturne vein; as, *e. g.*, in the Adagio of sonata pathetique, the Menuet in the sonata in E flat, op. 31, etc. To Field, however, is due the credit of having established the form of the nocturne as an independent piece for piano, in a tender, elegiac vein, and, both in point of difficulty and emotional range, keeping it within the resources of amateurs generally. Here, *e. g.*, is such a piece. (Plays Field's nocturne in B flat.) This piece, like all of Field's, is characterized by an extremely clear and limpid style, and a truly refined and delicate spirit.

Field was not insensible to the advantages of contrast, as we see in the following, where the second subject makes an admirable contrast with the first. (Plays Field's nocturne in D, No. 13.)

Mendelssohn, however, is the magician who first made known to amateurs generally the latent singing powers of the pianoforte. This he did in his famous works, the "Songs Without Words." No doubt the fortunate selection of title had much to do with their immediate popularity, which was very great, and has in fact continued ever since.

The first book of these beautiful works was published in 1829 and contained six pieces, in which the Mendelssohnian spirit is unmistakable. In the first we have a tender melody and a gentle and well-blended accompaniment, which, when well played, is truly charming. (Plays.) In the second we have a vein of sadness or melancholy, as well as the usual tenderness. (Plays.) The third is the well-known "Hunting Song," which may well enough be heard here for the sake of the contrast. (Plays No. 3.) No. 6 is a Venetian *Gondellied* in which one plainly hears the melancholy and passion of a decayed and fading race. (Plays.) Whatever meaning we may be led by their fanciful titles to attach to these pieces, they all speak unmistakably the voice of tenderness and sadness. Whenever we are in any similar mood these pieces chime in with our feelings, and utter the very tones we would ourselves have originated. This is the quality of popularity: to seem to say what every reader would himself have said (if only he had thought to do it). And this quality the Mendelssohn songs possess in the most eminent degree. Another example of the same spirit we have in the lovely Duetto in A flat, No. 18, which may be heard again if desired. (Let it be played if it is not clearly remembered from former citations.)

Chopin took up the nocturne form as Field left it, and imparted to it a greater depth and range of meaning. One of the simplest types of his is the second one, the lovely nocturne in E flat, op. 9, No. 2. This consists of a gentle melody and a delicate accompaniment of chords. It is extremely unpretending, yet it is one of the most perfect gems in this department of composition. (Plays.)

Here, in the 4th nocturne, he avails himself of a stronger contrast. (Plays nocturne in F, op. 15, No. 1.)

Another of the singing nocturnes of Chopin is that in B maj., op. 32, No. 1. (Plays.)

In the 13th nocturne there is a deeper meaning. It tells of greater depths of passion, and has stronger contrasts than those already heard. (Plays the nocturne in C minor, op. 48, No. 1.)

Two of the most admired of these works are those in G, op. 37. No. 1 in G minor is an elegy full of sadness and longing. It is relieved by an episode of pure uninverted triads, like a church piece. In this we have portrayed a deep and spiritual peace. (Plays.)

The second one, in G maj., is of a much more genial and cheerful character, delicate and tender. Owing to the preponderance of thirds and sixths it is extremely difficult to play well. (Plays.)

List of Illustrations.

1. Nocturne in B♭, Field.
2. Nocturne in D, No. 13, Field.
3. Nos. 1, 2, 3, 6 and 18 of Songs without Words, Mendelssohn.
4. Nocturne in E♭, op. 9, Chopin.
5. Nocturne in F, op. 15, Chopin.
6. Nocturnes in B, op. 32; C min., op. 48; and G, op. 37, Chopin.

LESSON THIRTY-THIRD.

THE HUMORISTIC AND THE PASSIONATE.

By the name Humor the Germans denote caprices, whims, moods, change; and not the ludicrous, as in later English usage. There is one side of the modern romantic school which can be appropriately named by no other term than humoristic. This is nearly the same as whimsical, the difference being that the latter term has acquired an objectionable meaning, like the "foolishly humoristic" or the "unreasonably humoristic." This element of musical expression frequently exceeds the bounds of beauty, and is indeed allied to realism, since *realism* in music is in fact nothing but musical expression made subservient to a strictly literal representation of natural sounds or common-place sensations. Humor in music frequently approaches the grotesque. The great exponent of this school is Schumann, whose fancy ran wild in every direction, and only in exceptional cases controlled itself according to the moderate and decorous.

Here, for example, are three little pieces from the Kinderscenen. (Plays successively, "From Strange Lands," "A Curious Story," and "Playing Tag," the first three pieces in the "Scenes from Childhood.") These little pieces, as you observe, are entirely unlike each other, and each one is complete in itself. The first a graceful little melody. The second a bright and rather sprightly and forcible little piece in march time. The third a sort of presto with very strong accents. It would be a very superior sort of clairvoyance in any one who should be able to guess the names of these pieces from hearing them played. Yet the names give a very decided assistance toward divining the author's meaning. Observe now the following: (Plays No. 5, "Happy Enough," No. 7, "Traumerei," and "Frightening," No. 11.) Among larger pieces of the humoristic type are to be mentioned the Schumann Phantasiestücke, op. 12. It is of the first of these that Franz Brendel remarks: "It brings us blessed enjoyment, vernal airs, and flowery savors." (Plays "In the Evening.") This dreamy nocturne is followed by a powerfully excited piece called "*Aufschwung*," "Soaring," a name intended to convey the idea of such a mental state as one falls into in

8

wakeful hours of night, especially after taking too strong tea, or a light opiate. Then the brain is preternaturally active, nothing seems impossible; the most brilliant conceptions throng the mind, one visits strange lands, rises into unknown regions, solves impossible problems. The sober light of day dissolves all these visions, but while they last they carry the bewildered visionary captive at their will. Such a piece is this: (Plays "Soaring.") Then follows a sort of musical conundrum, "*Warum*," "Why." It consists of a single motive many times slowly repeated, accompanied by a restless accompaniment of chords entering on the half-beat. (Plays *Warum*.) Then follows yet a different strain, called "Whims," of which we need no further explanation than the title. (Plays *Grillen*.)

In all these pieces we plainly see that the beautiful, as such, is not sought by the composer. They afford neither the sensuous charm of delicately-balanced phrases, sweetly-modulating chords, or any other mere gratification of a love for the well-sounding. Quite as little do they afford satisfaction in contemplation. Formal beauty they do not possess. Their distinctive merits are two: First, their coherence as music. Here comes along a new composer, Schumann, a hundred years later than Bach, and develops musical ideas in ways that are musically right and proper, and yet *new*. And, second, these humoristic pieces carry us along with them, move us, excite us, as the Bach pieces do not. You may pronounce them unbeautiful if you please, but they are musically right and genuinely expressive.

There is also a darker side of the picture. Observe now this: (Plays Schumann's "In the Night.") It is of this piece that Franz Brendel says: "It is a powerful night-piece, hobgoblin-filled, awful pictures, anxious waking-dreams; a state of soul the opposite of the 'Evening' formerly mentioned." This vein is not uncommon in Schumann, especially in his later years. It also appears in Chopin as the first part of the first movement of the sonata in B flat minor, op. 35, and in many other places. So also many of the Beethoven pieces must have sounded in this vein when they were new, before the listener's ears had become accustomed to the rapid modulations of these pieces and their restlessness. This spirit is also to be met with in Bach, as in the great organ prelude in A minor, and in many other pieces. This prelude, for example, seems to aim at representing a tossed and troubled spirit, like the waves of the sea. Neither the tuneful as such, nor still less the reposeful, could have been intended. They cannot be called beautiful since they are neither pleasing to hear, satisfactory to continually meditate upon, nor inspiring except as they widen the range of musical expression and serve for contrast, thereby heightening the beauty of other movements with which they are associated. This use, however, was not intended either by Bach or Schumann. The former wrote them for the purpose of expressing himself in this direction, which he saw to be legitimate and possible; Schumann, to satisfy his musical instincts in the same way, and also to gratify morbid moods.

List of Illustrations.

1. Schumann's Kinderseenen (Scenes from Childhood) op. 15. Nos 1, 2, 3, 5, 7, 11.
2. Schumann's "In the Evening," No. 1 in op. 12.
3. *Aufschwung*, or "Soaring," No. 2 in the same.
4. *Warum*, "Why?" the same.
5. *Grillen*, "Whims," from the same.
6. "In the Night," No. 5 in the same.
7. First part of Allegro in Chopin Sonata, op. 35.
8. Great Organ Prelude in A minor. (Vol. II. Bach's Organ Works, Peters' Ed.)

LESSON THIRTY-FOURTH.

THE FANCIFUL AND PLEASING.

Pieces of this class represent the lighter sentiments of social life, especially of polite society. We find in them symmetrical and graceful forms, permeated by a bright and pleasing spirit. They are refined and true, but they do not express the heroic or despairing moments of the soul. In consequence of their representing so completely the spirit of social life, they are eminently suitable for parlor performance. Observe this elegant waltz. (Plays Chopin's waltz in A flat, op. 34, No. 1.) This is the very spirit of the world and of society. Another example of the same kind is Rubinstein's Valse Caprice in E flat. (Plays.) Still another, and a famous one, too, is Weber's "Invitation to the Dance." (Plays.) This latter is more perfectly idealized than either of the preceding. The introduction is moderate and meditative, as if undecided whether to dance or not. Fanciful people have imagined that they saw in it the advance of the gentleman and his address to the lady, her acceptance, their quiet and fragmentary talk in the moment before the dance actually begins. Then the dance itself. At the close he re-conducts the lady gracefully to her seat, in the figure of the introduction.

Another example of similar spirit is the elegant Chopin Rondo in E flat, op. 16, which, though long and difficult, is conceived in the spirit of play, and represents the light and worldly side of feeling, yet with true refinement and earnestness. (Plays.) Were we to go further in this field we might bring forward the elegant Scherzo in B flat minor, op. 31, a very beautiful and poetic piece, which contains, perhaps, rather more of meaning than this list properly includes.

This field is practically illimitable. It includes all the lighter works of the greatest composers, except Schumann, who has left nothing properly belonging to it, and almost the entire production of very many smaller writers, such as Schulhoff, Jaell, Hunten, Leybach, Gottschalk, etc., etc.

Pieces of this class should be elegantly written and agreeably sounding. In the nature of the case they are perfectly easy to understand, for which reason we do not dwell upon them, but content ourselves with simply calling attention to them.

LIST OF ILLUSTRATIONS.

1. Chopin's Valse in A flat, op. 34, No. 2.
2. Rubinstein's Valse Caprice in E flat.
3. Weber's Invitation to the Dance.
4. Chopin's Introduction and Rondo in E flat, op. 16.
5. Chopin's Scherzo in B flat minor, op. 31.
6. Mill's 1st Tarantelle.
7. Raff's Valse Impromptu in B flat, op. 94.

LESSON THIRTY-FIFTH.

THE SENSATIONAL AND THE ASTONISHING.

In ordinary English usage, the term Romantic implies something "striking," "characterized by strong contrasts," "sensational," etc. Our studies thus far in this school of music are sufficient to show us the propriety of its name. In the previous lessons we have, indeed, come upon only the more reasonable and justifiable features of the romantic, in which the beautiful in some sense is the supreme object. Recent music, however, and particularly pianoforte music, contains many productions in which the sensational and the astonishing are the ends sought. Of this kind are concert pieces in general, especially the earlier works of Liszt, and most of the productions of other virtuoso players. Such, also, are very many orchestral works, especially some of Berlioz, Saint-Saens, Wagner's "Ride of the Valkyrie," etc.

In making the sensational their object, all of these exceed the bounds of the beautiful, and are of real use in art only in so far as they break new paths of technical accomplishment, and thereby provide means of expression which may afterwards be employed in artistic creation. In this way all great *virtuosi* have illustrated the capacity of their instruments, and in their works have provided useful studies for the mastery of peculiar difficulties. Of this kind, for example, are the Caprices of Paganini, which, while containing many musical and beautiful passages, are in general rather extravagant, and almost entirely wanting in symmetry and repose. They resemble tropical vegetation where in a humid soil and a dank atmosphere the most extravagant and fantastic growths are seen, luxuriant and beautiful in abounding vitality, yet oppressive to the senses.

In all these productions, moreover, there is a certain charm which recommends them to the player. It is not unlike what Ruskin calls " vital beauty, or the appearance of felicitous fulfillment of function in living creatures;" in other words, their remarkable adaptation to the instrument for which they were composed. The study of them has particular value in affording a free and dashing mode of playing.

The sensational in piano music dates from the discovery of the diminished seventh and its chromatic susceptibility. Thus in many of the earlier Liszt pieces there are passages which are neither pretty nor expressive, but which are merely *noise*. This kind we have illustrated in the " Lucia," for instance, and in the Rigoletto chromatic cadenza, described in Lesson XIX.

Another example is found in the cadenza near the close in Raff's Polka de la Reine. (Plays cadenza of diminished sevenths in the bass, and the ascending passages belonging to them; afterwards the entire piece.)

Of this kind are the cadenzas in the Chopin concerto, referred to in Lesson XIX. (Play if convenient.) In the Liszt concerto in E flat, we have many examples of this kind of work, put together much more loosely. (Play, if convenient.)

It cannot be denied that there is something satisfactory in the way in which these effects are planned. Thus in Liszt's " Rigoletto " fantasia we have opening passages which although brilliant and pleasing are not very difficult. Then follows the pretty melody, and, after the striking sequence of chromatic modulations, the cadenza already described comes in. The work then resumes the melody *pianissimo*, with very delicate and pretty runs, rising occasionally to *fortissimo*. Still the general build of these three pages is the *pianissimo*. At the close of this part there is a cadenza which is of extremely simple construction, but when well done is even more showy than that at the end of the first part. This, in turn, is followed by the octave finale, at first softly, but at the close working up to a brilliant and astonishing effect. The success of the piece lies in the care with which the brilliant passages are preceded with those of a soft and pleasing character, and this must be observed by the performer who expects to make a success with it.

This reserve—these long passages of really musical writing leading to astonishing and sensational passages, are the saving elements in *bravoura* pieces. The Liszt concerto is an extremely fragmentary work. It is written on a plan, and very cleverly too; but its primary elements are few, and it entirely lacks the artistic coherence and repose of such work as that in Chopin's concerto in E minor or in F minor. All of the Liszt *bravoura* pieces are written on the same plan, the climaxes being of occasional occurrence and carefully foreseen. Thus the well-known "Tannhauser March" opens brilliantly with the trumpet call, but presently subsides into a very reasonable and agreeably sustained presentation of the chorus. Gradually, however, the movement becomes more and more elaborate, and at last reaches an imposing effect.

All this modern virtuoso *bravoura* rests upon the idea of astonishing by mere sensation, and therein stands upon a lower plane than the cadenza formations of the older musicians. Bach, Handel, Beethoven and Mendelssohn, all were great performers who could entertain the most cultivated audiences by their masterly improvisations. But in their cadenzas they made their effect by the musicianship with which they elaborated and handled their themes, and not with any merely vulgar scrambling about the keyboard in apparently impossible passages.

Nevertheless the ways of Nature are not so crude after all; for every creature has its natural enemy which acts as a check upon its undue multiplication. So here, this sensationalism finally reaches bounds. Such a passage of sevenths as that of Raff's, already referred to, is the limit. This is mere noise, and just as bad and astonishing as any other hideous succession of chords played fortissimo on the bass of the pianoforte. So, also, Liszt in one piece and another covered the possibilities of radically different passages which would at the same time be playable, and therein effective. Hence in the later period of his creative activity he gave over the piano as a *bravoura* instrument, and applied his powers to the reproduction of pieces of every kind upon it, which had hitherto been supposed impossible. And in these, although a great technique and abounding courage are presupposed for the player, the emphasis is put on musical declamation and the imitation of orchestral effects, or at least their substitution by pianoforte equivalents (as in engraving such and such lines represent one color, and such and such another, though all in the engraving are in black and white). In this, while he by no means rises into the plane of original creation, he certainly entitles himself to respect by employing his powers for worthy uses. Three remarkable examples of this kind are afforded by Liszt's transcriptions of the Wagner "Spinnlied," "Isolde's Liebes Tod," and "Lohengrin's Verweis an Elsa." Another fine example is in Bülow's excessively difficult transcription of Wagner's "Faust Overture." These observations hold true of other virtuoso work since Liszt, such as the concert pieces of Tausig, Saint-Saens, etc.

It should be said of these experiments in the sensational that, like most of the prominent features of the romantic school, they have found their inciting cause in poetry, or the effort to represent by means of music something which, properly speaking, is neither in music nor in any strict and proper sense representable by it. This has already been suggested in the lesson on descriptive music, and comes more plainly in review in the next following discussion of Songs.

List of Illustrations.

1. Liszt's "Rigoletto."
2. Raff's "Polka de le Reine."
3. Chopin Concerto in E minor, op. 11.
4. Liszt's Concerto in E flat.
5. Liszt's "Tannhauser March."

PART SEVENTH.

STUDIES IN SONG.

LESSON THIRTY-SIX.

THE INFLUENCE OF POETRY UPON MUSIC.

Modern music owes its development to the co-working of three influences. The first of these is the better comprehension of the nature of music itself; the true relations of tonality, harmonic progressions, melody, and form to each other; and the logical methods of handling musical ideas merely as music, and aside from a definitely chosen emotional content seeking expression through them. The second operative force is the general progress in art conception, and especially the overmastering desire of the Romantic for a natural and valid means of expressing *feeling*, merely as such, and uncolored with conscious thought. The third of these forces is the influence of poetry upon music, and especially of the desire to express, by means of music, ideas not properly belonging to it, but suggested to it by poetry.

These three have operated simultaneously throughout the history of music. Yet it may be truly said that the first of them came soonest to expression; and this very naturally. For in the earliest times, when the development of music began, its relation to the other arts was not understood; indeed the meaning of art in general has only lately begun to be fathomed. So the musician worked by himself as a musician, seeking to comprehend the mysteries of this new form of art, and to reproduce his thoughts in it. Outside influences were not wanting here, particularly that of the church. On the whole, as already suggested in Chapter XXIII, the influence of religion has been of the highest advantage to art by raising and purifying its ideal. But Religion is one thing, and the Church sometimes another. And so while Religion has always performed this service to art, and has further extended her inspiration to music in particular, in the form of sublime hymns and canticles which become truly complete in the liturgy only when music's voice has modulated and shaped the hallowed utterance, the influence of the Church has sometimes tended in the direction of mere conventionality. They have it for a proverb in Germany, that when a composer has written all his original ideas, he can then compose only church music. And so the truly original musicians in every generation have developed and matured their talents in purely secular fields, and only in old age have brought a single wreath (often of flowers how precious! and gathered in fields, how far away!) and laid it with palsied but reverent hand upon the altar. So did Bach in his Passion Music and his one Mass; so also did Handel with his immortal "Messiah," a work in which we hear not the feeble and uncertain accents of age, but the sweet songs of hope and trust, as if the old composer had tasted before time the fountain of eternal youth, or that, like the servant of the prophet, his eyes had been opened so that he saw the mountains full of the chariots of the Lord. So was it with Mozart in his Requiem; and Beethoven with his colossal Mass in D minor. But as a rule, all the composers, who gave coherence and shape to music, arrived at their results by working in purely secular fields, where the swift-coming fancies might all find legitimate utterance. In particular the composers who wrote music, as music merely, were Bach, Haydn, and Beethoven; and, since them, Schumann and Chopin, though the latter is rather to be counted for a worker in one particular province of music, the pianoforte, than in the whole field of absolute and independent music.

The influence of the second of these operative forces has been silent and unconscious, as indeed, inspiration generally is. There has never been an authoritative declaration of the meaning of art, least of all by artists. Each man has builded, moulded, painted, sung or prophesied as the inner force impelled him. His life has gone into his works. When death overtook him he dropped his workman's tools, and sank unconscious into the bosom of mother earth. Sometimes, his very friends have not taken the trouble to count and reckon up his effects, and only the tardy justice of posterity has been able to gather up the precious tokens and place them in the pantheon of art. So was it with Bach, and Schubert; and so almost with Schumann and Berlioz.

Yet in one way this force has operated upon musical development, and that in great power; namely, in the extinction of other forms of art, leaving almost the whole ideality of several generations to seek expression through music. This comes out plainly enough in the dates. Michael Angelo and Raphael were nearly two hundred years before Bach and Handel. Dante was two centuries earlier still. Shakespeare was a hundred years earlier than Bach. Thus Bach, Handel and Beethoven had the stage to themselves for a century, during which there was no absolutely great master in any other form of art. In this way the world gained leisure to attend to music; and so it has been since, for during the last century there has never been a genius of the highest order outside of music. Thus, what music could do, as music, we must learn for the most part in the works of Bach, Haydn, Mozart, Beethoven, and Schumann. And in the very same works, also, we must measure its value as a form of art and an expression of the ideal. And this has been our labor in these studies hitherto. We now come to the point where we must enter upon the historical and practical study of the relation of music to poetry, and of the manner and extent of the action of poetry upon it. The subject is a very large one, and for full handling takes us over wide lapses of time and a considerable range of topics. In general, however, we shall obtain a fair idea of the course of this development if we attend carefully to the obsertations following.

In the union of poetry and music, both sides have to make important concessions. These are of so serious and so vital a character that, speaking in a broad sense, we might say that both poetry and music must needs sacrifice their most eminent qualities, as poetry and music respectively, in order to successfully unite themselves in the complex utterance of song. We are already, to some extent, prepared to understand this, by our studies in Chapter XXV. For, as we there saw, the distinctive excellencies of Poetry are its sense-pictures, and its power of awakening emotion by contrasts and collisions of persons, respectively living and acting out the opposing principles between which the collision takes place. The highest poetry, while always in sense-forms, is peculiarly and pre-eminently intensified by thought.

The first and perhaps chief difficulty Poetry has to contend with in uniting with music, is the long time consumed by musical utterance, a time from two to six times greater than speech,—and, it may be added, constantly increasing in the later composers, as we see, for example, in Max Bruch's Lay of the Bell, etc. Almost any poetical picture or scene runs through four lines, and sometimes through ten or twenty, but as all these lines do something towards completing the picture, they must all be retained in the mind at the same time. Ordinary reading passes so quickly as to permit the mind to do this without difficulty. But when this time is spun out too long, and especially when the unity of the description has been destroyed by the inception and completion of several musical periods to one period of words, the pictorial quality of the poetry is lost in the song. In like manner, the very form of musical utterance is fatal to the intelligible expression of any kind of reasoning, or deduction of conclusions from premises. Not even Beethoven would be able to set to music successfully such a passage as Portia's Plea for Mercy, in "The Merchant of Venice." Music, as we well know, is the expression of *feeling;* when poetry becomes directly expressive of emotion it becomes musical—provided only that its feeling is not outside of or contrary to music. Thus when hate, revenge, or remorse are the feelings seeking expression in the words, music can do nothing to aid them, for they are in their essence contrary to music, and if at all representable in sounds, representable only in harsh and hideous discords. Yet even this range must not be denied the opera; we can only limit its recourse to such extravagant measures, to its moments of brief and insuperable necessity, to be atoned for by many a bar of tuneful penance. Hence we may say in general that, in order to adapt itself to musical expression, Poetry must forego its reason, its long-spun descriptive passages, and, to a certain extent, its coherence. Its pictures must become mere outlines, such as a couple of phrases will compass; its thought sharp, incisive, terse, and never of an abstract character. And it is only when it speaks directly the language of the heart, that musical utterance becomes indispensable to its completeness. A true lyric requires music to fully express it. Of such sort are all true hymns, such as the "Gloria," the "Te Deum," the "Venite," "Jubilate." These without the voice of song are but birds or angels without wings.

On the other hand, Music has much to lose in a direct union with poetry. She, also, must part with her coherence in long forms. Such closely knit and legitimately developed musical creations as the great organ fugues of Bach, and the sonatas or symphonies of Beethoven are entirely foreign to the spirit of song. Here first music has to consider the compass and pitch of the voice, and its effectiveness in different registers. One recalls here the remark of the teacher, himself a distinguished composer, who, when a pupil brought him an anthem in which the tenor had the words "Praise the Lord" on G below middle C, crossed out the passage with the remark. "The tenor *can not* 'praise the Lord' below middle C," alluding, of course, to the non-effectiveness of the tenor voice at so low a pitch. So, also, music must provide the singer with opportunities for breathing, and interludes for rest after trying passages. She must not forget to confine herself within a practicable range of keys, for singers sing on melodic principles, and no singer sings or thinks a full score. These, with many other such like restrictions, inhere in the very nature of song, and hamper the musical composer extremely. The old proverb says that "necessity is the mother of invention"; so here the necessity of finding compromises or mutual concessions between music and poetry has at length led to several well defined types of song, which differ from each other in the manner and nature of the concessions made. These are (1) Simple Ballad, (2) The Recitative, (3) The Aria and Scena, (4) The German Thoroughly Composed Song, (5) The Arioso, and (6) the union of them all in The Oratorio and Opera.

In all these modes of union there are, however, certain principles that remain constant and must not be violated. These are the correct accentuation and emphasis of the words, according to the sense, and the correspondence of the music to the poetry in respect to feeling. All forms of song must observe these conditions. To this extent, at least, poetry is dominant. Besides, the musical phrasing must be made to correspond with the grammatical and declamatory necessities of the text, and this in all forms of vocal pieces. Besides these, there are important variations in style, resulting from the greater or less attention paid to the convenience of the voice. Thus Italian songs, in general, are carefully planned so as to suit the voice, and to require effect only at ranges of pitch in which effect is possible. Moreover, this entire school indulges itself less with chromatic and difficult modulations, and in general is much less elaborate, as music merely, than the German songs. The Italians consider the *voice* the main thing in singing; the Germans the *idea*. In thus ranging themselves under opposite principles, both parties fall short of their goal. The German ruins his song for actual delivery, by placing it badly for the voice. This appears continually in Bach, and Schumann, and frequently in other writers. The Italian's method of work, on the other hand, produces a composition in which the voice makes an agreeable effect; so that these works are cherished all the world over, as the most convenient show-pieces for singers. Nevertheless he works within so narrow musical limits as seriously to impair the value of his pieces from the musical side. And in general it is not too much to say that even the best Italian music sounds thin and unsatisfactory when compared with the best German music; while the common run of Italian work is thin indeed.

Yet, after all, the Italian certainly has the advantage in the matter of taste, and we find in the productions of such writers as Rossini, Bellini, Donizetti and Mercadante, as well as in the simple *cantileni* of less noted composers, a grace and elegance of style which, since Glück and Mozart, is no longer to be found in German song.

LESSON THIRTY-SEVENTH.

THE SIMPLE BALLAD.

The nearest example of the union of poetry and music is afforded by the simple ballad. Musically considered it consists of a symmetrically balanced and pleasing melody, of a quiet character, with words easily enjoyed by the common people. In this form of composition the melody is of the foremost importance, and in very many cases was first composed, and the words afterwards written to fit. As a rule, both words and music are pleasing, quiet, popular, and but a shade removed from the commonplace. Examples of this class are practically innumerable. We may begin with almost any specimen. Let it be Dr. Geo. F. Root's "Brooklet," from the "Curriculum." (Plays and sings.) Another example is "Joys that we've tasted," adapted to an Irish melody. (Plays and sings.) Other examples are the two by Mr. Root so popular many years ago, "The Hazel Dell" and "Rosalie, the Prairie Flower." (Sings "Hazel Dell.") This class also includes many songs of a sad and mournful temperament (as well as many sadly poor ones), such as "Pass Under the Rod," Mr. Root's "Vacant Chair," Miss Linsay's "Resignation," etc.

Of the same kind is Claribel's "O many a time I am sad at heart." (Sings.) The life of this song is mainly in its words. This was not so much the case in the earlier American songs of the same class, as is shown by the continual popularity of the music in cotillons, quadrilles, etc., after the words have been forgotten. This was also the case with Mr. Stephen C. Foster's "Uncle Ned" and "Massa's in the Cold, Cold Ground," "Old Folks at Home," etc. In all of these the distinguishing feature was the agreeable and easily-remembered melody. Another example, depending partly on its words and partly on its music for a deserved popularity is Claribel's "Five o'clock in the Morning." (Sings.) In this the music takes a wider range of harmonies than in any of the American examples referred to. In Claribel's "Come Back to Erin" we have a still more unmistakable example of a purely musical interest and that mainly in the melody. This melody has been sung and played, varied and arranged, all over the English-speaking world. (Sings.)

The apparent depth and meaning of these songs are very much increased when the words are deliberately and clearly spoken, and the melody delivered with artistic emphasis. An example of this was afforded by Nillsen's singing of "Old Folks at Home" in her American concerts, and in the practice of the popular singers in London, as well as Mme. Parepa-Rosa's "Five o'clock in the Morning," etc. Such a delivery would lend dignity and worth to any air, however empty. It is the result of thorough control of the voice and extended experience in the delivery of every kind of song.

LIST OF ILLUSTRATIONS.

1. The Brooklet, by Dr. Geo. F. Root, "Curriculum."
2. Joys that We've Tasted.
3. Hazel Dell. Dr. Geo. F. Root.
4. Pass under the Rod.
5. The Vacant Chair. Root.
6. Resignation. Miss Linsay.
7. O Many a Time I am Sad at Heart. Claribel.
8. Five o'Clock in the Morning. Claribel.
9. Come Back to Erin. Claribel.

LESSON THIRTY-EIGHTH.

RECITATIVE.

Our second type of song is one in which, clearly, the text receives primary consideration. By Recitative is meant a form of song to which the text is set to musical pitch and cadence, but not to a definite speed, rhythm, or in lyrically-adjusted phrases. In this form of song it is the sole task of the music to afford an impressive and suitable delivery of the words. In plain recitative the accompaniment consists only of simple chords. Of all writers, Handel was at times particularly fortunate in his recitatives, and nowhere more so than in the "Messiah." Observe the dignity of the following: (Plays and sings the recitative "Behold a virgin shall conceive," from " Messiah.") And this: (Plays and sings "Then shall the eyes of the blind be opened," also from the " Messiah.")

This form of song admits of great pathos. Handel affords a great example in the tenor recitative "Thy rebuke hath broken his heart." (Sings it.) In this the melodic cadences are extremely clever, and will be the subject of remark presently. Measured recitative differs from the plain, in having a measured accompaniment, and hence in requiring of the voice at least an approximate adherance to the measure. In one instance Handel has contrasted these two methods with fine effect. Thus in the "Messiah" we find the plain recitative " There were shepherds abiding in the field." This is followed by a measured recitative to the words "And lo! the angel of the Lord came upon them." And this, again, by the plain recitative "And the angel said unto them." And this, again, by the measured recitative "And suddenly there was with the angel." (Sings the two measured recitatives first, and afterward the four in succession.) One of the most beautiful examples of measured recitative is found in the opening number of the " Messiah," " Comfort ye, my people." (Sings.)

In all these examples the music is determined in the effort to furnish suitable expression to the words. To recur to an example already given, consider " Thy rebuke hath broken his heart." The very first upward inflection on the word "rebuke," and the downward sweep of the octave in "hath broken his heart," are extremely impressive. So, again, when the words come "but there was no man," the emphasis falls on the last word; but when the same words are repeated the emphasis falls on " was."

In many instances the phrases of recitative are interspersed or intercalated between descriptive phases of the accompaniment. Of this we have many examples in Haydn's "Creation." So we have it in Raphael's "Now furious storms tempestuous rage," which is preceded by the storm in the orchestra. And so successively are set "As chaff by the winds are impelled the clouds," "By heaven's fire the sky is inflamed," "And awful thunders are rolling on high," etc. This plan of structure suggests the Apostolic practice of afterward interpreting the prophecies just delivered in unknown tongues. In the same way is treated " In splendor bright." (Sings.)

Perhaps the most insignificant form of recitative is that where the voice recites on a monotone while the orchestra pursues a measured melody. In this case, of course, the text is little if at all considered. A convenient example of this is afforded by a passage in Ambroise

Thomas's well-known song from "Mignon," "Know'st thou the land," where a difficult and unmusical part of the text is treated in this way. Here, indeed, it is managed with real art, since it but serves to intensify the climax that follows. (Sings Mignon's song.) The musical structure of recitative is necessarily coherent, else it could not be sung. But it does not return upon itself in lyrically-arranged phrases.

List of Illustrations.

1. "Behold a virgin shall conceive." No. 7 of Handel's "Messiah."
2. "Then shall the eyes of the blind be opened." No. 17, the same.
3. "Thy rebuke hath broken his heart." No. 27, the same.
4. "There were shepherds abiding in the field." No. 14.
5. "Comfort ye, my people." No. 1, the same.
6. "And God made the firmament." No. 4, "Creation."
7. "In splendor bright." No. 13, "Creation."
8. Mignon's song from the Opera of "Mignon," by Ambroise Thomas.

LESSON THIRTY-NINE.

THE ARIA AND SCENA.

The aria is a regularly developed musical form. Its text is usually meagre. In the older works it consists of but a single complet, or at most of but two or three. The music seizes the emotional content of the text, and repeats it over and over, builds out of it, intensifies it in many ways. Examples are innumerable. Let us begin with Bach's "My heart ever faithful." (Sings.) In this we have, first and foremost, good music. And this also is elaborated out of very few motives. The first phrase returns with the persistence of a rondo. In the intermediate complets, which serve for episodes, the words are broken in two, the syllables separated, and elocutionary proprieties violated with impunity. Yet it is an extremely enjoyable piece of music. In this case we see plainly that music has given up little of its own.

Of the same kind is Handel's "Oh had I Jubal's lyre," except that he re there is an evident pleasure in providing agreeable passages for the voice, which, however, are in very good keeping with the emotional stand-point of the song. (Sings.) In other cases the text is treated more seriously, as in Handel's "He shall feed his flock," and "How beautiful are the feet." (Sings.) In both these, as indeed in the previous examples, we have consistently developed musical creations, which in point of form are the same as the gavottes, sarabands, etc. of the ancient binary order. In respect to musical development they partake somewhat of the spirit of the thematic, since the leading motives are often repeated, transformed, presented with various harmonies, modulated into new keys, etc., in a manner very different from what we find in the simple ballad.

The aria is also capable of being applied to descriptive purposes. Of this we have two very pretty examples in Haydn's "Creation," in the well-known soprano songs "With verdure clad," and "On mighty pens." (Sings, both, if convenient.) The descriptive part, it will be observed, is in the accompaniment rather than in the vocal phrases.

Mozart imparted to the aria the simplicity and grace of the people's song, and at the same time contrived for the most part to remain true to the spirit of his text. Some of these songs are of the most exquisite character, as for example, "*Vedrai Carino*" and "*Batti, Batti*," sung by Zerlina in "Don Giovanni." Of the same kind is the tenor aria "*Il mio tesoro*" in that opera. Another one of the same sort is "*Porgi amor*," in Mozart's "Figaro." In "*Dove sono*," of the same opera, we have a more varied treatment. An *adagio*, first part, changes to an *allegro*, closing part. (Let any of these be sung that can be conveniently produced. It does not particularly matter which, since all manifest in general the same traits.)

Another famous example of the aria is Beethoven's well-known song, "Adelaide."* (Sings.) This song is a fully developed piece of instrumental music, in which the voice is treated from a musical standpoint, merely, as if it were a violin or 'cello.

In Italian opera we have various kinds of aria, all, however, having the quality of adaptation to the voice. In these the well-sounding, the effective, the astonishing, the tuneful, are the chief points of concern. Thus in Bellini's "Norma" we have the lovely "*Casta Diva*," an air which is now out of style, and is indeed somewhat wanting in heart when compared with those of Mozart, but which, nevertheless, is tuneful and refined, and, when well done, an extremely pretty piece of singing. (Sings.) In Bellini's "Sonnambula" we have a similar song, "*Ah non Credea*," and, at the close, the famous war-horse of prima donnas, "*Ah non giunge*," where the voice becomes a mere instrument of rejoicing, and the text as such is very little regarded.

Again there is the *scena*, or scene, to be taken into account; a composition in which recitative, arioso, and aria alternate according

*The pronunciation required by the music is äd-ĕl-ă-ee-dĕ.

to the fancy of the composer, in order to meet unusual transitions in the text. Examples of this are found in the great dramatic scene for soprano in Weber's "Oberon," "Ocean, thou mighty monster," and in "Der Freyschutz," where the prayer occurs. In these the fullest resources of the orchestra are unsparingly employed to paint the dramatic situation

Throughout all forms of the aria, the music is consistently developed, as music. The general spirit of the text is seized and represented, but no effort is made to represent merely transitory shades of feeling, except in descriptive arias. When this is done it naturally deprives the aria of its power to absorb and carry along the listener, because such a lingering on separate ideas precludes attention to any single, grand, overmastering impulse of feeling; and *this* is what the aria has for its fundamental design to express. It is to be observed further of the examples here referred to, that they are all from masterworks, by great composers, and are, for the most part, the chief arias in the works in question. They represent, therefore, the highest conception of song in this direction, and for their adequate interpretation demand exceptional voices, thoroughly trained, and musical endowments of high order. Nevertheless, an inferior presentation of them will serve to familiarize one with their phraseology and mode of treatment. Only, if they fail of effect in such presentation, it must be remembered that they are really great works, and require to be heard many times.

LIST OF ILLUSTRATIONS.

1. "My heart ever faithful," Bach.
2. "O, had I Jubal's lyre!" Handel.
3. "He shall feed his flock," Handel.
4. "How beautiful are the feet." Handel.
5. "With verdure clad," from the "Creation," Haydn.
6. "On mighty pens," Haydn.
7. "Vedrai Carino," from "Don Giovanni," Mozart.
8. "Batti, Batti," from "Don Giovanni," Mozart.
9. "Il mio tesoro," from "Don Giovanni," Mozart.
10. "Dove sono," from "Figaro," Mozart.
11. "Porgi amor," from "Figaro," Mozart.
12. "Voi che sapete," from "Figaro," Mozart.
13. "Adelaide," tenor song, Beethoven.
14. "Casta Diva," from "Norma," Bellini.
15. "Ah non Credea," Bellini.
16. "Ah non giunge," "Sonnambula," Bellini.
17. "Ocean, thou mighty monster," from "Oberon," Weber.

LESSON FORTY.

THE THOROUGHLY COMPOSED SONG.

The simple ballad and the aria have this in common, that they both strive first for a symmetrically returning lyric melody. Each ballad or aria represents on the whole a particular phase of emotion, or state of feeling, from which no wide departure is made throughout the song. In the ballad this arises from the necessity of repeating all the stanzas of the words to the same melody; and in the aria it is a natural consequence of the paucity of words. An aria although frequently extended to six or eight or ten periods, rarely has more than two or three couplets of words. Thus, in placing the emphasis upon the *music*, rather than upon the text, both ballad and aria display a decided congeniality of spirit. The aria is a ballad, magnified or exalted to meet more important demands.

We come now to the study of a form of song which we owe chiefly to Schubert and Schumann, in which the text and music receive almost equal consideration, yet in such a way as to afford every part of the text a legitimate musical expression. This necessarily includes the idea of a spontaneous musical activity in the music, for as soon as it ceases to be free in its movement, it ceases to be expressive. The Germans call it the *durchcomponirte Lied*, or "song composed throughout." As there is no English equivalent of this expression in use, the title here employed is "thoroughly composed song;" and the meaning is that every stanza of the song has its own music, different from the others, and suited to the peculiar needs of the words. Unity is subserved by a return of the first stanza, or of something very like it, in the form of a refrain.

We get something of this in the earlier songs of Schubert, as the "Miller" songs. But it is in the grand ballad of the "Erl King" that we have one of the most shining examples. This ballad contains five speakers, the narrator, the boy, the Erl King and Erl King's daughter, and the father. Although the singer represents them all, each one has a particular form of expression. Thus the narrator has a plain figure accompanied by that wonderful figure of repeating octaves. The father speaks in a low voice; the son in a higher one, and with more wildness.

The Erl-King's daughter speaks caressingly, and this, also, the accompaniment intensifies. When the boy is touched by the Erl-King, he cries out with terror, and always a semitone sharp of the accompaniment. This is a touch of realism. Considered merely as music this piece is one of the most remarkable examples of the romantic school; it has been very popular in instrumental arrangements. But it is plain to see that the music has derived its most important suggestions from the words. (Sings.)

Another example, equally fine in its way, though not so diversified, is found in Schubert's "Gretchen at the spinning wheel." In this we have the monotonous whirling of the wheel, the sadness of Marguerite after meeting Faust, her dreams of love, and her fears she will never see him again, and especially the very effective climax at the word "kiss." (Sings.)

Schumann effects a still closer union between the text and the music. Indeed we might say that Schumann's genius consisted in his preternatural quickness in *thinking* music, and his intuitive realization of the true relation between music and emotion. Among the greatest of his songs are the six called "Woman's Love and Life." These are by no means of equal merit. Perhaps the very choicest is "He, the best of all, the noblest," in which the maiden tells the virtues of her love. This song is one of the most remarkable that exist. The interest of it is not in the vocal part alone. The melody is very far from completing itself within the usual lyric limits. The first period closes with a half-cadence into the dominant, and the subject is completed by the piano alone. The harmony is extremely fresh and varied. The principal motive appears in many forms, and modulations are unsparingly employed. Yet the song as a whole has a warmth, a vitality, an onward sweep, such as is hardly anywhere else to be found in a song. And especially the music is remarkably true to the text. (Sings.)

The next one gives us a different phase of the woman's heart.

"'Tis true, I can not believe it,
A dream doth my senses enthrall,"

After this follows the charming piece

"Thou ring upon my finger
Thou dear little golden ring,"

a song little if at all inferior to the great one before-mentioned. (Sings.)

The entire Schumann nature is to be found in his songs. One phase of it, although not strictly belonging here, we may characterize as the tender and deep. It is illustrated by the lovely little piece "Moonlight." (Sings.)

Again in "*Waldesgespräch*" (Woodland Dialogue), we have another example of a dual personality expressed by means of a change of style in the music. There are two speakers, the knight and the sorceress "Loreley." The knight speaks in a quick, martial motive; Loreley in more gentle accents and to a harp-like accompaniment. (Sings.)

There is another form of song nearly allied to these, called Arioso. By this is meant an aria-like form, which may be either a small and less intense aria, or a piece in which lyric phrases do not complete themselves by sequences and tonality into regular period forms. But instead thereof, the melody closely follows the words, and the periods are lengthened, shortened, modulated into other keys, or completed in any way that the feeling of the words seem to require. Mendelssohn uses the term arioso to denote a small and less complete aria. In this sense we have in St. Paul the arioso, "But the Lord is mindful of His own." (Sings.) Wagner is the great exponent of this form of writing. He has employed it with the greatest freedom, and, it may be added, with great propriety and beauty. A lovely example is Elsa's balcony song in "Lohengrin." (Sings.)

The thoroughly composed song and the arioso represent the latest advance in the union of music and poetry. As suggested in the Chap. XXXVI, both music and poetry have something to sacrifice in the union. If we attend closely to the texts of these later songs we shall find that the unmusical elements of poetry have been eliminated, and that the words now express sentiments congenial to music. On first sight the music seems to have retained its qualities better. But if we examine these later songs and arioso-pieces we shall find that clearness and definiteness of form have nearly departed from the music. The period-forms are so vague, and the modulations into so remote keys, and occur so frequently ("near and far," as the song has it) that it requires a special training in the most recent music in order to really enjoy them when heard as instrumental music merely. If such works are to be enjoyed, it is only when the voice and musical qualities of the singer have been cultivated to an extent adequate to these demands, and are employed in subjection to a strongly conceived and truly dramatic interpretation of the text. They require much more of a singer than the famous "voice, voice, *toujours* Voice."

Of the same general nature as the thoroughly composed song is the *Ensemble*, an important form in opera. The *ensemble* stands at that point in the drama where certain opposing principles have been introduced in the personages representing them, and here they are all brought upon the stage together. The problem for the composer to solve is to unite these contradictory impulses in the performance (or, as it seems on the stage, *production*) of a consistent and satisfactory piece of music, without causing the persons to violate their own individual characters and dispositions. In the nature of the case this problem is impossible of solution. For although a certain amount of individuality in the different parts of an ensemble piece can well enough be attained by skillful use of counterpoint, it remains certain that no piece produces a coherent impression, that does not present some leading idea, and therein a dominant emotion, which of course can not be done without practically extinguishing at least a considerable part of the opposing element. Many beautiful ensemble pieces are to be found in opera. In some the librettist has simplified the matter by leaving out the contradictions. In others the most antagonistic persons alternate with each other and presently join in as soprano and second, like society women who kiss in public and back-bite in private, and the music of the whole goes not as the text goes, but as the composer would have it. Wagner has attempted to meet this difficulty in other ways, as we shall see later. Some of the best ensemble pieces are to be found in Mozart's operas. There is one in "Figaro" which lasts forty minutes and includes some eight or ten pieces of music. The form is referred to here merely because it represents an additional phase of vocal writing, the study of which by composers has been of use in ascertaining how far it is practicable to go in music in the simultaneous representation of opposite determinations.

List of Illustrations.

1. The "Erl King," Schubert.
2. "Gretchen at the Spinning Wheel," Schubert.
3. "He, the best of all, the noblest," Schumann.
4. "Thou ring upon my finger," Schumann.
5. "Moonlight." Schumann.
6. "Waldesgespräch," Schumann.
7. "But the Lord is mindful of His own," from "St. Paul," Mendelssohn.
8. "Elsa's balcony song," "Ye Wandering Breezes" from "Lohengrin," Wagner.

LESSON FORTY-ONE.

THE OPERA AND ORATORIO.

Oratorio, as is well known, is a musical work for solo voices, chorus, and orchestra, on a sacred subject. It is sung without action, although the text is conceived in a dramatic spirit if not strictly in dramatic form. Of dialogue oratorio has very little if any. The nearest approach to it is in passages where an angel or other speaker delivers a message and a reply is made, but this is rare. The text deals with the large, the heroic or religious interests, and not with those of every day life. Indeed, oratorio was in the beginning an actual part of religious service. This was so with Bach's church cantatas, and the Passion Music.

Handel's oratorios were essentially concert works. As we shall see hereafter (in Chapter XLIII), Handel composed operas for some forty years before he began to write oratorios, and during most of that time had his own singers and theater. So, when actuated by some fortunate instinct, or by the neglect of the public, he began to write oratorio, he changed his style of composition but very little. The use of an English text, the vernacular of his audience, no doubt had a certain tendency to increase his verbal accuracy in adapting his music to it. But such airs as "O had I Jubal's lyre" from "Joshua," and "Rejoice greatly" from the "Messiah" are almost exactly of the same cut as the bravoura arias in his innumerable operas. So, also, very many of the smaller choruses are revamped from some of his former works.

Still, when all this has been said, the difference between Handel's oratorios and his operas is very great; not so much in exceptional moments as in the *average* of the oratorio, which is on a higher and more serious level than the opera. Then, too, between Handel's opera-music and his text there was often a certain contradiction, or at least what seems to be such in our day. The contrapuntal spirit was the habit of Handel's musical thought, and this spirit in its essential nature is suited to grave and elevated discourse. So when Handel fell into the sacred vein, it was not so much a change of style, a conversion, or a rising to a new plane of work, as a choice, fortunate though somewhat late, of a text suitable to the nature of his musical phantasy.

Yet when this change was made and the sacred words applied, and all the best and most elevated of his previous efforts fished up from their waters of oblivion and stood upon honest English feet in marching order, like Ezekiel's dry bones, which, also, the word of the Lord had clothed upon,—even then it is but rarely *sacred* music that comes to utterance, but *concert* music still; music to attract and please, music to elevate and edify;—but not music with which to worship. To demonstrate this position would take us too far. It must suffice here to call over the names of some of these works, leaving the student to confirm or overthrow our position at his leisure. They are "Solomon," "Joshua," "Judas Maccabeus," "Israel in Egypt," "Esther," "Deborah," "Susannah," "Theodora," etc. In some of these he reaches great heights. In particular is this the case in "Israel in Egypt" where those great double choruses must have been inspired by some idea of what his great contemporary Bach had done at Leipsic in his Passions Music.

Oratorio had at least one other decided advantage for Handel, and for the development of music after him. It put the emphasis on the chorus, and not on the solo. The operatic chorus is small at best. It is the peasantry of singers and must on no account usurp a leading interest in the drama. But in music there is a sense in which the Latin proverb is true, *Vox populi vox dei*—the voice of the people is the voice of God.

These Handel choruses have, indeed, a great advantage in their texts, which for the most part are well-known passages of scripture. The familiar word of some Biblical war-cry, such as "Sing to the Lord, for He hath triumphed gloriously," "Worthy is the Lamb," etc., awakens the historical associations that belong to it; these join in with the inherent majesty and impressiveness of the music, the effectiveness of its instrumentation and especially the deep, thrilling, pervading support of the organ, and all combine in introducing music to the public in a new light, that of the sublime.

Then, for once, it was permitted the almost inspired master to write with headlong haste all through that blessed fortnight, one great work, which stands, and will long stand, as a *ne plus ultra* of musical effort in the direction of the pathetic, the inspiring, and the sublime. The "Messiah" draws a part of its impressiveness, no doubt, from its noble text, which traverses the entire range of the most precious religious associations. And this also helped the composer, who here, at times, rises almost above himself. But to whatever source we may attribute its power over us, it is certain that in Handel's "Messiah" we have a work without which our idea of music would be much lower than it is, and the world would be by much the loser.

In the Bach "Passions Music" we have a different work, and one which is decidedly the expression of worship. But of this subject more is said in chapter XLII. Suffice it to point out here that oratorio is the field in which music has been furnished with the occasion and the means for exercising itself to its farthest bounds in the direction of the elevated, the heroic, and the sublime.

Opera is of the world, worldly. And this for two reasons : As a drama it deals with life, idealized, perhaps, sometimes made ludicrous, but in any case with *life*. Its trinity in unity is "the world, the flesh, and the devil." We have only to run over the librettos, if we have never seen the pieces for ourselves, to find in almost every one of them "the prince of this world" enthroned. Read the books of "Don Giovanni," "Figaro," "Robert le Diable," "Faust," "Il Trovatore," "Il Traviata," and almost all the rest. Then, in the second place, opera stands for an amusement. The opera composer must meet his public. They do not go to the play-house to hear sermons, nor to sing psalms, but to hear, to enjoy, and to be merry.

The opera is the great field in which, sooner or later, all worldly emotion comes to expression. As a form of art it is as blessed in abundant means as the oratorio. For although it lacks the massive chorus, it has a larger number of trained singers, and the advantage of action and spontaneous sympathy with the audience, as helps to inspiration. Librettist, composer, scene-painter, and singers, all combine to place before us a form of art which has in it every possible pleasure of the senses of hearing and sight, and along with this much of a finer and higher character.

From the very nature of the stage and the drama, opera was impossible in Handel's day. The prophet and founder of the modern opera, Glück, wrote his great works more than thirty years after Handel had laid down his operatic pen forever. Counterpoint needed to relax its severity somewhat in favor of the weakness of the flesh in chambermaids and valets upon the stage. Fugue, also, might find artistic justification in a fire, where the first engine company on the ground gave out the theme, the next answered it, etc., but for guests at an evening party it is but a tedious form of utterance. The opera needed the people's song. Glück took a great step in the true direction, and established the canons of operatic work. Mozart went beyond him ; and

Weber beyond him. In "Der Freischütz" we have the very people's song itself.

Besides the people's song, opera needed the neat and pleasing melodic and harmonic forms of Haydn and Mozart. With these it became fully equipped in its department, and went forth under its captains, such as Rossini, Meyerbeer, Weber, Bellini, Donizetti, Auber, Verdi, and last of all, Wagner, to conquer the world of secular music.

In its nature as a form of drama, dealing with men of the present or the immediate past, who in any case are presented on the stage as living before us, and in ranging through all varieties of plays, from roaring farce up through comedy to heroic and elevated phases of life (though these are always given from what, in stage parlance, one might call the "practicable" side as opposed to the "impractical" of oratorio), the opera calls upon music for every form and phase of its pleasant modulation, all its love and its hate, its rejoicing and its sorrow. And what the voice can not do, it offers to complete through the unrivalled riches of the modern orchestra; and in every time of "trouble," where music, as such, fails of power, it produces the "sheep-skin," its diploma of powers yet unexpended.

Thus the opera and oratorio together present us on the whole with every result that has been reached in the effort to clothe words with music, and are to be reckoned among the highest achievements in music. Yet, even in these, all that was said in the beginning concerning the influence of poetry upon music holds true; and all the limitations of vocal music as a form of art are here to be found illustrated. We have on one side Poetry, of which the practicable libretto is but a very small part. And on the other side Music, of which opera and oratorio are, to be sure, a larger part, yet still lacking very much of the elevated sentiment and the epic sweep of pure music, as found in the symphony. Nevertheless, vocal music retains for itself two great points of merit: It is the most understandable form of music, for even the unmusical can follow the words. And, second, through the effort to unite music to poetry, and to extend its range to an equal compass, the true relation of music to emotion has been worked out, and instrumental music itself has gained in freedom of form and range of expression.

Part Eighth.

Historical and Miscellaneous Sketches.

Chapter Forty-Two.

John Sebastian Bach.

Across this interval of nearly two centuries Bach's life appears to have been very dull and uneventful. He was born at Eisenach, Prussia, March 21, 1685, as Ritter says, "a musician of the fifth generation of one of the most musical families ever produced by any country." His entire life passed in the burgher-like simplicity of the middle class German. His mother died when he was very young; and before he was ten years old he had lost his father also. He then went to his elder brother, John Christopher, organist at Ohrdruff, who gave him his first lessons in piano playing. Bach had scarcely more than made a beginning (which must have been exceedingly easy to so gifted a nature as his) when he cast his covetous eyes on a paper-bound volume containing pieces by Frohberger, Kerl, Pachelbel and others. But such treasures of art were not to be trusted to a boy not yet twelve years old—at least not if the crusty John Christopher could help it—so he locked the book in a corner cupboard, and gave himself no further anxiety on the subject. But the little John Sebastian was of a persevering kind, as we shall see before we have done with him, and his little hand proved able to push through the lattice work door and reach the precious book. But how to make it his own. Why copy it, to be sure. But the awful John Christopher! "Do it at night," said the tempter. "But I've no candles," said the boy. "The full moon." "Sure enough," said plucky John Sebastian, "free to all." So for six long months every bright night found him diligently copying the for-hidden treasure—copying, we may be sure, with rare patience, and a singularly fine hand for a boy, for paper was scarce. Alas! just as the task was done, in an unlucky moment his brother found him out, and not only confiscated the original but the copy as well, and the poor John Sebastian had only the comforting recollection that at least he "had done his best."

After a while the brother died, and the boy was sent to the "gymnasium" (or grammar school) at Luneberg, and was soprano singer at St. Michael's church. While here he lost no opportunity of hearing good players. On one occasion he went to Hamburg (about forty miles away) to hear Reinken, who was at that time a famous organist, and again to Zell to hear the Prince's band there, and especially to become better versed in the French taste that prevailed. All the while he applied himself so diligently to the study of the organ and piano that at the age of eighteen (in 1703) we find him widely recognized as an undoubted master, and appointed court musician at Weimar. The following year he became organist at the new church of Arnstadt—probably because he could pursue his taste for the organ better there, for his duties as court musician involved only his services as violinist. In his new place he manifested the diligence that had all along characterized him. Wherever in all the country around there was a celebrated organist, there would Bach be sure to go in order to discover the charm and secret of his power. He went on foot to Lubeck to hear Buxtehude, a distinguished master there; and, too poor to take lessons, he even remained a full quarter of a year a secret hearer of that organist. All this time he diligently exercised himself in organ and piano playing, and in all schools of composition. He studied with the closest care all the older master works he could lay his hands on. He fervently desired to make a longer art journey into Italy, but poverty prevented. By degrees, however, he possessed himself of the chief works of Palestrina, Caldara, Lotti, and the other best writers of the Italian school. He had already learned the Italian art of singing, from Italian singers he had known in Hamburg.

With such diligence no wonder his fame spread abroad as that of a master. Accordingly we find him soon back to Weimar as Court organist, and later (1717) as chief music director. Here, doubtless, he composed many of his chief works for the organ and his orchestral suites.

About this time Marchand, Handel's master, died at Halle, and Bach was invited to succeed him. He even went to Halle to prove his qualifications, but for some reason did not take the place. Some time before this Marchand and Bach had been invited to play in contest before the king at Dresden, but at the last moment Marchand's courage failed him, for he had in some way found out that the young German had an unparalleled fluency of ideas combined with rare skill in treatment; so Bach amused and astonished for hours the great audience gathered by his wonderful performances. Passing over Bach's service as court music director under Prince Leopold of Anhalt-Cothen (extending through six years), and his journey to Hamburg to play the organ, where he excited the greatest wonder in the breast of the veteran Reinken by his masterly improvisations on the chorale, "*An Wasserflussen Babylon's*," we come to the year 1733 when Bach was appointed Cantor to the St. Thomas school in Leipsic, where he spent twenty-six fruitful and peaceful years. What good came of this quiet life will appear when we come to speak more particularly of his works. The chief episode of his Leipsic life was his visit to Frederick the Great, at Potsdam, in the year 1747. This visit was paid only after the most pressing invitations from the king, expressed through Bach's second son, Carl Philip Emanuel, who was at that time chapel master to the Princess Amelia. King Frederick was a flute player, and, like the most of the breed, thought himself a fine one. So every night, when not too busy with cares of state, he was accustomed to get his orchestra together and astonish them with his flute virtuosity. In this way he imagined himself greater than a king—a God-endowed artist. One night just as the musical hilarity was about to begin, a servant brought him the list of arrivals. "Gentlemen," said the king, solemnly, "Old Bach is come!" So, all stained with travel and tumbled and torn with the horrible stage-coaching of those days, with never a moment for a hasty bite of something to eat, with scarcely a glass of beer to soothe the inner man, the great king was confronted by a greater, the king of the organ, John Sebastian Bach. Bach, taken from one room to another by the king and assembled musicians, was compelled to inspect and play upon every one of the numerous Silbermann pianos in the palace. After Bach had improvised for a while he asked the king to give him a subject in which to work out a fugue, and the learning displayed in the work was highly admired by all present. He then selected a suitable subject and worked out extempore a fugue in six obligato parts.

The next day they made the tour of all the organs in Potsdam, in in order that the King might hear his organ-playing. On his return to Leipsic, Bach composed the subject he had received from the King in three and six parts, and had it engraved under the title "*Musikal-*

isches Opfer" (musical offering), and dedicated it to the inventor—certainly a neat and proper thing to do, and for which I hope the rather stingy King had the grace to make a fit acknowledgment.

Bach not only used his eyes enormously in reading and writing an immense mass of works in early youth, seriously undermining his sight by the moonlight writing, but in many cases he had engraved his own compositions. In consequence of all this application through more than sixty years, at last his eyes became much inflamed, and finally he lost his sight altogether. This so weighed upon his spirits that he continued to decline for fully half a year, and finally expired July 28th, 1750.

Bach was twice married. The first wife had seven children; the second thirteen, of whom eight were sons. Several of his children were musical, and one of them, Carl Philip Emanuel, was the forerunner of the Haydn and Mozart school of music. His theory was that the instrument must be made to *sing;* accordingly we find him content with shorter forms and less learned musical phraseology than that adopted by his father, whom, on his own ground, he modestly confessed himself totally incapable of rivalling.

As a piano player Bach was one of the greatest of his time. His touch was silvery, distinct and expressive, his legato playing extremely perfect, and his contrasts of power remarkable for that day. He had a short, thick hand, and Prof. Karl Klauser (of the seminary at Farmington, Conn.) says that as near as he can make it out from Forkel's life, Bach's touch must have been much the same as that employed by Dr. Wm. Mason—a touch which then, as now, produced the most lovely and varied tones from the piano-forte.

As an organ player Bach has had great injustice done him by those who suppose that every time he sat down to the organ he drew all the stops and "blazed away" by the hour on the full organ. Not he. The organ builders used to complain of his audacity in making combinations. They said he put stops together in the most unheard of and unorthodox manner. And all this is easy enough to understand. Bach was first a violinist, and there is no record of a violinist who could not appreciate melody. He was full of melody. Consider further that he was an orchestral writer of rare power—quite an innovator in his day, coloring his scores to the full scope of the instruments then employed. Besides, his very organ works themselves contradict this notion, for the full organ pieces do not make up more than half the volume of them; but we find trios for two claviers and pedale, and variations which you may be sure Bach "varied" in combination no less than in harmony and melody.

While Bach was Cantor of the St. Thomas Church he had two choirs and an orchestra at his disposal. Music was no small part of the service. The hearty singing of the German peasants and school children in the simple chorals, which Bach accompanied with such wonderful harmonies, and the well-trained choirs, combined to afford the composer rare facilities for the illustration of the musical ideas with which his solid-looking old head teemed. So on every feast day he brought out a new Cantata, a psalm set to music for one or two choirs, orchestra and organ, now and then a verse of a psalm-tune interspersed, in which everybody took part, and the freest use of solos that the subject demanded. Of these works about seventy have been published, ranging from twenty minutes in length to an hour—works which suggested Mendelssohn's "Hymn of Praise," "As Pants the Heart," etc.

To be sure but few of the common people knew what wonderful things they were hearing. Robert Franz tells that he once saw a very old man who was sexton of the St. Thomas Church while Bach was there. "And what did they think of his works?" asked the enthusiastic and reverential Franz. "Mr. Bach's compositions," said the sapient critic, "were very much alike."

The greatest work of this period was Bach's "Passions Music," according to St. Matthew. This consists of about two hours' music, solos, choruses, interspersed stanzas of hymn tunes descriptive of the passion of the garden and the cross. It was written for and first given on Good Friday evening in 1729, and does not seem to have been given again until Mendelssohn exhumed it a hundred years later, and gave it on Good Friday 1829. Since then it has been frequently done in Germany, and always on Good Friday in the St. Thomas Church in Leipsic. This work has become much admired in London, and was nibbled at bravely by the Handel and Haydn Society in Boston at their Festival in 1871, and finally given entire in 1877, largely, be it said, through the perseverance of Mr. Dwight and two or three other enthusiastic admirers of Bach.

When given at Leipsic, and as a religious service, the Passion Music is full of pathos and beauty. Let us imagine a vast, barn-like church, dimly lighted, with two galleries, one above the other. Far up in the upper gallery, with never a soul in sight, we hear the voices of the choirs and organ. The choirs occupy opposite galleries. At the appointed hour the gentle strain begins, "Come, ye daughters, weep for anguish," and presently breaks in the penetrating voice of a couple hundred school children, singing independently the choral, "O Lamb of God, all blameless," a tone and words as familiar there as the Old Hundredth here. The effect is totally indescribable. The gentle and cultivated tones of the choir as they thread the graceful strains of the counterpoint, the reed-like and lusty tones of the boys' voices, the coloring of the orchestra, and the sombre majesty of the organ—all this with never a performer visible; you sit there in the darkness and from some far-away shore the sounds come to you and overwhelm you with waves of music. Anon the chorus dies away and a piercing hautboy takes up a charming theme which a solo voice interprets, "I'll watch with my dear Jesus," and softly, yet richly, the chorus responds, "So slumber shall my sins befall."

And further on the whole congregation, choirs and instruments, all in tender devotion, take up the strain—

"O Head, all bruised and wounded
Hung up to brutal scorn!
O Head with shame surrounded
With crown of cruel thorn!
O Head, to honor wonted,
To splendor all divine,
Now outraged and affronted;
All hail, dear master mine!"

This indeed is religious art! Not these the utterances of the bright concert room, for the applause of the unthoughtful crowd; but here the Christian heart meditates on the mystery of redemption, and to celebrate that wondrous love tearfully brings every offering that the musical art affords.

Mr. John Hullah, in his lectures on "The Transition Periods of Music," holds that Bach's obscurity of expression is such as will forever debar him from wide popularity. This way of putting it does not seem to me fortunate. "Obscurity of expression" is not properly predicable of Bach. Nor has he any lack of melody. On the contrary, he is absolutely the most inexhaustible of all in this direction. It can not be denied that Bach carried the intellectual in music beyond the point where technical devices assist the expression of emotion—at least for our day. But let us not forget that while there are now few musicians who can handle contrapuntal forms well, in Bach's day this was a common accomplishment, and formulæ of expression which in his day were clear enough, and dramatic enough, are, in the light of this excitable nineteenth century, too cold.

And however Bach may stand with the public, he has been the great inspiration to all the best and most poetic of later musicians,—as for instance Mendelssohn, Schumann and Chopin—and this, across a century or so, is surely great honor. To the organist and violinist Bach's works are at once the best exercises for developing his art as a player, and the freshest and most characteristic pieces for his instrument. Yet not all Bach's compositions are great. But in the mass (the manuscripts make a pile over two feet high, and, it is computed, would occupy a copyist more than twenty years to copy them—although this, I dare say, is making it rather a fat thing for the copyist) masterworks of the purest conception are to be found, and that in large numbers.

I can not sum up Bach's works better than in the words of Wilhelm Rust, in Mendel's "*Conversations-Lexicon*," article "Bach."

"In all these works, from the greatest and richest in compass clear down to the smallest range of musical formations, Bach maintained his imperishable glory as the lofty representative of the Inner and Spiritual in art, as the boldest and mightiest herald of the ideal in art works. The great contrapuntal skill which holds performer and hearer in the chains of the most perfect polyphony, the mastership of the works in their organic development, and their value and thankfulness for the purposes of study, serve only as means for expressing his ideal. All these are the stuff through which he expresses the spiritual. The purely technical, therefore, can in no way be regarded as Bach's chief greatness, although many still suppose so. His greatness rests not in the ingenious forms of which, to be sure, he is master, so that no one before or since has expressed himself in them so easily and naturally, but rather in the noble, free and lofty spirit, which in its mighty flight is able to rule and control his thoughts and perceptions, and with equal ease strike the strings of a sought-for emotion, or rise into the boundless fields of free music. Deep moral earnestness is the very foundation of his music, and glorifies even his playful creations; aesthetic loveliness adds itself to him, as it were, of its own accord. Only such a strength, eminent in depth of thought, and equally skillful in expression, could possibly have produced such colossal structures and giant forms as Bach has left us in his great church works, which, in all their greatness, are created out of the deepest and most trustful piety."

PROGRAMME OF BACH ILLUSTRATIONS.

1. *(Moderately Difficult.)*

1. Prelude and Fugue in C minor, "Clavier" I. No. 2.
2. Loure in G, arranged by Heinze.
3. Sarabande in A, No. 5, Bach "Favorite Pieces," Peters, No. 221.
4. Gavotte in D, No. 3 in the same.
5. Song, "My Heart ever Faithful."
6. Invention in E minor, No. 7 of the 3-part Inventions.
7. Gavotte in D, arranged by Mason.

2. *(Difficult, Employing the Piano, Organ, and Violin.)*

1. Chromatic Fantasia and Fugue.
2. Air for G, string, (As played by Wilhelmj).
3. Courante in E minor, No. 7, from Peters, No. 221.
4. Organ Prelude in B minor, Organ works Vol. II, No. 10.
5. Chaconne for violin Solo.
6. Grand Prelude and Fugue in G minor, Organ works, Vol. II, No 4.
7. Meditation upon Bach's 1st Prelude, by Ch. Gounod, For organ, piano, and violin.

3. *(For Piano and Voice.)*

1. Chromatic Fantasia and Fugue.
2. Song, "My Heart ever Faithful."
3. Invention in F, No. 8, two part.
   Sarabande in A.
   Invention in E minor.
   Gigue in G, (No. 2 in Peters, No. 221).
4. Slumber Song from Christmas Oratorio.
5. Invention in C minor, 3 part.
   Loure in G, Heinze.
   Sarabande in F, No. 6, Peters, No. 221.
   Echo in B minor, No. 8 of the same.
   Gavotte in E major, Arr. by Tours.
6. Echo Aria from the Christmas Oratorio.
7. Grand Organ Fugue in G minor, Arranged for piano by Liszt.

CHAPTER FORTY-THREE.

GEORGE FREDERICK HANDEL.

At Halle, in Lower Saxony, Feb. 23, 1685, was born Bach's great contemporary, and, in after times, rival, Geo. Frederick Handel. His father was a physician and surgeon. The little George early showed an immense desire for music, and that to his poor father's discomfiture: "For," said the judicious sire, "music is an elegant art and fine amusement, but as an occupation it hath little dignity, having for its object nothing better than mere entertainment and pleasure." So he kept the boy out of school lest he should learn to sing, and taught him his Latin and humanities at home. But, by connivance of mother or nurse, they say, the boy contrived to get a dumb spinet hid away in the garret, and there, by night, taught himself to play. The "dumb spinet" was a very small piano-forte, of which the strings were wound with cloth so that when struck it gave forth only a mild tinkling sound. They were made for nuns who might want a little music in a quiet way without disturbing the lady superiors.

When still a small boy, scarce eight years old, his father made a trip to Weissenfels, to visit his eldest son, who was in the service of the Duke there. Of course he had no idea of taking the little George Frederick with him, for, at court, the boy would be almost sure to hear some music and so get further strengthened in his pestiferous liking for the shallow art. But as the good old doctor drove away in his chaise the boy ran after him a mile or two, and begged so hard to be taken that the father finally bundled him into the chaise and took him along "to get rid of him." Arrived at court, the boy was left to shift for himself while papa and the big brother were seeing the lions of the place. By a natural attraction the young musician soon found himself in the chapel, and, with the friendly aid of a good natured servant at the bellows, was soon in fine frenzy of harmony at the organ. By a lucky chance the Duke came along, and immediately perceived the real talent of the young player. And here, to his great horror, papa Handel found him a little later. But the Duke assured the old gentleman that the boy had a genuine talent for music which must on no account be hid; that he must put young George Frederick under strict training as a musician, and not try to thwart the plain design of Providence.

So, on his return to Halle, young Handel was put under the instruction of the great organist there, Zachau, who, for about three years, put him through a course of the heroic training those times delighted in. Towards the last of this course Handel wrote a cantata or motette every week—many of them, I dare say, poor stuff; for what else could be expected of a boy of ten, although they must have been technically correct to satisfy the conscientious old pedagogue. At length Zachau had not the heart to keep it up any longer, for a boy who could produce fugues with such facility and of so good an average of merit was already a master, and so Zachau told him. So Handel went next to Berlin, in 1696, and studied the opera school, under the auspices of the Elector. The next year old Dr. Handel died, leaving his family poorly provided for. George Frederick then went to Hamburg, where he hoped to earn a living as violinist in the opera orchestra. Being a rather poor player he got a very subordinate position, that of *ripieno* second violin (a sort of fifth wheel), and was regarded by the other players as a veritable dunce, for he was nineteen, large, awkward, rather shy, and a poor fiddler. But one day the leader was sick and the rehearsal likely to fall through; and Handel took his seat at the harpsichord (or piano) because he could best be spared from his place in the orchestra, and carried the rehearsal through with such spirit that the whole orchestra broke into loud applause.

On the strength of this recognition he appears soon as permanent conductor of the orchestra, and, along with his dear friend Matheson, a chief composer of opera for the Hamburg stage. Here presently he brought out "*Almira*" and "*Nero*," and, probably, "*Florindo and Daphne*," which he had already written while in Berlin. But it was Handel's great desire to visit Italy. So, refusing the liberal offer of Prince Giovanni Gaston de Medici to send him, he saved his money and was straightway able to go at his own expense, and in 1707, at the age of twenty-one, he entered Florence. Here, however, he stayed only long enough to compose the opera "*Roderigo*," for which he received one hundred sequins, when he immediately betook himself to Venice. Here he was received with open arms. The abounding vitality of his music and its sparkling and good natured originality was such as to secure for him the epithet "the dear Saxon" ("*Il Caro Sassone*").

Domenico Scarlatti was the great harpsichordist of all Italy at that time. He was a sort of Chopin of his day, imparting a new grace and scope to piano-forte music, yet not creating in such a masterly way as to conquer the after-coming generations. Handel, also, excelled as a harpsichordist, and the relative merits of the two artists were widely discussed. It was generally thought that Scarlatti played with more grace; but at the organ Handel was unquestionably the superior. Scarlatti himself, however, was not satisfied. One night at a masked ball a disguised player seated himself at the harpsichord and amid the noise and confusion played away unnoticed. But just then Scarlatti came in and at once his trained ear recognized the masterly touch. "It is either the Saxon or the Devil," said he. It *was* the Saxon. Whenever people used to praise his playing he used to pronounce Handel's name and, with the Italian grimace, cross himself. But Handel and Scarlatti became fast friends.

Here in Venice, Handel in three weeks composed an opera "*Agrippina*," which made a furore from Venice to Rome. Here he secured the patronage of Cardinal Ottoboni, whose band-master was the celebrated Corelli, a composer and violinist of somewhat refined and gentle nature, but of marked genius. Here Handel wrote five operas, of which we have no room to speak further.

In 1709 he was back again in Germany, at Hanover, where he was retained in the service of the Elector George of Brunswick, afterwards the English George I, at a salary of £300 a year. Here he fell in with some English noblemen, who invited him over to London. So with gracious leave of absence from the Elector, he came to London in the Autumn of 1710, where he found the Italian taste everywhere prevalent. To meet this he composed the opera *Rinaldo*, which was brought out in 1711 with immense success, and was forthwith arranged for pianos and barrel organs, and was thrummed, whistled and beat from one end of the kingdom to the other. Walsh, the publisher, is said to have made £1,500 out of the sale of the pieces of this opera. Within a few months Handel was back again in Hanover, but the quiet German Court was not much to his taste after the success in London. So again he got leave of absence for a visit to London, and in 1712 brought out an ode on the occasion of the Queen's birthday. The following year the peace of Utrecht gave occasion for the *T_e Deum* and *Jubilate* (both well known in England), and for these three the composer received a pension of £200 a year from Queen Anne, and forthwith Handel (to use a western phrase) "went back" on Hanover and its rather slow court completely and for good. Now this was all very well as long as the Queen lived, for the public was ready to hear and pay. But presently Queen Anne died, and, bad luck for Handel, George I, in very wrathful mood at the trick played him by his *quondam* chapel master, came over himself to reign. Handel was forbidden the court; but Handel's music was sung and played everywhere, and the new King not only knew good music when he heard it, but he knew Handel's music as well as he knew his robust frame and round face. So one day as the King went down the river in a state barge, a boat came after him playing some new and delightful music, which in the turn of the phrases was Handel's clearly enough. This was the celebrated "water music," well enough in its day, but now, in spite of its election and high calling, rather passed. But it appeased the ire of the King, and Handel's pardon was sealed with a new pension of £200 a year.

Mr. Haweis, in "Music and Morals," gives a pleasant picture of the society in which Handel moved at that time. "Yonder heavy, ragged looking youth, standing at a corner of Regent street with a slight and rather refined looking companion, is the obscure Samuel Johnson, quite unknown to fame. He is walking with Richard Savage. As Signor Handel, the composer of Italian music, passes by, Savage becomes excited, and nudges his friend, who only takes a languid interest in the foreigner. Johnson did not care for music; of many noises he considered it the least disagreeable.

"Toward Charing Cross comes, in shovel hat and cassock, the renowned ecclesiastic, Dean Swift. He has just nodded patronizingly to Bononcini in the Strand and suddenly meets Handel, who cuts him dead. Nothing disconcerted, the Dean moves on muttering his famous epigram:

> 'Some say that Signor Bononcini,
> Compared to Handel, is a ninny;
> While others vow that to him Handel
> Is hardly fit to hold a candle.
> Strange that such differences should be
> 'Twixt tweedledum and tweedledee.'

" As Handel enters 'Turk's Head,' at the corner of Regent street, a noble coach and four drove up; it is the Duke of Chandos, who is inquiring for Mr. Pope; presently a deformed little man in an iron-grey suit, and a face as keen as a razor, hobbles out, makes a low bow to the burly Handel, who, helping him into the chariot, gets in after him, and they drive off together to Cannons, the Duke's mansion at Edgeware There they meet Mr. Addison, the poet Gay, and the witty Arbuthnot, who have been asked to luncheon. The last number of the *Spectator* lies on the table, and a brisk discussion soon arises between Pope and Addison concerning the merits of the Italian Opera, in which the poet would have the better, if he only knew a little more about music, and could keep his temper."

The Duke had a private chapel, and appointed Handel organist in place of Dr. Pepusch, who retired with very good grace before one so manifestly his superior. The Duke's chapel became a very fashionable Sunday resort of those who wanted to worship God in great company and hear Mr. Handel play the organ. While in this position Handel composed what were called the "Chandos Anthems," numbering over a hundred pieces. These are interesting as marking his transition towards the oratorio; but they are never performed now, except for their historical interest. During his residence at Cannons, which extended to 1721, Handel composed his oratorio of "Esther."

In 1720 Handel was engaged by a society of noblemen to compose operas for the Royal Academy of Music at the Haymarket, of which "*Radamistus*" was one of the first fruits; on this followed "*Floridante*" in 1721 and "*Otto*" in 1753—the latter being considered the flower of his dramatic works. Of the favorite air "Affani del pensier," Dr. Pepusch remarked, "The great bear was certainly inspired when he wrote that song." This career of activity went on with full tide of fashionable favor for four years, including seven more operas. Then the fashion changed. At a rival theatre Dr. Pepusch brought out 'The Beggar's Opera,' composed of all sorts of bits from every source including much from Handel himself, and all the public went to laugh at and enjoy it.

Not disheartened, Handel posted off to Italy to get a supply of the best singers, determined to "fight it out on that line." But fashion is a fickle goddess, and it was many a struggling year before tough old Handel saw her smiling face again. New and better operas were given with new and good clothes; but the public did not respond. Giving operas with Italian singers is apt to try one's temper, as perhaps Messrs. Maretzek, Strakosch and Grau could inform us if they would. It is related that at a rehearsal, after repeated signs of insubordination that had terribly tried the composer's irascible temper, the famous Cuzzoni finally declined to sing "Falsa Immagine." Handel exploded at last. "He flew at the wretched woman and shook her like a rat. 'Ah! I always knew you were a fery tefil,' he cried; and I shall now let you know that I am Beelzebub, the prince of te tefils!' and dragging her to the open window, was just on the point of pitching her into the street, when, in every sense of the word she recanted.*"

The struggle against fate lasted until about 1741. In 1732, we read that "*Hester*, an English oratorio, was performed six times, and very full." Within the next seven years he wrote sixteen operas and

*Music and Morals.

five oratorios. Still, with strange blindness, Handel could not see that the public had done with his operas. He wrote ballet music (fancy Handel writing music for "the Black Crook" or "the Field of the Cloth of Gold") and lavished immense sums in scenery, "new clothes" and properties. But it was all in vain. In eight years he lost £10,000 in opera and was obliged to suspend payment and close the theatre. With failing health he betook himself, sick, discouraged and mad, to Aix-la-Chapelle. In 1727 he was much amended and returned to England, as Mr. Haweis suggests, "not like Mozart from Baden, to write his own requiem, but some one's else." It was the funeral anthem in memory of Queen Caroline that claimed his attention.

Resolute still, he tried the opera again, producing three successively; but each failed worse than the last. Still many were true to him. King George II, paid him well for his work, and taught the Prince of Wales (afterwards George IV) to love his music. "Southey tells us that Handel asked the boy, then quite a child, who was listening very earnestly to his playing, if he liked the music, and when the little prince expressed his delight, 'A good boy! a good boy!' cried Handel. 'You shall protect my fame when I am dead.'" The best writers, too, stood up manfully for Handel. Such were Gay, Arbuthnot, Hughes, Colley Cibber, Pope, Fielding, Hogarth and Smollett. "These were the men who kept their fingers on the pulse of the age; they gauged Handel accurately, and they were not wrong. At a time when others jeered at Handel's oratorios, these men wrote them up; when the tide of fine society ebbed, and left Handel high and dry on the boards of a deserted theatre, they occupied the pit ; when he gave his benefit concert they bought the tickets, and when his operas failed, they immediately subscribed and had them engraved."*

The people, also, were true to Handel. His music was played by bands everywhere throughout the kingdom. He became very popular as a player, and at every oratorio performance performed one or two "new organ concertos." The year 1739 was a very active one for Handel; in it he produced the oratorios of "Saul," "Alexander's Feast," and "Israel in Egypt." The latter is truly a colossal work, containing twenty-seven choruses, nearly all of which are double, that is, written for two choirs. This work has been given by the Boston Handel and Haydn Society several times, and perhaps elsewhere in this country. It is very grand, but many regard it as somewhat tedious on account of the preponderance of choruses. This succession of such mighty choruses

*Music and Morals, p. 167.

has always struck musicians with wonder. Mendelssohn regarded it as something almost superhuman. In the letters from 1833 to 1847, Mendelssohn recounts the use he made of a part of this oratorio in an entertainment of music and *tableaux* given at Dusseldorf, in honor of the Crown Prince. "They took place in the great hall of the Academy where a stage was erected. In front was the double chorus (about ninety voices altogether) standing in two semi-circles around my English piano; and in the room, seats for four hundred spectators. R— in mediæval costume interpreted the whole affair, and contrived, very cleverly, to combine the different objects in spite of their disparity.

"He exhibited three transparencies: 1st. 'Melancholy,' after Dürer, a motette of Lotti's, being given by men's voices in the far distance; then the Raphael, with the Virgin appearing to him in a vision, to which the 'O Sanctissima' was sung (a well known song, but which always makes people cry); thirdly, St. Jerome in his tent, with a song of Weber's '*Hor' uns, Wahrheit.*' This was the first part. Now came the best of all. We began from the very beginning of 'Israel in Egypt.' Of course you know the first recitative, and how the chorus gradually swells in tone ; first the voices of the *alti* are heard alone, then more voices join in, till the loud passage comes with single chords, 'They sighed,' etc. (in G minor), when the curtain rose and displayed the first tableau, 'The Children of Israel in Bondage,' designed and arranged by Bendeman. In the foreground was Moses, gazing dreamily into the distance in sorrowful apathy; beside him an old man sinking into the ground under the weight of a beam, while his son makes an effort to release him from it; in the background some beautiful figures with uplifted arms, a few weeping children in the foreground—the whole scene closely crowded together like a mass of fugitives. This remained visible till the close of the first chorus; and when it ended in C minor the curtain at the same moment dropped over the bright picture. A finer effect I scarcely ever saw.

"The chorus then sang 'The Plagues,' 'Hail Darkness' and 'The First-Born,' without any tableaux, but at the chorus 'He Led Them Out Like Sheep,' the curtain rose again, when Moses was seen in the foreground, with raised staff, and behind him, in gay tumult, the same figures who in the first tableaux were mourning, now all pressing onwards ladened with gold and silver vessels; one young girl (also by Bendeman) was especially lovely, who, with her pilgrim's staff, seemed as if advancing from the side scenes and about to cross the stage. Then came the choruses again, without any tableaux, 'But the Waters,' 'He rebuked the Red Sea,' ' Thy Right Hand, O Lord,' and the recitative 'And Miriam. the Prophetess,' at the close of which the solo soprano appeared. At the same moment the last tableau was uncovered—Miriam with a silver timbrel sounding praises to the Lord, and other maidens with harps and citherns, and in the background four men with trombones pointing in different directions. The soprano solo was sung behind the scenes, as if proceeding from the picture, and when the chorus came in *forte* real trombones and trumpets and kettle drums were brought on the stage and burst in like a thunderclap. Handel evidently intended this effect * * * "

In 1741 Handel composed his master work, "The Messiah," in seventeen days. For a detailed criticism on this work and the "Judas Maccabeus" I have no place. It must suffice to say of "The Messiah" that certain numbers of it are masterpieces of the most precious quality. Even the quaint and curious "And He Shall Purify" is one of the most characteristic morceaux to be found in the whole chorus repertory. The "Hallelujah" chorus is now everywhere known. Still those who have never heard this chorus with hundreds of voices, full orchestra and organ, have not yet heard Handel's "Hallelujah," but only a part thereof. It is generally known that Mozart added new wind parts to the score of the "Messiah." These additions in this chorus fill up seven staves, and impart a characteristic splendor to this noble creation, which the orchestra in Handel's time could not attain.*

There is no doubt in my mind that Handel was helped in the "Messiah" very much by the *text*, which contains the most inspiring passages to be found in all literature; besides, in his other works he only rarely rises to the heights he reaches in this one.

"The Messiah" was first produced in Dublin in 1742, for a charitable purpose, and it is interesting to note that this oratorio has contributed more money in charity, first and last, than any other work of art whatever. The production of these great oratorios was the turning point in Handel's fortunes. He speedily paid off his debts, and within the next seventeen years accumulated a handsome fortune. His last oratorio was "Jephtha," written in 1751, about which time he began to be blind, from the affection known as *gutta serena*. He was couched several times, but he finally lost his sight entirely. He continued to give oratorio performances, at intervals, until about a week before his death. He died in London, Good Friday, April 14, 1759, in his seventy-fifth year. His large property, amounting to something like £50,000 was all bequeathed to charitable institutions. Handel was

---

*(Those curious in this matter can obtain the full orchestral score of "The Messiah," in the Peters' edition, including Mozart's additions for about three dollars.)

never married, had no vices except an irascible temper, and seems never to have been in love but once.

As an organist, he was of the greatest eminence. The clearness with which he expressed his ideas, the dignity of his musical thought, so well suited to the organ, together with his decision and spirit as a performer, combined to make him immensely successful.

It is difficult to define the relative rank of Handel and Bach as great masters, and to weigh their influence on the course of musical development since. As Brendel well says, they were the culmination of musical progress in their age, but they represented opposite poles. Bach was a quiet home-body, writing always in a highly subjective manner out of the depths of his own feeling. Although the greatest organist of his times, and often listened to by kings and lords, he did not allow himself to change from the ideal of art that was congenial to his nature. Handel on the other hand, a bustling, energetic man, of a truly cosmopolitan taste, had it always for his task to please and attract the masses. Resources were not wanting. He controlled for nearly forty years the best singers and players in the world. His genius had every thing to favor it. To a German honesty and depth of artistic conception he united the Italian art of clear expression; yet all this with no sacrifice of the nobility of his art, and for a genius of such composition, England, the land of common sense, was, of all others, the field of action. Handel has done more to make the musical art respected by the public generally than any other composer. Bach has been the inspiration of musicians. Bach and Handel are the corner stones of Modern Music.

Handel was pre-eminently a composer of vocal music. In his recitatives he attains a dignified and truly musical declamation of the text, as we already saw in Chapter XXXVIII, and occasionally rises to true pathos. In his arias he is frequently diffuse. The leading motive is too many times turned over. Yet this fault is wellnigh universal in the classical aria, which is, as we know, merely a prolongation of a single moment in the dramatic movement. Besides, this prolixity only gave more opportunity to the prima donna. At other times, however, his arias are not too long, even for the rapid age we live in. In very many of them we find a close relation between the text and the music, and always a careful consideration for the voice. His style, although melodious and thus far Italian, was distinguished for its contrapuntal spirit, and its elevation and dignity, and was therefore especially suited to the oratorio. In his choruses he rises to the highest points yet reached in this form of art. Of this one finds very many examples, of which the "Hallelujah," "The Horse and His Rider," "The Hailstone Chorus," "Lift up Your Heads," and "Worthy is the Lamb" are known to all. His instrumental music is not so important. It is melodious, and of course well written, but in general somewhat diffuse. Even his famous organ concertos do not escape the charge of being commonplace.

Programme of Handel Illustrations.

1. (*Moderately Difficult, Employing the Piano and Soprano.*)

1. Fugue in E minor (" Fire Fugue").
2. "As when the dove laments her love," from "Acis and Galatea." Soprano.
3. Pastoral symphony, from " Messiah."
4. " How beautiful are the Feet " (from " Messiah"). Soprano.
5. Air and Variations in E. " The Harmonious Blacksmith."
6. Aria, " Lascia ch' io Pianga," from " Rinaldo."
7. *a.* Minuet from Samson.
   b. Chaconne in F.
   c. March from occasional Oratorio.
8. "I know that my Redeemer liveth." Soprano.
9. Hallelujah Chorus from the "Messiah."

(2. *Employing Soprano, Alto, Tenor, and Chorus with Piano-forte.*)

1. *a.* " Comfort ye my people."
   b. Every Valley shall be exalted. Tenor Solo.
   c. Chorus " And the Glory of the Lord."
2. *a.* Minuet from Samson.
   b. March from Joshua.
   c. Air Bourée and Double. Arr. by Mason. The Piano-forte.
3. "Hope in the Lord," Arr. by Mason. Soprano.
4. " O thou that tellest," from " Messiah." Alto solo and Chorus.
5. *a.* "Thy rebuke hath broken his heart."
   b. " Behold and see if there be any sorrow." Tenor.
   c. " But Thou didst not leave his soul in hell." From the " Messiah."
6. "How beautiful are the Feet." Soprano.
7. Hallelujah Chorus, or " Worthy is the Lamb."

CHAPTER FORTY-FOUR.

FRANCIS JOSEPH HAYDN.

Up to the time of which I am now about to write, the great creative geniuses, Handel and Bach, had devoted their efforts to vocal music; instrumental music had received a certain amount of attention, it is true, and the organ especially was carried no further until the time of Mendelssohn. But although Bach and Handel were not altogether above playfulness, it was of a sort essentially masculine and earnest. The light and easy-going spirit of modern society, which chiefly cultivates instrumental music, formed no part of Bach or Handel's nature, and hence it has no expression in their works. Nevertheless, what they had done went far to render instrumental music possible, as they imparted to music a degree of emotional coloring entirely unknown before their time. At the hands of Handel, also, melody had assumed more definite form. Both these men, also, were able to develop a musical thought in a purely musical spirit (that is, independently from words, and influenced simply by conditions of symmetry and contrast, as well as unity) to a masterly degree, which has never been surpassed. One of Bach's sons, Carl Philip Emanuel, began the career of instrumental music. He was wonderfully gifted in the art of improvising, for which he was amply qualified by the thorough training he had received from his father. Emanuel Bach was the father of the Sonata.

In March, 1732, in the village of Rohrau (not far from Vienna), a certain wheelwright, of a musical turn, was blessed with a dark and perhaps rather scrawny little son, to whom was given the name of Francis Joseph Haydn. Papa Haydn played a little on the organ and harp, and sang with a fine tenor voice. Sunday afternoons, when his official duties as sexton were over, he was accustomed to have a sort of concert with the aid of his wife. The little Francis Joseph was an interested assistant at these domestic celebrations, and soon learned to add his own piping little voice to the family concerts. At an early age he went to Hamburg with his cousin Frank, who promised to teach him music and Latin. When yet hardly eight years old the youngster became celebrated as a choir-boy, and very soon he was captured by

Reuter, the director of the music at St. Stephen's Church in Vienna, who used to make frequent tours in search of promising voices for his choir. Haydn afterwards said that all the time he was with Reuter (over ten years), never a day passed in which he did not practise from sixteen to eighteen hours, although the boys were practically their own masters, only being obliged to practice two hours.

When thirteen years old he composed a mass, which to his great chagrin was mercilessly ridiculed by Reuter. Haydn presently saw that a knowledge of harmony and counterpoint was essential to success in composition. But who would teach a penniless choir boy? For Haydn was absolutely as poor as poverty itself. Bread and cheese and an annual suit of clothes he had to be sure, but the authorities of St. Stephen's Church in Vienna preserved their choir boys as carefully from "the deceitfulness of riches," as many churches do their ministers now-a-days. But genius is indefatigable. Haydn found a copy of a treatise on counterpoint by Fux, in a second-hand bookstore, and by some desperate expedient contrived to get possession of it. Now Fux's book is in Latin, and not in the clearest form. But Haydn knew there were worse things in the world than bad Latin, and one of these was ignorance. So he "pegged away" at it, like the plucky little man he was, lying a-bed in cold days to keep warm, taking his diurnal portion of the sorry old book as conscientiously as he did his daily mass and dinner. About the time he had begun to get easy on the subject of counterpoint, Providence sent him another lesson.

In the *suite* of the Venetian ambassador at Vienna was the great Italian master and singer, Nicolo Porpora. Now Porpora was a crusty old person, and was not a man who at all looked like taking up a *protégé* in the shape of a seedy looking little choir boy. But if Porpora did not know Haydn, Haydn did know Porpora, and that he was the same great master who had been brought over to London to rival the mighty Handel, just now in the very glory of his fame. So Haydn got up early, cleaned the boots, brushed the coat, and curled the wig of the amiable master, whose only recognition of these services was a muttered "*fool*," when Haydn entered the room. But, as Sam Slick discovered, "soft soap" will tell if persevered in, and when to these civilities was added the fact that they were *gratis*, and when the boy had proved himself so useful in accompanying some of Porpora's songs, which the beauteous lady of the ambassador was fond of singing—at last the severity began to relent, and Haydn got many a word of sound advice, and with it the Italian taste in singing. Presently the ambassador recognized the young man's progress by a pension of fifteen dollars a month, and a seat at the secretaries' table. Haydn was now full of activity; as soon as it was light he made haste to the Church of the Father of Mercy, where he played first violin; from thence he hastened to the chapel of Count Hangwitz, where he played the organ; afterwards he sang the tenor at St. Stephen's. He then returned home and finished out the day at his piano. If there is any one lesson that the early lives of these composers teach more plainly than another, it is that laziness is not a sign of genius. *Hard work* is an indispensable condition of success in any business that is worth following. Haydn's voice broke when he was nineteen years old, and he found himself without employment. A wig-maker named Keller kindly received him as a son, and in this house Haydn gave himself more decidedly to composition. When he was twenty he published six instrumental trios, which attracted general attention. The individuality of his talent was more fully confirmed by his first quartette, which soon followed. Presently he left the house of Keller, and found a boarding place with a Mr. Martinez, on condition of his giving piano and singing lessons to his two daughters. In the same house lived the poet Metastasio, who, being fond of music, took Haydn into his friendship, having him daily to dinner and good converse. In this way Haydn picked up a great deal of general knowledge and some Italian, affording, I dare say, with his simple German nature, fully as much as he gave.

In 1758 he entered the employment of Count Mortzin, as leader of his orchestra. In this capacity some of his works attracted the attention of old Prince Esterhazy, who in 1760 appointed him *kapellmeister*. The old gentleman died a year after, but Haydn continued for thirty years in the service of his son Nicholas, who died in 1790. Within the ten years previous to this appointment, he had composed his opera "The Devil on Two Sticks," a number of quartettes and trios, and just now his first symphony, and here he is twenty-eight years old. Yet this short list of works was by no means all Haydn had written. He had produced an immense mass of pieces of every kind, which had merely served the purpose of giving him that facility of expression, that mastery over the technics of his art, without which a genius, however highly gifted, is curtailed in the most promising flights.

The thirty years that followed were monotonous in the extreme. About two months of every year were spent in Vienna; the other ten at the prince's quiet Hungarian estates. Haydn produced an enormous list of pieces, many of them of great beauty. They comprise 119 symphonies, 83 quartettes, 24 trios, 19 operas, 15 masses, 163 compositions for barytone (Prince Esterhazy's favorite instrument), 44 pianoforte sonatas, etc.

Haydn appears to have been unconscious of the immense reputation he had achieved throughout Europe, and was never more astonished than when, soon after Prince Esterhazy's death, a stranger burst into his room, saying, "I am Salomon of London, and am come to carry you off with me; we will strike a bargain to-morrow." "Oh, papa," said the youthful Mozart, "you have had no education for the wide, wide world, and you speak too few languages." "Oh, my language," replied the papa with a smile, "is understood all over the world." And so at the age of sixty, in the full maturity of his powers, came Haydn to London. Here in little more than a year he wrote six new symphonies, and many other smaller things. These symphonies were brought out as novelties, Haydn conducting in person, seated at the piano.

The bustle of London and the favor with which he was received struck Haydn favorably. "He tells us* how he enjoyed himself at the civic feast in company with William Pitt, Lord Chancellor, and the Duke of Lids (Leeds). He says, after dinner the highest nobility—*i. e.* the Lord Mayor and his wife (!)—were seated on a throne. In another room, the gentlemen, as usual, drank freely all night; and the songs and the crazy uproar and the smashing of glasses were very great. The oil lamps smelt terribly, and the dinner cost £6,000. He went down to stay with the Prince of Wales (George IV.), and Sir Joshua Reynolds painted his portrait. The Prince played the violoncello not badly, and charmed Haydn by his affability. 'He is the handsomest man on God's earth. He has an extraordinary love of music, and a great deal of feeling, but very little money.' From the palace he passed to the laboratory and was introduced to Herschel, in whom he was delighted to find an old oboe player. The big telescope astonished him, so did the astronomer. ·He often sits out of doors in the most intense cold for five or six hours at a time.'"

In 1792 Haydn returned to Vienna, where he brought out his new symphonies. In 1795 he was back again in London, and earned no less than 12,000 florins (five or six thousand dollars). He bought him a little home near Vienna, where he passed the remnant of his days in peace and quiet. In 1795 he began, and in 1798 finished his cantata or oratorio "The Creation," which we commonly speak of as his greatest work. Haydn died at the age of seventy-seven, in 1809, and was buried in the cemetery of Gumpfendorf, Vienna.

* "Music and Morals."

Haydn's works number about eight hundred, many of them of small value, yet all finished with great care. I hardly know whether in strict justice we ought to accord Haydn the greater honor as a vocal or instrumental composer; for, although his works in the line of chamber music and symphony have exercised the greatest influence upon composers, his "Creation" has been very influential (in this country at least) in educating the taste of the public. It is the one oratorio that receives the earliest attention of amateur societies, a pre-eminence it well deserves from the grace and sweetness of its ideas, and the elegance with which they are worked out. And although "The Creation" appears somewhat childlike and bland, for a work in severe style (especially when compared with Handel's "Messiah" or "Israel," Bach's "Passion's Music," or even Mendelssohn's "Elijah"), we can not deny the consummate grace of the lovely airs "With verdure clad," and "On mighty pens," or the almost operatic sweetness of the trio "On thee each living soul awaits," and the concerted duet "By thee with bliss." "The heavens are telling" has been universally a favorite.

Nevertheless the critic turns from this work, which in every trait except grace and sweetness has been far surpassed, to the quartettes; and here, as the conditions have remained substantially the same from his time until now, Haydn has not been so far out-ranked. Mozart had a livelier imagination, Beethoven and Schumann more of Bach's earnestness. Haydn's music, even in its most elaborate moments, is simple in its essential nature—the expression of a child-like, contented soul, so completely well bred as almost to seem never to have required training.

As an orchestral writer Haydn made enormous advances. He gave the symphony the systematic development of the sonata form, introduced many new combinations, and established the type of the *Andante cantabile* movement, which Mozart and Beethoven afterwards carried to so great a perfection.

His pianoforte compositions sound narrow and old fashioned.

In the mere fact of producing so much of a somewhat uniform texture, Haydn did a great deal for the cultivation of instrumental music. He seems always to have had a singularly accurate idea of the practical and the available. We may be sure both that he was a pleasant man to get along with, and an agreeable writer, or he would not have remained so long in one position.

Haydn attached small importance to the actual substance of the germinal ideas in his works. He had such consummate art that he could work up the most commonplace ideas into an attractive and beautiful whole. He said *the treatment* was every thing.

List of Haydn Illustrations.

(*Employing Soprano, Tenor, Bass, and the Pianoforte.*)

1. Sonata in E flat.
2. "My Mother Bids me Bind my Hair," Soprano.
3. Minuet in C (Oxen Minuet).
4. "In Native Worth," Tenor.
5. Variations on "God Save the Emperor" (Haydn Album, p. 38).
6. "Now Heaven in Fullest Glory Shone," Bass.
7. Symphony in D for four hands (No. 5 Peters' Edition).
8. Trio, "On Thee each Living Soul Awaits," Soprano, Tenor, and Bass.

CHAPTER FORTY-FIVE.

MOZART.

Rarely does it fall to the lot of a writer to undertake a more genial task than to sketch the short life of Wolfgang Amadeus Mozart, born at Salzburg, about a hundred miles from Vienna, January 27, 1756—a life of such marvellous richness as to give to a sober account the air of liveliest romance. Bach had died only six years before. Handel was in his old age and blindness, and died three years later; Haydn was in the very pinch of his hardest fortunes, living in the house with Metastasio, as previously recorded. Yet these proximities of dates look far more significant to us now than they could have looked a hundred years ago; for then there were many other composers of great talents who contested with these giants the claim to immortality. The century that has intervened has been very busy in analyzing and sifting their productions, and this has finally resulted in giving due honor to these great ones, who the more they have been weighed in the balance have proven themselves the more worthy.

Leopold Mozart, the father, was himself a musician of marked talent. He published an instruction book for the violin and held a place as court musician with the Archbishop of Salzburg. When Wolfgang was three years old his talent for music began to manifest itself. When he was four years old he could play a number of minuets and the like, and learned with wonderful facility. He found out for himself thirds and other concords. When yet under six years old his father found him one day writing something which he called a "concerto for the harpsichord." The father of course laughed at such a work by a mere baby, but the little fellow insisted that it was really a concerto, and on examination it proved to be written strictly according to rule, although so overloaded with difficulties as to be impossible. When a little over six years old he performed at the court of Francis I., at Munich, with his eldest sister, where his wonderful gifts excited the greatest astonishment. Still it is but just to say that child-virtuosity was of much easier attainment then than now, for the pianos of that day were very small, the touch light, and the compositions in vogue were of an amiable and unimpassioned character.

Presently young Wolfgang learned the violin, and surprised his father by playing correctly in a quartette. Of anecdotes of this kind the Mozart biographies are full. Suffice it to say, that during his first twelve years his talent shone out brighter and brighter, and on all hands he received the warmest approbation, yet he never became a spoiled child. He was of a gentle, confiding disposition, of a sweet and even temper, fond of play—a queer compound of manly talent and skill with childish tastes and habits. He spent some three years in traveling, visiting France, England and Holland—his public life as a youthful virtuoso being supplemented by regular and daily studies in musical theory, and the regular branches of a polite education. In this way he learned French, Latin and Italian. In 1767 or so he visited Vienna, and composed a small opera, which, however, was never performed. By the command of the Emperor, he wrote a mass for the dedication of the new Waisenhaus church, and conducted with *baton* in hand. When scarcely twelve years old, he was appointed concert-meister by the Archbishop of Salzburg, and within the next year wrote a number of masses.

But his father was anxious that Wolfgang should become known in Italy, which was at that time the fountain of musical inspiration. So in December, 1769, they set off for Italy, staying some months in Rome, Bologna, Florence Milan, etc. The Pope made him a "knight of the golden spur."

The most significant triumph of this tour was his admission as a member of the Philharmonic Academy of Bologna, at that time the highest musical authority in the world. At its head was the learned contrapuntist, Father Martini, and at his right hand the great singer, Farinelli, also a learned musician. These men and the members of the Academy generally recognized Mozart's genius as a performer, but no one could believe that a boy of twelve could pass triumphantly through the severe tests in counterpoint required of candidates for admission. Nevertheless, *Padre* Martini rightly judged that the extreme youth of Mozart made it necessary that his admission to the distinguished honor of membership should be justified to the world by the severest tests ever assigned. This task was the composition for four voices of one of the canticles of the Roman *Antiphonarium*. The work was to be treated according to severe rules, and performed within three hours in a locked-up room—the Academy waiting as patiently as they might in order to judge the work as soon as it was accomplished. Men who regarded themselves great masters had often failed in this task, consuming the whole time in the production of a few lines. It was therefore with no small misgivings that Father Martini delivered to the hopeful Mozart the task which was to announce his manhood in the most difficult department of musical theory. But great was his surprise, when after little more than a half hour the beadle came in saying that the young Mozart declared himself ready to be let out, having finished the task.

"Impossible!" said many of the members. "In the hundred years the Academy had been established such a case had never occurred." Nevertheless, when the committee proceeded to Mozart's room they received from him a manuscript, written in his usual neat and delicate hand; and after careful scrutiny they were compelled to admit that it contained no faults whatever. I may add that it took the old doctors about an hour to go through the paper thoroughly enough to convince themselves that Mozart's rapid work was faultless. The young composer was then led in, and the whole Academy greeted him with hearty applause, and recognized in him an accomplished *Maestro*, and a *Knight of Harmony*.

Now, the gratifying point of this transaction is, that this highly gifted boy, traveling from place to place, playing in public almost daily, found time for such thorough study as to be able at the childish age of twelve to meet and conquer the most learned theorists on their own ground. And better than this, he does not seem to have been puffed up by his success; to him it was not difficult, and while proud of the commendation of these learned men, and of having proven himself a master, we find his letters just as simple, and child-like, and modest as before.

After this Italian tour Mozart returned to Salzburg, which, however, he soon left for Munich. But his future ups and downs we have not room to follow; for, unlike Bach, Handel and Haydn, whose lives embraced long periods of twenty years and more passed in one place, Mozart was rarely more than a few years in a place, except his last ten years, which he spent in Vienna. It is the more difficult to bring his life into a sketch from the fact that he went much into society, and has left on record a large collection of letters which give a very graphic picture of life at that time. These letters fill two volumes, and are well worth reading. The little book called "Mozart's Early Days," lately published, gives a very lively and entertaining account of his life up to the time of his triumph in the Bologna Academy. Lee & Shepard also publish a book—"Mozart and Mendelssohn"—which not only gives a succinct account of his life, but a great deal of interesting information about his music. To these sources I beg to refer the reader for the details of Mozart's marriage and later life, assuring them that only in the life of Mendelssohn do we find equally rich musical materials.

In 1779 Mozart produced his opera, "Idomeneo," the first upon which his present fame rests. It was followed during the next ten years by "The Marriage of Figaro," "Don Juan," and "The Magic Flute," which comprise his master-pieces in this department of composition. These operas showed a marked advance over similar works of preceding composers, chiefly in their wealth of imagination and fancy, and especially in their geniality. They were in the first place *musical* to a high degree, and this in spite of the unquestionable science displayed in the concerted pieces. What was the state of music as left by Mozart's predecessors? Handel gave a clear form to melody, but we rarely find him successful in avoiding prolixity. His greatest songs are open to this charge. In the line of delicate sentiment he was also out of his element to a degree not always admitted by his admirers. He was fully successful only in a certain rude and genial energy, and in setting passages of such overpowering emotional import as to carry him beyond himself. In such airs as, "Oh, ruddier than the cherry," we find, to be sure, freshness to the last degree gratifying, yet it is not sentimental music.

Haydn, as we have already seen, developed *musical* life as such; for, in his manifold symphonies and quartettes, we find musical motives worked out in a manner at once elegant and musical, and essentially independent of words for their explanation. At the same time, Haydn was simply *genial* and *good natured* and not, in a high degree, *poetic* or imaginative, still less dramatic. His "Creation," indeed, was written after Mozart's death, and here Haydn builds on Mozart, notwithstanding that twelve or fifteen years before Mozart had built his first symphonies on Haydn's foundation.

In Mozart's operas we find the orchestra treated with a fullness greater than in the Haydn symphonies. An equally masterly working out of germinal ideas meets us here, but how changed! Mozart had rich imagination, and no small amount of the dramatic spirit. He had studied singing thoroughly, and well knew what was suitable for the voice. Still better, he knew what would please the public. And those amateurs who hold up their hands in blind worship of Mozart's operas (as some literary men do of every thing bearing the name of Shakespeare), imagining that he evolved them out of a prophetic inner consciousness, a striving after the ideal, with no consideration for the approval of the public of the day, show in this a strange ignorance of the man and his music. What is there in "Figaro," I ask, unappreciable by the Prague public of 1787? Nothing at all! Of this the best proof is that it was played *the whole Winter long* in that theater where first brought out. It is not the fate of prophetic masterpieces (music of the future) to succeed at once with the theater-going public like that.

Let it suffice for the operatic fame of Mozart to say that he first wrote melodies of matchless grace (see "*Vedrai Carino,*" in Don Juan) and the most genial and bewitching sentiment. It was the beautiful especially in its lighter aspects that Mozart came to reveal. These bewitching strains of opera, ground on hand organs, sung by amateurs, and strummed on pianos the world over, were exactly the new revelation needed to render music a household word among all enlightened people.

Mozart's indifference to all but music is further shown by his finding himself able to set such objectionable texts as "Figaro" and "Don Juan;" this, as we shall hereafter see, would have been impossible for Beethoven or Mendelssohn, or for any man of sensitive moral earnestness. Nor do I find myself able to attribute to Mozart the dramatic ability many think they find in his works. But to discuss this would take me too far. In the opera, then, we see Mozart reaching the highest triumphs of his age, namely, fascinating and individualized melodies, the loveliest instrumentation, and a high degree of dramatic contrast.

In the symphony his success was almost equally great—although he gives no foreboding of the transition from the purely musical symphony of Haydn to the tone-poem symphony of Beethoven. His great art is in the increased wealth of instrumentation he displayed, more dramatic contrast, and an incomparable elegance and fascination of style.

Mozart left a great many string quartettes, duos, etc., of the most lovely character. In this kind of composition he was eminently successful, as the instruments and the sphere of that kind of music were as well understood then as now.

His pianoforte sonatas, though much talked about in school catalogues and the like, are really old fashioned, narrow and meagre works: possessing, indeed, beautiful ideas, yet, on the whole, so far inferior to more recent productions as to convey but an extremely imperfect idea of Mozart's real powers.

Of his church writing much might be said. He left a large number of masses, nearly all composed before he was twenty, and, therefore, full of a lively spirit of cheerfulness and hope, but not characterized by the deep and reverent devotion of Bach or Handel. Mozart was not distinctively a *religious* writer, but a *worldly*. He was fond of dancing, of society, loved every beautiful woman, liked a glass of wine, and in every thing was the opposite of the ascetic, self-forgetful church composer. Still, these works contain many beautiful movements, and give another side of the richly endowed Mozart nature. The last of the so-called sacred works was the *Requiem*, written shortly before his death, under the circumstances so well known as not to require recounting here. This "Mass for the Dead" is a fitting climax to the life of the great composer.

One of the most useful services of Mozart was the addition of wind and brass parts to the score of Handel's "Messiah"—a helpful act which has undoubtedly done much to prolong the popularity of that sublime masterpiece. Mozart died on December 5, 1792, at the early age of thirty-five, worn out by hard work and too much society.

It deserves to be remembered that while this great master was endowed by God with a wealth of musical inspiration, so that in this respect no one has yet surpassed him, he found time to thoroughly study the works of his predecessors—especially of Bach, Handel, Glück and Haydn; and thought himself not above the drudgery of mastering the theoretical principles of his art; and in this way only did he contrive to leave on record such a brilliant list of beautiful creations.

PROGRAMME OF MOZART ILLUSTRATIONS.

1. (*Employing Soprano and Pianoforte*).

1. Symphony in C, "Jupiter," for 4 hands, The Piano.
2. Air, "Vedrai Carino" from "Don Juan," Soprano.
3. Air, "Voi Che Sapete" from "Figaro," Soprano.
4. *a.* March from the Magic Flute.
   b. Menuet in E flat, arranged by Schulhoff, The Pianoforte.
5. Air, "Dove Sono" from "Figaro," Soprano.
6. The Overture to "Figaro" for four hands, The Piano.

CHAPTER FORTY-SIX.

BEETHOVEN.

All our studies throughout this course have revolved around Beethoven. His works furnished a part of the illustrations of the very first lesson, and there is scarcely one of the thirty-seven practical lessons in the present course where his name does not appear. Not only is this the greatest name in Music, but it is one of the greatest that has appeared in Art. When men think of the grace and refinement and incomparable beauty of his work, they call him the Raphael of music, although such a title by right should belong to Mozart. When they listen to the Heroic Symphony or the Mass in D minor, they call him the Michael Angelo, or the Milton of music. But both these are misnomers. Others call him the Dante of the tone-art, or the Shakespeare. These, also, are unfruitful suggestions. There *is* no Shakespeare in music, nor can be; the arts are too dissimilar. For the same reason there is no Raphael, nor Tintoret, nor Angelo in tones. Mozart had a grace and sweetness equal to that of Raphael's. But besides these qualities there is in Mozart's work a simplicity and unaffected naivete peculiar to him. The grandeur and seriousness of Milton exist in music also, and in greater measure, but without the labored and somewhat pedantic form of Milton's phraseology.

What we do have in Beethoven is a genius of as pure a ray as the world has ever seen. He was not technically the most scientific of great composers. Bach, Handel, Haydn and even the genial and spontaneous Mozart, wrote smoother counterpoint, and traveled more easily within the lines of fugue. Yet Beethoven knew *Music* better than any of these, and left works which out-rank theirs in every direction except that of purely formal phraseology. What was it then, in which Beethoven excelled? And wherein lies the secret of the estimation in which he is held by the whole civilized world?

Beethoven's greatness as a composer, and his influence upon the development of music since his day, lies in one point, namely, his intuition of the *relation of music to emotion*. As already pointed out, Bach wrote more learnedly, Handel, at times, quite as heartily, Haydn as clearly, and Mozart as sweetly; but what Beethoven does is to avail himself of all these excellencies of form and substance, *in order to express feeling through them*. The greatest of his predecessors, Bach, also had feeling and expressed it in his Passion Music with great power. But his style is not easy, the phraseology is too learned. It seems to us cold. The composers after him relapsed his severity, as we have seen. Through Handel, the sons of Bach, Haydn, and Mozart — the World and Art were drawing nearer each other. In Beethoven they coalesce. And so it is the proud pre-eminence of this Master to have expressed his soul in music as fully and as exclusively as Shakespeare expressed his in his plays, or Raphael in his cartoons, and with such force and range of imagination, and such exquisite propriety of diction, that all the world immediately listens to him. Like all these geniuses of the very highest rank, his soul is in his works. His daily life is nothing. He is never a citizen, magistrate, a teacher, a writer, a talker, or a man of property; but always and only a creative Artist. In early life he was, indeed, a virtuoso, not through study and drudgery, but by sheer force of the overmastering inspiration within him.

The world used him, how shall we say? Well, or badly? If we reflect upon his humble origin, his steady elevation during his lifetime into the highest estimation ever accorded a musician and composer, his comparative immunity from want or the necessity of drudging toil either in teaching or playing, and this through the ready sale of the productions of his pen—we must say *well*. On the other hand, if we think of his lack of education or early training, his solitary life, his graceless nephew, his deafness and his suspicious and difficult habit of mind,—in these we recognize the unfavorable side of his relation to the world; and when we think that all this befell one whose creations have added delight and beauty to the daily lives, not only of his contemporaries and compatriots, but to that of the whole civilized world in three generations, we can not help perceiving here a certain dissonance the resolution of which we are not able to trace.

It is our difficult task, therefore, to outline the life of this man, to describe his surroundings and personal peculiarities, and to trace his mode of outward life, so as to bring him before our minds in some resemblance to the form he wore in the eyes of his neighbors and friends; and yet along with this, to trace, in his works, the transcendently beautiful operations of his mind and inner nature, and to hold them up as the true expression of the Beethoven soul, which they most certainly were. If in doing this we might also unite both pictures into one, so that we could think of Beethoven as a humbly-born, hardworking boy, of the most determined "grit," yet with a delicacy and sweetness of fancy which is absolutely nobler than even Shakespeare's (for Beethoven nowhere descends to coarseness), and then trace his growth to manhood, his steady pursuit of his one ideal, Music, the blessing that followed him in it, and that has followed us for his being in it; and crown the whole with the still nobler side of his nature in his unselfish and well-meant love and providence for a graceless relative, when he himself was, as we ordinarily say, "a crusty old bachelor" of fifty;—if we could bring all these together into a single consistent idea we should then have performed for the reader a service indeed.

Ludwig van Beethoven was born at Bonn, the *Residenz-Stadt* of the Electors of Cologne, in 1770. His father was tenor singer in the Elector's Chapel, an ill-natured, drunken fellow with a shiftless, easygoing wife. They lived in a very humble way, the annual income of the family being probably less than three hundred dollars. As Mozart was just then at the height of his celebrity, the father of our Beethoven was in no small degree delighted to observe the promising musical talent of the boy—a talent which manifested itself at a very early age. There was music in the family, unquestionably—Beethoven's grandfather having been an organist and a composer of creditable talent. So at the early age of five he was taken in hand by his father and set to work in the laborious German fashion to learn to play the piano and the violin. The crusty father is said to have pulled him out of bed in the middle of the night, to make him finish up the practice he had neglected. Nor was the practice sweetened for him; for the boy was not allowed to play melodies, many of which came to him even then untaught, but only the exercises then most approved for practice.

At that time the works of Bach held high honor for purposes of study, and the boy Beethoven was so thoroughly exercised in them that at the age of twelve he was perfectly familiar with the entire forty-eight preludes and fugues of the "Well Tempered Clavier," and could play them with the utmost facility. All this time he went to the public school, but owing to his father's ambition to bring him out as a musical wonder-child, his studies in letters were seriously neglected. When the boy was about eight years old his father turned him over to the teaching of one Pfeiffer, an oboe player and pianist, under whose kindlier direction he got along more rapidly and no doubt much more pleasantly. Presently the organist Neefe took him in hand and taught him the organ and composition, so that when twelve or thirteen years old he appears as author of three sonatas for piano, which are small, but very clever for a boy.

For some time, probably since his tenth year, he had played a viola in the orchestra. About this time he became assistant organist to Neefe, although the formal appointment was not received until he was about fifteen. When he was about thirteen, he began to act as pianist and assistant director in the orchestra during Neefe's absence, which frequently extended over several months. The duties of this position were not small. High Mass was performed in church three times a week besides Sunday, and on at least as many days there were elaborate vesper services. The theater gave a light opera or operetta three times a week, and comedies on other nights, for all of which music had to be prepared. This kind of activity seems to have continued until Beethoven was about twenty, interrupted only by his first visit to Vienna, where he somehow managed to go when he was about sixteen. Beethoven's duties as organist must have been very unthankful, since the old organ had been removed from the chapel, and in his time only a small chamber-organ stood in its place. That he had no special vocation for the organ appears plainly from his never having written anything for it. The particulars of his Vienna journey are rather hypothetical, especially the anecdote of his having played before Mozart and receiving lessons from him.

During all these years he attained no recognition in Bonn as a promising artist. On the several lists of the Elector's musical staff, the name of Beethoven figures as organist and player of clavier concertos, but amid many who are distinguished as of exceptional talent, he stands unnoticed and undistinguished.

The theater at Bonn produced a fine selection of works for that day, among which were the best of Glück's operas. On the whole we can hardly imagine a place better calculated to familiarize a young composer with every slightest peculiarity of the composers before his day, than Beethoven found in his six years' service as assistant director at Bonn. In the work of arranging and adapting the scores to the limitations and weaknesses of his orchestra, he could not fail to acquire rare tact, and a spontaneous comprehension of all effects of instrumentation. He played the piano part from the full orchestra score, and it was thus that he developed that lightning-like comprehension of the fullest scores, which he always manifested. Mendel says that Max Franz (the Elector, brother of Joseph II) when he appointed Beethoven second organist furnished funds for him to go to Vienna to make more extended studies.

During this Bonn life Beethoven early attracted the attention of the von Breunings, a wealthy and refined family of that town, and at their house he was always at home. No doubt it must have required a good deal of faith in the diamond concealed in his rough exterior, for the fine von Breunings to have made so much of so unpromising a customer as the boy Beethoven. He was moody, often irritable. He was the very prince of awkwardness, upsetting and breaking every fragile article he came near. Still there seems to have been a charm about him, for as we shall see later, he was through life a favorite among the best people, especially the ladies, of an elegant and ceremonious court. Here at the Breunings' he became familiar with the books and pictures denied him at home. Count Waldstein, also, was one of the friends he made in this early time, and who always remained true to him. It was Waldstein who recommended him to the notice of the titled relatives of his family when Beethoven came to Vienna to live; and it was to Count Waldstein that in 1803 the brilliant sonata in C, op. 53, was dedicated.

In personal appearance Beethoven must have been rather striking. He was of medium height (or rather under), thickset, a noble forehead, small, brown eyes, deeply set in, very profuse hair, generally "towseled," his dress of rather common texture originally, but now rich with the sedimentary deposits of many brushless months. His hands are well shaped, but the nails are not well kept. In movement he is quick and abrupt, often boorish. This want of politeness adhered to him through life. Still, it was his lot to associate with many eminent men, and from them he doubtless imbibed a great deal of cultivation. His manners must have been worse about the time of his departure from Bonn and first entrance into Vienna than afterwards.

As to his self-conceit, all testimony proves it. Nor is it difficult to account for it. It must have been perfectly apparent to Beethoven that he was able to improvise music of such rare power over the feelings that nothing of Haydn's or Mozart's or Handel's could be compared with it. We read remarkable stories of this faculty. As, for instance: "Ignace Pleyel had brought some new quartettes to Vienna, which were performed at the house of Prince Lobkowitz. At the close, Beethoven, who was present, was asked to play. As usual, he had to be pressed again and again, and at last was almost dragged by force to the instrument by the ladies. With an impatient gesture he snatched from the violin desk the open second violin part of Pleyel's quartette, threw it on the desk of the pianoforte and began to improvise. His playing had never been more brilliant, original and grand than on that evening. But through the whole improvisation, in the middle parts ran like a thread or *canto fermo* the notes, unimportant in themselves, of the accidentally open page, on which he built the noblest melodies and harmonies in the most brilliant concert style. Old Pleyel could only show his astonishment by kissing his hands. After such improvisation Beethoven would break out into a loud, merry, ringing laugh."

This is the spirit of his first entrance upon the Vienna life in 1792. Here he lived until his death, in 1827. At first he was the pupil of Haydn, who since Mozart's death, was king again. For these lessons his fee was exactly eight groschen, *eighteen cents!* Later he went to Albrechtsberger for lessons in counterpoint, and to Salieri for lessons in dramatic composition.

As early as 1800 he began to be hard of hearing, gradually increasing to almost total deafness as early as 1810. This affliction, as well as the false behavior of his two brothers, his nearest relatives, had the effect to cloud his mind with suspicion of all the people around him. In the period from 1792 to 1810, he produced a constant succession of the noblest works. Before he had got beyond the fifth symphony the critics had begun to talk of his "obscurity," "want of melody," etc., just as they did a few years ago of Schumann, and just as they do now of Wagner. Yet, he seems to have cared very little about it, and said that if it amused them to be constantly writing such things about him they might be freely indulged.

His personal habits were whimsical enough. One lodging was too high; another he left because the landlord was too obsequious. He would walk his room half the night through, " howling and roaring" the melodies that filled his imagination, and flooding the floor and ruining the ceiling and tempers of the occupants of the rooms below with the water he poured over his hands to cool his feverishness. He would hire a boy to pump water over his hands by the hour together. It is related *apropos* to his carelessness in money matters that "the waiters in the *cafés* in Vienna were content to be unpaid sometimes, if they were paid double and treble the next day. It was not worth while to quarrel with a privileged person, who always had the laugh on his side, and had been known to throw a dish of meat at the head of a waiter suspected of cheating. Here, after the close of his day's labor, he appeared at his best, and those who knew him speak of his loud laughter, his richness and originality of conversation, his wit, bold and reckless as his harmonies, his strong opinions, his interest in books and politics. On all hands we see the signs of the broad and wholesome humanity which formed the ground of his strangely mingled character, so much caricatured and so little understood by the retailers of anecdote, who can see in Beethoven nothing but an inspired artist, and a mixture of misanthropy and buffoon."* "To his friends he was a warm hearted, unselfish friend, not to be treated carelessly, much less to be played with or slighted; a friend whose friendship was worth a sacrifice, because it was founded on perfect sincerity, could endure no suspicion of insincerity in others. That Beethoven—great Mogul as he was, and capable of many unmannerly words and actions—was not unacceptable to those who loved good society, we may learn from the fact of his having always been well received by the great ladies of a ceremonious court. It was true that his dress was untidy to dirtiness; that he picked his teeth with the snuffers, upset inkstands into the pianoforte, and broke every thing he touched; and that he had been known to play off ill-bred practical jokes on some of his friends; but in spite of all incongruities, princesses and countesses—nay, personages of still higher rank—received him as an equal or a superior This result could hardly have been brought about by his music alone."†

From 1800 to 1806 Beethoven was in the height of his creative activity. During this time he produced the sonatas opus 22 to 57, the third and fourth symphonies, a number of chamber pieces (quartettes, trios, etc.), and the opera "Fidelio." This creative activity continued, with little falling off in speed, and with a decided progress in the quality of the work produced, down to 1815, by which time he had written all the nine symphonies except the last. These years were especially productive in smaller works—such as songs, bagatelles of various kinds, three sets of Scotch and Irish airs, arranged with ritornellos and accompaniments.

Beethoven was now forty-five years of age. He was in ill health, probably for want of proper care of himself. He was overrun with commissions from publishers, and had the most flattering offers to travel in different countries, of which, however, he was too fond of Vienna and too ignorant of the world to take advantage. At this period misfortune befell him, in the shape of a nephew—the son of his brother Carl—left in his guardianship. As already shown, there were undesirable streaks in the Beethoven family. This had not been mended by Carl's marrying a shiftless woman, of bad repute, and it was the product of this union that was left in the composer's care. He undertook the task in the loftiest spirit. Henceforth for eleven years the boy regulated all the affairs of Beethoven's

*"Lives and Letters of Beethoven."—*Edinburg Review*, Oct., 1853. †Ibid.

menage, and a most thankless time the old gentleman had of it. The very worst housekeeping bachelor that ever was was a prince of managers compared with Beethoven. He had not the slightest "faculty" for business. It discomposed him to be obliged to transact the most ordinary affairs. We may well imagine what a time he had of it with a reckless, ungrateful youth on his hands. His love was repaid with ingratitude, and, to crown all, the nephew seems to have been responsible for his uncle's death; for, when sent for a doctor, he carelessly gave the message to a billiard marker, who forgot it for a day or two, and when the doctor arrived there was no longer a possibility of cure.

These last years of Beethoven are sad in the extreme. That a man should have had so much greatness, yet so little comfort! That his inner world should have been so full of lovely fancies, which he has left on record for the gratification of aftercoming generations, and yet his own daily life have been so unblessed by woman's tenderness, and the amenities of home, is one of the mysteries of life. Yet we may be glad that Beethoven undertook the care of this boy, and stuck to it so manfully; for his letters and the whole history of this time place his character in a much nobler light of self-sacrifice than would otherwise have been the case. And as to the works we might else have had from this period, our composer has already left the highest monument so far in the world of music. Surely it is better for us to know that he was a noble-hearted, true man, than for us to have had another symphony. Besides, there is no doubt that this discipline, painful as it was, must have wrought a great softening and deepening in Beethoven's disposition.

In 1825 he imagined himself in poverty. Moscheles, who was then in London, wrote to him, and arranged for the London Philharmonic Society to give a concert for his benefit, in return for which he was to write them a tenth symphony. This concert was given and a sum of £100 made up and sent to Beethoven a short time before he died. The whole correspondence may be found in Moscheles' edition of "Schindler's Life of Beethoven," and in Moscheles' "Recent Music and Musicians."

Beethoven died March 29, 1827, at the age of fifty-seven, during a violent thunderstorm. He was buried at Wahring, a small village near Vienna, and was followed to the grave by an immense concourse of people (over twenty thousand, some say).

Beethoven's genius was distinctly that for expressing feeling. Feeling is the source of the all-penetrating unity, which is perhaps one of the most conspicuous marks of his work. We do not mean by this that he is always in a passion, or under the influence of some dark or disturbing mood. Far from it. The genius of his music is characteristically the *peaceful*, the *tranquil*. In these qualities he is hardly surpassed by Mozart. It is the unity and the repose of the great, the lasting, the true. Beethoven was extremely fond of the open air and the country. When the weather was fine he would spend whole days and half the nights wandering about the fields or stretched at ease in the shade of a tree. In these walks his eye was quick to notice every pleasant bit of landscape, every pretty flower, or effect of light, and if he had a companion, he remarked upon these things with warmth and force.

Such beauty and quiet took musical shape within him. Out came the memorandum book of music-paper roughly stitched together, and the walk and discourse gave place to that curious "howling and roaring" with which his labor of composition was always accompanied. His published works are full of ideas which may be traced sometimes for years, through wide and strange changes from the forms in which they at first suggested themselves to him to the shape in which they were at last employed. Those tranquil days under the pleasant sky are all expressed in his music. Of such a spirit are the pianoforte sonatas in E and G, op. 14, the "pastoral," op. 28, that in G, op. 31, and several of those for piano and violin, as well as the pastoral symphony, and the seventh and eighth. In deriving his inspiration from external nature as a source, Beethoven was like Schubert, in whom every movement of soul translates itself into tones. With Beethoven there is, however, this difference, that he selects the more significant for publication, and then shapes and prunes it with more care. Beethoven is never too long; certainly never tedious.

Another of the most remarkable peculiarities of Beethoven's music is the clearness and beauty of his orchestral coloring. No other composer knows better just where to throw in a few notes of the flute, a soft low tone of the horn, a clever bit of the bassoon, or just how to place a subordinate phrase in order to have it express itself without interfering with the blending and harmony of the whole. This delicious reserve is one of the most eminent traits of the symphonies, although no doubt, a part of it is apparent only, and due to the remarkable heightening and strengthening of orchestral coloring since his day.

Were we to attempt to measure up and estimate the place of these works on the scale of beauty, we should be first struck with their elegance, clearness and the agreeable nature of their sound. They have for pleasure of sensation all that they could have and still retain their distinguishing elevation of sentiment. In formal beauty, likewise, they hold an extremely high rank, perhaps as high as any. There is in Mozart a certain sweet and spontaneous grace, an unconscious sweetness, such as we rarely find in Beethoven; but Beethoven compensates for this lack, if lack there be, by a greater coherence and unity, through which he reaches a more serene repose, especially in the classical moments of his art.

And then, finally, we come to the symphonies. These are the thoughts Beethoven had while he lay under the trees out in the country. Far on into the night he would wander, and drink in his fill of the silent teaching of nature. Here in the symphonies we have them all. If in the pastoral symphony we have a moment of pleasantry in the bird song or two, it is thrown in only to bring us still nearer the inscrutable mystery of the growing grass; nearer to the trees, by their subtle chemistry building themselves up out of intangible air and the hidden riches of the ground; nearer to the light and fleecy clouds, and the golden and crimson sunset, fitly emphasizing the finished day, ever more to be numbered with the infinite ages of God; and, above all, nearer to the greater mystery of thoughtful life, the image of the Invisible, the sure witness of the Infinite. No other instrumental music so completely seizes and exalts the hearer.

The inner nature of Beethoven allies him to Bach. They were both *universal* musicians, innovators and experimenters in every direction, according to the light and resources of their respective generations. Both found in a particular style and form, a field which, on the whole, satisfied them and afforded room for the elaboration of their most beautiful ideas. Bach's was the fugue. There was no kind of musical production known to Bach's day which he did not to some extent try, except, perhaps, the opera. The suite, church pieces, organ works, and compositions for violin and almost every instrument, he produced in large quantities. But, after all, the one form which he always adopted, or came back to for a climax, was *fugue*. This great form, the *ne plus ultra* of musical logic, was not original with Bach. On the contrary it had been worked out by three centuries of experimenters and geniuses, until it assumed the form in which Bach found it, and in which it is in effect the valid and final solution of coherent tonality. Counterpoint, which is the basis of fugue, is the exhaustive solution of melodic invention. Bach's work was to seize this form and appropriate it to the needs of musical revelation. He filled it full of novelty, grandeur, caprice, humor, true musical feeling and beauty.

He exhausted it, completely filled up the capacity of the form, so that since Bach there is no longer any thing new to be said in Fugue.

In like manner Beethoven was a composer of sonatas. The *rôle* of his works embraces every kind of production known in his day; but the one form which he made his own, and in which his most beautiful and characteristic ideas are expressed, is the sonata. This form includes his thirty-three for piano solo, which would eternally have established his fame if they alone had constituted his serious works; nineteen sonatas for piano and other instruments; eighteen trios, mainly for piano and other instruments; twenty-three quartettes and quintettes; the sextette and septette, and the nine symphonies. In all, more than three thousand large pages of sonata writing. Beethoven, like Bach, was in every way progressive and an innovator. He experimented in all forms, and in all combinations of means of expression. Yet, on the whole, he was a composer of sonatas.

This form he found ready to his hand in the works of Haydn and Mozart. The form, as such, he accepted with little improvement. But he put into it such a wealth and many-sided possibility of expression as surpassed their efforts in every direction, and amounted finally to completely exhausting the subject. There have been, really, no genuine composers of sonatas since Beethoven. Every great master has tried it out of deference to public opinion, but the chief ideas and distinctive excellencies of all composers since Beethoven are expressed in other forms and not in the sonata. Even in symphony, where they have enjoyed the inestimable advantages of modern wealth in instrumentation, no one has been able to create works at all equal to his, or even such as add any thing essentially new and important to what he has said.

Again, Bach and Beethoven were both of them characteristically instrumental composers. Although both have written works employing the human voice in solo, ensemble and in great masses, and have therein reached the most sublime heights yet attained in musical creation, they have in all cases treated the voice like an instrument, and with almost total disregard of the conditions of its agreeable and pleasing exercise. This limitation, of course, is a detraction from their success, for if they were to use the voice at all, there was no valid reason why its convenience and inherent capacity should not be as much regarded as that of any other instrument. Bach and Beethoven are both of them exponents of the *inner* in music. While they both reach the highest mark of formal beauty, they do so accidentally, so to say; as an incidental result of the spontaneous expression of the inner and spiritual.

'Beethoven marks a giant stride in musical progress since Bach, in the direction of the humoristic. Bach himself was full of this spirit, and of playful phantasy, as all his works show. But the new forms developed or perfected by Haydn and Mozart, and the lessons taught by their disregard of scholastic tradition, and especially the vigorous flight of his own all-comprehending and untamed spirit, enabled Beethoven to go vastly farther than Bach in this direction, and to reveal music in its true nature as spontaneous expression of heart, feeling, and imagination. And thus he not only concentrated in himself and fulfilled all the tendencies and prophecies of musical history before him, and enriched the world with some of the most precious and immortal productions of the human spirit, but afforded in turn the most pregnant tokens of possibilities in music yet unrevealed — indications of new paths, which the great masters since have occupied themselves in exploring.

List of Beethoven Illustrations.

1. (*Moderately Difficult, Employing the Pianoforte and Tenor.*)

1. Sonata in G, op. 14, No. 2.
2. Menuet in E flat out of Sonata op. 31, No. 3.
3. Scherzo in C, out of Sonata op. 2, No. 3
4. "Adelaide." Tenor.
5. " Nicht zu Geschwind," out of Sonata in E, op. 90.
6. Rondo in G, op. 51, No. 2.

2. *Difficult.*

1. Sonata Appassionata, op. 57.
2. Air and Variations in A flat, op. 26.
3. "Adelaide." Tenor.
4. Sonata in A flat, op. 110.
5. Rondo Capriccioso, op. 129.

CHAPTER FORTY-SEVEN.

MENDELSSOHN.

Felix Mendelssohn was born in Hamburg, February 3, 1809. He was the son of Abraham Mendelssohn, a banker, a man of very refined tastes, and grandson of Moses Mendelssohn, the eminent Rabbi and philosopher. The name Bartholdy was his mother's, and was taken later in life as a condition of some property inheritance. Felix was the second of four children, of whom Fanny, the eldest, manifested the most remarkable talents in music. When Felix was only three or four years old the family removed to Berlin. At the age of eight he already played the piano well. The theorist Zelter was his teacher in composition, and Berger in piano playing. When only twelve he was pronounced by Zelter his best scholar. In 1824 Zelter wrote to Goethe: " Yesterday evening Felix's fourth opera was brought out here in a little circle of us, with the dialogue. There are three acts, which, with two ballets, occupied about two hours and and a half. The work was received with much applause. I can hardly master my own wonder how the boy, who is only about fifteen, has made such progress. Everywhere you find what is new, beautiful and peculiar — wholly peculiar."

In the year 1824 he became the piano pupil of Moscheles, and so began the long and delightful intimacy, which, like a golden thread, runs through the volumes of Mendelssohn's charming letters and Moscheles' " Recent Music and Musicians."

In 1829 Mendelssohn started to visit London. He made a long tour through many places of interest, especially in Italy, before he reached England. Among the new pieces he brought to show Moscheles, were his overture to " Fingal's Cave," " Walpurgis Night," and his G minor concerto for piano-forte and orchestra. In London, Mendelssohn was rapturously received. His organ playing excited the greatest astonishment, and remains to the present day a bright tradition with English musicians. Yet it is but fair to say that the opinion there held of his organ playing was by no means shared by the best authorities in Germany. There is very good reason for believing that his pedal technic was by no means superior, however charming his manipulation and registration may have been. Be this as it may, he undoubtedly gave a decided impetus to English organ playing, especially to the study of Bach.

Mendelssohn came to Leipsic in 1835, and remained there all but one year of the rest of his life. He assumed direction of the Gewandhaus concerts, which, henceforth, reached a delicacy unknown to them before. The oratorio of "St. Paul" was written for the Lower Rhine Musical Festival, held at Düsseldorf in 1836. It excited the highest enthusiasm.

In the Spring of 1837 Mendelssohn was married to Miss Cecilia Jeanrenaud, of Dresden, a daughter of a clergyman, with whom he lived very happily until his death.

"St. Paul" was brought out at the Birmingham festival, in 1838, where it at once took a high place. Three of his psalms, "As the Hart Pants," "O Come let us Sing," and the one hundred and fifteenth were the product of this period.

In 1843 the Leipsic Conservatory was opened with about sixty pupils. The teachers were Mendelssohn, Schumann (piano), David (violin), and Becker (organ). Other teachers were soon added. This renowned institution seems to have been chiefly the creation of Mendelssohn's brain, and to him it owes its character. It has turned out a vast number of pupils, all more or less well grounded in music. No school has had greater influence in this country. There is one drawback to the association of a man like Mendelssohn with such a school, namely: that after he leaves it his charming manner and peculiar ideas become the ideal which places subsequent directors, however talented, at a disadvantage. There is some reason to believe that the Leipsic school has not been entirely free from this failing. One good point about this school must not be overlooked: that there they always hold *content* for the first merit of a work. This, in a town enriched by the labors of Bach, and Mendelssohn, and Schumann, is what we might expect.

Space does not permit to follow closely Mendelssohn's subsequent career. It embraced a year's residence in Berlin, frequent visits to England, where he brought out "Elijah," in 1846, as well as constant appearances throughout Germany, as director, composer and pianist. His life was a ceaseless round of activity, and it is little wonder that the delicate frame wore out. He died in Leipsic, November 4, 1847.

In personal appearance Mendelssohn was rather under the medium size, graceful in walk and bearing. His forehead was high and arched, his nose delicate, slightly Roman; his mouth fine and firm, and his head covered with glossy, black, curly hair. His countenance was very expressive, and his whole manner fascinating in the extreme. He was the idol of men and women alike in every circle where he moved. He inherited large means, which he freely dispensed in the most delicate and unostentatious charities. His entire independence of the need of labor for sustenance gave no slackening to his ardor in composition. In my opinion, Mendelssohn's chief characteristics must have been his genial fancy, his exquisite taste and kind heartedness. In his charming letters from Italy and Switzerland we have these qualities fully exhibited. Two more delightful books than those of his letters do not adorn literature. The same qualities shine out in his music. Everywhere we meet a romantic and delicate fancy, a sprightfulness and ever-present sense of the beautiful, which carries us back to Mozart.

As a composer Mendelssohn built on Bach. By this I mean that Bach stood to him as a model of true greatness in music. It was not possible for such a nature as Mendelssohn's to emulate the lofty repose of Bach's greatest things. Still everywhere in his serious moments we find the traces of the influence of the sober old Leipsic cantor.

Mendelssohn's greatness as a composer lies in his oratorios and psalms. Brendel regards these as no longer *religious* works, strictly speaking, but as "concert oratorios," in which he thinks the worldly element comes forth. In this he is right to a certain extent. Handel's "Messiah" does not manifest this worldly spirit, because the subject forbade it. In the first place, this spirit manifests itself in a lingering over details, such as beautiful tone effects of one sort or another (just as the ribbon, the ornament, or other little piquancy of dress, betray a woman's instinct for being admired), and, for this sort of thing, the haste in which Handel wrote the "Messiah" left him no time. Besides, as I have before said, the text of the "Messiah" inspired in him an elevation of sentiment to which he was commonly a stranger. Moreover, the worldly element in music was then in its infancy. The foundation of it was there, namely, the taste of the public. The "Messiah," and all of Handel's oratorios were written for the concert, and not for religious use. In this he differs from Bach, who had nothing to consult but his own ideal. His pieces were written for church and played in church. Religious worship was their inspiration. It is the absence of the influence of the public that permits Bach's unquestionable prolixity, which, in our day, seems tediousness.

It is in "Elijah" that Mendelssohn most fully moves the public. The dramatic story, the picturesque contrasts, the richness and taste of its orchestration, its novel and fascinating choruses, and especially the beauty and graphic appropriateness of his melodies, give this oratorio a wonderful charm. One should read Mr. Dwight's glowing description of it, found at the end of Lampadius' Life of Mendelssohn. I confess that there is hardly a tedious moment to me in this lovely work. From the first recitative, "Thus saith the Lord," through the entire work, I find the rarest appreciation of beauty, and the rarest truth to the words. How overpowering the choruses, "Thanks be to God," and "Be not Afraid;" how sweet and lovely "He, watching over Israel;" how graphic the recitative where fire descends; how mighty the contrast in the quartette and chorus, "Holy, Holy, Holy, is God the Lord!"

In this oratorio Mendelssohn seems to have reached the acme of taste in the compromise he has effected between the religions and the merely beautiful. This same admirable taste manifests itself also in the psalms. Take, for instance, the "Hear my Prayer." Here we have a solo, "Hear my Prayer," the excited chorus, "The Enemy shouteth," and, finally, the altogether unique solo and chorus *obligato*, "Oh, for the Wings of a Dove!" Nothing could be more beautiful.

In his piano forte music, especially the "Songs Without Words" we have the same loveliness of fancy and sentiment. These are works which all tasteful people admire. The larger pieces no longer hold the position in the estimation of musicians they once did, although it would be impossible to find two more lovely pieces for ladies' performance than the "Rondo Capriccioso" and "Capriccio in B minor."

It is further in proof of the ruling quality of Mendelssohn's mind that the *scherzo* is his most perfect triumph. There we have a fairy-like playfulness truly exquisite and altogether *unique*. The "six organ sonatas" were made up for the English market. They have marked beauties and are ecclesiastical in tone; and, in spite of their peculiar "sonata" form, I hold them in high estimation. Besides, there was a justification for this irregularity (which, perhaps, I ought to explain, consists of their having but two movements in place of the usual four), in the congeniality of their spirit to religious service, and especially the benediction like effect of the soft and songful *andantes* forming their conclusions. In quartettes, quintettes and symphonies, Mendelssohn was also extremely successful, but it may be questioned whether he ever surpassed his lovely overture to the "Midsummer Night's Dream," the work of his boyhood.

LIST OF MENDELSSOHN ILLUSTRATIONS.

(*Employing a Soprano, Alto, and the Pianoforte.*)

1. Overture to the Midsummer Night's Dream (for four hands).
2. "On Wings of Music," Tenor (or Soprano).

3. Rondo Capriccioso.
4. "Jerusalem, Thou that Killest the Prophets," Soprano.
5. *a.* Hunting Song (No. 3).
   b. People's Song (No. 4).
   c. Spring Song (No. 27).
6. "O! Rest in the Lord," Alto.
7. " Duetto " (No. 18 in Songs without Words).
8. Duet, "Would that my Love," Soprano and Alto.
9. Finale from " Italian " Symphony, (four hands) Pianoforte.

CHAPTER FORTY-EIGHT.

CHOPIN.

Frederic Chopin was born at Zela-zola-Wola, near Warsaw, March 1, 1809, and died at Paris, October 17, 1849. Within these forty years were bound up the activities of one of the most remarkable spirits in music. In Chopin we have another example of precocious talent, such as are seen in Mozart, Schubert, and Liszt. At the age of nine he played in public a concerto by Gyrowetz, and improvised. His studies were begun under the direction of Ziwna, a passionate admirer of Sebastian Bach, and carried on later under Joseph Elsner, principal of the Conservatory of Warsaw. The records of Chopin's early life are extremely meagre. We know that he was then a fluent Bach player, to whom through life he remained devoted. We are also sure that even as early as sixteen he must have been a great virtuoso, not only equal to every thing that had been planned for the piano before his time, but already the author of the completely new methods indicated in the excessively difficult variations on *La ci darem la mano*, the first nocturnes, op 9, the early mazurkas and waltzes, and especially the great studies op. 10 and the two concertos. These studies have passed into the standard repertory of advanced piano-playing, and the two concertos, although weak in orchestral handling, are extremely brilliant and poetic for the piano, and have the great merit of complete novelty and freshness of style.

With these great compositions already finished, as well as many others of a character more immediately available, he set out for Vienna, Paris, and London, at the age of nineteen. He reached Paris, and there met Liszt, with whom he formed a devoted friendship. Here

Chopin found a congenial public. He was of a shy and delicate nature, proud, yet somewhat effeminate, and public appearance was distasteful to him. In manners cultivated and refined, and quick of intellect, Chopin immediately became the center of a considerable circle of artistic people, who esteemed him no less for his personal qualities than his remarkable musical gifts. He was overrun with pupils, of whom, however, he would take but a small number. In 1837 the lung disease, with which he had been threatened since childhood, developed itself. In company with his devoted friend, M'me Geo. Sand, to whom he had been introduced by Liszt, he resided at the island of Majorca for several years. Deceived by a show of returning health he came back to Paris, and, as already recorded, died at the age of Raphael and Mozart.

Chopin's music is not the *universal* music of the German composers, nor is it the humoristic music of the romantic school, although with both these it has something in common. It is a contradiction. He is wild, passionate, capricious, yet always graceful, subtle, refined, and delicate. Nothing could be less like Bach's music, yet it has much in common with it. Chopin's genius is especially for the piano. All the grace and elegant manner of modern virtuoso piano-playing come from him. Yet the inner life, the musical feeling which is the determining cause of this grace and refinement, comes rather from Schumann. Chopin was an innovator for piano in his matter and manner. He gave depth to the nocturne; enlarged the poetic range of the piano by his Polonaises, Scherzos, Impromptus, Ballades, and Etudes. His passages are new, ingenious and beautiful. Like Schumann he writes mainly for the pianoforte. Unlike him, he does so in a manner which completely harmonizes with the nature of the instrument, and, indeed, foresaw its latest improvements. Hence we find in Chopin's works the well-sounding always considered. Nevertheless they are not reposeful. Although the themes are fully developed, the harmonic structure and the rhythmic organization of these pieces gives them a character of restlessness and dissatisfaction. By so much they fall short of great art. In all of them it is rather the manner of saying which charms, than the actual idea itself. Psychologically considered they are unhealthy. There runs through them a vein of sadness and morbid feeling which renders them too exciting for the weak and nervous. Their most conspicuous external quality is the subtlety, the evanescence, of their harmonies. It is this which makes Chopin's music so difficult to remember. Its technical novelty was partly in a new and freer use of the pedal, and the effective employment of extended chords, and partly in better sustained and more brilliant passages, especially those constructed on the diminished seventh. As to its metrical structure, Chopin's music is lyric. His period-lengths are remarkably uniform, as compared with those of Beethoven or Schumann. The other qualities of his music appear best in the actual illustrations.

List of Chopin Illustrations.

1. *Moderately Difficult.*

1. Polonaise in C sharp min., op. 27.
2. Valse in D flat maj., op. 64.
3. Nocturne in E flat, op. 9.
4. Impromptu in A. flat, op. 29.
5. Prelude in D flat.
6. Valse in E flat, op. 18.
7. Nocturne in G min., op. 37.
8. Polonaise Militaire in A, op. 40.

2. *Difficult.*

1. Etudes out of op. 10, No. 8 in F, No 5 on the black keys, and No 12 for the left hand.
2. Nocturne in C min., op 48, or in G maj , op. 37.
3. Fantasie Impromptu in C sharp, op 66.
4. Andante Spianato and Polonaise in E flat, op 22.
5. Prelude in D flat.
6. Ballade in A. flat, op. 47.

CHAPTER FORTY-NINE.

ROBERT SCHUMANN

Robert Schumann was born in Zwickau, in Saxony, June 8, 1810. His father was a bookseller and publisher, a man full of energy and circumspection, and of decided literary tastes and ability. The boy was sent to school and began to learn music at an early stage. As early as the age of seven or eight he wrote some little dances, although ignorant of the rules of harmony. It is said that even then he was fond of sketching in music the peculiarities of his friends, and did this "so exactly and comically that every one burst into loud laughter at the similitude of the portrait." Schumann was scarcely nine years old when his father took him to hear Ignatz Moscheles, the famous pianist, whose playing made the most profound impression upon him. At the age of ten he entered the academy, and here formed a companionship with a boy about his own age, with whom he played many of the works of Haydn and Mozart, arranged for four hands. His father evidently encouraged his love for music, and gratified him with a fine piano and plenty of new music.

Presently the boys came across the orchestral parts of Righini's overture to "Tigranes," and forthwith mustered their forces for performance. They had two violins, two flutes, a clarionet, and two horns. Robert directed and undertook to supply the missing parts upon the piano. Their success encouraged them to undertake other tasks of a similar kind, which, also, Robert directed. He also set to music the one hundred and fiftieth psalm for chorus and orchestra, and this was given by the same performers, assisted by a chorus of such boys as could sing. In all these and such like exercises, the father recognized the plain indication of Providence that the son was intended for a musician, nor was he disposed to thwart the design. The mother, however, had a poor idea of the musical profession, and thought only of the hardships it carried with it.

As a boy Robert was full of tricks and sports. But at the age of fourteen a change came over him, and he became more reserved and prone to revery. This habit never forsook him through life. It was, perhaps, increased by the death of his appreciative and kind-hearted father, which took place in 1826, when Robert was but sixteen. In deference to his mother's wishes he matriculated at Leipsic as a law student in 1828.

Through his father's example he had already made the acquaintance of Byron's poems. He now became infected with a perfect fever for Jean Paul. Here, also, he made the acquaintance of Friedrich Wieck, and became his pupil in piano-playing. The daughter, Clara, then but nine years old, attracted him very much by her remarkable talent. Schumann left Leipsic for Heidelburg for a while, in order to attend certain lectures there. Now ensued a still more violent contest between law and music, which resulted at last in his return to Leipsic in 1830, for the purpose of devoting himself to music, which he began to do again under Wieck's instruction. But this course was not rapid enough for the impatient student, who imagined himself the discoverer of a secret by which the time of practice could be much shortened. The experiment, whatever it was, worked disastrously, and had the effect of destroying the use of the fourth finger of the right hand, and consequently in disabling him from piano-playing altogether.

He now devoted himself to composition, and produced his op. 1, variations on the name "Abegg," and directly his "Papillons," or scenes at a ball. In these his talent and originality were plain enough, as well as the lack of clearness. Incited by the criticism which these works met on all hands, he took up the study of counterpoint and composition, and little by little acquired smoothness of style. Thus he produced his two sets of studies after Paganini, op. 3 and op. 10, the *Davidsbündlertänze*, op. 6, the Toccata, Allegro, Carnival, op. 9, the sonata in F sharp minor, and the "Phantasie Stücke," op. 12. The latter set of pieces has become universally favorite, and shows Schumann's originality in a favorable light. They have already been analyzed in Chapter XXXIII, and need not here be taken up again.

One of the most remarkable of the works of this first epoch is the *Etudes Symphoniques*, an air, twelve variations, and a finale. These variations are not so much unfoldings of the theme, as associated or congenial ideas and images called up by it, as it is dwelt upon in the mind. It would be impossible to conceive any thing less like an ordinary set of variations. Instead of the usual, somewhat timid progression from one variation to the next, we here effect the boldest transitions. At times we lose the theme completely. Then it re-appears. This work is extremely interesting, because the forms are short, and the musical nature of the whole is of the most precious quality. Of similar excellence is the Kreisleriana, op. 16, and the Humoreske, op. 20.

In 1833 Schumann united with a few others in establishing the *Neue Zeitschrift für Musik* (New Journal of Music), as the advocate of progression, and as opposed to pedantry and (other people's) conceit. Like all journals devoted to art, it was published at a loss, but was kept up for several years, and to it the world is indebted for the preservation of Schumann's opinions and criticisms upon contemporary music. Two volumes of his writings are now available in English, and exhibit him in an altogether favorable light. Meantime his affairs of the heart made haste slowly. After several episodes, he finally settled down to the conviction that Clara Wieck was indispensable to his happiness. Father Wieck objected, for reasons not publicly stated, but probably on account of doubt of the lover's fixity of purpose and stability of talent. At length an engagement was allowed, and in 1840 Schumann burst out in song, composing in a single year one hundred and forty. Among them were those two sets "Woman's Love and Life," and "Poet's Love," which still remain among the most highly prized achievements in this line. In this year he was married to Clara Wieck, on the 12th of September.

He now turned his attention to orchestral instruments and produced his piano quartette and quintette, and his B flat symphony. This was followed by other orchestral works, and in 1851 by the symphony in D minor. In 1841 he became connected with the Conservatory at Leipsic as teacher of piano-playing, composition, and the art of playing from score. This continued until his removal to Dresden, which took place in 1844. He had already in 1840 composed his charming and highly romantic work "Paradise and the Peri." As soon as he arrived in Dresden he set to work on the epilogue to the Faust music. The incessant activity of his mind finally resulted in throwing it completely off its balance, and gave rise to distressing symptoms of melancholy. In 1848 he wrote his opera of "Genoveva," which, although full of beautiful music, is not well adapted for dramatic performance. Here also followed, in an order which we have no room to trace, the later compositions for the piano. In 1850 he removed to Düsseldorf as municipal director, and was received with a banquet and concert. His position here was pleasant, but he had as little talent for directing as teaching. In 1853 he and his wife made a concert tour through the Netherlands, where Schumann was delighted to find his music as well known as at home. "Everywhere," he writes, "there were fine performances of my symphonies, even the most difficult."

Still his malady increased. He imagined he heard a tone, which pursued him incessantly, and from which harmonies, nay whole compositions were gradually developed. He became sleepless, and cast down with melancholy. At length he threw himself into the Rhine, from which he was with difficulty rescued. He was removed to a private asylum at Endenich, where he died two years later, July 31, 1856.

"Robert Schumann was of middling stature, almost tall, and slightly corpulent. His bearing while in health was haughty, distinguished, dignified and calm; his gait slow, soft, and a little slovenly. While at home he generally wore felt shoes. He often paced his room on tiptoe, apparently without cause. His eyes were generally down-cast, half-closed, and only brightened in intercourse with intimate friends, but then most pleasantly. His countenance produced an agreeable, kindly impression; it was without regular beauty, and not particularly intellectual. The fine cut mouth, usually puckered as if to whistle, was, next to the eyes, the most attractive feature of his full, round, ruddy face. Above the heavy nose rose a high, bold, arched brow, which broadened visibly at the temples. His head, covered with long, thick, dark-brown hair, was firm and intensely powerful, we might say square.*"

As a composer Schumann is one of the most important in the entire history of music. Liszt acutely remarked, "Schumann *thinks* music better than any other since Beethoven." We have already seen that Bach established modern tonality by taking it as he found it already developed for him in Fugue, and applying it to the expression of musical feeling, the vital element which had been generally wanting in the music written before his day. After Bach, nothing new was done for music but to invent clearer forms, and to master its use as the expression of light and deep feeling according to the demands of the classical school. We have also seen that Beethoven, in some of his works, goes beyond the classical idea, and actually enters upon the province of the romantic. This he does in the stronger contrasts of his works, especially in the pianoforte sonatas, op. 13, 110 and 111. Yet in these works which are so full of feeling, and expressed with such masterful power, there is after all a certain repose and classical dignity beyond which they do not come. These elements are still more noticeable in his opera "Fidelio," where there was room for him to have expressed himself in a truly romantic manner. But no! here, as elsewhere, he is distinctly the instrumental composer, considering the music first and the text afterwards. That the music is far above that of any Italian opera, comes not from Beethoven's seizure of the text, but from his range of expression as a musician. It is as *music* that "Fidelio" surpassed other operas, and not as a poetico-musical interpretation of a highly poetic and suggestive text. The same peculiarities of Beethoven's music are still more perceptible in the symphonies, where he is always moved by musical considerations as such. Nothing tempts him from the strictly appropriate and suitable development of his theme. True, he does this with consummate beauty, and sets it off by the most delightful contrasts, but in all he is reposeful, elegant, beautiful. The very fineness of the work makes it ineffective to common minds. Yet, how much more effective to those who have the ears to hear.

Schubert is in many respects to be counted a romantic composer. Yet we have but to study his music deeply to perceive that his romanticism is spasmodic and temporary, while the natural range of his thought is according to the methods of the classical. Thus while in his great romantic songs, like the Erl King, he is distinctly a romantic

*Von Wasielwski.

writer, as soon as the stimulus of poetry is withdrawn he develops his musical ideas at great lengths, strictly in the classic method. This is to be seen everywhere in Schubert's instrumental works, and he is especially the *longest-winded* composer of all. No one else is so unwearied in turning over the same idea; and, it may be added, no one else does so with such elegance and grace.

Schumann, on the contrary, is romantic in the very essence of his musical thought. When he is writing to a text he is graphic and flexible in conforming to the spirit of the words. But when he is writing instrumental music merely, he is equally direct and full of humor. The classical method of developing musical ideas is contrary to his nature and impossible for him. All through his life he made the most strenuous efforts to write elegantly, and according to the canons of form. He disciplined himself in counterpoint and fugue under the best masters of his day, and studied eagerly Bach and Beethoven. Yet he could never develop an idea easily and naturally according to the fashion of the classic. His fugues are forced, his counterpoint spasmodic, and his sonatas his poorest work. His songs are at times badly placed for the voice, and entirely unlike every thing that a song ought to be — if we may believe the critics who wrote upon them in Schumann's life-time. Yet they have made their way and are now accepted as among the most successful efforts yet made to unite poetry and music. So also in the instrumental pieces. These little, fantastic, irregular compositions are now played and enjoyed all the world over, although they do not contain a single element of the "grateful" salon piece for the pianoforte.

Yet the classical moment in music had not passed by in Schumann's day. Beethoven's later sonatas were as yet a sealed book. Mendelssohn, although on the whole to be counted for a romantic composer, handled musical ideas with an ease and classical elegance, limited only by the inherent lightness of the ideas themselves. Chopin, a still more poetic writer, and the inventor of very many entirely new ways of proceeding, yet develops his ideas in his own new ways, somehow not unlike the spirit of the classical model. Chopin is everywhere new and original; but he has also a certain epic breadth. He writes long movements, which are well sustained, and thoroughly satisfactory in point of formal beauty.

Schumann, doubtless, would have agreed with the late Edgar A. Poe, that "a long poem is a contradiction in terms." There is never a long piece of music in Schumann. But instead thereof, short pieces, strongly differentiated and contrasted, and out of them are built up, mosaic-wise, long movements. So it is in his pianoforte concertos, sonatas, his quartettes and symphonies. The distinguishing greatness of Schumann, then, is not in his large pieces, for in all of them he is one way or another hampered. In the pianoforte concerto, for example, there are no effective passages. It is in places difficult enough, but it is very far from a bravoura piece. Even the cadenza is as far as possible from any thing likely to bring down the house. Yet it is one of the most delightful works ever written, and full of the most beautiful ideas, although, to be sure, these are mainly for the piano.

It is another peculiarity of Schumann's genius, that he is on the whole a pianoforte composer. Although he wrote a large amount for other instruments and for the voice, his piano works are the ones on which his fame chiefly rests. And it is curious to observe that while this is the case, he has never written "gratefully" for the pianoforte, but always the new and original. Hence his piano pieces had to wait a long time for their merits to become known. One might almost say that they had to wait for a generation of players able to understand them and do them justice.

Schumann is essentially the music *thinker*. He writes well for no instrument whatever, nor even for the voice. The entire art of piano playing, and especially of early technical practice, has had to be re-modeled in order to provide the technical ability with which to properly render these works of his. His symphonies not only are made up out of bits, like all his long pieces, but are badly written for the strings, the very foundation of the orchestra. Yet the music has in it such force and freshness, that these works hold their position, not only against the more reposeful and elegant works of Beethoven and the classical composers, but against modern works also, even though in some cases much better written. Bach established the musical vocabulary within which the entire classical school expressed itself. In like manner Schumann did this for the romantic school. Nothing essentially new has been added to musical phraseology since Schumann, but only to master the use of his new modes of expression. What these are it would be difficult to point out. If we examine the harmony we can not say that Schumann uses any chord that may not be found in Bach. Nor is the novelty in period formations. But perhaps, if in any single element, in the manner of motive-transformation. In this respect the difference between Schumann and Bach or Beethoven is world-wide. In Bach there is, to be sure, a fresh and thoroughly right thematic development, and so in Beethoven. In the latter his fantasy sometimes carries him to great lengths, as in the Rondo Capriccioso,

But in Schumann this fantasy becomes much more fantastic and humoristic. In many cases it is so violent as to forbid his adhering to a single idea and working it out thoroughly. Instead of that he flies restlessly from one idea to another, and to yet another, until the listener wearies of it. So he violates all canons of beauty, and destructive criticism breaks all her vials of wrath upon him. Yet the strongest of these pieces has something true and tender in it. When a Rubinstein produces the key that unlocks the magic door, we enter and find here a world of tenderness and fanciful beauty. So has it been with the apparently most unjustifiable of these works, like, for example, the Carnival, the *Faschingsschwank aus Wien*, and so on.

It is Schumann who has in one effort taught the musical world two lessons: that there is *poetry* in music, and that there is *music* in the pianoforte. His creative activity busied itself along the line where poetry and music join. Although an imaginative and fanciful person, he had a true instinct for valid and logical expression in music. So, even in his most far-fetched passages, the melodic and harmonic sequences, although new, are inherently right, and entirely compatible with those of Bach and Beethoven. Hence whatever ground his music has gained, it has held. On the other hand he had also a fancy in which every fantastic idea found congenial soil. The proper, the conventional, the allowable, meant nothing to him. He gave loose rein to his humor and followed it whithersoever it led. Nor yet in this did he lose his balance. For at the bottom he had the key to the riddle, which we have before several times pointed out: *the relation of music to emotion*. And so while his fancy took him far, and into many new paths, his fine musical sense kept him from passing beyond what was inherently right in music, as such. That he often passes beyond the limits of the symmetrical, the well-sounding, or even the agreeable, we can afford to forgive for the sake of the vigor of his imagination, and the inherent sweetness and soundness of his disposition. And it is these which on the whole have supported and justified his works.

LIST OF SCHUMANN ILLUSTRATIONS.

1. (*Moderately Difficult, Employing the Pianoforte and a Soprano.*)

1. "The Entrance," "Wayside Inn," and "Homeward" from the Forest Scenes, op. 82.
2. "The Hat of Green," Soprano.
3. *a.* Romance in F sharp, op. 28.
   b. Hunting Song.
4. "O Sunshine," Soprano.

5. Nachtstücke in C and F, op. 23.
6. "Moonlight," Soprano.
7. "End of the Song," from op. 12.

2. Difficult.

1. Etudes Symphoniques, op. 13, Theme, variations 1, 2, 3, 7, 11, 12, and Finale.
2. "Thou Ring upon my Finger," Soprano.
3. "Aufschwung," "Warum," and "Ende vom Lied," from op 12.
4. "He the Best of all, the Noblest," Soprano.
5. Novellette in F, No. 1, Romance in F sharp, and Novellette in E. No. 7.

3. Illustrations of the Romantic

1. SCHUMANN.—*a.* Novellette in E, No. 7.
   b. Prophetic Birds.
   c. Traumeswirren.
   d. Warum.
   e. Ende vom Lied.
2. SCHUBERT.—"The Erl King," Soprano.
3. CHOPIN.—*a.* Scherzo in D flat, op. 31.
   b. Nocturne in F sharp, op. 15.
   c. Ballade in A flat, op. 47.
4. SCHUMANN.—"He the Best of all, the Noblest."
5. CHOPIN.—Polonaise in A flat, op. 53.

CHAPTER FIFTY.

LISZT.

Liszt is one of the most remarkable personages who has yet appeared in music. His life is briefly told by Francis Heuffer, in Grove's "Dictionary," as follows:

"Franz Liszt was born October 22, 1811, at Raiding, in Hungary, the son of Adam Liszt, an official in the imperial service, and a musical amateur of sufficient attainment to instruct his son in the rudiments of pianoforte-playing. At the age of nine young Liszt made his first appearance in public at Oedenburg, with such success that several Hungarian noblemen guaranteed him sufficient means to continue his studies for six years. For that purpose he went to Vienna, and took lessons from Czerny on the pianoforte, and from Salieri and Randhartinger in composition. The latter introduced the lad to his friend Franz Schubert. His first appearance in print was probably in a variation (the 24th) on a waltz of Diabelli's, one of fifty contributed by the most eminent artists of the day, for which Beethoven, when asked for a single variation, wrote thirty-three (op. 120). The collection, entitled Vaterländische Künstler-Verein, was published in June, 1823. In the same year he proceeded to Paris, where it was hoped that his rapidly growing reputation would gain him admission at the Conservatoire in spite of his foreign origin. But Cherubini refused to make an exception in his favor, and he continued his studies under Reicha and Paër. Shortly afterwards he also made his first serious attempt at composition, and an operetta in one act, called 'Don Sanche,' was produced at the Académie Royale, October 17, 1825, and well received. Artistic tours to Switzerland and England, accompanied by brilliant success, occupy the period till the year 1827, when Liszt lost his father and was thrown on his own resources to provide for himself and his mother. During his stay in Paris, where he settled for some years, he became acquainted with the leaders of French literature, Victor Hugo, Lamartine and George Sand, the influence of whose works may be discovered in his compositions. For a time also he became an adherent to Saint-Simon, but soon reverted to the Catholic religion, to which, as an artist and a man, he has since adhered devoutly.

"The interval from 1839 to 1847 Liszt spent in traveling almost incessantly from one country to another, being everywhere received with an enthusiasm unequaled in the annals of Art. In England he played at the Philharmonic Concerts of May 21, 1827 (Concerto, Hummel), May 11, 1840 (Concertstück, Weber), and June 8, 1840 (Kreutzer-sonata). Here alone his reception seems to have been less warm than was expected, and Liszt, with his usual generosity, at once undertook to bear the loss that might have fallen on his agent. Of this generosity numerous instances might be cited. The charitable purposes to which Liszt's genius has been made subservient are legion, and in this respect as well as in that of technical perfection he is unrivaled amongst virtuosi. The disaster caused at Pesth by the inundation of the Danube (1837) was considerably alleviated by the princely sum — the result of several concerts — contributed by this artist; and when two years later a considerable sum had been collected for a statue to be erected to him at Pesth, he insisted upon the money being given to a struggling young sculptor, whom he moreover assisted from his private means. The poor of Raiding also had cause to remember the visit paid by Liszt to his native village about the same time. It is well known that Beethoven's monument at Bonn owed its existence, or at least its speedy completion, to Liszt's liberality. When the subscriptions for the purpose began to fail, Liszt offered to pay the balance required from his own pocket, provided only that the choice of the sculptor should be left to him. From the beginning of the forties dates Liszt's more intimate connection with Weimar, where in 1849 he settled for the space of twelve years. This stay was to be fruitful in more than one sense. When he closed his career as a virtuoso, and accepted a permanent engagement as conductor of the Court Theater at Weimar, he did so with the distinct purpose of becoming the advocate of the rising musical generation, by the performance of such works as were written regardless of immediate success, and therefore had little chance of seeing the light of the stage. At short intervals eleven operas of living composers were either performed for the first time or revived on the Weimar stage. Amongst these may be counted such works as *Lohengrin*, *Tannhäuser*, and *The Flying Dutchman* of Wagner, *Benvenuto Cellini* by Berlioz, Schumann's *Genoveva*, and music to Byron's 'Manfred.' Schubert's *Alfonso and Estrella* was also rescued from oblivion by Liszt's exertions. For a time it seemed as if this small provincial city was once more to be the artistic center of Germany, as it had been in the days of Goethe, Schiller and Herder. From all sides musicians and amateurs flocked to Weimar, to witness the astonishing feats to which a small but excellent community of singers and instrumentalists were inspired by the genius of their leader. In this way was formed the the nucleus of a group of young and enthusiastic musicians, who, whatever may be thought of their aims and achievements, were and are at any rate inspired by perfect devotion to music and its poetical aims. It was, indeed, at these Weimar gatherings that the musicians who now form the so-called School of the Future, till then unknown to each other and divided locally and mentally, came first to a clear understanding of their powers and aspirations. How much the personal fascination of Liszt contributed to this desired effect need not be said. Amongst the numerous pupils on the pianoforte, to whom he at the same period opened the invaluable treasure of his technical experience, may be mentioned Hans von Bülow, the worthy disciple of such a master.

"The remaining facts of Liszt's life may be summed up in a few words. In 1859 he left his official position at the Opera in Weimar owing to the captious opposition made to the production of Cornelius' 'Barber of Bagdad,' at the Weimar Theater. Since that time he has been living at intervals at Rome, Pesth, and Weimar, always surrounded by a circle of pupils and admirers, and always working for music and musicians in the unselfish and truly catholic spirit characteristic of his whole life."

Liszt's position in the world of art is one that is altogether peculiar and unexampled. He appeared in Paris just at the time when Thalberg had made a profound impression by the ease of his playing and the remarkable results attainable from the piano. What Thalberg did was to carry a melody in the center of the compass of the instrument, principally with the two thumbs, and to surround it with an elaboration of passage-work entirely unheard of before. The melody so carried was not left to itself, or merely pounded out, but made to sing, and delivered with the utmost refinement of phrasing, as if, indeed, the player had nothing whatever to do just then but to play that melody. There was in all of Thalberg's pieces a certain similarity of style, and in his performance a certain coldness.

All this, which Thalberg did so beautifully and elegantly, yet so coldly, Liszt did spontaneously, and with an endless caprice of color and shading as the mood chanced. Besides these things, to which, indeed, he attached little importance, Liszt's exuberant fancy broke out in every direction, especially towards the new, the startling, the astonishing. For his calmer moments he had his work ready to his hands in the elegant but dramatically suggestive compositions of Chopin, and these Liszt played with a fire and strength far beyond the feeble powers of Chopin himself.

As a player Liszt gathered up and combined within himself all the excellencies of piano-playing known before him, and added to this, his inherited capital, a perfectly tropical luxuriance of elaboration in every direction.

The possibilities latent in the diminished seventh and the chromatic scale, were very plainly suggested in Mozart's wind-parts of Handel's "The People that Walked in Darkness," but they remained a sealed book to the pianist until Chopin showed them at their true value on the pianoforte. This new path attracted Liszt, who has effected a thousand transformations on these elements, most of them much simpler and less subtle than Chopin's, but perhaps on that very account all the more effective in concert. And so we find in Liszt's transcriptions and paraphrases of songs and orchestral works, not only very effective solos for virtuoso performance, but also an actual and very influential enlargement of the available field of the piano, and, more and more in his later works, a demand upon the player for intelligence and musical discrimination of touch. In his earlier transcriptions he is concerned with operatic melodies, and those mainly of Verdi, Rossini and Meyerbeer. In his later works he traverses the whole range of musical literature. Symphonies, quartettes, masses, operas, oratorios, and, last and least promising of all, Wagner's "Art-Work of the Future,"—all these re-attire themselves in habiliments of pianoforte passages, and pose for drawing-room use.

Liszt has been the great music teacher of the last forty years. He has never received a dollar for musical instruction, but has given his services in pure love for the art. All good pianists owe much to him; not only to the silent but forcible inspiration of his printed works, but also still more to his personal example and criticism. As long ago as 1852 he had a class of seven or eight young men at Weimar, all of whom have since become famous. Among them were Hans von Bülow, Carl Klindworth, Joachim Raff, William Mason, Dionys Prückner, and Joseph Joachim. Later additions were Edouard Remenyi and Carl Tausig. Not only were pianists here, but violinists, singers, painters, sculptors, poets, and literary men of all kinds, all of whom found something inspiring and helpful in this magical and unconventional atmosphere. Since 1853 it is safe to say that every concert pianist in the world has been for a longer or a shorter time with Liszt.

A wrong idea of Liszt as a pianist is held by those who suppose that his playing is characterized by great force and extravagance. Imagine a very tall and slender man, more than six feet, with enormously long arms and fingers. He sits bolt upright, his long legs bent at a sharp angle at the knee. The trowsers are held down by straps. His face bears an ascetic expression. His hair is long, white, and floats upon his shoulders. His eyes are half-closed, and he scarcely ever looks at his hands. He sits perfectly still. Those long fingers go meandering over the key-board like gigantic spiders. You shudder at the sight. He seems to be playing slowly. The touch is everything but *legato*. This he does with the pedal. Yet in this easy, nonchalant fashion he is improvising the most wierd or impressive harmonies, or plays at first sight the most difficult productions of other virtuosi. Nay! he even takes a full score of a pianoforte concerto by some new author, and plays it from the cramped and obscure handwriting as coolly and vigorously as if he had written it himself, and at the very same first sight reads also the orchestral parts, and makes spoken comments on the instrumentation as he goes along! This, which sounds like a rhapsodical description, is literally true of Liszt. A virtuoso pupil brings him a fugue on which he has spent much practice. Liszt thinks it too slow, and plays it at the proper tempo. The youngster takes it home and works at it six weeks before he brings it up to the rapid tempo. If now he were to bring it again to Liszt, he would be just as likely to play it again in yet double speed.

Liszt seems to have been expressly designed for a sort of appreciative older brother to all new and original composers. For this use his temperament exactly suits. The points in their work that criticism sticks at, are, of course, the new and sometimes the very turning-points of their lasting value. These points Liszt seizes by intuition. Imperfections of a trifling character, or even of a serious kind, so they do not interfere with the main idea of the work, have no power to withdraw his attention from vital points. It was Liszt who first joined with Schumann in recognizing the genius of Schubert. It was Liszt who even went beyond Schumann and every other critic in recognizing the high artistic significance of the works of Berlioz and Wagner.

As a composer Liszt has worked in every field. He is never reposeful. His works are generally fragmentary. They are characterized by intense contrasts and sensational transitions. All available resources he uses unhesitatingly. His influence in art will be very great, but as a composer it will probably be limited to his own generation. His power is rather in his personal inspiration to other men of genius, than in a vocation for a distinctly new artistic utterance, except, indeed, upon the pianoforte.

PROGRAMME OF LISZT ILLUSTRATIONS.

(*Employing two Pianists and a Soprano.*)

1. Concerto in E flat, with second pianoforte accompaniment.
2. Song, " Thou'rt Like a Lovely Flower."
3. *a.* Waldesrauchen, Concert Study.
   b. Spinning Song from " Flying Dutchman."
4. " Mignon's Song."
5. *a.* Polonaise Heroique in E.
   b. Schubert's " Wanderer."
   c. Second Hungarian Rhapsody. (Rivé King Edition.)

CHAPTER FIFTY-ONE.

WAGNER.

In the old University city, Leipsic, was born on May 22, 1813, one Richard Wagner, who for many years has seemed to the older and more conservative musicians to be turning the world upside down, but who in the outcome bids fair to add another name to the list of Leipsic celebrities. Wagner was the son of a police magistrate, and a relative of the distinguished tragedienne, Johanna Wagner. The boy was intended for the law, and pursued his studies at the St. Thomas school until he was about seventeen. Long before this, however, as he tells in his autobiography, he heard Weber's "Freyschütz" and a symphony of Beethoven, and thenceforth he forsook the Shakespearean tragedies it had been his pleasure to compose, in favor of symphonies and overtures. One of the latter was actually performed at the Leipsic theatre, but the effect of it was somewhat marred, Wagner says, by the big bass drum, which he had brought in on the accented part of every third measure throughout the piece; whereat, when the audience fairly realized it, there was most derisive laughter.

In 1830 Wagner entered as a music-student at the University. In this year he carried a symphony of his to Dionys Weber in Vienna, who praised the talent he displayed in it, and advised him to study. Three years later he went to Warzburg, where his brother Albert lived, and wrote there his first opera, "Die Feen." In 1837 he went to Königsburg as musical director, and two years later he was writing on his "Rienzi," at Dresden. Later he went to Paris, and on the way read the legend of the "Flying Dutchman," and in the sea voyage encountered the storm he has represented in the overture to that opera. In Paris he nearly starved, and was reduced to the necessity of writing pianoforte potpourris to boil his own pot. He left Paris in 1842. In 1844 and 1845 he wrote "Tannhäuser," and very soon afterwards his "Meistersinger von Nürnburg," and had sketched "Lohengrin." "Rienzi" was brought out for the first time in Berlin in 1847, with great success. As early as this he was already at work on his poem of "Siegfried's Death." In the year 1848 he was mixed up in the political revolution, and compelled to fly to Switzerland. The following year he brought out his important pamphlets "Art and Revolution," "The Art-Work of the Future," and was at the same time engaged in the study of the "Niebelungen Lied." As already recounted in the notice of Liszt, it was at Weimar that "Tannhaüser" and "Lohengrin" first found their success. The former sprang into popularity and in 1853 was performed in Leipsic, Frankfort a. M., Schwerin, Düsseldorf, Cologne, Bromberg, Posen, Freyburg, Königsburg, Danzig, Bremen, Hamburg, Riga, Cassel, Darmstadt, etc.

About 1870 Wagner began to plan seriously for the first Bayreuth Festival, which took place August 13-17, 1876. For this a theatre had been erected, complete in all its appointments, at an expense of over half a million dollars. The orchestra was composed of the best musicians in Germany, to the number of one hundred, and the singers embraced the most distinguished artists—all of whom volunteered their services for the occasion. The audience was from every part of the world. The scenic effects were of the most elaborate and gorgeous description. In this magnificent manner two performances of his great quartette of operas the "Ring of the Niebelungen" was performed. This festival was repeated in 1878.

As an artist Wagner stands in a three-fold capacity: as a musician, in which his influence has been on the whole in the direction of the *realistic*, and beyond the romantic. The Romantic, as we saw in the earlier parts of this work (Chap. XXI), rests in a suggestiveness of poetic idea, rather than in an actual representation of the external world; whereas Wagner, without attempting the impossible in seeking to represent actual inanimate existence by means of tones, has many times represented the forces and effects of nature with remarkable cleverness, as, for example, the storm in the "Flying Dutchman," the sunrise in "Lohengrin," etc. Besides, in representing emotion he carries it to the verge of literalism. As an orchestral writer he is an innovator, and one of the greatest masters the world of music has ever seen.

Wagner has also claims as a poet, and literary man. As to the literary value of his works, opinions in Germany differ. But there can be no question as to the remarkable freshness and suggestiveness of his writings on music, a part of which have lately been translated into English. As a scenic artist, he has very much improved the mechanisms of the stage, and introduced the most complete spectacular effects yet contrived. Personally, Wagner represents the opposite disposition to that of Liszt. For whereas Liszt is generous and quick to recognize merit in all, and the last to claim any for himself, Wagner is so entirely absorbed in his own ideas as to have little time to study those of other men. Perhaps I shall make plainer my estimate of Wagner by comparing his operatic works with those of his predecessors.

The day of Wagner's triumph draws near. The Bayreuth Festival, the persistent quarreling between his adherents and classic musicians, the efforts of the Thomas orchestra, all have done something to bring it on. It is the peculiarity of Wagner's operas to hold their own wherever they once gain a foothold. Such is the splendor of their instrumentation, the magnificence of their stage effects, and especially their remarkable unity, that they not only improve on acquaintance, but make almost all other operas pale in comparison. Their masterly unity is the great point in their favor. They exhibit no discrepancy between poet and composer, nor between both and the stage-manager; but the same master mind that conceived the plot, elaborated the dialogue, and the musical declamation that fitly expresses it. The same skill seized the orchestra, greatly enlarged it, enriched its treatment, and handled it in complete subjection to the dramatic idea. The music is intense, and even if the listener fails fully to comprehend it, he can but feel that the fault is with him, for the masterly grip of the composer is expressed in every strain.

Wagner is the legitimate successor of Meyerbeer. He is the heir, who having buried the dead body with all proper respect, lives on the property bequeathed him, which with rare skill he manages to increase four-fold.

Meyerbeer was an artist in *effects*. There is scarcely a line of really heartfelt musical inspiration in all his writings; yet such are the stage effects, and the brilliancy of the scoring, along with the somewhat over-strained rhythms, that his operas form excellent stage pieces for large theatres. Meanwhile the spectator feasts his eyes, is impressed by the gorgeousness of it all, and wonders why he is not affected, wonders why he is even (shall he say it?) a little bit bored. He dares not attribute this feeling to his musical superiority, for he well remembers hearing "Der Freyschütz" with pleasure only the night before. Two nights afterwards he heard "Lohengrin" with enjoyment. Why then does he stumble at Meyerbeer? The explanation is to be found in the change of standpoint which the composers have effected, without mentioning the fact, until Wagner perceived it and explained it. Such operas as "Fra Diavolo" and "Wm. Tell" are written to amuse. The former is a comedy. The music is melodious, and the kind of melody that fits into easy harmonies, and carries with it a sense of play. Wagner's music, on the other hand, carries with it a sense of work, and very hard work it is too. The Gluck operas were designed as music-dramas. This was also Mozart's idea of "Don Juan." In this idea he was exactly contrary to the author of the libretto, Da Ponte, who designed merely a comedy. Mozart was himself too good natured, and too much a man of his time to fully carry out his own inner conviction. Besides, the world had wrestled faithfully with the *working* music of Bach, and was just then ready only for something that could be enjoyed without work. In his ensembles Mozart discards well-turned tunes, and elaborates long finales of inherently dramatic music, rising finally to a powerful but not showy climax. On the other hand, his peasants and smaller characters speak in melodies of the most deliciously simple cut, and these, while dramatically true, serve at the same time to amuse the audience. Thus the Mozart standpoint is not consistent with itself; and hence, in spite of their beauty, the Mozart operas do not fully satisfy either party. Beethoven in his "Fidelio" intended to be true to the drama, and his music in that opera is of the most refined and poetic description. Still Beethoven was too good a musician to be a good opera composer. In his idea, repose was an element of beauty. Now repose shows itself in music in the well-rounded return of melodies upon themselves, and in the intervention of simple passages to serve as contrasts with the more noble and passionate, in the same way that the delicious idiocy of the grave-digger in "Hamlet" relieves the attention and serves to emphasize the subtilty and high intellectual quality of much that occurs in the same connection. It was impossible for Beethoven not to regard musical symmetry. Yet this must be disregarded if the opera is to be really a drama. Another element of repose in Beethoven, and in all the composers before Wagner, is the simplicity of the harmonies. Dissonances do not abound. This and the decided tonality of almost every period makes the harmonic structure clear, and by so much assists the hearer. All the Italians have written opera first for the voice, and secondly to amuse.

The Wagner music-drama, on the other hand, is not an amusement, and was not designed to be. It is a work of art; a powerful achievement of the imagination, acting through a combination of musically declaimed speech, dramatic action, and an orchestra controlled solely for the purpose of heightening the effect. Wagner's standpoint is consistent with itself, whether the true one or not. He does not seek effects merely as such, but only where they truthfully belong to the drama. He neither sacrifices to the prima-donna by means of encore-compelling cadenzas, nor to the groundling with airs that may be whistled. If the singers make effects they must do so through the intelligence and power of their declamation, and by the intensity and truth of their action. Such demands as these for a time disabled both singers and hearers. Wagner has had to wait twenty-five years for a generation of singers who have mastered the art of the lyric stage in this conception, and even now their number is small. So also audiences and critics had to be educated to the new order of things, before they could recognize the merit that showed itself in the new way.

Let us consider two of Wagner's operas. "The Flying Dutchman" was written thirty years ago. Wagner had only set out on the new path. He had not then mastered his own idea. His arioso style was not yet smooth. But the dramatic structure of the play is simple, effective, and well contrasted. It was originally designed to be played in a single act. This for the sake of unity. It is now played in three. The first is in the little bay where the ships of Daland and Vanderdecken have taken refuge from the storm. Here are male choruses, the pilot's beautiful song, the monologue of Vanderdecken, and the dialogue between him and Daland. The second act takes place in Daland's house, and makes us acquainted with Senta, and afterwards brings in her would-be lover, Eric, and later the Dutchman himself. In this act there is a female chorus. The third act takes place on the quay, the peasants on shore, the Dutchman's ship, which presently sets sail and departs. The stage situations are simple, plausible, and effective. Already here is a music-drama with a conceivable plot. The musical contrasts in this work are fine. The work opens with the sailors' chorus, bold, wild, and original; then follows the pilots' song, wh'ch comes very near the spirit of the Italian aria. Much that follows between Vanderdecken and Daland is a little tedious, but the act concludes with the sailors' chorus that opened it. In the second act the music brings Senta's very striking ballad, the legend of the "Flying Dutchman," the spinning chorus of the girls, as well as much that is less intelligible. If the standpoint be once conceded that opera is a music-drama, and not simply a "play," there is nothing in this work but possesses interest. Wagner has not over-stepped the ability of music. His next opera was "Tannhäuser," and then came, three years afterwards, "Lohengrin." "Tannhäuser" goes farther in the new direction. Several of its numbers are great. But it is in "Lohengrin" that his genius takes a bolder flight. The unity of this piece is complete. It does not present the aspect of a series of disconnected numbers strung together by a chain of recitatives, but from first to last it is consistent with itself. In this work Wagner has attained a high mastery over his favorite ideal, the dramatico-musical declamation. This varies very much in style. Some of it is lyric in everything except the rounding of the periods; other parts run into a well-cadenced recitative of entirely new cut, accompanied by a flowing melody, or rather a melodiously-flowing river of orchestration. The latter is in itself a study. Leading motives already appear in it; these striking bits of melody are each one associated with an important moment in the drama. Each is worked into the musical comment upon the moment to which it belongs. Later, when the consequences of such a moment begin to appear, this motive returns with greater or less emphasis. Such, for example, is the striking bit of melody in which Lohengrin in the first act solemnly enjoins Elsa never to ask his name. In the third act, when Elsa begins to approach the fatal question, this motive begins to occur in the instrumentation. At first it is hinted at obscurely. Then it comes stronger and stronger, until finally just before the fatal question, it is given out boldly and with solemnity. So speaks conscience to the wavering heart; except, unfortunately that conscience, lazy jade, is too apt to reverse the order of emphasis, speaking weaker and yet weaker as the fatal moment of yielding nears.

'Lohengrin" is a true drama. Though founded on a myth, it deals with the eternal conflict between good and evil. This conflict here is veiled somewhat, and in this the nobility of the drama is elevated. For although the ending shows the separation of Lohengrin and Elsa, brought about by the evil working through Ortrud, the effect is reached without any loss of virtue in the hero and heroine who have occupied our attention. The ending has genuine pathos without tragedy. The different acts are symmetrically balanced over against each other. The evil stands in Ortrud and Frederick. The first act shows the wager of battle and the triumph of the right. The second act has the evil for its motive. The evil begins and well-nigh ends it. The third act shows a fictitious triumph for the evil. Yet it brings also the death of Frederick. The scenic effects are splendid. The first scene is extremely brilliant, and the entrance of Lohengrin is beautiful. The second act opens with a long duet between Ortrud and Frederick. This takes place in the night, on the steps of the church, where the bright moon casts a dark shadow. The subject matter of the dialogue is hate and vengeance, and it ends with Ortrud's profane appeal to false gods, uttered in the very shadow of a temple to Jehovah. The contrast here implied is forcible and poetically conceived. The scene is long, partly, perhaps, in order to allow the impression of the first act to subside. Then enters Elsa on the balcony, and her song of love is one of the purest and most beautiful on the stage. One analyzes it in vain to find its secret. It is not in the song alone, nor in the accompaniment, nor yet in the scenic effect; but rather, perhaps, in one of the most perfect unions of all these elements ever accomplished by any composer. Part of the effect is due doubtless to the contrast with the scene immediately preceding. The following bit of stage effect, where the warders blow their trumpets from the towers of the castle at the approach of dawn; the gradually increasing light, the music that accompanies it, the gathering of the people in the square—all these have no bearing on the developement of the story. They form a splendid scenic effect that serves to relieve the attention preparatory to what follows.

Wagner has himself pointed out that Shakespeare expected impossibilities from his actors. Men of mediocre minds, untrained and hampered by the necessity of daily toil, are required to assume heroic parts, where keen wits and strong passions are clothed in noble human forms, such as it is impossible for them with their experience and low imaginations to conceive of, much less to fitly personate. He says that this must always be the case in master-works of imagination, and he has not hesitated to go perhaps farther in this direction than even Shakespeare. For the dramatic part finds its actor when it finds intelligence, flexible mimicry, good declamation and suitable personnel combined. But Wagner goes further. With these important qualifications must coincide the infinitely rarer one of a phenomenal voice of the proper range. Now your singer begins by training his voice. To train his voice he goes to Italy. If he has time or ambition, perhaps he does a little something in the way of training his intellect. As a rule, however, he stops with his throat, or if beyond that, with his arms and legs. Hence, we may expect that an adequate appointment of principals in "Lohengrin" will be something like ten times more rare than an adequate support for Booth or Barrett in "Hamlet" or "Shylock."

To the chorus Wagner has been still more cruel. He has written for the militia of the stage, evolutions possible only to regulars in complete training. On the whole, the orchestra has come up to its part in this compound work rather more promptly than the others. "Lohengrin" is no longer impracticable for orchestral players. The weak point in the Wagner drama, the fallacy that underlies its whole conception, is a misapprehension of the capacity of music. Music is the language of love and of serious and noble affection. It may become so little musical as to express apprehension and grief. But *hate* is discord, bold and biting. Dissonance is a discord that is musically cured by what is called "resolution," or its subsidence into consonance. Thus sorrow and trouble are cured into peace. But hate can not subside into love; it is contrary to love. Hence, the sounds that properly represent it are not those of "sweet bells jangled out of tune," but rather the mutterings and crashings of on-coming doom. Such a scene as that between Ortrud and Frederick, in the second act of "Lohengrin," can be made interesting only by an Ortrud rarely gifted with passion and dramatic art; and the interest then excited is but a hellish fascination. Such a scene is an ungrateful strain upon the attention, and it is questionable whether it has any business with music at all.

Another weak point in this drama is its lack of repose. As we have already seen, the old operas afford a sense of repose by the arias which suspend dramatic movement and attract the musical attention. In the Wagner drama, on the contrary, there is no suspension of the action except where an act is completed. In accordance with this, the musical-declamation falls into what Wagner calls an "endless melody," which to a certain extent, is a contradiction of terms.

Still the entire parts of the King, Elsa, and Lohengrin admit of being well done. They are not impossible, any more than Portia and Shylock are impossible. They ask merely for endowments and genius —endowments being the body, and genius the soul.

Nothing is more conspicuous in Wagner than his lack of wit or humor. He is always grimly in earnest. Doubtless in his estimation, wit is out of place in a noble work. But here he might have drawn a lesson from Shakespeare. Surely playfulness is not farther from a noble imagination than sensuality. Yet this he has not scrupled to depict in "Tannhaüser," and still more decidedly in some of his later works.

Be the final out-come what it may, the Wagner drama makes a powerful appeal to the senses and the intelligence. Unquestionably it has genius. Whether, on the whole, it is worth the trouble, who shall say? Meanwhile, there is room down-stairs for the average opera. The world will always contain those who, as it has been said, "go through life like flies, seeking only to be amused." For them the

Wagner "Art-Work of the Future" will never possess beauty or even intelligibility. But earnest souls, whether agreeing with the composer or not, will always recognize in Richard Wagner an earnest man, a genius, and a Great Master.

Wagner Illustrations.

(Employing two Pianos, a Soprano, Tenor and Chorus of Female Voices.)

1. Overture to "Tannhäuser." 8 hands, two pianos.
2. Elsa's Balcony Song from "Lohengrin."
3. Romance. The Evening Star; from "Tannhäuser." Tenor.
4. Elizabeth's Song from "Tannhäuser." Soprano.
5. Grand March from "Tannhäuser." Liszt (piano solo).
6. Spinning Song from "Flying Dutchman." Female chorus.
7. Ride of the Valkyrie. For two pianos.

CHAPTER FIFTY-TWO.

CONCERT PROGRAMMES AND THEIR EFFECTIVE COMPOSITION.

In selecting pieces for a musical performance, the first consideration, properly, should be their adaptation to the end proposed in the performance or production of the music. Thus, for example, a performance may be intended to illustrate the work and genius of a particular composer. In that case the first consideration is to select a sufficient number of his best works to represent him in the strongest light. Or it may be desired to contrast the genius of two different composers, in which case, of course, care will be taken to select the most characteristic pieces of both. Or the production of music may be designed to give pleasure and zest to an evening gathering in a parlor. Or it may be intended to illustrate the varied powers of a great pianist, in which case the selections must cover a wide range. And so we might go on for pages, enumerating the possible purposes for which musical illustration is sought. But it must suffice to lay down clearly the law, that every performance of music must have an intelligent purpose, in order to produce an intelligent effect; and that this purpose must be regarded in the selection of every piece upon the programme.

In the second place, the *means available* will enter into and modify the conclusions arrived at under the principle just enunciated. Thus it may happen that some aspect of Bach's work is the point of consideration, while the performance is to take place in a town or room where there is no organ. In this case, of course, a pianoforte arrangement of the work must serve, or a different piece altogether be chosen. Or it may be that some of the difficult works of Chopin or Liszt are wanted, while yet there is no player available to perform them well. In such a case easier pieces must be taken, or four-hand arrangements of the same, or an abler performer secured. The genius of Handel may be in question, where there is neither chorus nor even a solo singer available, and consequently it becomes impossible to represent him, except inadequately, in an instrumental performance of pieces written for voices. In all these and such like complications, which are innumerable, concessions must be made on both sides, until a practicable mean is reached. Only we may be very sure that no concert or musical performance can produce a satisfactory effect unless it consists of intelligently chosen pieces, practicable for performance by the players or singers available.

Then, in the third place, the pieces *must be intelligently arranged* in the programme. This involves several different principles, one or more of which are violated in almost every programme. The first of of these is the law of *contrast*. Music expresses feeling. Feeling is merely modification of consciousness. There is no absolute scale of emotion. Mirth seems like insanity if too long continued. Grief becomes tolerable after a while. The human system attunes itself to the key. Thus it is with the weather. On a clear day, a slight beclouding is immediately noticed. On a rainy day the very same sky may be so much above the general dullness as to brighten anticipation with the hope of fair weather.

The second law is that of *progression* in the emotional determination of the music. This law is almost universally disregarded in programmes. Let us reflect upon our own habits of mind. We begin the day brightly, indeed, but seriously. A whole day's work lies before us. Presently we become fatigued and rest a bit. Towards night the serious thought of the morning gives place to the sense of duty well done, and the feeling of deserved repose. It is then that we gladly turn ourselves to enjoyments and pastimes for which in the morning we had little appetite. Or, to put it in another way, at the beginning of a concert the audience is fresh and interested. It is then that the serious work should be heard. Later, the air in the room becomes impoverished, and the listener tired. It is then that they revive under the magical excitement of the well-sounding, the lively and the sensational.

Again, progression must be carried farther, even to *climax*. In this a misconception may easily lead to undesirable results. The climax must be sought along the line of natural emotional progress, as already defined. For the programme to close with a great and serious work, like Bach's Chromatic Fantasia and Fugue, after light salon pieces, and sensational pieces by Liszt, might, indeed, be a climax in the line of the intellectual, but it could not possibly succeed; because this composition of Bach's is of a highly intellectual structure, and can be satisfactorily followed only by similar vigor of mind, which, as already pointed out, is not to be reasonably expected in an audience fatigued by a long programme. The climax which can most easily be reached is one of physical effect; as, for example, when all the singers, after having previously appeared in solos or duets, unite in an *ensemble* piece to close a part. This practice has much to commend it. In "recitals," where only a single singer or player takes part, this form of climax is of course impossible. But the same result can be reached in another way, namely, by bringing the most sensational pieces toward the end of the programme.

When different composers are represented, the historical order is in general the best, because the development of music has been from the intellectual and artificial to the well-sounding, the emotional, the expressive, and the more completely beautiful; and, even beyond this, to the sensational and astonishing. Yet this historical order may frequently be varied with good effect. Sherwood, the pianist, sometimes introduces Handel's "Fire Fugue" into the middle of a programme, after one of the lighter sonatas of Beethoven, or even more modern compositions. So placed, it has the force of a complete contrast with the pieces before and after it, and while it relieves the emotional tension and thereby heightens the beauty of the pieces in immediate proximity to it, it is heard for itself as little more than a piece of virtuoso finger-work.

It is impossible to give examples of programmes suitable for models, since the circumstances vary so much. It must serve our present purpose to point out the principles which properly should be considered in selecting and arranging the pieces, and beyond these to refer the student to the study of entire operas and oratorios, which are in effect completely original programmes, determined after much study, by men who not only appreciated music, but possessed creative ability in it. One would do well to study the programmes of Mr. Theo. Thomas, who possesses a fastidious taste, and has had the advantage of almost unlimited experience and observation. The illustrations at the end of the chapters in this book are not to be taken for model programmes, since they have not been made for the sake of the music as a whole, but only for the sake of such and such phases of it, which form the subjects of the different chapters.

CHAPTER FIFTY-THREE.

THE PSYCHOLOGICAL RELATIONS OF MUSIC.

The limits within which this chapter is necessarily concluded, do not permit a thorough discussion of the psychological relations of music, even if the present state of knowledge regarding sense-perception were such as to make it possible. There are, however, certain points which need attention, on account of the practical bearing they have upon the co-ordination and adaptation of educational means.

Attention must first be called to the extremely complex activities of the mind involved in the perception and enjoyment of music, especially of the finer kinds. A piece of music, if only a single period of simple melody, reaches the brain in the form of individual sense-perceptions, which are there somehow taken account of and perhaps remembered entire; at all events compared in various ways, whereby their coherence is realized. These comparisons are of several orders: such as those of *pitch*, whereby tonality or coherence in key is perceived; *rhythm*, whereby all the tones are compared with some unit of time, and all the phrases with each other, so that in the out-come the melody is perceived as determinate in measure, motivization and symmetry of structure; and *power*, whereby the intensity of the cause is estimated. These comparisons of pitch, moreover, are greatly complicated by the harmonic treatment, and by the orchestral coloring, if the music be for the orchestra. All such comparisons go on unconsciously, or rather sub-consciously, and consciousness takes cognizance only of the result, as complete periods and forms are turned over to it.

Different grades of music make very different demands upon these three classes of comparison. Light, popular music is simple, and extremely limited in the range of its harmonies and the complexity of its melodies. The memory of a single phrase-rhythm, and of the three principal chords of the key, exhaust the catalogue of its demands upon the mind. A fugue deals with a single subject, and hence from a melodic point of view is easy to follow; but its harmonic structure is highly elaborate, and the subject itself dodges about so from one voice to another, that the unwary easily misses it. A sonata is longer, and contains more subjects, is even more diversified in harmonic treatment than a fugue. Hence, though not so severe, because not dealing exclusively with a single subject, it makes, in some respects, even greater demands upon the attention.

Aptitudes for performing these comparisons and co-ordinations of elementary sense perceptions, vary extremely in individuals, and in many cases fail entirely in one department, or more. Absolute inability to perceive pitch-relation is very rare; but an inability to follow anything more than an easy digression from one key to another is very common, probably from failure in harmonic perception. Rhythmic sense is frequently imperfect, although this is the simplest of the acts involved in music. All rhythm in music consists of multiples or relations of *twos* or *threes*. Relations of *two* and all its multiples by itself are almost universally intelligible; relations of *three* are frequently beyond the individual. Thus in all the so-called failures in the musical ear of pupils, the teacher will do well to observe carefully in what department of perception the failure takes place, and in a great majority of cases means can be found for supplying the missing link. This is to be done by a course of *exercises in hearing*, after the general plan of the object-lessons in the early parts of this course; which, indeed, will be found helpful in many cases where positive deficiencies of aptitude are unsuspected by the teacher. The Mason system of rhythmical treatment of exercises is also very helpful in cases where the sense of rhythm is imperfect.

An attentive study of the lines of perception indicated in the first twenty chapters of this course, will serve to explain what we already knew by observation, namely, that the finer and more highly developed forms of music are appreciable only by persons of active mind, nor even by these generally, except after more or less practice. We have also seen that music is intimately connected with, or related to, that great class of modifications of consciousness we call *emotions*, which extend from those almost imperceptible shades of elation or depression occasioned by trivial matters or atmospheric influences, to the mightiest movements of the soul, wherein the whole being is overwhelmed by the surges of passion, agony or grief; or borne aloft on the swellings of delight, joy, or blessedness and spiritual triumph.

Human life is made up of such emotional transitions, and the greater part of them take place within us through the operation of causes of which at the time we are frequently unconscious.

The relation of music to emotion lies partly in the rhythm, the pulsation of which hastens or retards the human pulse, while the motivization intensifies and varies the stimulus. With this the melodic content chimes in. A preponderance of accent or emphasis on the strong tones, or on the sad tones of the scale, also has great power. Then, too, music has positive value in its ability to interest and occupy the mind, or at least to awaken it to activity. An eminent barrister speaks of an evening at the opera as the best preparation for a trying case in court. The reason of this is doubtless to be found in the absorbing character of the opera as an amusing and complicated body of sense-perceptions, which causes him for a time to forget his case and thereby rest his mind; and in the stimulative effects of the rhythms prevalent in opera, which have the effect of quickening the activity of the mind, by means of which much of his thinking is done for him subconsciously—as we all know in what are sometimes called the automatic activities of the brain. In this and many similar cases we have a suggestion of a possible value of music as a mind quickener; which also tallies with the well-known fact, already adverted to, that the higher and finer kinds of music are enjoyed only by those of active mind.

Again, the psychological relations of musical performance deserve attention, even if what we can say takes only the form of suggestion. A musical performance, as upon the pianoforte, is in fact a lengthy and elaborate series of muscular operations, the proper co-ordination of which is accomplished by means of various combinations into secondary reflexes. In an important piece all the scale and arpeggio passages, and most of the accompaniments are either partly or completely automatic in character, and the melody notes only are purely the product of direct volition. It is in this way, by concentration of attention upon the melody notes, which after all contain the real idea, that music is interpreted to the listener. Now this, which seems so easy in the saying, carries with it important conclusions, which have a most significant bearing upon elementary education, especially upon the pianoforte. And this more especially, upon the mode of study and practice.

In all elementary musical study there are at least three interests which go hand in hand, and must receive equal attention. They are: First, the *technical* or the mechanical ability to perform the necessary motions; second, the *musical*, or the ability to think of the melodies, chord sequences, time relations, etc., that compose the piece; and third, the *feeling of these* as expressive of something.

The technical progress depends upon the practice of suitable exercises for developing the muscles of the hand and arm, and especially those which render the touch flexible and expressive (like Mason's two-finger exercises); and then in the case of any particular piece, *the practice of it in slow time, very many times in succession*, taking the utmost care to fully perform every muscular motion in its right order, and with occasional trials of the passage at the proper speed in order to ascertain how nearly complete the mastery of it has become.*

The musical comprehension of a work and a true feeling of its emotional meaning are best reached by committing the piece to memory and playing it without notes. In this way, sooner or later, it becomes absorbed into the musical life of the student, and not only is felt and enjoyed at its own value, but also facilitates the comprehension of other pieces. In this connection, also, it may serve to remind the reader of the great value of opportunities for hearing music, such as are by far too scarce in this country, and even where available too much neglected, especially by students.

This chapter is to be regarded as suggestive rather than complete, and as indicating a line of thought which deserves to be more thoroughly explored.

*See Mason's Pianoforte Technics, "The Mind in Playing," for further discussion of this point.

INDEX.

Antecedent, 30.
Adieux, the Ab. and Ret., Beethoven, op. 84; 34.
Architecture, Oriental, 77.
Architecture, 81.
Aria, and Scena, 128, 130.
Astonishing and the Sensational, 116.
Art, Design of, 54.
    Conditions of its Enjoyment, 61.
    Content and Form of, 61.
    Religion and Philosophy, 74.
    and Sense, 74.
    and Religion, 75.
    Ancient, 76.
    Symbolical, 77
    Classical, 78,
    Romantic, 79.
    Romantic, Conflict in, 79.
    Romantic, Keynote of 79.
    Design and Scope of, 59.
Bach, 2 pt. Inventions, No. 1: 11, 48, 94.
    Prelude, Bm, W. T. C. Bk. II., 11.
    2 pt. Inv. in F, No. 8: 12, 14, 44, 48, 146.
    Fugue in G min., W. T. C. I.: 14, 16, 48.
    Inventions 1, 4 and 8: 16.
    Gavotte in D (Wm. Mason), 17, 146.
    Gavotte in D min., 17, 29, 33.
    3 pt. Inv. in E min., No. 7: 5, 25, 146; 41.
    Fugue in C min., No. 2, W. T. C., 48, 146.
    Illustrations of, 146.
    Italian Concerto, 106.
    Passacaglia, in C min. for Organ, 106.
    Organ prelude in A min., 115.
    Loure in G, 146
    Song, My Heart Ever Faithful, 146, 130.
Ballad, The Simple, 125.
Bellini, Operatic Illustrations, 130.
Battle of Prague, Kotzwara, 54.
Beautiful, Perceived by Contemplation, 62.
    Nature of, 63.
    in Spiritual Perception, 68.
    in Reflection, 69.
    in Classic Music, 101.
    Perception of one of the Highest Faculties, 74.
Beauty, Formal, 67.
    Psychological Rank of Perception of, 74.
Beethoven, 168.
    Op. 2, No. 1: 10, 11, 13, 14, 22, 24, 28, 30, 33, 36, 39, 48, 96, 100.
    Op. 2, No. 2: 33, 44, 96.
    Op. 2, No. 3: 15, 33, 36, 94.
    Op. 7: 7, 11, 25, 94, 98.
    Op. 10, Son. in C min., 39, 41.
    Op. 10, Son. in D, 94.
    Op. 13; 11, 12, 13, 14, 22, 24, 28, 30, 44, 98, 100.
    Op. 14, No. 2: 20, 30, 94, 98.
    Op. 20, Septette, 100.
    Op. 22, Son. in Bb, 6, 39.
    Op. 26, Son. in Ab, 20, 36.
    Op. 27, No, 2: 106
    Op. 28, Son. pastorale, 41, 54, 94.
    Op. 30, Son. in G for P. F. and Violin, 96.
    Op. 31, No. 1, in G, 39, 41, 96.
    Op. 31, No. 2: in D. minor, 10, 11.
    Op. 31, No. 3: in Eb, 15, 96, 100.
    Op. 51, Two Rondos, 36, 98.
    Op. 57, Son. app. 20, 39, 44, 48, 96.
    Op. 81, Sonata, 54.
    Op. 90, Sonata, 13, 14.
    Op. 129, Rondo Capriccioso, 98.
    Vari. on Gretry's "Une Fièbre Brûlante," 20.
    Symphonies, 2d, 5th and 7th, 100.
    Sonatas for Piano and Violin, 106.
    List of Illustrations, 179.
Chopin, List of Illustrations, 186.
    Life, etc., 183.
    Op. 9. Nocturne in Eb, 44
    Op. 11, Concerto in E min., 4 , 57, 119.
    Op. 16, Rondo in Eb, 116.

Chopin, Op. 1 . Valse in Eb, 2.
    Op. 22, Pol naise in Eb, 119.
    Op. 26, Polonaise in C sharp, m, 110.
    Op. 29, Impromptu in Ab, 2, 2.
    Op. 31, Scherzo in B min., 4, 43, 116.
    Op. 34, No. 2 . Valse in Ab, 116.
    Op. 35, Sonata, 115.
    Op. 40, Polonaise in A, 22, 25, 3 , 44, 110.
    Op. 42, Valse in Ab, 52.
    Op. 53, Polonaise in Ab, 110.
    Op. 64, Valse in Db, 23.
    Polonaises, 107.
Cadenza from Liszt's Rigoletto, 57.
Cadenza, 49.
Cadence, 13.
Carnival of Venice, 22.
Cascade, Pauer, 25.
Classic, The Playful in, 93.
    The Tender and Soulful in, 94.
    The Rondo, 97.
    Music, the Beautiful in, 101.
    Music, Transition from Romantic to, 101.
Coda, 33.
Counterpoint, 16.
Consequent, 30.
Content, 42.
Contemplation, The Satisfactory in, 65,
Chivalrous, The, 107.
Claribel, Songs, 126.
Descriptive Music, 52.
Elaboration, 37.
Emotional, 45.
Fugue, 15.
Form, 26.
Forms, Open and Closed, 28.
    Unitary, 29.
    Irregular Period, 30.
    Binary, 32.
    Ternary, 34.
Field, Nocturne in B , 44, 112.
Faust Waltz, Liszt, 52.
Fanciful, The, and Pleasing, 115.
Gentle, The, and Sentimental, 111
Greek Ideal, The, 78.
Handel, Chaconne and Var, 48.
    Capriccio in G minor, 48.
    Messiah, Selections, 128, 130, 147.
    O Had I Jubal's Lyre, 130.
Harmony, 67.
Haydn's 5th Symphony, 96.
    Creation Selections, 129, 130.
    Illustrations, 161.
Hobby Horse, Schumann op. (S: 54.
Humoristic, The, and the Passionate 113.
Imitation, 14.
Intellectual, 45.
Idealized, The, 51.
Ideal, The, 54, 58.
    Phases of, 55.
    Greek, The, 78.
    in different Arts, 81.
    and its Phases, 55.
Infinity, 73.
Influence of Poetry upon Music, 120.
Liszt's Rigoletto, Cadenza, 51, 119.
    Polonaise Heroique in E, 110.
    Concerto in Eb, 119.
    Tannhäuser March, 119.
    Life, etc., 194.
    Illustrations, 190.
    and Thalberg compared, 1.7.
Lyric, 10, 12.
Mills' 1st Tarantelle, 116.
Motive, 10.
Mendelssohn, Sw. W., No. 1. 11, 29.
    Chorale from St. Paul, Sleepers wake, 17.
    Hunting Song, 21.
    Rondo Capriccioso, op. 14, 98.

Mendelssohn, Life, etc., 180.
    List of Illustrations, 183.
    Aria from St. Paul, 134.
Measure, 21.
Merz, K, Leonore Polka, 22.
    Pearl of the Sea, 52.
Motivization 24.
Mason, Wm., Dance Rustique, 28.
Mozart, Son. in F. (No 6 Peters' Ed.), 41.
    Andante for Quintette, 96.
    Larghetto in D, from Clarinet Concerto, 96.
    Andante from 5th Quintette, 106.
    Life, etc., 162.
    Operas, 165.
    Illustrations. 167.
    Operatic Selections, 130.
Moderation, 68.
Messiah, The, 154.
Music as Related to other Arts, 86.
    Limitations of, 89.
    Classic, the Beautiful in, 101.
    Influence of Poetry upon, 120.
Opera, The, 135.
Oratorio, The, 135.
Oriental Architecture, 77.
Painting and Sculpture Compared, 85.
Painting, 83.
Passage, 43.
Passionate, The Humoristic and the, 113.
Pauer, Cascade, 25.
Period, 9.
Period-group, 32.
Phrase, 10.
Philosophy, Art, Religion and, 74.
Playful, The, in the Classic, 93.
Pleasing, The Fanciful and the, 115.
    in Sensation, 64.
Principal, 32.
Psychological rank of the Perception of Beauty, 74.
Psychological Relations of Music, 211.
Programmes, How to Plan, 208.
Poetic Music, 52.
Poetry, 88.
    Content of, 91.
    Kinds of, 92.
Proportion, 67.
Poetry, Influence upon Music, 120.
Pulsation, 21.
Purity, 64
Raff, Op. 94, Valse Impromptu in B♭, 116.
    Polka de la Reine, 119.
Religion and Art, 75.
    Art and Philosophy, 74.
Regularity, 67.
Repose, 71.
    The Touchstone for False Art, 73.
Recitative, 126.
Rhythm, 21, 23.
Rhythmic Motion, 23.
Rigoletto, Liszt, Cadenza, 51, 119.
Romantic Illustrations, 194.
    Art, 79.
    Art, Conflict in, 79.
    Art, Keynote of, 79.
    Art, Transition from, to Classical, 101.
    The Chivalrous, 107.
    The Gentle and Sentimental, 111.
    The, Humoristic and Passionate, 113.
    The Fanciful and Pleasing, 115.
Rondo, 34.
Root, Geo. F., The Brooklet, 126.
    Hazel Dell, 126.
    Vacant Chair, 126.
Rubinstein's Valse Caprice in E♭, 116
Ruskin on Beauty, 63.
    on Infinity, 73.
    on Moderation, 68.
    on Purity, 64.
    on Repose, 71.
    on Symmetry, 65.

Ruskin on Unity, 69.
Schumann, Life, etc., 186.
    List of Illustrations, 193, 194.
    Contrasted with Beethoven and Bach, 192.
    Op. 2, Polonaise in D, 110.
    Op. 12, Aufschwung, 31, 115.
    Op. 15, Scenes of Childhood, 54, 115.
    Op. 16, Kreisleriana, No. 2, 36.
    Op. 21, Novelette in E. No. 7; 11, 29.
    Op. 24, No. 1, in C, 22.
    Op. 24, No. 4, in F, 22.
    Op. 28, Romance in F sharp, 44.
    Op. 68, Spring Song, 15.
    Op. 68, Hobby Horse, 54.
    Op. 99, Novelette in B minor, 11.
    Traumerei, 29.
    Songs, 134.
Schubert, Dances, 11, 28.
    Menuetto in B min., Op. 78: 10, 11, 13, 14, 22, 33, 44.
    Waltz, No. 1, 22.
    Sonata in C, 31.
    Op. 90, I., Impromptu in C min., 48.
    Op. 90, II., Impromptu in E♭, 48.
    Op. 142, Impromptu in B♭, 106.
    Songs, 134.
Sentimental, The Gentle and, 111.
Second, 32.
Sequence, 48.
Sensuous, The, 51.
Scenes from Childhood, Op. 15, Schumann, 54.
Sensation, The Pleasing in, 64.
Satisfactory in Contemplation, The, 65.
Sense, Art and, 74.
Sculpture, 82.
Sonata, piece, 36.
Song-group, 37.
Sonata, 40.
    Plan of, 40.
    Unity in, 41.
    The Cycle of, 98.
Sculpture and Painting Compared, 85.
Soulful and Tender in the Classic, 94.
Sensational and Astonishing, 116.
Scena and Aria, 128.
    and Aria, Illustrations of, 130.
Scarlatti, D., 148.
Strauss, Blue Danube, 52.
Storm, The, H. Weber, 54.
Song, The Thoroughly Composed 134
    Illustrations of
Suggestive Music, 52.
Symmetry, 66.
Symbolical Art, 77.
Thematic, 10, 12.
Third, 34.
Titania, Lefebre-Wely, 48.
Time, 67.
Tender and Soulful, The, in the Classic, 94.
Transition from Romantic to Classical, 101.
Thomas, A., Mignon, 128.
Unity in Variety, 67.
Unity, 69.
    of Separate and Distinct Things, 70.
    of Origin, 71.
    of Membership, 71.
Voice, 14.
Variations, 18.
    Defined, 20.
    Formal, 20.
    Character, 20.
Variety, Unity in, 67.
Weber, "Der Freischütz," Waltz, 22.
    Polocca Brillante, Op. 72, 110.
    Ocean, Thou Mighty Monster, 130
Wieck, Clara, 189.
Wagner, R., 200.
    Aria from Lohengrin, 134.
    Illustrations, 208.
Zachan, 148.

AND

CONDENSED ENCYCLOPEDIA

OF

*MUSICAL TERMS, INSTRUMENTS, COMPOSERS,
AND IMPORTANT WORKS.*

Designed to Accompany "How to Understand Music."

BY

W. S. B. MATHEWS.

Copyright, 1880.

CHICAGO:
DONNELLEY, GASSETTE & LOYD, PRINTERS.
1880.

PREFACE.

Every musical student, teacher, amateur, and newspaper critic has frequently experienced the need of a handy little book of reference, in which he might be reasonably sure of finding the pronunciation and definition of terms, description of instruments, the names, composers and dates of important works (such as oratorios, operas, cantatas, symphonies, etc.), and the names, nationality dates, and general characteristics of all the principal composers. The present work is offered for general use as such a dictionary, and a sort of condensed encyclopedia of music.

Its difference from other musical dictionaries may be inferred from the following memorandum of its mode of preparation, and its contents. Taking Mendel's *Musikalisches Conversations-Lexicon* (11 vols. 8vo. Berlin 1870—1883) a list of titles was made under each initial. That work is sufficiently rich in the explanation of terms, and especially so in larger articles, such as "Assyrian Music," "Hebrew Music," "Harmony," as well as German biography. To the list of titles thus made, were then added the most desirable ones from Grove's "Dictionary of Music and Musicians" (London 1879—1881, 2 vols. 8vo). To this source are we indebted for the names of operas, etc., descriptions of instruments, and the English biographical matter. Next, Stainer and Barrett's "Dictionary of Musical Terms" (8vo. pp. 456, Ditson & Co. 1879) was gone through, as well as Mr. Ludden's excellent and remarkably complete "Pronouncing Dictionary of Musical Terms" (J. L. Peters & Co. N.Y.) The additions from these latter sources were considerable. Even this did not suffice to complete the list. Names were overlooked, and some which were obviously desirable, were not to be found in any of these works. These omissions were supplied in a measure through the promptings of Mr. G. Schirmer's very complete "Catalogue of Music," and by personal correspondence. In the nature of the case, the satisfactory selection of titles for inclusion in a handy book like this, is a matter of difficulty, if not impossibility. The explanations given above will perhaps serve to condone the shortcomings yet remaining.

The definitions and characterizations of musicians have been freely taken from the sources indicated above, where, in turn, they had been just as decidedly acquired from previous writers. So also with the pronunciations of terms from foreign languages; when practicable they are here taken from Ludden or from Zell's encyclopedia. While they may not give an accurate idea of the true pronunciation of the terms, according to vernacular usage, they at least may lay claim to the merit of making as fair an approximation thereto as the type and popular character of this book permitted. To the whole is added an explanatory Synopsis of Musical Notation and a list of the principal Melodic Embelishments, with the proper manner of performing them, carefully prepared from the best authorities. Titles improperly omitted from this will be added to subsequent editions in an appendix.

W. S. B. MATHEWS.

DICTIONARY.

A, or **Ab.** (Ital. prep.) from; of; also a name of a pitch.

Abbreviations. These are the more usual. Look for definitions under the words themselves.

A cel., for accelerando; *Ac omp.*, Accompagnement; *Adgo.* or *Ado.*, Adagio; *ad lib.*, ad libitum; *all' ot.*, all' ottava; *Allo.*, Allegro; *Allgrto.*, Allegretto; *Anan.*, Andantino; *Andte.*, Andante; *ar..., coll'* are; *Arpio.*, Arpeggio; *a. t.*, à tempo; *Basso*, Contrabasso; *C. B.*, Contrabasso; *c. 8va.*, coll' ottava; *C. D.*, colla destra; *C. L.*, col legno; *C. S.*, colla sinistra; *Cad.*, Cadenza; *cal.*, calando; *c. B.*, col Basso; *Clar.*, Clarinetto; *Claro.*, Clarino; *Co.*, Corno; *cres.*, crescendo; *D.*, destra, droite; *D. C.*, da Capo; *D. S.*, dal Segno; *decrs.*, decrescendo; *dim.*, diminuendo; *div.*, divisi; *dol.*, dolce; *espr.*, espressivo; *f.*, forte; *Fag.*, Fagott.; *ff.*, fortissimo; *Fl.*, Flauto; *Fp.*, forte piano; *fz.*, forzando; *G.*, gauche; *L.*, laeva; *leg.*, legato; *lo. luc.*, loco or luogo lusing.*, lusingando; *manc.*, man an; *marc.*, marcato; *m. d.*, mano destra; *m. d.*, main droite; *mez.*, mezzo; *mf.* or *m.f.*, mezzo forte; *mezz.* forte piano; *m' ito.*, moderato; *m. v. muzo*, mezza voce; *Ob.*, Oboe (Hautbois); *p.*, piano; *ped.*, pedale; *perd.*, per dendosi; *P. F.*, Piano-Forte; *pf.*, più forte; *pizz.*, pizzicato; *pp.*, pianissimo or più piano; *rall.*, rallentando; *rf.*, *rfz.*, rinforzando; *rit.*, ritardando; *riten.*, ritenuto; *S. sin.*, sinistra; *scherz.*, scherzando; *seg.*, segue; *sem.*, sempre; *sfz.*, sforzando; *sim.*, simile; *smorz.*, smorzando; *sost.*, sostenuto; *s. S.*, senza Sordini; *s. T.*, senza Tempo; *sta.*, staccato; *string.*, stringendo; *T.*, tasto, tenore; *T.*, tutti, tempo; *ten.*, tenuto; *Timp.*, Timpani; *tr.*, trillo; *trem.*, tremoland; *Tromb.*, trombone; *Tromp.*, Trompette; *T. S.*, tasto sol; *u. c.*, una corda; *unis.*, unisono; *V.*, Voce; *Va.*, Viola; *vara.*, variazione; *Vo.*, Violino; *Vello.*, Violoncello; *V. S.*, Volti subito.

Abbandono, con (Ital. ä-bän-do-no), or **Abbandonatemente.** With abandon, with enthusiasm.

Abend Musik (Ger.) Evening music.

Abert, J. J. (ä-bêrt), a German orchestral and operatic composer, born at Kachowitz, in Bohemia, 1832. Best known by his orchestral transcriptions of Bach's organ fugues.

Ab Initio (Lat. in-ish'-io). From the beginning.

Abt, Franz, the popular German song-writer ("When the Swallows," etc.) b. Dec. 22, 1819, at Eilenburg, Prussia. Visited America in 1872, and conducted at the Gilmore Jubilee.

A capella (Ital. kä-pel'-lä). In church style; *i. e.*, voices only, without accompaniment.

A capriccio. Ital. cä-prëe'-cho. At caprice; at pleasure.

Accelerando (Ital. ät-sel-än-rän'-do). Accelerating; gradually hastening the time.

Accent, an emphasis or stress on a particular notes or passages, for the purpose of rendering the meaning of a passage more clear. The principal accents in music are (1) the measure accent, occurring on the first of every measure; (2) the motet accents, a vary on the emphatic note of a phrase, or a most important word in a phrase; (3) ordinary rhythmic accents, on the first note of smaller groups contained in the full measure, as e. g., on the first note of triplets, etc.

Accidental, one received, a name given to a sharp, flat, or naturals in music outside the signature.

Accentuato (Ital. ät-ts än-tu-ä'-tö). Accented.

Accompagnamento (Ital. ak-kom-pan-yä-men'-to). Accompaniment; parts used in sounding with and supporting the leading voice.

Accord, to sound well together. See consonance. *A chord.*

Acoustics are sciences. The science of sound.

Accordion, a well known instrument, the tones of which are produced by "free reeds." Large instruments of this class have a compass of about four octaves.

Acis and Galatea (ä'-sis, gä-lä-tê'-ä). A pastoral cantata by Handel in 1720.

Adagio (Ital. ä-dä'-jo). Literally *at ease, leisurely*. A slow and tender movement, slower than *andante*, but not so slow as *largo*. See "Tempo."

Adagissimo (Ital. ä-dä-jis'-sï-mö). Superlative degree of adagio.

Adam, Adolph Charles, a French composer of light operas (Le Postillon de Longjumeau, etc.), newspaper critic and professor of composition at the Conservatoire; b. 1803, d. 1856.

Adams, Thomas, a distinguished English organist and composer; b. 1785, d. 1858.

Ad Libitum (Lat.) At pleasure; *i. e.*, slow or fast.

Adler, Vincent, a young composer living in Paris, belonging to the school of Stephen Heller. Author of many interesting piano pieces.

A due (Fr.) For two. (Used in orchestral scores.)

A dur (Ger. ä-dür). The key of A major.

A moll (Ger.) A minor key of.

Eolian Key, one of the "church modes," having the tones A B C D E F G A; the natural minor scale.

ā *ale*, ă *add*, ä *arm*, ē *eve*, ĕ *end*, ī *ice*, ĭ *ill*, ō *old*, ŏ *odd*, ô *ore*, oo *moon*, ū *lute*, ŭ *but*, ü *Fr. sound*

Æolian Harp, a harp played by the wind. Should be of thin pine, 3 ft. long, 3 in. deep, 5 broad, with beech ends for insertion of pitch and tuning pins. Is strung with 12 catgut strings passing over low, hard-wood bridges, and tuned in perfect unison. Placed in a window open enough to receive it, and somewhat obliquely to the wind, it produces the most delightful chords.

Æschylus (Ger. es'-ke-lus), a Greek (Attic) philosopher, born B. C. 525.

Affetuoso (Ital. äf-fĕt'-oo-ō'-zō), or **Con affetto**, with feeling.

Agilita (Ital. ä-jĭl'-ĭ-tä). Agility, quickness.

Agitato (Ital. äj-ĭ-tä'-tō), or **Con Agitatione**, agitated, disturbed; commonly implies hurrying.

Agnus Dei (Lat. äg-nŭs dā-ee). Lamb of God; part of the service of mass.

Air, a melody or tune. See Aria.

Al, All, Alla (Ital.) To the; in the style of.

Alberti, H. (äl-bär'-tee). At once poet, organist and composer. Born at Lobenstein 1704. Died 1657.

Albani (äl-bä'-nee). The stage name of a favorite soprano. See Lajeunnesse.

Alboni, Marietta (äl-bō'-nee). The most celebrated contralto of the 19th century. Born Censensa, Italy, 1824. Sang with the greatest éclat throughout Europe. Visited America in 1852. Her voice was large, rich and true, and her method delightful. Lives in Paris.

Alceste (Fr. äl-sĕst'). Tragic opera in three acts by Calzabigi and Glück, 1761.

Albrechtsberger (äl'-bretchts-bŭr'-gĕr), Johann Geo. Contrapuntist and teacher of sacred music, composer and organist, born 1736, at Klosterburg, near Vienna. Died Vienna March 7, 1809. Among his pupils were Beethoven, Hummel, Weigl, Seyfried, etc.

Alexander's Feast, an "ode" of Handel's to Dryden's words, 1736. Re-scored by Mozart, 1790.

Alkan, Charles V. Born at Paris, 1813. Pianist and composer, chiefly of études and caprices for piano. His studies are extremely difficult, and are important. Has published op. 72.

Alla Breve, indicated 2-2, a form of common time, taken somewhat faster and beat with two beats in a measure.

Allegro (Ital. äl-lā'-grō), literally "cheerful." A tempo mark, indicating a quick movement. See Tempo.

Allegretto (Ital. äl'-lĕ-grĕt'-tō). Diminutive of allegro; cheerful; not so quick as allegro. See Tempo.

Allegrezza (Ital. äl-lĕ-grĕt'-zä). Gayety; cheerfulness.

Allegri (äl-lāg'-ree), Gregorio, a priest at Fermo, 1580-1652. Author of a celebrated "Miserere" used at the Pontifical chapel during Holy week.

Allemande (Fr.) One of the movements of the suite. It is of German origin, and was not a dance.
2. Also used as equivalent to Deutscher Tanz, a dance resembling the waltz.

3. A German national dance of a lively character, in 2-4 time.

Al Segno (Ital. säu'-yō). From the sign; return to the sign ——, and play from there to "Fine."

All Unisono (Ital. oo-nĭ-sō'-nō). In unison.

Alto (Ital.) literally, "high." The highest male voice, having a range above the tenor. The low female voice now commonly called by this name is properly *contralto*, which see.

Alto Clef, see Clef.

Amabile (Ital. ä-mä'-bē-lĕ). Lovingly; tenderly.

Amati (äm-ä'-tee). A celebrated family of violin makers, who lived and worked at Cremona. Their best work was: ANDREA, about 1550; NICOLO made basses; ANTONIO and GERONIMO, sons of Andrea, 1550-1635; NICOLO, 1596-1684, the most eminent of all the family; GERONIMO, his son, an indifferent maker.

Ambros, August W. (äm'-brōz). Born 1816, in Bohemia. A brilliant writer on musical topics, and author of a fine Musical History, four volumes of which have appeared. Died June 28, 1876.

Ambrosian Chant, the ecclesiastical mode of saying and singing Divine service, set in order by St. Ambrose for Milan cathedral, about A. D. 384.

Ambrosian Hymn, the *Te Deum*.

Amoroso (Ital. äm-or-ō'-zō). Lovingly, tenderly, with warmth.

Amphion, one of the oldest Greek musicians; flourished about 1300 B. C.

Anapest, see "foot."

Andante (Ital. än-dan'-tĕ, from *andare*, to walk.) Going, moving along at a moderate pace. See "Tempo." Also used as the name of a piece of music in andante movement.

Andantino (Ital. än-dan-tee nō, diminutive of the preceding). A movement somewhat quicker than *andante*. Sometimes used to denote a slower movement than *andante*. (Mendel.)

Andrè, Johann (än'-drä), the head of an extensive musical family. B. 1741, d. 1799. Author of many works of almost every kind. JOHANN A., his son, 1775-1842, also a prolific composer, and teacher of the piano and violin; JOHANN B., his son, pupil of Aloys Schmitt, a resident of Berlin; JULIUS, son of J. A., an organist and writer for the organ.

Angelica, angelic. **Vox Angelica**, angelic voice, the name of an organ stop, free reed.

Anlagnier, Antonin, a French composer of popular piano pieces. Born 1800 at Manosque, educated in the Paris Conservatoire, and later a music dealer there.

Anima (Ital. än'-ĭ-mä), **con anima**, with life.

Animato (Ital. än-ĭ-mä'-tō). Animated.

Anna Bolena (bo-lā'-na). Opera by Donizetti, 1831.

Auschuetz, Karl (än'-sheetz). B. about 1831. Died in New York about 1875. An opera and orchestral conductor and composer.

Answer, the imitation of a previous phrase.

ale, ä add, ä arm, ē eve, ĕ end, ī ice, ĭ ill, ō old, ŏ odd, ō dove, oo moon, ŭ lute, ŭ but, ŭ Fr. sound

4

Antecedent, a phrase proposed for imitation. The first section in a period.

Anthem, a sacred motet for use in Divine service.

Anticipation, the entrance of a single note of a chord in advance of the remaining notes, thus making a dissonance with the chord into which it thrusts itself.

Antienne (Fr.) An anthem. Also used as the name of a soft and quiet organ piece.

Antiphony, responsive singing, between two choirs or the priest and choir.

Antiphonarium Romanum, Roman Antiphonary, the Romish collection of antiphons.

A piacere (Ital. ä pē-ä-tshä'-rĕ) At pleasure, faster or slower.

Appassionato (Ital. äp-päs-sē-ō-nä'-tō), Impassioned; passionately. Beethoven's sonata op. 57 was thus named by Cranz, the publisher.

Applicatur (Ger. ap-plik-a-tūr). Application, as *pedal applicatur*: pedal marks for applying the toe and heel.

Appoggiatura (Ital. ap-pod-jīä-tū'-rä), from *appoggiare* to lean upon. A melodic ornament consisting of a dissonant tone occurring on the accent and resolving into the true melodic tone one degree above or below. The *long A.* occupies half the time of the note it leans upon, and is written as a grace note. The *short A.* is played as quickly as possible; written as a grace note with a stroke through the stem. See Appendix, pp. 78 and 79.

Appoggiatura Double, a melodic ornament consisting of two grace notes before a melody note. Played rapidly, and in time taken from the principal note.

Aptommas, two Welsh brothers, harpists. B. 1826 and 1829.

Arendelt, Jacob, a singer, teacher and composer, at Rome about 1539. Born in the Netherlands. Author of madrigals, masses, etc.

Arco Ital. är'-kō), The bow of stringed instruments. **Coll' arco**, or **arcato**, with the bow, as opposed to *pizzicato*, which see.

Arditi, Luigi (loo-ee-gee är-dee'-tee). Born at Crescentino in Piedmont, 1822. Author of several operas, overtures, songs, etc. Conductor of Italian opera in London, Vienna, etc. Visited America several times.

Ardito (Ital. är-dee'-tō). Warmth; ardor.

Aria (Ital. är'-ïä). Air. See Lesson s xxx, xxxv.

Arietta (Ital. är-ī-ĕt'-tä). A little air. Lesson xiv.

Arioso (Ital. är-ī-ō'-zō). In style of an aria. Lesson xxvii.

Arion, a Greek musician, fabled to be the son of Neptune and Oncea. Lived about 620 B. C.

Armide (är-meed'). One of Gluck's greatest operas. Produced in Paris Sept. 23, 1777.

Arne, Thomas A., Mus. Doc. An English composer of glees, anthems, and the music of several operas or stage pieces, music to Shakespeare's Tempest, to cantatas "Judith" and "Abell," etc. 1710-1778.

Arne, Michael, son of preceding, 1741-1+86. A conductor and popular composer of operas, etc., in his day.

Arpeggio (Ital. är-pĕd-jō). A melodic figure composed of the tones of a chord struck successively. A broken chord.

Arnold, Samuel, Mus. Doc., born in London, 1740. Died 1802. An organist, conductor and author. Composed many dramatic works.

Art of Fugue, The (*Die Kunst der Fuge*), a wonderful work of Sebastian Bach's, containing eighteen fugues, all on one subject. Composed in the last year of his life.

Ascher, Joseph born in London, in 18—. Died 1869. A fashionable pianist and composer of drawing-room pieces.

Assai (Ital.) A flat. (Ab.)

Assai (Ital. äs-sä'ī). Very, e. g., **Allegro assai**, very fast, etc.

Assoluto (Ital. äs-sō-lū'-tō). Absolute. **Prima donna assoluta**, absolute, or first, prima donna.

Athalia (äth-äl-ī-ä), The third of Handel's oratorios 1733.

Athalie (Ger. ät-tăl-y). Overture, march and six vocal pieces (op. 74) to Racine's drama, composed by Mendelssohn, 1845.

A tempo (Ital. ä těm-pō). In time.

Attwood, Thomas, English composer of dramatic and cathedral music; conductor and organist; a favorite pupil of Mozart, and one of the first English musicians to recognize the genius of Mendelssohn. 1717-1838. Buried in St. Paul's Cathedral, under the organ.

Attacca Ital. ät-täk-kä). Attack. **Attacca subito**, attack the following immediately.

Atto (Ital. ät-tō). Act.

Auber, Daniel-François-Esprit, born 1784 at Caen. Died 1871. Auber was the most popular of the French composers of this century. Auber was composer of a large number of operas, among the best of which are "Crown Diamonds," "Fra Diavolo," and "La Muette de Portici" (Masaniello). His works are characterized by bright and sparkling melody, and pleasant and piquant instrumentation, though Wagner says he uses the orchestra like a mighty guitar (implying Auber's lack of thematic treatment). He was made Director of the Conservatoire by Louis Phillippe, and remained so until his death. A. was genial and witty.

Audace (Ital. ä-oo-dä'-tshě). Same as *arditto*.

Auflösung (Ger. ouf-lö-sūng). Resolution (of dissonances).

Auftact (Ger. ouf-täkt). The unaccented beat of the measure.

Augmentation, the extension of a phrase or subject by lengthening the time of all its notes, imitating quarter notes by halves, etc.

Ausdruck (Ger. ous-drūk), Expression.

Ave Maria (Lat. ä-vě mär-ee-ä). "Hail Mary." The angelic salutation, Luke 1, 28.

ä *ale,* ä *add,* ä *arm,* ē *eve,* ĕ *end,* ī *ice,* ĭ *ill,* ō *old,* ŏ *odd,* ō *dove,* oo *moon,* ū *lute,* ŭ *tut,* ü *Fr. sound*

Authentic, certain of the ecclesiastical modes. They are:

No.	Mode.	Compass.	Final.	Dominant.
1	Dorian	D to D	D	A
3	Phrygian	E to E	E	C
5	Lydian	F to F	F	C
7	Mixolydein	G to G	G	D
9	Æolian	A to A	A	E
11	Ionion, or Iastian	C to C	C	G

Azor and Zemira, or The Magic Rose, in three acts. English version of Spohr's *Zemire und Azor*, produced at Covent Garden, April 5, 1831.

B. the name of a pitch. In Germany the name B is applied to the tone B♭, and B is called H.

Bach, Johann Sebastian (bäkh), one of the greatest masters who have ever appeared in music. B. 1685, d. 1750. Bach's ancestry for a century had been musicians, and several of them eminent. See chapter on Bach.

Bach, Wilhelm Friedmann, called also the Hallé Bach, oldest and most talented son of John, born at Weimar 1710. Was noted for his originality as a composer and improviser, but owing to dissipated habits he left comparatively few works. Died at Berlin, 1784.

Bach, Karl Philipp Emanuel, third son of J. S., born at Weimar 1714. Studied law, but as he had been educated in music from childhood, he presently betook himself to it as his calling, and became kammermusiker and cembalist at the court of Frederick the Great. As composer, director, teacher and critic, his influence was very great. He belongs to the transition period from his father to Haydn. His works are remarkable for refinement and elegance rather than power. Died 1788.

Bach Society, in London, devoted to the study and promulgation of Bach's works. 1849–1870. Its library is now in the Royal Academy of Music.

Bach Gesellschaft, a German society for publishing Bach's works, of which some thirty volumes are now issued. The idea originated with Schumann and Hauptmann.

Bache, Francis Edward (bāk), born at Birmingham, Sept. 14, 1833, died there Aug. 24, 1858. A talented young composer, a student at Leipsic, who died before his talent was fairly developed. Author of several piano pieces, a concerto, etc.

Bachelor of Music, a degree conferred complimentarily by American colleges. At Oxford and Cambridge (Eng.) a candidate for degree must pass certain written and *viva voce* examinations in harmony, counterpoint, principles of orchestration, etc, and present a good vocal composition containing pure five-part harmony and good fugal counterpoint, with accompaniment for strings, sufficiently long to occupy from 25 to 40 minutes in the performance. Fees about £18.

Badinage (Fr. bäd'-in-äg). Playfulness.

Badarzewski, Thekla, born at Warsaw 1838. Died 1862. Immortalized by her composition, "*Prière de la Vierge*," "Maiden's Prayer."

Baertauze. (Ger.) Dance of the Bayardiers; female dancers in the East Indies.

Bagatelle (Fr. băg-ă-těl), a trifle. A name applied to short compositions.

Bagpipe, a famous instrument of great antiquity. It consists of a combination of fixed tones, or "drones," which sound continuously when the instrument is played, and a "chanter." The drones are made by three pipes with reeds, tuned differently in different parts of the country; A A A, G D A, G D G, etc. The chanter is an instrument akin to the oboe, with a compass of only nine notes, not tuned accurately, but approximating the scale of the black keys of the piano. The wind is furnished by a wind-bag or sack, worked by the left arm.

Baker, B. F., born about 1820. Author of a text-book of Harmony and several books of psalmody.

Balfe, Michael William, born at Dublin 1808, died 1870. A prolific composer of songs and operas, the best of them being "The Bohemian Girl," "Siege of Rochelle," "The Enchantress," "Talisman," and "Puritan's Daughter." Balfe was a fine melodist but a careless composer.

Balatka, Hans, a fine German musician, teacher and conductor, in Chicago. Born about 1830.

Ballad, from the Italian *ballata*, a dance. *Ballata*, a dancing piece; *Suonata*, a sounding piece; and *Cantata*, a singing piece.— *Grove.*) In Italy the ballata was a song to be sung while dancing. A poem in narrative form, adapted to be sung to some ballad tune.

Ballade (Fr. băl-läd'). A ballad. Capriciously applied by Chopin to four pieces of pianoforte music.

Ballerina (Ital. bäl-ler-ee-nä). A female ballet-dancer.

Ballet (Fr. băl-lā). A suite of elaborate dances for performance on the stage. The term B. is applied equally to the music, to the dancers, and to the dances.

Ballo in Maschera (Ital. bäl'-lō in mäs'-ker-ä). "The Masked Ball," opera by Verdi, 1859.

Band, a company of instrumental players. See "String band," "Brass band," "Wind band," "Military band."

Banjo, an American instrument of the guitar kind, the body covered with parchment like a drum-head. It has five or six strings, tuned: A, E, G sharp, B, E, or G, D, G, B, D, G, the lowest string being in the octave below middle C. Its pitch is an octave lower than its notation.

Bar, a line across the staff to mark the measures. In England often applied to the measure itself.

Barbaja, Domenico (bär'-bä-yä), an Italian opera manager, who introduced most of Auber's and Rossini's operas to the world at San Carlo theatre in Naples and La Scala in Milan. 1778–1841.

Barber of Seville. English name of an opera by Rossini, 1816. Also opera of Paisello 1785.

Barcarole (Ital. bär-kă-rōl), a boat-song. A piece written in the rocking movement of a boatman.

ā ale, ă add, ä arm, ŏ eve, ĕ end, Ī ice, Ĭ ill, ō old, ŏ odd, ö dove, oo moon, ŭ lute, ŭ but, ü Fr. sound

Bargiel. Woldemar (völ -dē-mär bär -gēel), Step-brother of Mme. Clara Schumann. Born in Berlin 1828. A teacher and an elegant composer of pianoforte pieces, chamber music, etc. B. stands too near Schumann for his own talent to have fair play.

Baritone, a male voice of medium range and large body of tone. Also the name of the smaller bass saxhorn, in B♭.

Baritone Clef, the bass clef applied to the third line of the staff.

Barnby, Joseph, a prominent English composer of church music, glees, songs, etc. Born about 1837. For some reason omitted from Grove's Dic. and Mendel.

Barnett, John F., an English pianist and composer of three Cantatas, "The Ancient Mariner" 1867, "Paradise and the Peri" 1870, "Raising of Lazarus" 1873, "Lay of the Last Minstrel" 1874; also of several concertos, overtures, quartettes, etc. Born Oct. 6, 1838.

Barrel Organ, of various design and construction. Some are merely enlarged music-boxes, others small orchestrions, in which the tones are produced by reeds or pipes. All are controlled by means of a *barrel*, or cylinder, on the surface of which pins are set at such intervals that a revolution of the cylinder opens the valves and so produces the tones of a piece. By sliding the barrel a minute distance, another set of pins come into operation and thereby the tune is changed. In orchestrion organs the crank not only revolves the cylinder, but also works the bellows.

Bartholdy, see Mendelssohn.

Barytone, a stringed instrument of the violin family, having six or seven catgut strings stretched over the fingerboard, and from nine to twenty-four metal strings which act sympathetically. Has a weak but pleasing tone. Has given place to the violoncello.

Bass (bās), the lowest part in harmony. Also the lowest male voice.

Basso Profundo (prō-fun'-dō). The lowest male voice, of deep quality of tone.

Basset Horn (Ital. *corno di bassetto*), a bass clarinet in F, reaching from F below the bass clef. Written for by Mozart and Mendelssohn.

Bass Clarinet, a low clarinet ranging upwards from E below middle C. A slow-speaking, hollow-toned instrument.

Bass Clef, the sign of the bass staff. Represents F next below middle C.

Bass Tuba, th lowest of the saxhorn family. That in E♭ reaches E♭ of the 16 ft. octave. The B♭ Tuba, B♭ in the 32 ft. octave, three octaves below middle C.

Bassini. Carlo, an Italian teacher of singing, living in New York from 1864 or thereabouts. Died in 1871.

Bass Horn, see Serpent.

Bassoon (bä-zoon), Ger. *Fagott*, a wooden double-reed instrument of 8 ft. tone. Its compass is from 16 ft. B♭ to A♭ on 2d space of treble. Is the natural bass of the oboes and clarinets, *i. e.*, the "wood."

Basso Cantante (Ital. kän tän'-tō). The singing bass, or principal bass singer, as distinguished from the *basso buffo*, comic bass, and the *basso profundo*, or very low bass.

Basso Continuo, a bass running through the whole piece, from which, with figures, the accompaniment used to be played. See Thorough Bass.

Bass Posaune (Ger. Pō'-sown'-ē). The bass trombone.

Basien et Bastienne, a German operetta in one act. Mozart 1768.

Bass Viol, English name of the violoncello.

Baton (Fr. bä-tonh). A conductor's stick for beating time.

Battle of Prague, a descriptive sonata by Kotzwara, 1792. One of the most famous pieces of programme music.

Battle Symphony, English name for Beethoven's "Wellington's Sieg oder die Schlacht bei Vittoria," op. 91. 1813.

Battement (Fr. bät-tē-mon). An old embellishment similar to the mordente, but made with the note below.

Battishill, Jonathan, an English composer of songs, glees, catches and anthems. 1738-1801.

Baumbach, Adolph, A German piano forte teacher and prolific arranger of piano pieces, living some time in Boston. Came to Chicago about 1869. Died 1880.

B dur (Ger. dūr). B major.

Bearings, the few notes a tuner lays down carefully as guides. Usually the middle octave.

Beat. An embellishment of the mordent kind.
  2. The conductor's motion in indicating the time.
  3. The throbbing effect of dissonance, produced by the occasional interference and consequent extinction of a vibration. The number of beats per second is equal to the difference between the rates of vibration in the notes.

Becker, Paul, a German piano teacher and fine musician, resident in Chicago since 1855, where he was for many years the leading exponent of classical music.

Becker, Carl Ferdinand, organist and professor at the Conservatorium of Leipsic. Born 1804, died 1877. Especially learned in musical literature.

Beer (bār). Original name of Meyer Beer.

Beethoven, Ludwig van (lood vig fan bā-tō-vn). 1770-1827. See Part VIII.

Behr, Fr., a German composer of light pieces.

Begleiten (Ger. bĕg-lī-tĕn'). To accompany.

Beggar's Opera, a celebrated piece, written in 1727 by Gay. Its songs were all written to old melodies, or to the most popular airs of the day. It had an immense success.

Bell, the expanded opening in which most brass instruments terminate. Also applied to organ pipes, as in the "bell diapason," "bell gamba," in which all the pipes end in a bell.

Belisario (bĕl-I-sär-Iō). Italian opera in 3 acts by Donizetti, 1836.

Bellezza (Ital. bĕl-lät-zä). Beauty of tone and expression.

Bellicoso (Ital. bĕl-lI-kō-sō). Warlike.

ā *ale*, ă *add*, ä *arm*, ē *eve*, ĕ *end*, ī *ice*, ĭ *ill*, ō *old*, ŏ *odd*, ȯ *dove*, oo *moon*, ū *lute*, ŭ *but*, ü *Fr. sound*

7

Bellini, Vincenzo (vin tchǎn'-dzō bĕl-lee'-nee). Italian composer of operas, the best of which are " Sonnambula," " I Puritani " and " Norma." His writing is characterized by delicate and graceful melody, and great refinement. Bellini died very young, perhaps before his powers were fully developed; still he represents the simple, natural side of Italian music, where the music exists for itself alone, paying very little attention to the text, a school which was even in his day giving place to the stronger style of Verdi and Wagner. 1802–1835.

Bellows, the wind receptacles of organs.

Bells, musical instruments of metal, sounding by percussion. Extremely ancient. Bell metal consists of copper and tin, 3 to 1.

Belly, the upper side of violins, that next the strings.

Belshazzar, an oratorio by Handel, 1745. 2. Dramatic piece by Mr. J. A. Butterfield, 1871. Written for amateurs.

Bemerkbar (Ger, bĕ-märk'-bär), marked; to be played in a prominent manner.

Be mol (Fr. bĕ-mŏl). B flat.

Ben, Bene (Ital. bĕn, bā -nĕ). Well.

Benedict, Sir Julius, born at Stuttgart, Nov. 27, 1804. " One of the most eminent foreign musicians settled in England since Handel's time." Author of several operas, the oratorios of " St. Cecilia " and " St. Peter." One of the most eminent conductors of the present time. Lives in London. Visited this country with Jenny Lind in 1850.

Benedictus (Lat.) The song of Zachariah, Luke i.

Bendel, Franz, piano virtuoso and composer of a vast mass of piano music, among the best of which is his " Am Genfer See," also his op. 8, 45 and 47. Visited the United States and played at 2d Peace Jubilee in 1872. Died about 1874. B. 1833.

Bennett, William Sterndale, Mus.Doc., M.A., D.C.L., one of the greatest English composers since Purcell. Born 1816. B. was a great friend of Mendelssohn's, whose style influenced him very much. Composer of many piano works, two concertos, 1840, for piano and orchestra, cantata " The May Queen," 1858, and an oratorio " The Women of Samaria," 1867. (Given in Boston in 1874.) His works are characterized by elegance and finish rather than power. Died Feb. 1, 1875.

Ben pronunziato (ital. prō-noon-tsē-ä'-tō). Pronounced clearly and distinctly.

Berceuse (Fr. bair-sŭrs'), a cradle song. Characterized by a rocking and monotonous accompaniment, and great delicacy.

Berens, Hermann (bā'-rĕns), born at Hamburg 1826. A good pianist and a successful popular composer. Resides in Stockholm, Sweden, where he is very active in all departments of musical work. D. 1880.

Berger, Ludwig (lood-vĭg bair-gĕr), a fine pianist and composer in Berlin 1777–1838. Pupil of Clementi. B. was teacher of Mendelssohn, Taubert, Henselt, and Fanny Hensel. A prolific writer.

Berge, William (hăr-gā), a piano-teacher, organist, and arranger of pieces in New York.

Bergmann, Karl, a 'cellist and conductor, born at Eisenach in Saxony, 1821. Came to America with the " Germania " orchestra in 1850. In 1857 he removed from Boston to New York, where he occupied a leading place as conductor of the "Arion," " Philharmonic," etc. Died 1877.

Beriot, Charles Auguste de (bē'r' -ī ō), a celebrated violinist, born in Belgium 1802. Died 1870. In 1835 he married the famous singer Malibran. Author of many pleasing works for piano and violin.

Berlioz, Hector (bair'-lYŏz), a great French composer, critic and *littérateur*. Born Dec. 11, 1803, died March 9, 1869. Composer of many overtures, symphonic poems, etc., of the " programme " order, in which all the resources of the modern orchestra are employed with consummate mastery for the portrayal of poetic, bizarre, piquant, or profound sentiment. Berlioz seems like a genius of great power, in whom a vivid imagination is not restrained by good judgment. As a writer about music he is one of the most gifted of the present century. His place as a composer is not yet settled. His greatest dramatic work, " The Damnation of Faust " 1846, is only just receiving its due recognition.

Bertini, Henri (bār-teen'-ee), a pianist of French family, born at London 1798. Settled in Paris 1821. Died at Meylan 1876. B. was author of more than 200 compositions, of which his piano-school and " études " had wide currency. They are now superseded.

Bes (Ger. bĕs). The note B double flat, enharmonic with A natural.

Best, William T., the eminent English virtuoso organist, born at Carlisle 1826. Since '55, organist of St. George's Hall in Liverpool. Composer of many church services and many skillful and effective " arrangements " for the organ; also of a large " organ school," B. has been called " the Liszt of the organ," a title more complimentary than exact.

Beyer, Ferd. (bī'-ĕr) 1803–1863. A prolific " arranger " for the piano-forte.

Bianca, or the Bravo's Bride, a grand opera in 4 acts, by Balfe. 1860.

Bianca E Faliero (bee-än'-kä ā fal-yā'-rō). Opera by Rossini, 1819. A failure.

Bind, see Tie.

Birmingham Festival, triennial. The most important in England. Among the great works written for it were " Elijah " in 1846, " Eli " 1855, " Naaman " 1864. Profits go to hospital funds. Last one occurred in 1879.

Billert, Karl, a German composer of psalms, songs, overtures, symphonies, etc. A prominent and active musician. 1821 —.

Bilse, Benjamin (bĭl'-sĕ), one of the most famous conductors of the present day. Born 1816. His famous orchestra at Berlin, has 70 men. B. is also a composer of dance music.

Bird, H. D., organist in Chicago. Born about 1837.

Bis, twice; equivalent to *encore*, " again."

Bishop, Sir Henry Rowley, a popular English composer of songs, stage pieces, operas, one oratorio (never performed), etc. 1786–1855.

ā *ale*, ä *add*, ü *arm*, ĕ *eve*, ĕ *end*, Ī *ice*, I *ill*, ō *old*, ŏ *odd*, ò *dove*, oo *moon*, ū *lute*, ŭ *but*, ü *Fr. sound*

Blaze (called Castil-Blaze), François (blāz), a French writer upon music in "Le Menestrel," and in books. 1784-1857.

Blasinstruments (Ger. from *blasen*, to blow). Wind instruments, which see.

Blassmann, Adolph J. M., born 1823 at Dresden. An accomplished musician, composer and director at Dresden.

Blechinstruments (blĕk). Brass instruments.

Blow, John, Mus. Doc., a voluminous English writer of church music, odes, songs, etc. 1648-1708. Organist of Westminster Abbey, where also he was buried.

Blumenthal, Jacob (blū'-men-täl), a fashionable piano teacher in London, and composer of light pieces and popular songs. Born at Hamburg 1829.

B mol, the German name of the key of B flat minor.

Bocca ridente (It. bō'-kä re-dän'-tě). Smiling mouth. Applied in singing to a position of mouth believed to be favorable to the production of a good tone.

Boccherini, Luigi (lwee'-gee bōk-ĕr-een'-ee), a highly gifted Italian composer of chamber music, of which he left a vast amount, and of masses, songs, cantatas, concertos, etc. An extremely melodious and pleasing writer. 1740-1805.

Boehsa, Robert N. C. (bōk'-sä), a composer and eminent harpist, 1789-1855. As a composer, "too prolific for his own fame." As a man, "irregular and dissipated to the last degree."

Boge (bō-jě). A bow for stringed instruments.

Bohm, Theobald, a famous flute-player at Munich, and inventor of the flute which bears his name. Born 1802. Author of a well known set of 32 studies for Flute.

Boieldieu, François Adrien (bwäl'-dū), born 1775 at Rouen. B. made his debut in Paris as an opera composer with "Famille Suisse" in 1797, which had a run of 30 nights. His famous "Califfe de Bagdad" was produced in 1798. "La Dame Blanche" 1825. This latter opera up to June 1875 had been performed 1,340 times. B. was the greatest master of French comic opera. He died in 1834.

Bolero (bō-lār'-o) A brisk Spanish dance, similar to the polacca. It is in 3-4 time, in eighth notes with two sixteenths on the last half of the first beat of the measure.

Bologna (bōlōn'-yä). The seat of the earliest music school in Italy, founded 1482.

Bombardon, or **Bombard**, now applied to the lowest of the sax-horns. See Bass-tuba. 2. The name of a reed pedal-stop in the organ, generally of 32 ft., large scale, rich tone and frequently on a heavy wind pressure.

Bones four pieces of the ribs of horses or oxen, held in the hands and struck together rhythmically, like castanets.

Boosey & Co., music publishers in London. Established about 1820.

Bordese, Luigi (lwee'-gee bōr-dā-sĕ), a light opera and song composer of the present time. Born in Naples in 1815.

Bordogni, Mar. (bor-dō'-nyē) one of the most celebrated singers and masters of singing of recent times. Born in Bergamo 1789, died 1856. Author of many songs, also of studies for the voice, etc. 1802 32 years from 1824, professor of singing in the Paris Conservatoire.

Bourdon (bōōr'-dōn). An organ stop, usually of 16 ft. pitch, consisting of stopped wooden pipes, otherwise called "stopped diapason."

Bouche Fermee (Fr. boosh fŭr mā'). The mouth closed

Bottesini, Giovanni (jō-vän-nee bōt-tās-see-nee), a celebrated virtuoso contrabassist. Born in Lombardy 1823. Author of several successful operas, as well as quartettes, symphonies, etc.

Bourree (oor-rā). A dance of French origin, similar to the gavotte, but quicker, having only two beats to the measure. Found in suites.

Bow. Used to set in vibration the strings of the violin family. Consists of a stick of Brazilian lance-wood. From 175 to 250 hairs are put in a violin bow. The present form was perfected by Tourte near the close of the 18th century.

Bowing (bō-ing). The art of using the bow.

Boyce, William, Mus. Doc., an English composer of church music, odes, oratorios, a few pieces for the theatre, and a collection of standard music for the cathedral. 1710-1779.

Brabangonne, La (brä-bän'-son-nŏ). The national air of the Belgians, dating from 1830.

Brace. A vertical line for connecting the staves of music performed simultaneously in a set.

Brahms, Johannes (yō-hän'-nes brähms), one of the greatest living composers. Was born at Hamburg, 1833. He was the son of a musician, and his education commenced early. B. has composed a large number of works, all of masterly workmanship, and they are rapidly becoming current throughout the musical world. They consist of very many songs (over 100), piano forte pieces, quartettes and other chamber music, variations, and two symphonies which have been received with enthusiasm wherever performed.

Branle, an old English dance.

Brass Band. A band furnished with brass instruments of the sax-horn family. The proper appointment of such a band requires.
BAND OF EIGHT.—1 E♭ Cornet, 2 B♭ Cornets, 2 E♭ Altos, 1 B♭ Tenor, 1 B♭ Baritone, 1 E♭ Bass
BAND OF TWELVE. - 2 E♭ Cornets, 2 B♭ Cornets, 3 E♭ Altos, 2 B♭ Tenors, 1 B♭ Baritone, 1 B♭ Bass, 1 E♭ Bass.
BAND OF SIXTEEN 3 E♭ Cornets, B♭ Cornets, 3 E♭ Altos, B♭ Tenors, 1 B♭ Baritone, 1 B♭ Bass, 3 E♭ Basses.
The addition of oboes and clarinets transforms a "brass" band into a Military band, which see.

Brassin, Louis (bräs-ähn), one of the most noted piano virtuosos of the present time. Was born in Brussels in 1840. Was a student at Leipsic, and later teacher of piano at Stern's conservatory in Berlin. B. is a talented composer, and an exceedingly good interpreter of music, both old and new.

Bratsch. The German name for the viola, or tenor viol.

ā *ale*, ă *add*, ä *arm*, ĕ *eve*, ĕ *end*, ī *ice*, ĭ *ill*, ō *old*, ŏ *odd*, ŭ *dove*, oo *moon*, ū *tute*, ŭ *cut*, ü *Fr. sound*

Bravura (Ital. brä-voo'-rä). Courage; bravery. A style of music in which *effect* is sought for.

Breit (Ger. brīt). Broad.

Breitkopf & Härtel, a Leipsic firm of music publishers, which on Jan. 27, 1869, celebrated its 150th anniversary, the business having descended from father to son.

Brendel, Dr. Karl Franz, musical critic and lecturer on the history of music in the Conservatory at Leipsic; succeeded Schumann as editor of the "Neu Zeitschrift fur Music." 18:1-1868.

Breve, a note equal to two whole-notes (semibreves); not now used except in church music.

Bridge, the wooden contrivance used to support strings of stringed instruments, and to communicate their vibrations to the soundingboard.

Brio (Ital. bree'-ō). Spirit; vigor; force.

Brillante (Ital. and Fr.) Brilliantly.

Bristow, Geo. F., director and music teacher in New York. Born 1825. Author of two symphonies, an opera, etc.

Brindisi (Ital. brin'-dee-see, *far brindisi*, to drink a health). A drinking song.

Brisson. François, a French composer of piano pieces.

Broken Chords, chords the tones of which are sounded separately instead of simultaneously.

Bronsart. Hans von, a distinguished pianist, a pupil of Kullak and Liszt, and music director at Hanover. Born 1830 in Königsburg. A talented composer, his concerto in F sharp minor having been much played by Bülow.

Bruch, Max (brūkh), one of the most eminent living German composers, especially in respect to large vocal works, such as his "Loreley," "Frithjof," "Odysseus," "Flight of the Holy Family," "The Lay of the Bell," etc. To this must be added his two violin concertos, a symphony, etc. Bruch is a master of the orchestra, an earnest and serious composer, highly gifted in melody no less than harmony, and witha, a genius. B. 1838.

Buck, Dudley, born at Hartford, Conn. 1837. His studies in composition were mainly made with Julius Rietz at Leipsic and Dresden, where also he was an organ pupil of Schneider. His first "Motette Collection" was published in 1867, and marks an epoch in American church music. His second in 1871. Buck has also written very much church music for Episcopal choirs, and three important choral works: "Don Munio," the "46th Psalm," and last "Scenes from the Golden Legend," which gained the $1,000 prize at Cincinnati in 1880. He has also written several chamber compositions, overtures and two symphonies. Buck must be regarded as one of the most distinguished American composers. In 1871 he became organist at the Boston Music Hall. In 1875 he removed to Brooklyn, where he still resides.

Buffo (Ital. boof-ō). Comic.

Buelow, Hans Gu'do von (bū'-lō), the great pianist, born at Dresden, 1830. Became pupil of Liszt in 1851. Made his first concert journey in 1853. Since then resident in Berlin, Dresden, etc. Visited America in 1876. Bülow is one of the most learned musicians of the present day, a great conductor, and a pianist with no superior (except perhaps Liszt). B. has a profigious memory, knowing by heart almost the entire classical literature of music. He is also a composer of important works.

Burden, a chorus or refrain in old songs.

Burgmueller, Norbert, born at Düsseldorf, 1810. Died in 1836. He left a symphony and several other works of decided value and promise.

Burla, Burlesca or **Burlesque**, a musical joke.

Burletta (Ital. būr-lĕt'-tä). A musical farce.

Burney. Charles, Mus. Doc., 1726-1814. A cultivated and genial Englishman, best known by his "History of Music," 1776-1789. Wrote before modern music was developed; it is no wonder, therefore, that his erudite work contains little of present value.

Burrowes. John F., London, 1787-1852. Best known by his piano-forte and thorough bass "Primers," two of the most successful and worst text-books ever made.

Busby. Thomas, Mus. Doc., a laborious English composer and writer of works about music, now forgotten. 1755-1838.

Butterfield, J. A., born in England, 1837. Author of popular songs and several dramatic pieces, "Belshazzar" 1871, "Ruth" 1875, "A Race for a Wife" 1879.

Buxtehude, Dietrich, a celebrated organist and composer, whose playing Bach went to Lübeck to hear. 1637-1707.

Byrd. William, a prolific English composer and publisher. 1538-1623.

C, the key note of the natural scale. It is the Ionic scale of the church modes. The name of a certain pitch (see "Pitch"). The sign of common time, 4-4.

Cabinet Organ, a reed organ. (This name is owned by the Mason & Hamlin Organ Co., who were the first to use it.)

Cabinet Piano, a small upright piano. The large upright pianos are sometimes called "cabinet grand."

Cabaletta (Sp. kä bäl-āt tä). A lively melody in triplet time and rondo form.

Cadence (from *cado*, to fall). The close of a strain or piece of music. Cadences are "perfect," "imperfect," "half" and "plagal." See Lesson iii.

2. Also the name of an old embellishment resembling the mordente.

Cadenza (Ital. kä-dänt'-zä). A more or less elaborate bravoura passage, introduced by a performer just before the close of a piece. In concertos, cadenzas are sometimes extended to several pages.

Cæcilia (sē-sīl'-iä). A German musical periodical founded by Gottfried Weber. 1824-1848. (See *Cæcilia, St.*)

Ca Ira (sä ēē-rä). The earliest of French revolutionary songs.

Calando (Ital. from *calare*, to descend). With decreasing force.

Caldara. Antonio (käl-dä'-rä), born at Venice 1678. Died 1768 (or 1736, date disputed). Wrote 69 operas and oratorios.

Califfe de Bagdad (Fr.) Comic opera in one act. Lib. by Saint-Just. Music by Boieldieu, 1800.

Callcott, John W., Mus. Doc., an English composer of glees, anthems, etc., and a musical grammar. 1766-1821.

Calmato (Ital. kăl-mä'-tō). Calmed; quieted.

Calore Ital. kăl-ō-rē). Heat; warmth.

Camera (Ital. kam-er-ä). Chamber, or room. Applied to compositions *(sonata di camera)* to distinguish them as secular.

Campanini, Italo (kam-pan-ee-nee), the great tenor, born at Parma in 1846. Studied at Parma and Milan. Debut in leading characters in 1870. Knows the tenor roles of more than eighty operas.

Campanella Ital. kam-pan-el-la, a small bell. A piece of music suggesting little bells.

Canon (Grk.) A musical form in which a second voice exactly repeats the melody of another (called the antecedent) at any pitch. Canons are in unison (antecedent and consequent at the same pitch) in the octave, second, third, fourth, etc. Also in *contrary motion*, where the consequent repeats the antecedent backwards, and *inverted* the ups and downs of the antecedent reversed).

Cantabile (Ital. kan-tä'-bil-ĕ, from *cantare*, to sing). In singing style.

Cantata (Ital. kan-tä-tä). sung. A composition for voices with or without orchestra. Sung without action.

Cantate Domino Lat. kăn-tä'tō domi-In-ō). "O sing unto the Lord,' Ps. 98.

Cantilena (Ital. kăn-tĭ-lā-nä). A short, song-like piece for voice or instrument. A ballad.

Canto (Ital. kan'tō), song. The melody. **Bel Canto**, beautiful song.

Cantor (Lat.) Precentor. The director of a choir.

Cantus Fermus (Lat.) The fixed melody. A subject to which counterpoint is to be added.

Canzona (Ital. kan-zō'-ña). A song in a particular Italian style.

Canzonetta (Ital. kan-zō-net'-tä). A little canzona. A light and airy little song.

Capella Ital. kä-pĕl'-lä). A chapel.

Capelle (Ger. kä-pel'-ĕ). See Kapell.

Capellmeister (Ger. mis'-tĕr. See Kapellemeister.

Capo (Ital. kä-pō). The head or beginning.

Capo tasto, or **Capo dastro** Ital.) A small piece attached to the neck of a guitar to shorten all the strings in order to facilitate playing in difficult keys.

Capriccio (Ital. kä-prĭt-zīō), or **Caprice** (Fr. kä-prēs). A freak, whim or fancy. A composition irregular in form.

Capriccioso (Ital. ka-prit-zīō'-zo). Capriciously.

Capulletti e Montecchi (Ital. kä-pool-lĕt-tee ĕd mon-tāk'-kee). "The Capulets and the Montagues." Italian opera in 3 acts, from Shakespeare's Romeo and Juliet, by Bellini Venice, March 12, 1830. A fourth act was added by Vaccai.

Carafa, Michele ka- -fä, a popular Italian opera and pianoforte composer. Born at Naples 17 5. Made professor of composition at the Paris Conservatoire in 1822. Died 1876.

Carcassi. M treo (kär-käs' see, an eminent guitar virtuoso. Born about 1792. Died in Paris 1 5.

Carillon kär-ĭl' lōn, a hinge of bells. A set of bells so arranged as to be played upon.

Carissimi. Giacomo (jāk-ō'-mo kär ees -sImee, a celebrated Italian composer of church music and oratorios, in which he greatly improved recitative and accompaniments, and left many works deserving to be better known than they are at present. Born at Rome 1604. Died 1674.

Carlberg. Gotthold (gŏt'-hōl i kä̂l -bärg, a German teacher, conductor, editor and composer, residing in New York. Born about 1837. A sharp and rather sarcastic writer in excellent English.

Carnaby. Wm., Mus. Doc., an English composer of vocal music. 1772 1 .).

Carnaval (Ital.) carnival. The title of a set of fantastic pieces of Schumann, op. 9.

Carnaval di Venise, a popular Venetian air, to which grotesque variations have been written by Paganini and many others.

Carter, Henry, an English organist living in New York. Born perhaps about 1840.

Carter, Thomas, an English composer of operas, a singer and pianist. 1735-1804

Cary, Annie Louise, a celebrated contralto singer, born in Maine in 1846.

Catalani. Angelica (än-gĕl'-ō-kä kät-ä-lä'-nee), a great singer born 1770. Died 1849. She had a soprano voice of great compass, purity and power, and prodigious execution.

Catch, a round for three or more voices, the singing of which was extremely fashionable in the reign of Charles II.

Catel, Charles Simon (kä-tel '\, born 1773, died 1830. A French theorist, teacher of harmony, and composer of military music and operas. Best known by his treatise on Harmony.

Catgut, the name given to the material for certain strings. It is derived from the intestines of the sheep; never from the cat.

Cathedral Music, music composed for the English cathedrals.

Cavaillie (kav-al-lō), a family of distinguished organ-builders in the South of France. The present representative of the name is Cavaille Coll, the distinguished Parisian organ-builder.

Cecilia, St., a young Roman lady of noble birth, a Christian and a martyr of the second century. She has been long regarded as the patron saint of music and musicians, although there is no authentic evidence of her having had any musical accomplishment whatever.

Celeste Fr. sĕ-lest). An organ stop or tremulous effect, produced by a set of reeds or pipes slight y lower than the true pitch.

Celtic Music was entirely melodic in character, no harmony being employed, except perhaps a drone (as in the bag-pipe). The scale consisted of five tones: Major, C d e g a; minor, A c e d g, and D e g a c. Several of the Scotch and Irish melodies, especially those in the minor keys, are of Celtic origin.

ă *ale*, ä *add*, ä *arm*, ē *eve*, ĕ *end*, ĭ *ice*, ĭ *ill*, ō *old*, ŏ *odd*, ū *dove*, oo *moon*, ŭ *late*, ŭ *but*, ü *Fr. s und*

Cembalo (Ital. chem-bal-ō). A dulcimer. The addition of keys made it Claviercembalo, which see.

Cembal d' Amore. "cymbal of love," an old form of the Clavichord, which see.

Cenerentola, La (Ital. chěn-er-ān'-tō-lā). An opera on the story of Cinderella by Rossini, libretto by Feretti. Produced in Rome, 1817.

Chaconne (Ital. *Chiaconna*). An obselete dance, probably of Spanish origin. It is in 3-4 time, moderately slow, and in form of variations. Bach's Chaconne from his 4th sonata for violin solo is a very celebrated example.

Chamber Music, is the name applied to all that class of music specially fitted for performance in a room, rather than in a large hall or church. The "chamber" quality refers chiefly to the serious and elevated character of the thought, and the consequent difficulty of finding a congenial audience.

Chanson (Fr. shäng-sŏng). A little poem or song.

Chansonette (Fr. shan-son-ĕt). A little chansonne.

Change, any order in which the bells of a chime are struck. 2. A change of key.

Chant, a musical utterance in definite pitch, the rhythm of which is entirely determined by the needs of the words.

Chant. Single, a chant, the music of which consists of but a single couplet. Each phrase consists of two parts, a chanting note and a cadence.

Chant. Double, a chant consisting of two couplets.

Chapelle (Fr. shăp-ell), the chapel. Originally the musicians of a chapel; afterwards extended to include the choir and orchestra of a church, chapel or palace. See Kapelle.

Chappell, William, a learned English musician, born in 1809 in London. Author of "Popular Music in the Olden Time," etc.

Character of Keys, a supposed difference in the emotional effect of keys, which, if it really exists, is probably due to absolute pitch. C was pure, simple ; D maj., the tone of triumph ; E maj., joy, etc.

Characteristic Tones, the fourth and seventh of the key, because these tones determine the tonic.

Chasse (Fr. shäs), the chase, hunt. Applied to music imitative of the spirit or actual sounds of the hunt.

Chef (Fr. shĕf), chief. As *Chef d' attaque*, leader of the 1st violins in an orchestra.

Cherubini, Maria C. Z. S. (ker-ū-been-ee), an Italian composer born at Florence 1760. In 1822 he became Director of the Paris Conservatoire. Died 1842. C. was a prolific and talented composer in almost every department, but is best known by his treatise on "Counterpoint and Fugue," now superseded, and his favorite opera, "The Water-Carrier."

Chickering & Sons, an eminent firm of piano-makers, established in Boston, Mass., by Jonas Chickering 1823.

Chiming. A bell is said to be chimed when she is swung through the smallest part of a circle possible so as to make the clapper strike. Ringing tunes.

Chiroplast (ki-ro-plăst). An apparatus invented by Logier in 1814, designed to facilitate the acquisition of a correct position of the hands at the piano-forte. The C. consisted in effect of a wrist-guide in two parallel bars, between which the wrist was moved, and finger-guides in thin plates of metal, confining each finger to the vertical plane over the particular key which that finger was to strike. Bohrer's "hand-guide" accomplishes a much better purpose.

Chladni, Ernst F. F. (klăd'-nee), a German philosopher, 1756-1827. One of the first investigators of sound, and the father of the modern doctrine of acoustics.

Chopin, François Frederic (shō-păn), born in Poland March 1, 1809. Died 1849. See Chapters on Chopin.

Chorus, a body of singers. A composition to be sung by all the singers.

Chorale (kōr-äl). A sacred song in slow and sustained tones.

Choral Fantasia (kō-răl făn'-tă-slä). A compositiion of Beethoven's, op. 80, for piano solo, orchestra, solo quartette and chorus. 1808.

Choral Symphony. Beethoven's 9th symphony, in the finale of which a chorus is introduced. 1824.

Choralbuch (Ger. kō-ral-bŭkh). A book of chorals.

Chorister, a choir singer, or leader.

Chord, a harmonic combination of tones, all related to the chief tone called the *root*. In consonant chords the root is the greatest common measure of the series of vibrations composing the chords. Dissonant chords have one or more intruding tones not related to the root These afterwards retire in favor of tres lve into the consonant tone or tones they displaced.

Choir, a body of singers. The part of a cathedral set apart for the performance of ordinary daily service.

Chorley, Henry F. (kōr'-ly), an English journalist, author and art-critic. 1808-1872. From 1830 to 1868 he was associated with the "Athenæum." Author of numerous sketches, vacation letters, novels, etc., and libretti.

Choron. Alexander E. (kō'-rŏn), a French teacher of music, especially singing, and author of numerous articles, prefaces, etc. 1771-1834.

Christus, an oratorió projected by Mendelssohn to form a trilogy with "Elijah " and " St. Paul." He finished only 8 numbers of it.

Christus am Oelberge. Christ on the Mount of Olives. Oratorio by Beethoven.

Chromatic, literally *colored*. The name given to tones intermediate between the tones of a key. Also applied to tones written with accidental sharps or flats.

Chromatic Scale, a scale composed of twelve equally separated tones in an octave. The scale produced by the keys of a pianoforte struck consecutively from left to right, or the reverse.

---

ale, ā add, ä arm, å eve, ĕ end, ī ice, ĭ ill, ō old, ŏ odd, ö dove, oo moon, ū lute, ŭ but, ü Fr. sound

12

Chromatic Diesis (dī-ĕē -sĭs). A Greek interval equal to 27-26.

Chromatic Fugue, a fugue with a chromatic subject.

Chwatal, Franz Xaver, a prolific Bohemian composer of quartettes, symphonies, instruction books, etc. Born 1808.

Chrysander, Friedrich, the illustrious Handel scholar and editor of his works. B. 1826 at Lübthee.

Church, John, a large music publisher of Cincinnati. B. about 1830.

Ciaconna (Ital. tchä-kon -na). A chaconne.

Cimorosa, Domenica (che-mō-rō -zah), an Italian musician and composer of some 90 operas, the best of which is the *Il Matrimonio Segreto*. 1749-1801.

Cinque (Fr. singk). Five.

Cis (Ger. tsiss). C sharp.

Cittern, or **Cithera**, an instrument somewhat resembling the guitar. Of the greatest antiquity. Mentioned by Homer. It as wire strings, and is played with a plectrum.

Clapisson, Antoine Louis, an Italian composer, born 1808. Composer of 16 operas. D. 1866.

Claque (Fr. kläk). An organized body of hired persons distributed through a theater to create applause.

Clari, Giovanni (jō-vän'-nee klär'-ee), an Italian composer of church music. 1669-1746.

Clarinet, a musical instrument consisting of a small conical tube of wood about 24 inches long, with a trumpet-shaped bell. The tone is produced by a vibrating reed in the mouthpiece. It has a reedy quality, and about three octaves compass. Much used in orchestral scores and military music.

Clarke, John, Mus. Doc., an English composer of church music, songs, etc. 1770-1836.

Classical, a term used somewhat vaguely in music. See Chapter XXVI.

Clavecin (kläv -ĕ-sĭn). The French name for harpsichord.

Clavicembalo (kläv -I-tchĕm-bä -lō). Italian name for a harpsichord.

Clavichord, or **Clavier** (kläv'-I-kord, or kläv-eer'). A keyed instrument, shaped like a square piano-forte. Strung with brass wire, vibrated by means of "tangents," instead of hammers.

Clef (klĕf), a key. A character written at the beginning of a staff to determine the pitch. The C clef represented middle C. The G clef represents the G next above middle C, and is now always written on the second line. The F clef, on the fourth line, represents F next below middle C.

Clementi, Muzio (mūd-zio klem en'-tee), An Italian pianist and composer. Born at Rome 1752. Died in England 1832. Clementi was one of the greatest pianists of his day, and the author of a set of studies, "The *Gradus*," etc., still indispensable to the virtuoso. He was author of many sonatas and other pieces, and his sonatas were highly prized by Beethoven. Clementi lived through the most memorable period in music. "At his birth Handel was alive; at his death Beethoven, Schubert and Weber were bu

ried." His writings are characterized by great freshness, clearness and individuality.

Clemenza di Tito, La (klĕm-en-zī dee tee-tō). "The Clemency of Titus," Mozart's 23d and last opera. 1791.

Climax, the summit. A point of culmination in power r interest.

Col (Ital. kōl), with, or at the same time with. As *colla parte*, with the part; *colla voce*, with the voice.

Coloratur (Ital. kol-or-ä-tūr), coloration. Runs or embellishments introduced in singing.

Combination Tones, tones produced by the coincident vibrations of two tones sounding together. Thus c' and g' sound at together on a reed organ, produce middle C f r a combination tone, which may be plainly heard.

Combination Pedals, pedals serving to draw or retire organ-stops, and thus change the "combination."

Come (Ital. kō'-mě), how, as. *Come sopra*, as above, etc.

Comes (Lat. kō -meěst, the companion. The "answer" in fugue. A name given to the subject when it answers in another voice.

Comic Songs, songs with ludicrous words.

Comettant, Oscar (kom-met tan), a French composer, pianist and musical critic n *Le Siecle*. B. 1819. C. is an easy a d humorous writer and a great traveler. Auth r of a few piano pieces and several books on musical or semi-musical subjects.

Comma, a minute interval, represented by the ratio 80-81. Thus, e.g., if E be tuned four perfect fifths above 8-foot C, it will be exactly a comma sharper than the same E tuned two octaves and a major third above the same C.

Common Time, or 4-4, a measure consisting of four units, each written a quarter note. Primary accent on "one;" secondary accent on "three."

Commodo (Ital. kŏm-mō -dō). Easily; comfortably.

Communion Service, a set of anthems for P. E. church service.

Complementary Interval, that which added to any interval completes the octave. Inversion, is the change from an interval to its complement. Complements follow according to the two rows of figures here given, the sum of the names of any interval and its complement being *nine*:

```
1  2  3  4  5  6  7  8
8  7  6  5  4  3  2  1
```

Perfect intervals have perfect complements. All others go by contraries. Major, minor, augmented, diminished.

Compound Intervals, intervals greater than an octave.

Compound Stops, a name given to organ stops having several pipes to each key. See Mixture.

Compound Time, a measure composed of two or more simple triple measures. 6 3 2, 9-3 1, 12 3 4. See "Rhythm" in "Mason's Technics."

Composition, a musical work. The art of composing music.

Con (Ital. kōn), with. **Con Brio**, with spirit.

Concert, a musical entertainment deriving its name from the concert of the musicians.

Concerto (Ital. kon-tshūr -tō, Ger. *Concert*, kōn-sairt). A solo piece for some instrument, with orchestral accompaniment. Classical concertos are written in sonata form.

Concertante (Ital.) In style of a concerto.

Concertini (kon-sur-tee´-nō). A portable instrument of the accordeon family. Is hexagonal in shape, a key-board at each end, and an expansive bellows between the two. Compass of three octaves, capable of great variety of effect.

Concerted Music, music in which several instruments take important parts.

Concert Meister (Ger. kon-sārt mīs -tĕr). The leader of the first violins in an orchestra.

Concert Spirituelle (Gr. kon-sair spĭr-ĭt-oo-ĕll´). Sacred concerts. A famous institution in France, consisting of "sacred" concerts on Sunday evenings in the opera house. From 1725 to 1791.

Concert Pitch, the pitch usual at concerts—slightly higher than the ordinary pitch. See "diapason."

Concone, Guiseppe (gwŏ sŏp´-pĕ kon-kō´-nĕ), a well-known Italian composer of songs and exercises; best known by these and his duets. Born at Turin, 1810, D. 1861.

Concord, see consonance.

Conductor, director of a concert. It is the conductor's duty to study the score, correct the parts and see that they are clearly marked, beat time for the orchestra and chorus at rehearsal and performance, and generally be responsible for the due interpretation of the composer's intentions.

Consecutive Fifths, parallel progression of two voices at the interval of a fifth. Universally forbidden, except an imperfect fifth following a perfect.

Consecutive Octaves, parallel motion of two voices at the interval of an octave. Admissible when intended for strengthening a melodic phrase. The doublings which occur in the performance of a full score are unobjectionable if the four-part harmony is pure.

Consequent, the more or less exact imitation of an antecedent. The second or concluding section in a period. (See Lessons x, xi and xii.)

Con Sordini (Ital. kŏn sŏr-dee´-nee). With mutes. See *Sordino*.

Conservatory, an institution for preserving and fostering musical culture. The principal conservatories in Europe are those at Leipsic, Stuttgart, Frankfort-on-the-Main, Paris, Berlin, etc.

Consonance, the agreeable relation of sounds. Consonance depends on the frequency of coincident vibrations in the consonant tones. The most perfect consonances are the octave 2-1, the fifth 3-2, the fourth 4-3, the maj. third 5-4, the minor third 6-5, etc.

Contra Bass, the double bass, the largest of the violin family. Also the name of a 16 ft. organ stop of metal pipes.

Contra Dance, country dance. An English dance, in 2-4 or 6-8 time, consisting uniformly of eight measure phrases. Derives its name from the dancers being arranged over against one another *(contre)*. A series of five or six contredances form a QUADRILLE.

Contra Fagott (Ger.) The double bassoon.

Contralto (Ital.) The lowest female voice, distinguished by depth and fullness of the chest registers. The head register is commonly difficult of use.

Contrary Motion, a contrapuntal term signifying the movement of two voices in opposite directions, up and down.

Cor, or **Corno** (Ital, kor -nō). A horn.

Cor Anglais (Fr. kŭr än-glä). English horn, a tenor oboe. It has a wailing and melancholy tone.

Corda (Ital. kor-dŏ), a string, or chord. **Una Corda**, one string; *i. e.*, with the soft pedal.

Corelli, Arcangelo (ar-kăn -gel-ō kŭr-ell ce), an Italian violinist and composer, born 1653, died 1713. Author of many pleasing and melodic pieces for violin and string quartettes.

Cornet, a brass instrument of the sax-horn family, with three valves. Also an organ stop of the "mixture" family, which see.

Coro (Ital. kō -rō). A chorus.

Cosi Fan Tutti (kō -see fän toot-ee). An opera buffa in two acts, libretto by Da Ponte, music by Mozart. 1790.

Costa, Sir Michael (mik ell kŏs -tŏ), the celebrated English conductor, born at Naples in 1810. The composer of a number of operas. Costa became director of the Italian opera in London in 1833. Author of two oratorios, "Eli" and "Naaman," etc., etc.

Cotillon (Fr. ko-tĭl -yōn). A country dance.

Cottage Piano, an upright piano-forte.

Counterpoint, the "art of combining melodies," or of composing one or more independent melodies capable of serving as accompaniment to a given subject called the *cantus fermus*. See Lesson v. Double counterpoint is one which may be inverted in the octave, tenth, twelfth, etc., without giving rise to faulty progressions. The interval of the inversion gives the name to the counterpoint, as "of the octave," "of the 10th," "the 12th," etc. The best practical treatises on C. are those of Ritcher, Lobe, and Dr. Bridges.

Counter subject, the principal counterpoint to the "subject" in fugue. Each voice on completing the subject takes up the countersubject, while the answering voice takes the subject (or answer).

Couperin, François, called "Le Grande," a French composer of clavecin music, who exercised important influence on his successors. 1668-1733.

Coupler, a mechanical device for connecting the keys of two key-boards on an organ so that they may be played as one. The usual couplers are "swell to great," "choir to great" (played from "great"), "swell to choir" (played from "choir"), "swell," "great," and "choir to pedals" (played from pedals). There are also super-octave and sub-octave couplers acting on another octave of the attached key-board.

ā *ale*, ă *add*, ä *arm*, ō *eve*, ŏ *end*, ī *ice*, ĭ *ill*, ō *old*, ŏ *odd*, ū *dove*, oo *moon*, ū *lute*, ŭ *but*, ü *Fr. souna*

Courante (Fr. koor-änt, from *courir*, to run). A dance of French origin in 3-2 time, quick movement.

2. The Italian courante is more rapid, in running passages allegro or allegro assai in 3-8 or 3-4 time. The second movement in a *suite*.

Covent Garden Theater, in London, opened Dec. 7, 1732. Several times burnt and re-built. One of the two principal opera houses in London.

Cowen, Frederic Hymen, born at Jamaica Jan. 29, 1852. Author of several operas and many popular songs. Lives in London.

Cox and Box, a musical farce by Sir A. Sullivan.

Covered Fifths, an implied parallelism by fifths, produced by the progression of two voices to a perfect fifth by similar motion.

Cracovienne (Fr. kråk-ō-vee-yăn). The national dance of the Polish peasantry around Cracow. It has a rather sad melody in 2-4 time, and is accompanied by singing.

Cramer, J. B. (krä'-mēr), one of the principal founders of the modern pianoforte school, born at Mannheim Feb. 24, 1771. Lived mainly in London. Died in 1858. A prolific composer of sonatas, concertos, etc. Known now mainly by his famous "studies," though these are losing ground.

Cramer, Henri, a talented composer of light pieces, operatic potpourris, etc., for the pianoforte. Born 1818. Has resided chiefly at Frankfort-on-the-Maine and Paris.

Creation, The, an oratorio by Haydn. Produced 1798. An extremely elegant and melodious work, but neither "sacred" nor "sublime."

Credo Lat. kre'-dō), "I believe." The creed. One of the movements in a mass.

Cremona, a town in Lombardy famous for its violin-makers, the Amati, which see; also Stradivari and Guarnerius.

2. Sometimes applied to an organ stop as a corruption of "krum horn."

Crescendo (Ital. krĕs-shĕn' dō). Increasing (i. e., in loudness). Indicated by *Cres.* or ━━━━.

Cristofori (kris-tō'-fō-ree), a harpsichord maker at Padua, the inventor of the pianoforte. B. 1651, d. 1731.

Croft, William, Mus. Doc., an English composer and organist of the Chapel Royal. 1677-1727. Buried in Westminster Abbey. Distinguished for his anthems.

Crooks, short pieces of tubing for insertion between the mouthpiece and body of a horn, to lower the pitch by lengthening the tube.

Croisez, Pierre (pee-ār' krois-sā), a French composer of parlor pieces, lessons, etc. B. 1814.

Crotch, William, Mus. Doc., English composer, principally of church music and occasional "odes." Also of an oratorio, "Palestine." 1775-1847.

Crotchet, old English name of the quarter note.

Crown Diamonds, opera of Auber, 1841.

Cruvelli, J... a celebrated dr... prano, who debut t... place at Venice 1847.

Crwth (krooth). A Welsh instrument of the violin family, 23½ inches long, 10½ in... wide, and 2 inches high. Very ancient. Played as late as 1800.

Csardas (tschär'-däs). A national dance of Hungary, in two movements, an andante and allegro. Liszt's Hungarian Rhapsodies are founded on old csardas.

Curschmann, Karl F., born at Berlin, June 21, 1805. Died 1841. A popular song-writer.

Curwen, Rev. John, the great educator and apostle of the Tonic Sol-Fa method of singing. Was born at Heckmondwike in Yorkshire, Nov. 14, 1816. He was educated for the ministry, but in 1844 his attention was attracted by M. s. Glover's school at Norwich, and he set about elaborating the system of the Tonic Sol-Fa (which see). Its success was wonderful, and in 1862 he established the T. S.-F. College for the education of teachers. Mr. Curwen's labors had the effect of introducing hundreds of thousands of persons in England to the great oratorios and cantatas of Mendelssohn, Handel and Bach, who otherwise would never have known them. He was essentially an organizer and teacher. Died May 30, 1880, in London.

Czar und Zimmerman, Czar and Carpenter, opera of Lortzing, founded on the story of Peter the Great. 1854.

Cymbals, a Turkish instrument of percussion, consisting of two thin circular metal plates.

Cyclic Forms, such as the suite, sonata, cantata, etc. See Lessons xxi and xxvi.

Cyther, see Zither.

Czerny, Karl (tchär'-nī), an excellent pianoforte teacher and composer at Vienna. 1791-1857. Among his pupils were Beethoven's nephew and Franz Liszt. He was a kind and simple in his manner of life, and gentle in manners. C. composed an immense amount, little of which has artistic value. His once famous "studies" are rapidly falling into disuse. They do not prepare for the romantic school of piano-forte music, nor even for Beethoven.

D, key of, consists of the tones D, E, F sharp, G, A, B, C sharp, D.

Da Ital. dā, also compounded with the article *dal, dalla*, fr. m. from the, through, etc. **Da Capo**, fr. m. the beginning.

Da Capo al Fine — dā kä'-pō äl fe-nĕ, fr. m the beginning, ending at the word *Fine*.

Dactyl (dăk'-tīl). A poetic foot (— ◡ ◡). Ex.: Brightest and best of the sons of the morning — |.

Dactylion (dăk-til'-i-on). An apparatus designed for strengthening the fingers in piano practice, invented by Henri Herté, but now disused. It consisted of a wooden bar parallel with the keys, and from this were suspended, by elastic bands, rings through which the fingers were passed, so that in pressing the keys increased force had to be employed in order to overcome the pull of the elastic cords.

Dal Segno (Ital. däl sān yō). From the sign; i. e., return to the sign 𝄋 and repeat as far as the word *Fine*.

Dame Blanche. La (däm blänsh), The White Lady. Opera comique in 3 acts by Boieldieu, the libretto by Scribe, founded on Scott's "Monastery." 1825. Played the 1000th time Dec. 16, 1862.

Damp. to extinguish a vibration by pressing upon the string.

Dampers. cushions of felt resting on the strings of the piano-forte in order to prevent vibration. When a key is pressed the corresponding damper rises; when the key returns to its place the damper falls on the string and extinguishes the tone.

Damper Pedal, or simply Pedal or Ped., a mechanism in the piano-forte, commonly but improperly known as "loud pedal," which raises all the dampers at once, thus allowing the vibrations of the strings to continue until gradually extinguished by the resistance of the particles.

Dance Music. music to dance by, or to suggest dancing. All musical forms, except recitative, had their origin in dances or songs.

Dannreuther. Edward (dän-roit'-er), born at Strassbourg Nov. 4, 1844. When 5 years old moved to Cincinnati, O. Began his studies under Dr. F. L. Ritter, and continued them brilliantly at Leipsic, where he held all the scholarships. Settled in London in '64, where he "holds a high position as piano-forte player, teacher, littérateur, lecturer, and a strong supporter of progress in music." D. translated Wagner's "Music of the Future."

David. Felicien (dā -veed), one of the most prominent French composers. Born at Cadenet in 1810. Died Aug. 29, 1876. David was laborious rather than gifted. His most successful work was his "Desert" 1844, an "ode-symphony," a descriptive piece in three parts, partly vocal and partly instrumental. His other greatest works are "Lalla Rookh" and a popular comic opera, "La Perle du Brasil" 1851.

David. Ferdinand, the celebrated violin teacher at Leipsic. Was born Jan. 19, 1810, and died 1873 D. was a great friend of Mendelssohn, and was by him appointed concertmeister of the Gewandhaus orchestra in 1836, a position he held until his death. As a teacher David was strict but inspiring. Among his pupils are nearly all the prominent violinists of the present day, foremost of them, of course, being Joachim and Wilhelmj. As a virtuoso he was one of the most solid, and as a leader he had the rare quality of holding together and animating the orchestra. D. edited with additional marks of expression and traditional *nuances* almost the entire classical repertory for the violin (Edition Peters). "He was particularly fond of intellectual pursuits, was eminently well-read, full of manifold knowledge and experience."

Davidde Penitante. II, a cantata for three solo voices, chorus and orchestra, by Mozart, 1785.

Davidsbuendler (dä'-vĭds bĭnd'-ler). An imaginary association of Schumann and his friends, banded together against pedantry, "old-fogyism" and stupidity in music.

Day. Alfred, M. D., author of an important theory of Harmony, proposing considerable changes in its terminology, some of which have since been accepted. London. 1810-1849.

De (Fr. dŭ), or **d'.** of.

Deborah, an oratorio of Handel's. 1733. No less than 14 of its airs and choruses are transferred from other works of Handel.

Debutant (Fr. dā'-bü-tähn). One who makes a first appearance.

Debut (Fr. dü -bü). A first appearance.

Decani (Lat. dū-kā-nee). Used in antiphons to designate the singers on the Dean's side of the choir, which in a cathedral is the south side.

Deciso or **Decisamente** (Ital. dĕ-see' sō or dĕ-see-sa-men-te). Determined; decided.

Declamando (Ital. dĕk-lū-man-dō). In declamatory style.

Declamation. the delivery of text with suitable emphasis and intelligence.

Decrescendo (Ital. dā-krĕ-shän-dō). Decreasing; with gradually diminishing force.

Degrees of the Staff, eleven in number, viz.: the five lines and six appertaining spaces.

Degrees in Music, are two, Bachelor and Doctor. The former is conferred only on examination and proof of fitness. (See Bachelor.) Doctor is also conferred on examination at Oxford and Cambridge, but in this country as an honorary distinction.

Dehn. Siegfried Wilhelm (dān), a teacher of harmony, musical writer, and editor of many of Bach's works. Born at Altona 1796. Died at Berlin 1858.

Deliberato (dā-lee-bū-rā-tō). Deliberately.

Delioux. Charles (dĕl'-I-oo). A French pianist and composer.

Delicato or **Con delicatezza** (dĕl-I-kä'-tō or dĕl-I-kä-tĕd-zā). Delicately, or with delicacy.

Demi-semi-quaver, a thirty-second note.

Deppe, Ludwig (lood'-vĭg dĕp-pō), a distinguished conductor and teacher of music, and especially of the piano-forte, concerning which he holds many new theories, or, as his enemies think them, "hobbies." Born Nov. 7, 1828.

Des (Ger.) D flat.

Destra (Ital.), right. **Mano destra,** the right hand.

Dettingen Te Deum (det'-ĭn-gen), written by Handel to celebrate the victory at Dettingen, 1743.

Deus Misereatur. "God be merciful unto us," Psalm lxvii.

Deux Journees. Les, comedy lyric in 3 acts. Music by Cherubini. 1800. Known in Germany as " Der Wasserträger," and in English "The Water-Carrier." Beethoven thought the book of this opera the best in existence.

Devrient. Eduard Phillip, a distinguished baritone-singer and musician. and a particular friend of Mendelssohn. Born at Berlin 1801.

Devil's Opera, in two acts. Music by G. A. Macfarren. 1838.

Diabelli, Anton (dee'-ä-bĕl'-lī), head of the firm Diabelli & Co., music publishers in Vienna, and composer of piano-forte and church music. Born at Salzburg Sep. 6, 1781. Died 1858.

ū *ale*, ä *add*, ä *arm*, ē *eve*, ĕ *end*, ī *ice*, ĭ *ill*, ō *old*, ŏ *odd*, ō *dove*, oo *moon*, ū *lute*, ŭ *but*, ü *Fr. sound*

Diamants de la Couronne, Les, "The Crown Diamonds," comic opera in 3 acts. Words by Scribe, music by Auber, 1841.

Diapason (di-ă-pā'-son). Originally meant through an octave. In French it means "standard of pitch." In English, the name of the most important stop in an organ. (See Organ.)

Diatonic, "through the tones," *i. e.*, through the tones proper to the key without employing chromatics. Applied to scales and to melodies and harmonies.

Dibdin, Charles, an English actor, singer, and prolific composer of popular stage pieces, among which are some 60 operas, etc. 1745-1814.

Dictionaries of Music. The best are the large German *Conversations-Lexicon* of Mendel (11 vols.); "*Biographie Universelle des Musiciens*," by J. L. Fetis (8 vols. 8 vo.), and Grove's "Dictionary of Musicians" (2 vols. large 8 vo., Macmillan & Co., 1879-80), to which the present summary is largely indebted.

Diesis, a very small interval, about an eighth of a tone. Its ratio is 125 128. It occurs between two tones, one of which is tuned a perfect octave to a given bass, and the other three perfect major thirds above the same bass.

Dies Iræ (dē-āz ē-rā). "Day of Wrath," a celebrated old Latin hymn, which is the second number in the Mass for the Dead.

Dilettante (Ital. deel-a-tänt-a, from *delitare*, to love). One who feels an especial interest in an art without making it his principal business. Also used in an unfavorable sense, of one who *pretends* to a considerable knowledge of an art which he has never learned.

Diminished Intervals, those derived from minor or perfect intervals by chromatic diminution; *e. g.*, perfect fifth, C G; diminished fifth, C G♭.

Diminution, a term used in counterpoint to denote the repetition of a subject in notes of less value, as halves by quarters, etc.

Diminuendo (Ital. dim-in-oo-ăn'-dō). Diminishing in power.

Dinorah (dee-nō-rā'. The Italian title of Meyerbeer's opera, otherwise known as "Le Pardon de Ploermel," in 3 acts. 1859.

Direct, a mark formerly used at the end of a page in music to warn the player of the first note over the leaf.

Direct Motion, motion of parts in harmony in similar direction.

Dis (Ger.) D sharp.

Discant, originally the counterpoint sung with a plain song. Thence the upper voice in part music. In earlier English, *air*.

Discord, the inharmonious relation of sounds. D. depends on the want of common measure between the two sets of vibrations producing the discord. D. and dissonance are often used as synonymous, but not properly. The latter is a discord properly introduced and resolved.

Dissonance, a discord. A combination of notes which on sounding together produce beats. (See Discord.)

Dissoluto Punito, Il Ossia il D n Giovanni. Full title of Mozart's famous opera in which by the last part of its name. See *D n Giovanni*.

Dittersdorf, Karl Ditters von, a distinguished violinist and prolific composer of operas, popular in their day, and an intimate friend of Gluck and Haydn. Born at Vienna, 1739. Died 1799.

Divertimento (Ital. dee-văr-tee-măn'-tō). Divertisement. A name given by Mozart to 22 suits of pieces, ranging from 4 to 10 movements each, for strings, wind and strings, and various chamber combinations.

Divertissement (Fr. The same as the preceding. Applied to a kind of short ballet; also to potpourris.

Divise (Fr. dē-vee-sā). Divided. Used in scores where the 1st violins or soprani are divided into an upper and lower part.

D Major, a key containing the tones D, E, F sharp, G, A, B, C sharp, D.

D Minor, a key containing the tones D, E, F, G, A, B♭, C sharp, D. The relative minor of F major.

Do (dō). The syllable applied to the first tone of the scale in sol-faing.

Doctor of Music, the highest honorary degree in music. The candidate at Oxford or Cambridge must pass an examination in Harmony, Eight-part Counterpoint, canon and imitation in eight-parts, Fugue, Form, Instrumentation, Musical History, a critical knowledge of the scores of the standard works of the great composers, and so much of the science of Acoustics as relates to the theory of Harmony. An "Exercise" is required in advance, which may be sacred or secular, in good eight-part fugal counterpoint, with accompaniments for full orchestra, of such length as to occupy from 40 to 60 minutes in performance. After passing the previous examination the candidate must have his composition publicly performed with orchestra and chorus in Oxford or Cambridge at his own expense, and deposit the MS full score in the library of the Music School. The fees amount to about £50.

Döhler, Theodor (lŭh'-ler), of a Jewish family, born at Naples 1814. Died at Florence 1856. An accomplished pianist and composer of salon music.

Doigte (Fr. doig-tā, *doigter*, to finger. Fingered; *i. e.*, the proper finger-application marked.

Dorring, Karl Heinrich so ring, an eminent composer and pianist of the present time. Born 1834 at Dresden. D. is author of pieces in various departments; piano pieces, masses, songs, and articles about music.

Dolby, see Sainton-Dolby.

Dolce (Ital. dōl chā). Sweetly. Also the name of an extremely soft 8 ft. string-toned organ stop.

Dolcissimo Ital. dōl chees' 1 mō. Superlative of the preceding.

Dolente (Ital. dō län' tō, also *dolentamente*, *dolentissimo*, *con dolore*, *con duol*, all of which mean substantially the same thing. In a plaintive, sorrowful style; with sadness.

Doloroso (Ital. dō lor ō sō). Grievingly.

Dom Choir (dŏm). The choir of the dom or cathedral church. The three celebrated evangelical choirs of this name in Germany, are those of Berlin, Hanover and Schwerin.

Dominant (dŏm'-in-ant). Ruler. The name now given to the fifth tone of the key, counting upwards from the tonic. The D. is the key next in importance after that of the tonic, and is the one into which modulation is first made.

Domino Noir, Le (dŏm'-in-ō nwar). The Black Domino. Opera comique in 3 acts. Words by Scribe. Music by Auber. 1837.

Donizetti, Gaetano (gä-tä'-nō dŏn'-Y-zět'-tī), one of the most distinguished Italian composers of light operas. Born at Bergamo 1798. Died 1848. D. was a composer highly gifted with melody and with sparkling sentiment, as well as with a certain amount of dramatic ability. His success was early and decided, and lasted all his life. His principal operas were "Anna Bolena" 1831, "Elisir d'Amor" 1829, "Lucrezia Borgia" 1834, "Lucia di Lammermoor" 1835, "Belisario" 1836, "Poliuto" 1838, "La Fille du Regiment," 1840, "La Favorita" 1842, "Linda de Chamounix' 1842, "Don Pasquale" 1843.

Don Carlos. 1. Opera seria in 3 acts, by Costa, 1844.
2. Grand opera in 5 acts, by Verdi, 1867.

Don Giovanni (dŏn jō-vän'-ee, in German, "Don Juan"). Opera buffa in 2 acts by Mozart. Produced at Prague Oct. 29, 1787. (The overture written the night before.)

Don Pasquale (päs-kwäl'-ā). Opera buffa in 3 acts, by Donizetti, 1843.

Don Quixote (kē-hō'-tä). Comic opera in 2 acts, by G. A. Macfarren, 1846.

Donna del Lago, La (lä -gō). The Lady of the Lake. Opera in 2 acts. Music by Rossini, 1819.

Doppel Schlag (Ger.) A Turn, which see.

Doppio (Ital.) Double; *e. g., doppio movimento*, at double the movement—twice as fast; *doppio pedale*, with pedals doubled.

Doppel Flote (Ger. dop'-pĕl flŭt'-ā). Double flute. An organ stop composed of wooden stopped pipes with two mouths.

Doric Mode, or **Dorian**, a church mode from D to D in naturals. Many old German chords are written in this key, as "Vater unser." "Wir glauben all," etc.

Dorn, Heinrich (Ludwig Edmund), a musician of the present in Germany. Born at Königsberg, Prussia, Nov. 18, 1804. Dorn is one of the first conductors of his day, a melodious composer of operas (10 in number), many symphonies, overtures, piano-forte pieces, etc.

Dot, a point placed after a note to indicate that its length is to be increased one half. A second dot adds half as much as the first.

Double Dot, two dots after a note, adding three-fourths to its value.

Double Bar, two lines, or one heavy line, across the staff to indicate the end of a strain, or of line of text in church music. The double bar does not properly have any reference to measure.

Double (Fr.) A turn. Also an old name for variation.

Double Bass, the violon, the largest of the violin family.

Double Chorus, a chorus for two choirs and eight-parts; as, *e. g.*, in Handel's "I-rael in Egypt."

Double Concerto, a concerto for two instruments at once.

Double Flat, *bb*, two flats before the same note, representing a depression equal to two semi-tones. B*bb* being the same on the piano as A natural.

Double Fugue, a fugue on two different subjects which are afterwards combined and worked together.

Double Mouthed, an organ pipe having two mouths, in front and rear.

Double Tonguing, a method of articulating applicable to flutes and cornets. Effective in staccato passages, but requires long practice.

Double Sharp, *x*, a character representing a chromatic elevation equal to two semi-tones.

Dowland, John, Mus. Bac., an English composer and musician, author of many books of songs and airs. 1562-1626.

Down Beat, the downward motion of the hand in beating time, marking the beginning of the measure.

Dragonetti, Domenico (dō-měn-ee-kō dragon-nět-tee), one of the greatest known performers upon the double bass. Born at Venice in 1755. A friend of Haydn, Beethoven, Sechter, the theorist, etc. D., at the age of 90, headed the double basses at the Beethoven festival at Bonn, in 1845. Died in London, 1846.

Drama, a play for the stage.

Drammatico (It.) In dramatic style; *i. e.*, with forcible and effective expression.

Drei (Ger. drī). Three.

Dressel, Otto (drī -sěl), a refined and elegant pianist and highly cultivated and poetical musician, born at Andernach-on-the-Rhine in 1826. He made his higher studies with Fr. Hiller in Cologne, and Mendelssohn in Leipsic. Came to Boston 1852, where he has ever since resided, and where his influence has been highly important. Has composed much piano-forte music, as well as songs, chamber quartettes, etc.

Dreyschock, Alexander (drī'-shŏk), born at Zachi, in Bohemia, Oct. 15, 1818. Died in Venice 1869. Dreyschock was an extremely correct and remarkably brilliant virtuoso pianist. He traveled throughout Europe, giving concerts with great success, for about twenty years, after which he settled at Prague as a teacher. Among his American pupils were Nathan Richardson (about five years), and Wm. Mason (one year).

Droit (Fr. drwăt). Right. *Main droite*, right hand.

Drone, the name given to the three lowest pipes of the bag-pipe, which sound continually while the instrument is being played. They usually give two octaves of the key-note D, and the fifth A.

Drouet, Louis F. P. (droo-ā), one of the most famous flute-players and composers for the flute. Born at Amsterdam 1792. Died 1873.

Drum. Drums are of several kinds; (1) a single skin on a frame or vessel open at bottom, as the Tambourine, Egyptian drum, etc.; (2) a single skin on a closed vessel, as Kettledrum; (3) two skins, one at each end of a cylinder, as the side-drum, snare-drum, etc.

D String, the third open string on the violins, the second on tenors, violoncellos, and three-stringed double basses, and fourth on the guitar.

Duet (dū-ĕt'). A piece of music for two performers.

Duetto (Ital. du-ĕt'-tō). A duet.

Duettino (Ital. dū-ĕt-ee'-nō). A little duet.

Dulciana (dŭl-sĭ-ān-ä). An organ stop of a sweet, string-like quality of tone. In the great or choir organ for accompanying solos in the swell.

Dulcimer, a trapeze-shaped instrument of about three feet in greatest width, strung with fine brass or iron wires, from three to five wires to each note. Its compass was 3½ octaves, and it was played by means of small hammers held one in each hand. The D. is the prototype of the piano-forte.

Dulcken, Madame Louise (dŭl'-kĕn), a great piano-forte player, sister of Ferdinand David, born at Hamburg, March 20, 1811. Was pupil of Grund. Married in 1828, and removed to London, where she resided the rest of her life. She was "an executive pianist of the first order, with remarkable brilliancy of finger, an intelligent and accomplished woman, and a very successful teacher." Queen Victoria was one of her pupils. Died April 12, 1850.

Dulcken, Ferdinand, son of the preceding, born at London about 1837. Taken by Mendelssohn to Leipsic at an early age, where he was educated under the immediate supervision of Mendelssohn and his uncle, Fer. David. Dulcken is a good pianist, a superior accompanist, a good conductor, and a remarkably talented composer and arranger.

Duo (Ital. dū-ō). Two, hence a duet.

Duo Concertante (kŏn-tsher tän' tĕ). A duo in which each part is alternately principal and subordinate.

Dupont. Auguste (dū-pōnt), a prominent Belgian piano virtuoso and composer. Born 1828. Since 1853 professor of piano in the Brusse's Conservatorium. Author of string quartettes, piano trios and sonatas, études, salon pieces, etc.

Duprez, Gilbert (dū-prä', a famous tenor in Paris, 1825-1849, and professor of singing at the Conservatoire, 1842-1850. Born 1806.

Durchfuehrung (Ger. dŭrk-fee-rŭng). Carrying out, or elaboration of motives. See Lesson xv.

Dur (Ger. dūr). Hard. German name of the major mode.

Dussek, J. L., one of the most renowned pianists and composers of the latter part of the 18th century. Born at Czaslav 1761. Died 1812. Author of many elegant pieces for the piano.

Dux (Lat. dŭks). The subject in fugue.

Duvernoy, Charles, a French composer and elementary teacher in the Conservatoire. B. 1820.

Duvernoy, J. B., a well known as a teacher and piano composer in Paris, author of many studies, an elementary school, etc.

Dykes, Rev. J. In B., Mus. D., diks, 1823-1876. Auth'r of several services and hymn tunes. Vicar of St. Oswald, Durham, Eng.

Dwight, John S., one of the most cultivated and in fact for many years the reading musical critic of America, was b'rn in 1822. Graduated at Harvard. Was one of the members of the "Brook Farm" community, and in 1852 founded h's *Journal of Music* in Boston, which he still edits, and which has been perhaps the most powerful single agent in awakening a love of music in this country. Mr. Dwight is a highly cultivated gentleman, and was educated for the pulpit; has also evinced the possession of decided poetic ability.

Dynamic, relating to force, or power. The dynamic degrees range from pp., the softest possible, to ff., or as loud as possible.

E (Ital. ā), or, before a vowel, Ed, and. Also the name of a pitch, which see.

Ear for Music, the ability to recognize and remember modulated successions of sound.

Eberl, Anton (ā'-berl), a distinguished pianist and composer, contemporaneous with Beethoven, and friend of Gück and Mozart. Born at Vienna 1766. D. 1807. Author of operas, symphonies, sonatas, etc., all more or less successful in their day, but n w forgotten.

Echo, the reflected repetition of a sound.

Echo Organ, an obsolete contrivance for securing soft effects in organ-playing. The pipes of one manual were encl sed in a box, thus giving a soft and distant effect. The addition of moveable shades or shutters, giving the power of crescendo or decrescendo, produced the *swell* organ.

Eckert, Karl (ĕk'-ĕrt), violinist, pianist, composer and conductor. Born at Potsdam 1820. Studied with Mendelssohn. Composed an oratorio, "Judith" 1.41. In '51 accompanied Sontag in her tour through this country. At present head director at Berlin, in which capacity he is distinguished.

Eclat (Fr. ā-klä). A burst of applause. Expressions of approbation.

Eclogue (ĕk-lōg). A poem or song of a simple or pastoral nature. An idyl.

Ecole (Fr. ĕk-kōl). School.

Ecossaise (Fr. ĕk-kŭs-sä'). In the Scotch style. A dance originally in 3 2 or 2-4 time, accompanied by the bag pipe. In modern form it is a species of contredance in quick 2-4 time.

Eddy, Hiram Clarence, an eminent organ virtuoso and musician, head of the Hershey School of Music, in Chicago. Born 1851 in Greenfield, Mass. Pupil of Dudley Buck and later of Haupt, of Berlin. Mr. E. has performed the unprecedented feat of 100 executive programmes of organ music, *without repetitions*.

E dur (Ger.) The key of E maj.

Egmont. Beethoven's music to Goethe's tragedy of that name. An overture, 2 songs, 4 entr'acts, Clara's death melodram, and a finale—10 numbers in all. op. 84. 1800.

Egghard, Julius, pseudonym of Count Julius von Hordegan, a talented virtuoso pianist and composer of parlor pieces for the piano. B. 1834 at Vienna. Pupil of Czerny. Died 1867.

Eguale (Ital. ā-gwä'-lě). Equal; even; alike.

Egualment (Ital. ā-gwäl-män -tě). Equally, evenly.

Ehlert, Louis (ā'-lert), pianist and composer, but chiefly known as a cultivated critic and writer upon music. His "Letters upon Music" (1859, translated by F. R. Ritter, and re-printed by Ditson, 1870) contain notices of the chief musicians and their works, and picturesque observations upon them. Also composer of symphonies, etc. B. 1825.

Ehrlich, Heinrich (hīn'-rĭk är'-lĭk), a distinguished pianist, teacher and writer, born 1824. Since about 1858 he was the first teacher of piano in Stern's Conservatory in Berlin. As a player, is distinguished for his Beethoven interpretations. Is also the author of several successful novels of a semi-musical character.

Eichberg, Julius (ĭkh'-bärg), a distinguished violin virtuoso and teacher, head of the Boston Musical Conservatory (1867), and for many years principal of musical instruction in the Boston public schools. E. is author of two operas, "The Doctor of Alcantara" and "Rose of Tyrol," both of which are often given; but is most celebrated for his success as a teacher of the violin, in which he is one of the greatest. Born 1828 in Düsseldorf.

Eisenhofer, Franz X. (īs'-sĕn-hō'-fĕr), a German song-writer, 1783-1855. Is most distinguished for his songs for male voices and cantatas for the same, of which he generally wrote the words himself.

Eine Feste Burge (īne fĕs'-tĕ būrg). "A sure defense," Luther's version of Ps. xlvi. Hymn written 1530. Tune probably 1538. The form now in use is that given by Bach in several cantatas.

Eisfeld, Theodore, for many years one of the leading musicians in New York. Born 1816 in Wolfenbüttel. Came to New York in 1848.

Eisteddfod (Welsh, ĕs-tĕt'-ĕ-vŏd). "Sitting of learned men." Musical and literary festivals held by the Welsh in all parts of the world ; originated in the triennial festivals of the Welsh bards in 1078.

Elegante (Fr. ĕl-ā-gän'-tě). Elegantly, tastefully.

Elegy (Ital. *elegia*, Fr. *élégie*). A poem of sad and touching character, generally commemorative of some lamented decease. A piece of music in similar vein.

Elevation, a voluntary suitable for use at the elevation of the Host.

Elevatezza (Ital. ĕl-ĕ-vä-täd'-zä). Elevation, sublimity.

Elijah, an oratorio by Mendelssohn, first produced at the Birmingham Festival, Aug. 26, 1846.

Elisa, *ou le Voyage au Mont Bernard*, opera in 2 acts. Music by Cherubini. 1794.

Elisir d' Amore (ā-lee'-sēr däm-ōr'-ĕ). "The Elixir of Love," opera in 2 acts by Donizetti. 1829.

Ella, John, an English violinist, founder of the "Musical Winter Evenings," and originator of "analytical programmes." Author of a memoir of Meyerbeer, and "Musical Sketches." B. 1802.

Elson, Louis C., born at Boston, Mass., 1848, of German parents. Studied with Karl Gloggner, Castelli, Kreissmann, and others. Is a successful teacher of piano and singing at Boston, a musical critic, poet and litterateur.

Elvey, Sir George J., Mus. Doc., born 1816. A composer of church music in England.

Embouchure (Fr. äm'-boo-shur). The part of a musical instrument applied to the mouth. Hence used to denote the disposition of the lips, tongue, etc., in producing a tone.

Emerson, L. O., a well known teacher of music, conductor of conventions, and author of 35 successful books of psalmody, chorus collections, anthem books, a method for voice, for organ, etc. Born at Parsonsfield, Me., Aug. 3, 1820.

E Moll (Ger.) The key of E minor.

Emperor Concerto, a title gratuitously bestowed on Beethoven's concerto in E flat, op. 73. 1809.

Emperor's Hymn, music by Haydn, also used as theme for variations in his quartette, op. 76, No. 3.

Empfindung (Ger. ĕmp-fĭn'-doong). Sensation.

Eucke, Heinrich (ŏnk'-ĕ). A talented pianist, arranger and composer, pupil of Hummel. B. 1811. Died at Leipsic, 1859.

Encore (Fr. ong-kōr). Again; used for demanding repetitions in concerts.

Engedi (ĕn-gā'-dee). See "Mount of Olives."

Energia (Ital. ĕn-erd-jee-ä) Energy.

Energico (Ital. en-ār-jee-kō). With energy.

Engel, David H. (ŏng-gĕl), organ virtuoso and composer in Germany. B. 1816.

Engel, Gustav, a distinguished teacher of singing in Berlin. B. 1823. E. is also a writer of musical works and on philosophical subjects.

Engel, J. Karl, musical conductor and composer in Berlin, and composer of dances, marches, etc. B. 1821.

English Opera. Opera by English composers. Or, (2) opera in English.

English Horn, the tenor oboe in F.

English Dances, contredances, ballads, hornpipes, etc.

English Horn, a species of oboe a fourth or fifth lower than the common oboe. See *Cor Anglais*.

English Fingering, called also American fingering, see Fingering.

Enharmonic (ŏn'-har-mon -ic). The relation of pitch between tones having different names but sounding alike on tempered instruments ; C sharp and D flat, F flat and E, etc.

Enharmonic Organ (or "perfectly tuned"). An organ invented by Messrs. Alley & Poole, of Newburyport, Mass., about 1848, so constructed as to play in perfect tune in all keys. It contained 48 tones to the octave. Is described in Silliman's *American Journal* about 1850. Was practicable in plain music.

Enharmonic Scale, the name of an imaginary, or at least undetermined, scale employing enharmonic intervals.

Enharmonic Modulation, a change of key involving an enharmonic change of chords.

Ensemble (Fr. on-säm-bl). Together; the whole. The total effect of the combined forces.

Entrée (Fr. ohn-trā). The entrance; introduction.

Entfuehrung aus dem Serail (ĕnt-fee-rŭng ous dem sär-īl). A comic operetta in 3 acts by Mozart, 1782.

Erard, a famous family of piano and harpmakers in Paris, established 1777, when Sebastian Erard made the first piano-forte ever made in France.

Eolian, see Æolian.

Epic, an extended poem on a heroic subject.

Episode, a digression. A part of a piece not founded on the principal subject or theme.

Epode, an after-song. A burden or refrain.

Erben, Henry, an eminent organ-builder in New York. Established about 1835. Died in 1878.

Erdmannsdoerfer, Max, a talented director and composer in Germany, born 1848.

Erk, Ludwig Christian (ărk), a musical director author of school songs, etc., in Berlin. A prolific writer. B. 13-7.

Erkel, Franz, a distinguished Hungarian composer of the present time. B. 1810. Author of several operas, etc.

Ernani (är-nä'-nee). Italian opera in 4 acts by Verdi, founded on Victor Hugo's "Ernani." 1844.

Ernst, Henry William, celebrated violin player and composer of pieces for the violin. Born at Brünn, 1814. D. 1865.

Eroica. The sinfonia eroica is the 3d of Beethoven's symphonies, op. 55. 1804.

Eroico (Ital. är-ö'-ī-kō). Heroic.

Es (Ger.) E flat. **Es moll,** E flat minor.

Escudier (es-koo'-dee-ā) brothers, Marie and Leon, French critics of music in "La France Musicale." 1819 and 1821.

Eschmann, J. K., talented composer for the piano, highly esteemed by Schumann. Born 1825. Is a piano teacher in Zurich.

Eslava, Miguel Hilario, one of the most distinguished Spanish composers and musicians of the present time, was born in 1807. Was composer of operas, church music, etc. D. 1878

Espirando (Ital. es-pīr an'-dō). Used in the same sense as *perdendosi,* dying away; *i. e.,* gradually softer and slower.

Espressivo (Ital. es-pres-ee'-vō). Expressively.

Esser, Heinrich (ĕs'-ĕr), a well known German composer of popular songs, born 1818. In 1847 was director of the Royal Opera in Vienna. Died 1872.

Essential, the necessary or indispensable. In harmony the essential tones are those belonging to the chord, one of each. The doubles or repetitions of these, and the auxiliary notes are not an essential part of the harmony, although they may be to the effect.

Esther, Handel's first oratorio, 1720. 2. Cantata by Wm. B. Bradbury, words by C. M. Cady.

Esterhazy, a distinguished musical family, living partly in Vienna and partly in Hungary, who for very many years kept up a complete orchestra. Of this Haydn was director for about 30 years. This and the supp rt of his private opera cost the prince, in 1790, 40,000 florins $20,000.

Et Incarnatus (Lat. In-kär-nä-tŭs, "and was born." A part of the Credo, in the Mass.

Etoile du Nord, L', "The Star of the North," grand opera in 3 acts. Music by Meyerbeer. 1854.

Et Resurrexit, "and rose again." Part of the Credo.

Etude (Fr. ā-tūde). Study. Etudes are of several kinds: (1) Mechanical, such as those of Czerney, Köhler, Kalkbrenner, Herz, etc. (2) Mechanical and artistic, as when a new method of practice is proposed to facilitate certain artistic effects. Such are the Clementi Gradus (best in Tausig's arrangement for the classical school; the Chopin studies and Liszt's studies in transcendent execution, for the new school. (3) Studies in musical effect, such as: Bach's "Clavier" and Kunst der Fugue; Heller's Art of Phrasing; Schumann's etudes symphoniques, and studies founded on Paganini's caprices. (4) Studies for elementary instruction, among the best of which are those of Lœschhorn, op. 66, for forming the execution.

Etwas langsamer (Ger. ĕt'-väs läng-sä-mĕr). A little slower.

Euler, Leonhard (oil-er), a great mathematician and acoustician, one of the first who investigated the scientific principles of vibrations in tones. Born at Basel, 1707. D. 1783.

Euphony, sweet sound.

Euphonium. A brass instrument, the B flat bass sax-horn. Usually furnished with 4 or 5 valves.

Euryanthe (yoo'-rĭ-än-thē, Ger. pronunciation oi'-ry-än-the). The 6th of Weber's 7 operas. 1823.

Evers, Carl, a pianist and composer residing in Vienna. B. 1819. Author of sonatas, fugues, fantasias, etc.

Extempore Playing, the art of working up a subject without premeditation. In this art the old masters, Bach, Handel, Beethoven, Mendelssohn, etc., were very proficient. It depends on natural musical feeling, and a mastery of the art of musical expression by means of much practice in writing. The extempore playing of uninstructed players is generally egregious nonsense, and ought not to be tolerated in church or society. Among American musicians the most distinguished for ability in extempore performance, are Dudley Buck and Wm. Mason.

Expression, the utterance of feeling.

Extravaganza Ital. ex-träv-ä gänt-zä). A cadence or ornament in bad taste. A work of art in which the accepted laws are caricatured or violated for a purpose.

Eyken, John A. van (I'-kĕn), a distinguished Dutch virtuoso organist, and a very talented composer. Born 1823. Died at Elberfield 1868. Author of many compositions, among the best of which are his organ sonatas.

Extreme Keys, an old term implying those keys having many sharps or flats, as B, F sharp, Db, Cb, etc.

F, the fourth of the key of C. In French, *Fa.* The name of an absolute pitch. See table of pitches in appendix. F holes are the holes in the belly of the violin.

Fabri, Annebale Pio, a famous tenor of the 18th century, who was also a fine musician. Born at Bologna 1697. Died in Lisbon 1760.

Facilita (Ital. fä-sīl'-ī-tä, or Fr. *Facilité*), made easy. An easy arrangement of a passage.

Fackletanz (or *Marche au Flambeaux*), a torch-light procession. The music, for military band, is in 3-4 time, polonaise rhythm. Meyerbeer has written four.

Fagott (Ital. *Fagotto*), German name for the bassoon.

Fair Rosamond, a grand opera in 4 acts. Music by John Barnett, 1837. Also a name applied to a melody of Schubert's, on which he has composed variations in his Impromptu in B flat, op. 142.

Faisst, Immanuel (fīst), a distinguished German organ virtuoso, theorist and composer. Born 1823 in Esslingen. F. founded a school of organists in Stuttgart in 1847, and busied himself with organizing a conservatory there, which he accomplished in 1857, and was made director of it in 1859. Best known as a musical educator.

Fa-la, an old English refrain. Also applied as a name to pieces ending with it.

False, in music, signifies incorrect.

False Relation (or Cross relation) is the occurrence of a chromatic contradiction between two voices in composition; as when one sings C, and the other immediately follows it with C sharp. The false relation is corrected when the C sharp is given to the voice that had C.

Falsetto (Ital. fäl-sĕt'-tō). The head register of the voice, especially in men, where it has a feminine quality.

Falstaff, a comic Italian opera in 2 acts, by Balfe. 1838.

Fandango, an Andalusian dance accompanied by the guitar and castanets. Originally in 6-8 time, slow tempo, mostly in the minor. Later in 3-4 time, written with six 8ths to the measure, the second being divided into triplet of 16ths.

Fanfare (fän'-fär). A short, lively and loud piece of music for trumpets and kettledrums, used on state occasions to announce the entrance of important dignitaries.

Faniska (fan-is'-kä). Cherubini's 21st opera, in 3 acts. 1806.

Fantasia (Ital. fän-tä'-zī-a, Ger. *Fantasie,* fän-tä-zee), a fantasy. A composition following no regular form.

Fantasiestueck (Ger. fän-tä-zee'-steek). Fantasy piece, a name adopted by Schumann to characterise various pieces, for piano alone and with other instruments.

Fantastico (Ital. fän-tas-tee'-kō, Fr. *Fantastique,* fan-tas-teek). Fantastic. In an irregular and capricious manner.

Farce (*farcio,* related to the Latin *farcire,* to stuff). A play stuffed full of fun.

Farandola (Ital. fär-än-do-la, Fr. *Farandoule,* far-an dool). A peasant's dance in the south of France and adjacent parts of Italy.

Farinelli, Carlo Broschi (fär-In-el'-lee), a celebrated male soprano, one of the most beautiful voices ever heard. Born at Naples, 1705. D. 1782. F. was a good musician, an incomparable artist, and an intelligent and highly esteemed man.

Fasch, Carl (fäsh), founder of the Singakademie at Berlin. 1736-1800.

Faschingsschwank (fäsh'-ings-swänk). Carnival-pranks, the name of Schumann's op. 26, for the piano-forte.

Faure, Jean Baptiste (för), the most distinguished baritone singer of the present time, as well as a good musician, a fine actor and a man of culture. Engaged chiefly at Paris. B. 1830.

Faust (fowst). Opera in 5 acts by Gounod. 1859. There is also a "Faust" by Lindpainter 1832, Prince Radziwill 1836, and Spohr 1813.

Faust, Karl, a favorite German dance composer whose works exceed 200 in number. B. 1825. F. was in 1836 band-master in the 36th Inf. of the Prussian army. Later in 1869 music director in Waldenberg.

Faux-bourdon (Fr. fōs boor-dōn). False bass. A simple accompaniment once sung by ear to the plain song.

Favorita, La (fäv-ōr-ee'-tä). The favorite. Opera in 4 acts by Donizetti. 1842.

Favarger, René, a French pianist and composer of parlor pieces. Died in Sept. 1868 in Paris.

Feierlich (Ger. fī'-ĕr-likh, from *Feier,* a feast). In festival style. Grandly.

Fermata (Ital. fūr-mä-tō). A pause, or hold.

Fermo (Ital. fär'-mo). Firm.

Feroce (Ital. fa-rō'-tshĕ)or *Con Ferocita,* with ferocity, ferociously.

Ferrara, an Italian city, for very many years the seat of influential schools of instruction in music, of which the oldest was founded in 1600.

Ferrari. Benedetto (fĕr-rä'-ree), an Italian musician and composer of words and music for a species of drama. 1597-1681.

Fervente (Ital fär-vän'tĕ), fervently, with warmth.

Fernando Cortez, opera in 3 acts, by Spontini. 1803.

Fes (Ger. fĕs), F flat.

Fesca, Freidrich Ernst, a popular German composer, born at Magdeburg 1789. Produced very many works of chamber music and songs, which are melodious and beautiful, though not deep. D. 1826.

Fesca, Alexander, son of the preceding, was also a promising composer of chamber music, songs, an opera, etc. 1820-1849.

ā *ale,* ă *add,* ä *arm,* ŏ *awe,* ē *end,* ī *ice,* I *ill,* ō *old,* ŏ *odd,* ō *dove,* oo *moon,* ū *lute,* ŭ *but,* ü Fr. *sound*

Fetis, Francois Joseph, (fā -tēe), the learned, laborious and prolific musical litterateur, author of a "Biographie Universelle des Musiciens" and "Histoire général de la Musique," as well as several operas, theoretical works, and many critical essays, Born at Mons 1784. Died at Brussels 1871. Fétis was founder of "La Revue Musicale" in 1827. His Biographie is marred by many errors of dates.

Festivo (Ital. fĕs-tee -vō), festively, solemnly.

Festoso (Ital. fĕs-tō -zō), joyously.

Fiasco (Ital. fee-äs -ko), applied to a failure in performance.

Fidelio, *oder die eheliche Liebe* (fī-dā -līo) "Fidelio, or Conjugal Love," Beethoven's single opera, in 3 acts. Op. 72. 1804.

Field, John, born at Dublin, July 26, 1782. Died at Moscow 1837. One of the most charming pianists of his day, a good composer, and deservedly celebrated as the founder of the "nocturne" as a separate musical form.

Field Music. Military music (which see .

Fierrabras (feer'-räb-räs), an opera in 3 acts by Schubert. 1823.

Fier (Fr. feer), or *Fiéro*, (Ital. fū-ä -rō), proud, fierce.

Fieramente (Ital. feer -ä-měn -tē), proudly, fiercely.

Fife, the smallest variety of the simple flute, possessing but one key. Higher octaves are produced by over-blowing. Used in military music.

Fifth, the interval between any tone of the scale and the next but three above or below C G, D A, E B, etc. The perfect fifth has the vibrational ratio 2 : 3.

Fifteenth, the interval of two octaves. An organ stop of diapason tone, 2 ft. pitch. Used only in chorus effects, for brightening the somewhat dull tone of the 8 ft. stops by strengthening their overtones.

Figaro. (See Figaro's Hochzeit.)

Figaro's Hochzeit. Opera in 3 acts, by Mozart. 1786.

Figurante (Fr. fīg -u-ränt), a ballet-dancer, who takes an independent part in the piece.

Figure, a motive. Any short succession of notes, or group of chords, used as a model in sequencing. See Lessons 1, 2, and 19.

Figured Bass, a bass furnished with thorough bass figures indicating the accompanying chords. Used in scores as a convenience to the accompanist, and an additional assistance in correcting typographical errors. Many of Handel's arias have no other written accompaniment, the composer filling it out from this short-hand.

Figured Chorale, a harmonized choral, having one or more of the parts contrapuntally developed and ornamented.

Fille du Regiment. La (feeldu Rēgiman). "The Daughter of the Regiment," opera in 2 acts, by Donizetti. 1840.

Finale (Ital. fēn-ä -lē), the finale, the closing movement. Of sonata finales see Lesson 15. Opera finales consist of several single pieces strung together in cumulative succession, until a climax is reached.

Fine (Ital. fēen ē -, the end. Placed over a bar indicates that the piece ends there after a *da capo*.

Fingering, the mode of applying the fingers to the keys in the execution of passages. The mode of designating the fingers by numerals. *American* fingering uses dots those thumb and four fingers by 1 2 3 4. *Foreign* fingering denotes the thumb by the numeral 1. The same scale would be marked in the two ways as follows, the same fingers being indicated in both methods.
American. 1 2 3 1 2 3 4.
Foreign. 1 2 3 1 2 3 4 5.
Foreign fingering is gradually superseding the other on account of the constantly increasing use of foreign copies of classical music, especially the Peters' Edition.

Fink, Christian, a distinguished organ virtuoso and composer for the organ and voice. Born 1831 at Dettingen, near Heilbronn.

Fink, G. W., a German composer and poet. Born 1783. In 1827 became editor of the "Allgemeine Musikalisches Zeitung," in Leipsic. D. 1846.

Fioratura (Ital. fee -ōr-ä-tūr), flowerets, ornaments, arpeggios, shakes, turns, etc., introduced by singers into airs. A similus trated in the small-note runs, in the melodies of Chopin's slow movements.

Fis (Ger. fees). F sharp.

Fischer, Karl A., a distinguished organ virtuoso of the present time, in Dresden. Born 1829 at Ebersdorf. Author of many organ compositions, a sinfonie for organ and orchestra, an opera Lorely, etc.

Fitzwilliam Music, a collection of MS. music left the University of Cambridge in 1810, by Viscount Fitzwilliam, containing the Virginall-book of Queen Elizabeth, much church music, afterwards published by Novello, etc.

Flageolet, the modern form of the old 1, straight flute, or *flûte à bec*, shaped like an oboe or clarinet ; the tone is produced on the principal of a stopped pipe.

Flat, a character signifying depression of pitch. To depress the pitch.

Flauto, Italian name for flute.

Flautino (Ital. flaw teen -ō), a little flute. A light organ stop of 2 ft. pitch and flute quality, commonly in the "swell."

Flauto Traverso (träv-er'-sō , a flute, so named in distinction from the old *flute à bec*, or, "flute with a beak," or flageolet. An organ stop, generally of wood and 4 ft. tone, harmonic in quality (i.e. made to speak the octave of the true pitch of its pipes by over-blowing). Sometimes of 8 ft. pitch, in which case it is nearly the same as the "melodia," but more brilliant.

Fliegende Holländer. Der (fle-gĕn-dĕ hŏl-lĕn-dĕr), "The Flying Dutchman," opera, in 3 acts. Words and music by Richard Wagner, 1843.

Florio, Caryl, pseudonym of Mr. W. J Robjohns, an organist and composer, residing in New York. Born about 1850.

Florid Counterpoint, a counterpoint consisting of an alternation of all the primary varieties, as "note against note," "two against one," "four against one," and "syncopation," in successive measures.

ā *ale*, ŭ *add*, ä *arm*, ē *eve*, ĕ *end*, ī *ice*, ĭ *ill*, ō *old*, ŏ *odd*, ō *dove*, oo *moon*, ū *lute*, ŭ *but*, Ü Fr. *sound*

23

Florid, music in rapid figures, trills, runs, roulades, etc. Variations are the readiest examples of florid writing.

Flotow, Friedrich (flō'-tō), a German opera composer, born April 27, 1812, at Mecklenberg. Resides at present in the neighborhood of Vienna. F. is the author of no less than 14 or 15 operas, of which "Stradella," "Martha," "L'Ombre" have been extremely successful. Flotow is a pleasing melodist and a genial musician.

Fluegel (Ger. flōō'-gĕl), a wing. The name of the grand piano-forte, suggested by its shape.

Fluegel Horn, a brass instrument of the Bugle kind, used in the German armies. The F.H. now used is a Bb cornet with pistons and a horn mouth-piece.

Flue-work. Organ pipes in which the tone is generated by the wind passing through a fissure, *flue*, or wind-way, and striking against an edge above, all belong to the Flue-work, as distinguished from the Reed-work, which see.

Flute, called also German Flute, to distinguish it from the *flute a bec*, a kind of flageolet. Produces three octaves of tones from D below the treble staff. The Boehm flute is an important improvement in the mechanism of the keys, having the effect of equalizing the difficulty of playing in different keys. An organ stop now made in 8 ft., 4 ft. and 2 ft. pitch, and of several qualities.

Flute d'Amour (Fr. flut dăm-oor'), a flute of light and pleasing tone. Used also as name for a 4 ft. organ register.

Foot, a measure in prosody. 2. That part of an organ pipe below the mouth. Also used as part of the pitch designation, as 8 ft., the normal form. See Pitch.

Fontana, J. (fōn-tä'-nä), a composer of pleasing salon pieces for piano.

Fontaine, Henri L. S., a noted piano-forte virtuoso and composer. B. 1816 at Wisniowiec.

Foerster, Emanuel Aloys (fūrs'tĕr) a German composer of chamber music, and a theorist. Born 1748. Died at Vienna 1823. Held in high esteem by Beethoven.

Form, the organization of musical ideas into phrases, sections, periods, period-groups and complete forms. See Part Second. Also in general, the external part of an art-work. See Chap. 22.

Formes, Karl (fōr'-mĕs), a celebrated bass singer, born 1810. Came to America in 1857. Led rather an irregular life.

Forte (Ital. fōr-tĕ), loud.

Fortissimo (Ital. fōr-tees'-sĭ-mō), superlative of the preceding. As oud as possible.

Forte-Piano in its abbreviation fp. signifies a first note *forte*, and all the rest *piano*. Much used by Mozart.

Fortzando (Ital. fōrt-zän'-dō). Forcing. A sudden force, emphasis or accent on a particular note or chord.

Forza del Destino, La (fōrd-zä dĕl dĕs-tee'-nō). Tragic opera by Verdi. 1862.

Fourth, the interval between any tone of the scale and the next but two above or below. The perfect fourth has the vibrational ratio 3 : 4.

Fra Diavolo (frä dī-äv'-ō-lō). Opera in 3 acts by Auber. 1830.

Fradel, Charles (frä'-dĕl), a German musician, piano teacher, composer and arranger, for many years resident in New York. Born in 1821.

Franz, Robert, the most distinguished song-writer, and one of the foremost musicians of the present time. ,Born June 28, 1815, at Halle, Händel's birth-place. Franz studied music against his parents' wishes; when his first set of 12 songs (1843) were published they attracted the favorable notice of Schumann and afterwards of Gade, Mendelssohn, etc., after which he had a pleasanter time. His hearing becoming affected, he was obliged to relinquish (in 1868) his employment as organist and lecturer on music at the University of Halle. Franz is the author of very many songs, and of many other compositions. Besides which, he has added missing parts to several of the scores of Bach and Handel, thereby rendering them available for modern use.

Free Reed, a reed in which one end of the vibrator or tongue swings entirely through the opening in the metal socket at each vibration. Opposed to "impinging" reed, in which the vibrator beats upon the socket. Free reeds are used in accordions, flutinas, melodeons, harmoniums, reed organs, and in free reed organ pipes, the chief of which are the "euphone" and "vox angelica."

Free Fugue, a fugue in which the rules are not strictly observed.

Free Style, or simply **Free Composition**. Composition in which the rules of part writing are not observed, and no stated number of voices is maintained.

Freischuetz, Der (frī'-sheetz), "The Freeshooter." Opera in 3 acts by Weber. 1821.

French Horn. The orchestral horn, a brass instrument consisting of a very long tube curved into a circular form, and furnished with valves like a sax-horn. It produces a beautifully clear and mellow tone, or it can be blown brilliantly like the trumpet. Very difficult of intonation.

French Sixth. A name sometimes applied to the sharp 6th, 4th, and 3d.

Frescobaldi, Girolamo, the most distinguished organist of the 17th century. Born at Ferrara about 1587. Was organist of St. Peters, at Rome, from 1615. Published many works for the organ and for voices, the last of which appeared about 1657.

Frets, small pieces of wood or metal fixed transversely on the fingerboard of the guitar and lute for the purpose of marking the place for applying the fingers.

Froberger. Johann Jacob, (frō-bär-gĕr), an eminent court organist, born at Halle. Was appointed court organist to the Emperor Ferdinand III , in 1635-1695. Was a pupil of Frescobaldi.

Frisch (Ger.), lively.

Froelich (Ger. frü-lĭsh), joyous, gay.

Fugato (Ital. fū-gä'-tō), an irregularly constructed movement in fugue style.

Fughetta (Ital. fū-gĕt'-tä), a short, but strictly composed fugue.

Fugue, or **Fuga** (fūg), from *fugare* to fly. A composition developed from a single subject which is taken in turn by each voice, answering each other according to certain rules.

Fugue, Double, a fugue with two subjects, both of which are finally introduced together.

Full Anthem, an anthem in which there are no solos, or duets, but continually chorus.

Full Chord, a chord lacking none of its tones. A chord with many doubles, extending through several octaves.

Full Organ, implies generally the use of all the stops in the Great Organ. To this may be added the principal registers of the other manuals.

Full to Fifteenth, a direction for the use of all the stops of the Great Organ, except the mixtures and reeds.

Full Score, a complete score. See Score.

Fundamental Bass, a bass consisting of the roots of the chords only. See Root.

Funèbre Fr. fu-nābr), funeral, mournful. *Marche funèbre,* funeral march.

Fuoco (Ital. foo-ō'-kō), fire, energy, passion.

Fuocoso (Ital. foo-ō-kō-zō), fiery, ardent, impetuous.

Furia (Ital. foo'-rē-ä), fury.

Furie (Fr. fü-rē), fury, passion, rage.

Furore (Ital. foo-rō-rē), fury, passion, rage.

Fuss (Ger. foos), a foot.

Furniture, a name formerly applied to certain mixture stops, in the organ.

Fux, Johann Joseph, a celebrated theorist, author of the *Gradus ad Parnassum*, a treatise on composition, written in Latin in the form of a dialogue, for many years the standard text-book in harmony. F. was a prolific composer of sonatas, masses, motets, hymns, dramatic works, etc., all of which are now antiquated. Born at Gratz in 1660. Died at Vienna, 1741.

G (in Ital. and French *Sol*), the fifth of the scale of C. Keynote of a scale. Name of a pitch.

Gabriel, Virginia, pseudonym of an English lady, the author of many popular songs.

Gabussi, Vincenzo (gä-boos-see), composer and teacher of singing. Born at Bologna 1804, and educated there. He went to London in 1825, where for about 15 years he was a teacher of singing. Returning to Bologna he brought out his opera "Ernani," in 1840, and "Clemenza de Valois," without success. Died in London, 1846.

Gade, Neils (gä-dē), one of the most gifted and accomplished of living composers and conductors, was born Oct. 22, 1817, at Copenhagen. Studied music early, in 1841 he was "crowned" for his "Ossian" overture, and went immediately to Leipsic, where he was warmly received by Mendelssohn and introduced to the public. In 1845-6 he acted as sub-conductor to Mendelssohn at Leipsic, but in 1848 he returned to Copenhagen, where he still lives. G. has published 7 symphonies, 5 overtures, several cantatas, etc. His music is melodious, pleasing, refined, poetic, and in a style similar to Mendelssohn's.

Gaertner, Carl, a German musician, a teacher of the violin and singing. Born about 1830. Came to Boston in 1852, where he has since resided.

Galop (gäl-ō), a spirited round-dance in 2-4 time, usually in binary form.

Gamba, Viola da, (Ital. *gamba,* leg), a knee violin, an obsolete stringed instrument, resembling the violoncello, but originally furnished with frets like the guitar. It had 6 or 7 catgut strings, the lowest 3 spun with wire. Tuned D below the bass staff, G, C, E, A, D, and G.

Gamba, or, **Viol da Gamba,** an organ stop of 8 ft. pitch and I string quality of tone. Generally in Great Organ.

Gamut, the scale. The word means *gamma* and *ut*, the latter the first tone of the scale, and the former the letter which represented it. Now obsolete.

Gauche (Fr. gōzh), left, as *gauche main,* left hand. (From the same root as "gawky," awkward.)

Garcia, Manuel (gärts-zeeň), a Spanish teacher of singing, the original investigator into the anatomy of the vocal organs and the physiology of singing, and the first to use the laryngoscope. Born at Madrid 1805. Came to America with his father, the celebrated tenor, and his sister Malibran, in 1825. In 1847 he was appointed teacher of singing at the Paris Conservatoire, and among his pupils were Jenny Lind, Kate Hayes, etc.

Gardiner, Wm., author of the interesting but desultory book "The Music of Nature," and other writings about music, was born at Leicester, England, 1770. Died in 1853.

Gavotte (gä-vōt), a French dance, deriving its name from the Gavots in Dauphine. It is in common time, moderately quick, in the ancient binary form.

Gazza Ladra, La (gäd zä lä-dră), "The Thieving Magpie," a comic opera in 2 acts, by Rossini. 1817.

Gedacht (Ger. ga-däkt), covered.

Gedacht-Work, all the flue pipes of an organ that are closed or covered at the top.

Gegensatz (Ger. gä-gēn-sätz), against-piece, a contrast.

Geigen Principale (Ger. gī-gēn prin-si-pāl') from *geigen*, a string-toned diapason organ stop, of 8 ft. pitch. Usually in the church.

Gemshorn, a string-toned organ stop, generally of 8 ft. pitch. The name is not now much used. Its pipes were metal, small scale, with bells.

Gemuender, George, one of the most distinguished and successful violin-makers of the present time. Born 1816 in Ingelfingen in Wurtemburg. Came to London in 1851 and some ten years later to New York or Brooklyn, where he still resides. G. has re-discovered several of the ancient processes.

Geschwind (Ger. gĕ-schvĭnd), quick; rapid.

Gewandhaus (Ger. gĕ-vänd'-h ws). The name of a famous series of classical concerts, given every season in Leipsic since 1723.

Ghys, Joseph (geez), a distinguished Belgian violinist and composer, born 1804. Died at St. Petersburg, 1848.

Giardini. Felice de (jẽr-deen'-ee), an eminent violinist, born at Turin 1716. Came to London in 1750, where he made a great success, and afterwards became a popular conductor. Author of many chamber compositions. D. 1796.

Gibbons. Orlando, Mus. Doc., an old English cathedral composer. 1583-1625.

Giga (Ital. jee'-gä). A jig, or lively dance in triplets, either 3-8, 6-8, 3-4, 6-4, or 12-8.

Gigue (Fr. jig). A jig.

Giocoso (Ital. jĭō-kō'-zō). Jocosely; humorously; playfully.

Gioja (Ital. jĭo-yä). Joy; gladness.

Gipsy's Warning. The, opera in 3 acts by Sir Julius Benedict. 1838.

Giuramento. Il (joor'-a-män'-tō), "The Oath." *Dramma serio* by Mercadante. 1837.

Giusto (Ital. joos-tō), just. In equal, steady time.

Glæser. Franz (glā'-zĕr), composer and opera director, born in Bohemia 1798, studied at Prague, and in 1817 became opera director at Vienna. Here he brought out his best opera, "Des Adlers Horste" 1833. In 1842 he was called to Copenhagen, where he died in 1861.

Glee, a piece of unaccompanied vocal music for at least three voices, and for solo voices, usually for men. [Grove.] The word is from An.-Sax. *gligg*, music, and glees are in every vein of feeling.

Gloria in Excelsis. "Glory be to God on High," otherwise known as the "angelical hymn." Part of all the great Christian liturgies.

Glover. William Howard, an English violin player, opera composer and song-writer, in the latter of which capacities he is generally known. Born 1819. Died in New York 1875.

Gluck. Christopher Willibald Ritter (glŭk), was born July 2, 1714, at Weidenwang in the Upper Palatinate. In 1736 went to Vienna, where he was seen by Prince Melzi, who engaged him for his private band and took him to Milan to study. His first opera, "Artaserse," was written in 1741. In 1745 he went to London as composer of operas for the Haymarket theatre. He made no success in England, and returned to Vienna in 1746. After six years of insignificant activity here, he produced in 1762 his "Orfeo," in which he entered upon the period of his real maturity; in this he composed "Alceste," "Armide" and "Iphigenia," the latter of which was the greatest dramatic work composed up to that time. Gluck brought out this work in Paris in 1774. In 1780 he returned to Vienna where he died of apoplexy, Nov. 15, 1787. Gluck's influence on musical development has been very great. The dramatic principles which he promulgated have never been disputed, and but little has been added. As a melodist he was not unlike Mozart, but much less spontaneous.

Goddard, Arabella, one of the most distinguished English lady pianists. Born 1838. Studied with Kalkbrenner and Thalberg, and Mr. J. W. Davidson, Editor of the London "Musical World." She made continental concert tours in '54 and '55. In 1860 she was married to Mr. Davidson. Visited America in 1873. Lives in London.

Godfrey, a family of English band-masters. *Daniel,* the well-known waltz composer, took his band to the United States in 1872. Born 1831. Master of band of the Grenadier Guards since 1856.

God Save the King, the English national air. First sung by Henry Carey, the composer, in 1740.

Godefroid. Felicien, a distinguished French harp virtuoso, and composer for the harp and piano. Born 1818, was educated at the Conservatoire, and has made many brilliant concert tours. Lives independently at Paris.

Goekel, August, a noted German pianist and composer. B. 1831. Studied at Leipsic 1845 and after. Was in America 1853-1856. Author of many pleasing and elegantly written works.

Goldbeck, Robert, a talented composer and pianist, and a brilliant critic, *littérateur* and teacher, now living (1880) in St. Louis. Born in 1835 at Potsdam. Studied with Henri Litolff, and in 1851 went to Paris. In 1856 to London, where through Alexander von Humboldt he was introduced to the Duke of Devonshire, through whose patronage his operetta, "The Soldier's Return," was brought out at Drury Lane. Came to New York 1857, and in 1868 to Chicago, where he lived until 1873, at the head of his conservatory, and composed many important compositions, especially a quintette and trio, and some much admired part-songs.

Goldmark, Karl, a brilliant Austrian composer, born in 1832 in Hungary. His first compositions, a psalm, overture, etc., were produced in 1851. His best known works are his "Sakuntula" overture, and selections from his opera, "The Queen of Sheba."

Gollmick, Karl G., born 1796, died 1866 at Frankfurt. Was a pleasing composer for the piano, author of several text-books in singing, etc., and a teacher of music.

Goldschmidt, Otto, pianist, composer and conductor, was born 1829 at Hamburg. Studied at Leipsic. Married Jenny Lind in 1852. At present occupies a prominent place in England as Vice-Principal of the Royal Academy of Music, and author of an oratorio, "Ruth" (1867), a piano-forte concerto, songs, part-songs, etc.

Golterman, George Eduard, an eminent player and composer for the 'cello, born in Hanover in 1825. In '78 celebrated his 25th anniversary as conductor at Frankfort.

Golterman, Louis, professor of the 'cello at Prague. B. 1825 in Hamburg.

Gong, a Chinese instrument, made of bronze.

Goss, Sir John, Mus. Doc., an English composer of melodious and well written church music. Born 1800. Died May 10, 1880.

Gossec, François Joseph, a French composer of operas and the originator of symphonies for orchestra. A very celebrated musician in his day, and still held in honor in France. B. 1733. D. 1829.

Gotterdämmerung (got'-er-däm-er-ŭng), "The Twilight or Morning of the Gods." The fourth and last piece in R. Wagner's "Ring des Nibelungen." 1876.

ä *ate,* ă *add,* ä *arm,* ē *eve,* ĕ *end,* ī *ice,* ĭ *ill,* ō *old,* ŏ *odd,* ô *dove,* oo *moon,* ū *lute,* ŭ *but,* ü *Fr. sound*

Gottschalk, Louis Moreau, a distinguished American pianist. Born in 1829, at New Orleans, a pupil of Ch. Halle and Chopin at Paris in 1846. He made brilliant concert tours through Europe in 1847; in 1854 and after he played in all parts of the United States, Central America and South America. He died in Rio de Janeiro in 1869, where he occupied an important artistic position. Gottschalk was of a semi-Spanish nature, loved the passionate and effective, and as a composer is genuinely melodious and original, though rarely deep or very tender.

Gottschalg, Alexander Wilhelm, a German organist, arranger, and *littérateur*, born 1827, at Mechelroda, near Weimar.

Goudimel, Claude (goo-dē-měl), a celebrated French composer and teacher. Born in the early part of the 16th century, supposed to have been a teacher of Palestrina. Author of church music, etc. Was killed at the massacre of St. Bartholomew, 1572.

Gounod, Chas. (goo-nō), the popular composer, was born in Paris, June 17, 1818. His mother was a distinguished pianist. G. was pupil of Halevy, etc. In 1836 he took the "Prix de Rome." In 1852 he became conductor at the Orpheon in Paris, but it was only after a number of failures in other productions that his "Faust" in 1859 placed him in the front rank of living composers. Gounod has resided much in England. As a composer he is learned, ingenious and masterly in orchestration, and his works are on the whole rather sensuous and intoxicating than inspiring. His songs are extremely and deservedly popular.

Gow, Neil, a Scotch composer, born in 1727. Died 1807.

Graben-Hoffmann, Gustav (grä-ben), a German song-composer and teacher of singing at Dresden. Born 1820 at Bonn.

Grace Notes, the English name for ornaments in singing, or in melody in general, such as appogiaturas, after-notes, etc. 2. A small note.

Gradual, a short anthem sung at High Mass, between the Epistle and the Gospel for the day. Also used by French composers as title for organ pieces.

Gradual, The Roman, a volume of Ritual music, containing the plain song melodies for use throughout the year.

Gradus ad Parnassum, the title of two eminently instructive works in music. 1. Fux's treatise on counterpoint and fugue, 1725. 2. Clementi's 100 exercises in all styles of piano-forte playing, 1784. (See Etudes.)

Grammar of Music, the laws of musical speech. Embracing Tonality, Harmony, Counterpoint, Fugue, Form and Orchestration, or the entire art of musical composition. This mass of material has never yet been thoroughly systematized and set in order.

Grand Piano, the long piano-forte, with three legs, and keyboard at the large end. Its merits are longer bass strings and consequently more pervading tone, larger sounding-board, more powerful action, and greater carrying power of tone.

Grand Concert, properly a concert in which an orchestra plays the accompaniment. First so called in 1777.

Grand Opera, ... in which ... logic is carried on in recitative.

Grand Prix de Rome, a prize offered by the Paris "Académie" ... e Art ... the successful competitant to a pension for studying at Rome.

Grandioso (Ital. grän-dǐ-ō-zō). Grandly, in a dignified manner.

Graun, Heinrich, born 1701, died at Berlin, 1759. Author of many operas and other works, chief of which are his "Te Deum," and "Der Tod Jesu," a Passion cantata. G. was a fine contralto-artist, and a good harmonist.

Grave (Ital. grä-vō), grave. A slow and solemn movement. A low pitch.

Gravita (Ital. grä-vē-tä). Gravity; majesty.

Grazia (Ital. gräd-zē-ä). Grace; elegance.

Grazioso (Ital. gräd-zē-ō-zō). Gracefully.

Greatorex, H. W., an American author of a collection of psalmody. Lived in U. S. A.

Greatorex, Thomas, an English composer of church music, and organist (1819) of Westminster Abbey, in which he is buried. 1758-1831.

Great Organ, the principal department of the organ, embracing all the most powerful stops, controlled by the hands from the keyboard called "Great." Large churches had formerly two or more organs; a large one, for voluntary playing, in the tower, and a soft one, for accompaniment, in the chancel. This is perhaps the origin of the term as applied to the most powerful part of large organs.

Great Octave, the German name for the notes between 8 ft. C and the B next above (9 notes below middle C).

Greene, Maurice, Mus. Doc., an old English composer of church music. 1696-1755.

Greensleeves, an old English ballad and tune mentioned by Shakspeare (Merry Wives, ii, 1; v. 5).

Gregorian Modes, the musical scales set in order by Pope Gregory the Great, A. D. 590.

Gregorian Tones, or tunes, the melodies for Plain Song, for the Roman Ritual, established by Gregory the Great. (590.)

Greek Music, appears to have been chiefly melodic. Its notation is so imperfect that antiquarians entirely disagree in their interpretations of the same melody. It is literally "all Greek to us."

Gretry, André (grā-trē), was an extremely prolific, popular and gifted composer of some 50 operas, many symphonies, etc. Born at Liège 1741. Died at Paris 1813.

Griesbach, John Henry, an English 'cellist, teacher, composer of an oratorio, "Belshazzar's Feast," overtures, operettas, etc. Born at Windsor 1798. Was 14 times director of the Philharmonic Society. D. 1875.

Grieg, Edward (grēg), composer and pianist. Born June 15, 1843, at Bergen, in Norway, is a pleasing and romantic composer of songs, overtures, sonatas for piano solo and piano and violin, a concerto for the same and orchestra, etc. Was educated at Leipsic. Is teacher and conductor at Christiania.

Grisi, Guilia (jIool-Iā gree-zee), one of the most celebrated operatic singers (soprano). Born at Milan, 1810, made a brilliant debut in 1829, and Bellini wrote his Adalgisa in "Norma" for her. From 1834 until 1861 she sang in London and throughout Europe. Was married to Signor Mario, the great tenor, by whom she had three daughters. Died 1869.

Grossvatertanz. "Grandfather's Dance," a curious old German dance, the conventional signal of the end of dancing in German balls.

Group. several short notes connected by their stems. A figure of tones, a motive.

Ground Bass, a set bass, on the repetitions of which, by means of variations, etc., an entire composition is built up. An old device.

Grutzmacher. F. W. L. (grutz'-makh-er), a distinguished German 'cellist, and composer for his instrument. Born at Dresden 1832. Lives at Dresden.

Guarnieri, or **Guarnerius** (gwü-nā-ri-us), a family of celebrated violin-makers, living in Cremona. They were: Andreas, whose best work was made between 1662 and 1680; Peter, 1670-1717; Antonio, best work 1725-1745; Joseph *del Gesu* (so called from the letters I. H. S. on his tickets).

Guglielmi, Pietro, a favorite Italian composer, 1727-1804. His son *Pietro* was also a popular composer of operas, etc. 1763-1817.

Guillaume Tell (gweel'-yōm těl), "William Tell." Opera in 4 acts. Rossini's 34th and last. 1829.

Guilmant, Alexander (geel-mān), a' distinguished French organ virtuoso and composer, son of an organist, born at Boulogne, March 12, 1837. Organist of the church of the Trinity at Paris.

Guitar, a well known stringed instrument of very limited musical resources, but vastly romantic associations. Strung with six strings, tuned E A D G B G. Practical only for vocal accompaniment, and in very limited range of harmony.

Gung'l. Joseph, a favorite dance composer of the present time, born 1810 in Hungary. He has a celebrated orchestra in Berlin. Visited America in 1848.

Gruppetto (Ital. groo-pět-tō). Literally " a little group," *i. e.,* a turn.

Guida (Ital. gwee'-dā). A guide or direct, an obsolete mark.

H (hā), the German name for B natural. Their B is our B flat. The key having five sharps.

Habeneck, Francoise Antoine, a French violinist, conductor, and professor of the violin at the Conservatoire, etc. H. was the first to introduce Beethoven's symphonies in France. B. 1781. Died 1849.

Haberbier, Ernst (häb'-ěr-beer), a distinguished German virtuoso pianist, was born at Königsberg, Oct. 5, 1813, the son of an organist. Made concert tours in Europe in 1850-'52, and in 1866 was living as director of music at Bergen in Norway. Died March, 1869. H. was remarkable for his brilliant "interlocking" passages.

Halevy, Jacques F. F. E. (jūk hāl-ěv-ū), a Jew, whose real name was Levi. Born in Paris, 1799. Studied with distinction at the Conservatoire, and by 1828 became a prominent composer of operas in Paris. His greatest was " La Juive" (1835). Died 1862.

Half Beat, a name applied to the second half of a time-pulse.

Half Note, an open note with stem, formerly called minim.

Half Step, the interval produced by two successive keys on the piano-forte. This term is indefinite, and stands for any kind of a semitone, whether diatonic or chromatic. Varies from 24 . 25 to 16 : 15.

Half Shift, a position of the hand in violin playing between open and first shift.

Halle, Chas. (hāl-ā'), the celebrated classical pianist, born April 11, 1819, at Hagen. Studied with Rink at Darmstadt, and later with Cherubini, Chopin, Liszt, etc., at Paris. Settled in London in 1849, since which he has played in public every season, and is a leading teacher of piano. Hallé has played in public the entire 33 sonatas of Beethoven, twice in two successive seasons.

Händel, Geo. Friedrich (hěn'-děl). See Historical Sketches. Born 1685. Died 1759.

Hand Guide, a mechanical contrivance affixed to the piano-forte, designed to facilitate the acquisition of correct position and movements of the hand and wrist. The least objectionable is Böhrer's.

Handel and Haydn Society, a celebrated vocal society of mixed voices, at Boston, which has been one of the most important influences in the elevation of American musical taste. Founded 1815. Still active.

Hamlet, Grand opera in 5 acts. By Ambroise Thomas. 1868.

Hammer, that part of the piano action which strikes the strings for the purpose of producing vibrations. Hammers are now made of light wood, covered with felt made from the finest wool. The felt is put on by hydraulic pressure.

Hammer Clavier, the piano-forte.

Hanover Square Rooms, a celebrated concert hall in London, opened in 1775, variously remodelled, and finally sold for a club house 1875.

Hamerik, Asger (äs-ger hům'-ěr-eek), a distinguished Danish composer, born April 8, 1843, at Copenhagen. Was educated in Germany and England, and composed operas, of which he wrote both words and music himself. In 1872 he became Musical Director of the Peabody Institute in Baltimore, Md. Several of H's. compositions for orchestra have been played with great favor by Theo. Thomas.

Hanslick, Eduard, a prominent pianist, and a discriminating and celebrated critic and writer on music in the Vienna " Freie Presse" Born Sept. 11, 1825, at Prague, was a pupil of Tomaschek, and educated in law at the University of Vienna. Attracted attention as a critic as early as 1848. In 1859 and after, he has given several courses of lectures on the History of Music.

Harmonica, a musical instrument the tones of which are produced by vibrations of circular glass plates strung on a horizontal spindle, revolved by means of a treadle. The lower edges of the plates dip in a trough of water. The tones were obtained by rubbing the plates with the tips of the fingers. The tone was delicate and pleasant, but had little artistic value.

2. This name is now given to a set of glass rods or bars strung on tapes and struck by hammers.

ā *ate,* ā *add,* ü *arm,* ē *eve,* ĕ *end,* ī *ice,* ĭ *ill,* ō *old,* ŏ *odd,* ô *dove,* oo *moon,* ū *lute,* ŭ *but,* ü *Fr. sound*

Harmonics, the overtones which form part of complex tones. Supposing C to be the fundamental, the harmonics would be as shown in the following table:

Fundamental.	Octave.	Fifth.	Octave, 2d.	Third.	Fifth.	Seventh flat.	Octave, 3d.	Ninth.	Third.
1	2	3	4	5	6	7	8	9	10
C	C	G	C	E	G	B♭	C	D	E

2. The soft, flute-like tones obtained from a vibrating string, by lightly touching it with the finger at proper points of division.

Harmonic Flute, a flute stop in the organ, over-blown so as to speak the octave above its normal pitch, thus acquiring a clear and ringing quality. Of metal or wood, the latter called "traverse flute."

Harmonic Stops, organ stops not of the foundation pitch; such as octave, twelfth, fifteenth, mixture, etc.

Harmonic Musik (Ger. här-mō-nee' moo-zeck'). The wind instruments in the orchestra.

Harmonic Progression, movement from one chord to another.

Harmonium, a reed instrument of the seraphine family, in which the vibrations are occasioned by wind forced out from the bellows through the reeds; whereas in reed organs the wind is sucked in through the reeds. Invented by Alexandre Debain in 1840.

Harmony, the legitimate association or combination of sounds. The theory of H. involves the formation and permutations of chords, and their proper connection and movement according to the principles of tonality. Usually acquired by much practice in writing after "figured bass."

Harmonic Sequence, a sequence or successive repetitions of a harmonic figure; e. g., the chords of C G, A E, F C, etc., a sequence of descending fourths.

Harmonic Figure, a determinate succession of fundamentals or inversions in harmony; e. g., let the figure be of two chords, the second fundamental ascending a fourth. The bass then is C F, or D G, or E A, or F B♭.

Harmston, J. W., a popular composer of salon music.

Harold en Italie, the 4th of Berlioz's 5 symphonies, op. 16, 1834. A descriptive work in four movements. 1. Harold at the Mountains. 2. March of the Pilgrims and Evening Prayer. 3. Serenade; 4. *Orgie de Brigands.*

Harp, one of the oldest instruments, representations of which occur in the decorations of tombs at Thebes, supposed to date from about the time of Joseph. The simple harp produces the tones of the diatonic scale only. Double action harps afford sharps and double sharps by the action of pedals moving pins on revolving disks in such a way as to shorten the string and raise the tone. Each pedal sharps all the notes of the same name throughout the compass of the instrument. This action was invented by Sebastian Erard. The harp is tuned to the key of C♭.

Harper, a celebrated family of English trumpeters, of whom the elder, Thomas, was born 1787, and was the greatest trumpeter in England from 1806 to his death in 1854. His son Thomas succeeded him in all his positions. The elder Harper played a slide trumpet, and produced a pure, brilliant, even tone.

Harpsichord, the predecessor of the grand piano. Had from 4 to 5½ octaves. The wires were made to vibrate by means of plectra or quills acting on the strings by friction instead of percussion, as in the piano-forte. Invented as early as 1600. Gave place to the piano-forte about the beginning of the present century.

Hærtel, Benno, a talented German musician, and teacher of theory in Joachim's Royal Academy of Music at Berlin. B. 1846.

Hartmann, Freidrich, a noted song composer and director. Born 1805.

Hartmann, Johann Peter Emil, a distinguished Danish piano-forte, vocal, orchestral and operatic composer, born at Copenhagen 1805. Lives at Copenhagen.

Harvard Musical Association, The, in Boston, a society designed to promote musical culture by giving classical concerts, etc., in Boston and Cambridge. Organized 1837, largely through the efforts of Mr. John S. Dwight, who is still secretary (1880).

Haslinger, a distinguished firm of music publishers at Vienna, founded 1826. One of the original publishers of Beethoven's works.

Hasse, Johann Adolph (häs -sĕ), for a third of the 18th century one of the most popular dramatic composers in Europe. Born 1699 at Bergedorf, Hamburg, where his father was schoolmaster and organist. In 1724 became pupil of Porpora at Naples, and afterwards of Alessandro Scarlatti. Began his career as opera composer at Naples. In 1731 he went to Dresden, where he lived as kapellmeister until 1760. Died in Venice 1783. He wrote more than 100 operas, besides masses, cantatas, psalms, symphonies, and a host of smaller works. He was a great singer and a fine pianist, and had an inexhaustible flow of pleasing melody.

Hasse, Faustina Bordoni, wife of the foregoing, a great operatic singer, noted for the beauty of her voice, her exquisite method, pleasing manners and amiability. 1700-1783.

Hatton, John Liphot, born in Liverpool 1809, is one of the foremost composers in England at the present time. Has composed music for several of Shakspeare's plays, anthems, part-songs, operas, and last the sacred drama "Hezekiah," produced at the Crystal Palace in 1877. Hatton is a fine accompanist, and visited this country in that capacity in 1848, and again with Parepa in 1867.

Hauk, Minnie (hawk, or howk), born in New York to a German father in 1852. Made her debut as *Amina* in Sonnambula in 1868. From 1869, she sang for several years in Vienna, Berlin, Paris and Brussels in a large range of parts. Revisited America with Mapleson in 1879. Her voice is a mezzo soprano of great force and richness.

Haupt (Ger. howpt). The head or chief.

Haupt, Karl August (howpt), one of the most distinguished German organ virtuosos of the present time, was born in 1810 at Cunau. Studied at Berlin with A. W. Bach and Dehn, and appeared in public in 1831. Has made many concert tours to France and England, and throughout Germany, and for many years has occupied a commanding position in Berlin as organist and teacher of organ and theory. Among his American pupils are Prof. John K. Paine, of Harvard, Mr. H. C. Eddy, of Chicago, and Samuel P. Warren, of New York.

Hauptmann, Moritz (howpt'-män), the great theorist, was born in 1792 at Dresden. Studied the violin, on which he distinguished himself, and was from 1812 to 1818 a violinist at Dresden, and again from 1822 at Kassel, where also he taught theory, and had among his pupils Ferd. David, Curschmann, Norbert Burgmüller, Kiel, etc. In 1842 he became cantor of the St. Thomas school and church, in Leipsic, and teacher in the Conservatory, where he maintained his rank as one of the greatest theorists of his time. Died 1868. He was a fine composer of songs, motettes and church works. He laid great stress upon two æsthetic requirements, unity of idea and symmetry of form.

Hauptwerk (Ger. howpt'-vărk). The Great Organ.

Hautbois (Fr. hō-bwä). The oboe.

Hautboy (Eng.) The oboe.

Hawkins, Sir John, born 1719, was educated for a lawyer, but being fond of music wrote words for cantatas, etc., and finally his General History of the Science and Practice of Music, in 5 vols., 1776. This has been reprinted by the Novellos. H. was one of the executors of Dr. Johnson's will. Died 1789, and was buried in Westminster Abbey.

Haydn, Francis Joseph (hī'-dn), father of the string quartette and symphony, was born near Vienna 1732. Died 1809. See Historical Sketches, p. 157.

Haydn, Michael, younger brother of the preceding, was a fine musician, and a successful composer, although his fame has been too much over-shadowed by his greater brother. Born 1737. Died 1806.

Hayes, Catherine, a very popular Irish soprano, born in 1825. Died 1861.

Head Voice, the falsetto register, which in men has more or less the quality of the female voice, and in women a flute-like quality.

H dur (Ger, hä dŭr) the key of B major.

Hebrides, The. One of the names of Mendelssohn's concert overture in B min. op. 26, Called in Germany "Fingals Höhle," and "Die einsame Insel." 1831 or 1832.

Heftig (Ger. hĕf'tĭg), vehement, boisterous.

Heiter (Ger. hī-tĕr), serene, bright.

Heiss (Ger. hīs), hot, ardent.

Heimkehr aus der Fremde, German name of Mendelssohn's operetta, "The Son and Stranger."

Heller, Stephen, the universally known and elegant composer of etudes and salon pieces for piano, is an accomplished pianist. He was born May 15, 1815, at Pesth. Since 1838 he has resided in Paris, rarely playing in public, but highly esteemed as teacher and composer. His studies op. 45, 46 and 47, as well as the older set op. 16, have been in universal use among piano students, and for elegance and refinement of diction they are not equalled by other works of similar difficulty. They are, however, open to the pedagogic objection of being extremely unprogressive, easy and difficult ones strangely alternating.

Helmesberger, Joseph, a member of a distinguished musical family in Vienna, was born in 1828, appointed violin professor and director of the Conservatory at the early age of 24. In 1860 he was appointed first violin at the Imperial opera, etc. He leads quartette parties every season. His playing is noted for grace, poetic quality, refinement, and brilliancy.

Helmholtz, Hermann L. F., the celebrated investigator of sound, and the physiology of music, was born at Potsdam, 1821. Is professor in the Berlin University. His great work, "Tone Sensations," is now translated into English.

Helmore, Rev. Thomas, an English clergyman, author of several works in church music devoted mainly to the restoration of the Plain Song. B. 1811. Educated at Oxford.

Henkel, ——, a prolific composer of organ and church pieces, was born at Fulda, 1780. D. 1851. His son, *Geo. Andreas,* was born 1805, and was also a prolific composer. D. 1871. A younger brother, *Heinrich,* b. 1822, is a distinguished organist, and in 1844 was elected organist of St. Eustache, in Paris. Lives at Frankfort-on-the-Maine.

Henschel, George, born Feb. 18, 1850, was first a pianist, but at present the leading baritone singer in England. Is also a prolific and talented composer.

Hensel, Fanny Cecile, an elder sister of Mendelssohn, was born 1805. Was a fine player and a good musician. Died 1847.

Henselt, Adolph, one of the most distinguished virtuoso pianists of the present day, but so nervous that he rarely plays in public, was born May 12, 1814, in Bavaria, and since 1838 resident in St. Petersburg. H. was a pupil of Hummel, but is distinctly a virtuoso of the modern school. H. is a fine musician, and a very successful teacher. As a composer he has decided originality and poetic value, though perhaps not such as will rank him permanently with the highest. His pianoforte concerto is regarded as one of the most difficult ever written.

Heptachord, a scale or system of seven sounds.

Herculaneum, opera in 4 acts, by Felic. David, 1859.

Hercules, a musical drama or 'oratorio, by Handel, 1744.

Herold, Louis Joseph Ferdinand, one of the most gifted of the French opera composers, was born at Paris 1791, the son of a pianist. His earliest success was in 1813, but he composed a large number of operas before he achieved a cosmopolitan success in "Zampa" in 1831. H. died young, just at the maturity of his powers, in 1833, aged 42.

ā *ale,* ă *add,* ä *arm,* ē *eve,* ĕ *end,* ī *ice,* ĭ *ill,* ō *old,* ŏ *odd,* ò *dove,* oo *moon,* ū *lute,* ŭ *but,* ü *Fr. sound*

Herrmann, Gottfried, a many-sided German musician and composer, born 1808 at Sonderhausen, educated by his father, a violoncellist, and afterwards with Spohr, Aloys Schmitt, etc. Since 1839 he has occupied a very high position as conductor, opera composer, and teacher of singing, not only at Sonderhausen and Lübeck, but in many festivals, etc.

Herschel, Frederick William (Sir William Herschel), the great astronomer, was born at Hanover in 1738, and at the age of 14 was placed in the orchestra as oboeist. He came to England with the regiment about 1757, and was stationed at Durham. He soon became organist at Halifax, and afterwards at Bath. While living here he turned his attention to astronomy, and pursued his studies in the intervals of his professional duties for many years. In 1781 his discovery of the planet Uranus by means of the great telescope which he had built, procured his appointment of private astronomer to the king, and a pension of £400, whereupon he abandoned the musical profession. D. 1822.

Hertz, Michael (mĭk-ĕl härtz), piano virtuoso and composer, is one of the most talented young musicians in Germany. Was educated at Leipsic, and at present teaches at Berlin. Born 1844 at Warsaw.

Herz, Henri, a much admired composer and pianist, was born in 1806 at Vienna, and learned music of his father. In 1816 he was entered at the Paris Conservatoire, and two years later began to compose. His concert tours from 1831 to 1834 were made chiefly in Germany and France. In the latter year he came to England, and in 1846 to 1850 to the United States and South America. In 1851 he was back in Paris and professor at the Conservatoire, which he relinquished in 1874. He set up a piano factory of his own in 1853, and his instruments hold high rank. As a composer he has always written in the mode of the day.

Hesse, Adolph (hĕs'-sŏ), a great organist and elegant composer for the organ, as well as in most other forms of music. He was born at Breslau, Aug. 30, 1809, and in 1831 became organist there. He made concert tours to Paris, England and throughout Germany. Died August 5, 1863.

Hexachord, a scale of six sounds, having a semi-tone between the third and fourth, and major seconds elsewhere. 2. A lyre of six strings

Hexameron, a set of six pieces, or songs. This name is given to Liszt's Variations on "I Puritani" for two pianos.

Hidden Fifths, fifths produced by the progression of two voices to a perfect fifth through similar motion.

High Mass, a mass sung with full ceremonial.

Highland Fling, a step in dancing peculiar to the Scotch Highlands. Also the dance itself. The music to which it is danced is the Strathspey

Hiller, Ferdinand, one of the most eminent living German composers and musicians, was born of Jewish parents at Frankfort-on-the-Maine, Oct. 24, 1811. He studied the piano, violin, and composition, partly with Hummel at Vienna. From 1828 to 1835 he lived at Paris, composing and teaching, and was intimate with Rossini, Chopin, Liszt, Meyerbeer, Berlioz, Nourrit, Heine, etc. He was the first to play Beethoven's E flat concerto in Paris. After living some time at Leipsic and Dresden, he organized the Conservatory at Cologne, where he has resided ever since. His most distinguished pupil is Max Bruch. Hiller writes in a classical style, and has published 183 works, of almost every kind; chief of them being his "Destruction of Jerusalem," "Spring Symphony," and Piano concerto in F sharp. Hiller is a polished and genial man, who has never lacked friends

Hiller, Johann Adam, a very active, productive, and influential German musician, was born at Wendisch-Ossig, in Prussia, 1728, and lived independently at Leipsic, actively employed in promoting public concerts. As a composer he is credited with having enlarged the scope of the *Lied.* Died 1804.

Himmel. Freid Heinrich, a melodious, but unimaginative composer, born 1765, died 1814.

Hodges. Dr. Edward, an English musician and organist, was born at Bristol, 1796, and was organist of Clifton church. In 1838 he came to New York and became organist of St. John's, and in 1846 at Trinity. Returned to England 1863. Died 1867. His daughter, *Faustina Hasse Hodges,* is an organist, as is also his son, Rev. J. S. Hodges.

Hoffmann, a celebrated name in literature and music in Germany. Among the chief composers by this name were: *Ernst Theodor,* a highly original composer and *litterateur,* as well as jurist, b. 1776, d. 1822. H. was an extremely clever but fantastic newspaper writer, and many of his pieces have been translated, one by Carlyle. He wrote also 11 operas, a requiem, two symphonies, etc. *Karl Julius A. H.,* b. 1801 at Ratisbon, lives at Lobschütz, and is author of "History of Musicians in Silesia from 960 to 1830," also of several other musical histories, as well as very many compositions, songs, chorales, piano pieces, concertos for different instruments, an operette, etc. *Johann George,* an organist and founder of musical theory, born 1700, died 1780. Composer of many church cantatas, 400 serenades, concertos, etc. *Ludwig,* a clever composer, b. at Berlin, 1830, where he lives as teacher of singing, conductor, etc. *Heinrich Anton,* violin virtuoso and conductor, 1770-1842. His brother, *Phillip Karl,* was a pianist and prolific composer. 1769-1820.

Hofmann, Heinrich (hin'-rĭk), a talented and progressive composer of the present time. Born Jan. 13, 1842, in Berlin, where he studied piano and composition with Kullak, Dehn, and Wüerzt, and still resides. Is the composer of operas, symphonies, songs, and especially a number of very successful cantatas for chorus and orchestra, "The Fable of the Fair Melusine," "Cinderella," "Loreley," etc., which have been extremely successful. Hofmann is a pleasing composer, and a good colorist with orchestra.

Hoffman, Richard, a distinguished piano-forte virtuoso, teacher and composer in New York. Born in Manchester, England, May 24, 18—. Came to New York in 1846 or 1847, where he has since held high rank as teacher and pianist.

Hoffman. Edward, brother of the preceding, a popular writer of light salon pieces.

Hohlflote (Ger. hōl-flō'-tŭ), hollow-toned flute. An organ stop producing a thick and hollow flute-tone. Usually of 8 ft.

Hohnstock, Karl, a distinguished pianist, violinist, and musician, of Philadelphia. Born 1828 at Brunswick. Came to Philadelphia in 1848.

Holden, Oliver, one of the original American psalmodists, a carpenter by trade. Published his "American Harmony" about 1790. Died at Charlestown, 1831.

Holmes, Alfred, a talented composer and fine violinist. Born at London 1837. Died 1876. His principal works were his symphonies, "Robin Hood" and the "The Siege of Paris."

Home Sweet Home. This melody occurs in Bishop's opera of "Clari," 1823. It is designated as a "Sicilian Air," but is very possibly Bishop's own.

Homophony, the same in sound. Equivalent to *unison*, and opposed to Polyphony, or manifold sound. Now commonly applied to music in which the parts all move together, instead of imitations, etc., as in polyphonic style.

Hook E. & G. G., and Hastings, a firm of organ builders, established in Boston about 1835, and for the last twenty years occupying the foremost place among American builders. Their work is remarkable for sweetness and purity of voicing.

Hopkins, Edward John, an English organist and composer of church music, born at Westminster 1818. Died at Ventnor 1873

Hopkins, E. Jerome, an indefatigable teacher of chorus singing, and eccentric pianist and organist in New York, son of the late Bishop Hopkins, of Vermont. H. publishes "*The Orpheonist,*" a curious musical periodical.

Horn, French Horn, one of the most characteristic and important brass instruments in the orchestra. Is composed of a tube 17 feet in length, rolled into a spiral form. Modern instruments are furnished with valves on the same plan as those of the cornet, and crooks for the purpose of changing the pitch of the whole tube. The tone of the horn is peculiarly soft and pure. It is an extremely difficult instrument to learn to play, and the instruction books are said by players to be incorrect.

Horneman, Johann Ole Emil, a Danish composer, b. 1809, d. 1870, at Copenhagen.

Horneman, a young German composer, educated at Leipsic, well known by his pretty overture to "Aladdin." Born about 1850.

Hornpipe, an English dance in common time, rather quick.

Horsley, William, Mus. Doc., an English organist and glee and church composer. Born 1774, died 1858.

Hucbald (hŭk' băld), a monk of St. Amand, in Flanders, born about 840, died 932, aged 92. The author of the earliest treatise on harmony which has come down to us. Owing to the imperfect notation he employs, there is some doubt as to the real intention of his music. But on the whole it sounds to us dreadfully crude. It consists of parallel 4ths and 5ths.

Huguenots, Les. Opera in 5 acts, by Meyerbeer. 1836.

Hullah, John, LL.D., a distinguished teacher of singing and musical educator in England. Born at Worcester 1812. Came early to London, where he has lived ever since. In 1838, after composing several small operas, Mr. Hullah turned his attention to the popular instruction in vocal music in which he has ever since been engaged. Hullah advocates the "fixed Do," as distinguished from the " movable Do " of the Tonic Sol-Fa schools. He is the author of many text-books of music, lecturer and professor of vocal music in Queen's College, London, and Inspector of Training Schools for the United Kingdom. His lectures on Musical History are very interesting. (2 vols.)

Humor (Ger. hŭ-mor). Whim; fancy.

Humoreske (Ger. hŭ-mŏr-ĕs-kĕ). A title adopted by Schumann for his piano-forte piece, op. 20.

Humphry, Pelham, an English composer of anthems, songs, etc. B. 1647. D. 1674.

Hummel (hŭm'-mĕl), J. N., a celebrated pianist, and an elegant and in some sense, classical composer for the piano, was the son of a musician, and born at Presburg, 1778. About 1786 He became an inmate of Mozart's house, and for two years enjoyed his instruction. He traveled several years as a concert pianist, studied composition at Vienna with Albrechtsberger, was from 1804 to 1811 Capellmeister to Prince Esterhazy in Haydn's place, and afterwards lived at Weimar, with frequent journeys to Russia, France, England, etc. Died at Weimar, 1837. He wrote 3 operas, 2 masses, much piano music etc. He had good musicianship, elegance of style, but little force and concentration. As a pianist he was for some time the rival of Moscheles at Vienna.

Hunten, François (hoon-těn), a French pianist and composer, author of many light pieces for piano, studies, etc. B. about 1810.

Hurdy-gurdy, an obsolescent instrument, somewhat resembling a viola or large violin. The strings are made to vibrate by means of the friction of a wooden wheel let into the belly, just above the tail-piece, and revolved by means of a crank. Two of the four strings are used for melody strings, or chanters, and are stopped by means of keys on the fingerboard. The other two are drones and sound continuously when the instrument is played. It is essentially a peasant's instrument.

Hutchinson Family, a family of natural singers, born in Milford, New Hampshire. Four of the brothers, born from 1818 to 1828, were very noted as temperance and antislavery singers throughout the Northern States and England from 1846 to 1858. Later they were broken up, and are now represented by *John* and his family and *Asa* and his family. They had musical voices and sang simply.

Hymn, a song of praise to Deity. A lyrical poem for singing in church.

Hymn of Praise, The, a cantata by Mendelssohn, in 1840.

Hyper (Gr. hī-pĕr). Above.

Iambus, a poetical and musical foot, consisting of one short and one long syllable.
Idea, a theme or subject.
Ideal, that which is expressive of the idea. See Part IV
Idomeneo Re di Creta (ee-dō-mān-ā-ō rā dee kree-tā). "Idomeneo, King of Crete," opera seria in 3 acts, by Mozart. 1781.
Idyl, (i'-dil), or Idylle (Fr. ee-dīl'), a short poem in pastoral style; an eclogue.
Il (Ital cel.) the.
Im (Ger. *in dem*), in the.
Imagination, the faculty of forming lively images within one's mind, of scenes, histories, sounds, plays. It is the same as *Phantasie.*
Imboccatura (Ital. eem-bōk-kā-too-rā). The mouthpiece of a wind instrument.
Imbroglio (Ital, eem-brōl'-yō), confusion, want of distinct ideas.
Imitation, the repetition of a melodic figure or motive called *antecedent,* previously appearing in another voice. Imitation takes place "in the unison," *i.e.,* at the same pitch, in the second, third, fourth, etc., above or below. *Strict imitation* is an exact repetition of the antecedent; *Free imitation* an approximate imitation, one or more of the intervals being enlarged or diminished.
Immer (Ger. Im'-měr). Always, ever.
Imperfect, less than perfect. Applied to intervals to denote that they are too small.
Imperfect Consonances, the major and minor thirds and sixths, as well as their compounds with octaves.
Imperfect Cadence, a full cadence in which the soprano ends on the third of the chord.
Impeto (Ital. eem-pē'-tō). Impetuosity, vehemence.
Impetuoso (Ital. eem-pā-too-ō'-zo), Impetuously, vehemently.
Impresario (Ital. eem-prě-zā'-rē-ō). A manager of operas or concerts.
Impromptu (Fr. ăhn-prōmp'-too). An extemporaneous production. A light and spontaneous composition.
Improperia (Lat.) The Reproaches. A series of antiphons and responses used in the solemn service of the morning of Good Friday.
Improvisare (Ital. ēm-prū-vě-zā-rē). To improvise.
Improvisateur (Fr. ăhn-prō-vō-zā-tūr). An improviser.
Improvissatore (Ital eem-prō-vō-sā-tō-rě). One who sings or declaims in verse or music extemporaneously.
Improvisation, the act of singing, playing, or composing music without previous preparation. The composition so produced.
In alt, tones above the F of the 5th line of the treble staff.
In altissimo (Ital. āl-tees'-sō-mo). The octave above the preceding.
Incalzando (Ital. een-kāl-zān'-dō). Somewhat quicker than the preceding part).
Incarnatus est (Lat. In-kär-nā-toos ěst), "and was born." A part of the Credo, usually set to slow music.

Indeciso (Ital. een-dě-tshee'-zō). Undecided, wavering; with unsteady time.
Index, the old name for "direct," which see.
Indifferente (Ital. een-dif-fě-răn'-tě). Coldly, indifferently.
Infinite Canon, also called *Endless Canon.* A canon without proper ending, each part leading back to the beginning, like a *round.*
Inflection, any change of pitch or modification of the tone of the voice.
Infra (Lat. In'-fā). Beneath.
Inhalt (Ger. ēn-hält). Content; meaning.
Innig (Ger, In'-nīg). Cordial, fervent, sincere, devout. Used by Beethoven and Schumann in the last senses.
Innocentemente (Ital. een-nō-tshān-tī-mān'-tě). Innocently; in a simple and artless style.
In Partita (Ital, pār-tee-tā). In score. See "Score."
In Questa Tomba (Ital, een kwō's-tā tōm'-bā), "In this Tomb." A celebrated contralto song of Beethoven's. 1808. Also effective for bass. Much sung by Mr. M. W. Whitney.
Inquieto (Ital. een-kwō-ā'-tō). Restless, uneasy.
Instante (Ital. een-stān'-tě). Instantly.
Instantemente (Ital. een-stān-tě-mān-tě). Vehemently, urgently.
Institute, Prix de l' (prees dū līn-stī-tūt), "Prize of the Institute." A prize founded by Napoleon III in 1859, of 20,000 francs, awarded biennially to the member of the Institute most deserving of it. It has once been taken by a musician, Felicien David, in 1867.
Institute, any body or society established under law for a particular purpose.
Institute Nationale, a great national institution in France, established by the Directory in 1795. It consists of 5 Departments: 1, *Académie Fransaise,* 2, *Inscriptions et Belles-Lettres,* 3, *Sciences,* 4, *Beaux Arts,* 5, *Sciences Morales et Politiques.*
Instrument, in general a tool. In music an apparatus for producing musical sounds. Orchestral instruments consist of the *strings,* violin family; the *wind* (*wood*), flutes, oboes, clarinettes, and bassoons, and (*brass*), horns, trumpets, trombones, ophicleid, tuba, etc. *percussion,* drums, triangle, cymbal, tambourine, etc. All wind instruments are regarded as descended from the pipe, and all stringed instruments from the lyre.
Instrumentation, the art of writing for orchestra. Berlioz has a book on the subject. See also the 2nd Vol. of J. C. Lobe's *Kompositionslehre.* Also a primer of the Novello series.
Intendente (Ital. een-těn-dān'-tě). Director, conductor.
In Tempo (Ital. tŏm'-pō), in time. *i.e.* resuming the proper movement after a ritard.
Interlude, a short passage played between the stanzas of a song or hymn. Also a light play introduced between the acts of a drama.

ā *ale,* ă *add,* ä *arm,* ō *eve,* ě *end,* ī *ice,* ĭ *ill,* ō *old,* ŏ *odd,* ō *dove,* oo *moon,* ū *lute,* ŭ *but,* ü Fr. *sound*

Intermezzo (Ital. een-těr-mät'-sō). An interlude, or intermediate piece between two others. An interlude, a name frequently employed by Schumann to designate short and not very important pieces. An *I.* was originally of a light and pleasing character.

Interval, difference of pitch between tones. Intervals are named from the number of degrees of the scale they include. A *second* is the interval between any tone of the scale and the next above or below. A *third* takes to the next tone but one, etc. The representation of an interval is determined by its nature. A second is represented by two notes on adjacent degrees of the staff; a third by two notes on successive lines, or successive spaces, etc. Intervals which sound alike, as the minor third and augmented second, are introduced and resolved differently. Like different words of the same sound, they can not be determined when standing alone, as *ail* and *ale; plain* and *plane: so* and *sew: can* to be able, and *can* a receptacle. The manner of their use explains their meaning, and the true spelling thereupon follows. The principal intervals in perfect intonation are represented by mathematical ratios, those of the tempered scale are not easy to determine, and almost impossible to produce on different instruments twice alike, owing to the difficulty of tuning. (See "Temperament," and "Scale ratios.") The ratios of the principal intervals, beginning with the most consonant, are *octave* 2:1; per *fifth* 3:2; per *fourth* 4:3, maj. *third* 5:4; min. *third* 6:5; maj. *second* 6:7, 9:8, and 10:9, according to its place in the scale; min. *second* 14:13, 15:14, 16:15.

Intervals, Perfect. The unison, octave, 4th and 5th which occur between the tonic and the 4th, 5th, and 8th of the major scale. These are called *perfect* because they have perfect "complements," and because they are the only consonant intervals of those denominations.

Intervals, Major. Seconds, 3ds, 6ths, 7ths, and 9ths, between the tonic of the major scale and the corresponding diatonic tones.

Intervals, Minor. Seconds, 3ds, 6ths, 7ths, and 9ths, a chromatic semi-tone smaller than the major intervals of the same name.

Intervals, Augmented. A chromatic semitone larger than major or perfect intervals.

Intervals, Diminished. A chromatic semitone smaller than perfect or minor intervals.

Interrupted Cadence, called also evaded cadence, a cadence that is interrupted by the unexpected entrance of some other chord (usually the sixth degree) where the tonic was expected.

Intonare (Ital. een-tō-nä'-rě), To pitch the voice; to sound the key note; to intone.

Intrada (Ital. een-trä'-dä). An introduction.

Intrepido (Ital. een-trä'-pē-dō). Intrepid, bold.

Introduction, a short preparatory movement.

Intonation, the pitch. Also the introductory notes of the Plain Song where the precentor is hunting for the key.

Introit (In-trō -It, or Fr. ähn-trwä), Entrance, a hymn or anthem sung while the priest enters within the rails at the communion table, or at the opening of the service. Anciently sung while the faithful were entering the church.

Invention, a name given by J. S. Bach to certain small piano-forte pieces in two and three parts.

Inversion, a turning upside down. In *harmony* the change from an interval to its complement. Also the substitution of the 3rd, 5th, or 7th of a chord as bass, instead of the root, the natural bass. In *counterpoint* the interchange of voices, the higher becoming the lower, and *vice versa*, at some pre-contrived interval, which may be the octave, ninth, tenth, or twelfth. In *melody* the repetition of a motive or phrase, with its ups and downs reversed. In the inversion of a chord, the "combination tone" remains unchanged, hence the identity of the chord is unaffected by it.

Ionic Key } One of the church keys, having the tones C D E F G
Ionian Mode } A B C, being in fact our major scale.

Ipermestra, an opera libretto, by Metastasio, which has had 18 composers. Among them Sarti, Jommelli, Hasse and Gluck.

Iphigenie en Aulide, "Iphigenia in Aulis," tragic opera in 3 acts, by Gluck. 1774.

Iphigenie en Tauride, "Iphigenia in Tauris," tragic opera in 4 acts, by Gluck. 1779.

Irene (i-reen). An English version of Gounod's "*Reine de Saba.*" 1865.

Irlandais (Fr. eer-lähn-dä'). An air or dance tune in the Irish style.

Irish Music, is noted chiefly for its sweet and pathetic melody, and for its wild and devil-may-care dance tunes.

Irresoluto (Ital. ee-rŭ-zō-loo'-tō). Irresolute, wavering.

Isochronous, in equal time.

Isotonic System, a system of tuning in absolutely equal temperament.

Istesso (Ital. ees-tä'-sō). The same.

Isouard, Nicolo, a prolific French composer of operas, distinguished by melody and freedom from vulgarity. 1775-1818.

Israel in Egypt, the 5th of Handel's oratorios. 1738. This work contains a greater number of bare-faced plagiarisms from other composers than was perhaps ever offered in a great work by a man of genius. It is distinguished, nevertheless, for grandeur and monotony.

Italian Music was formerly noted for its scientific cleverness, and always for its melody and pleasing quality. See Lessons xxxix and xli.

Italiana in Algieri, L', "The Italian in Algiers." Comic opera by Rossini. 1813.

Italian Sixth, a name sometimes given the chord of the augmented sixth and maj. third, as D6 F B.

Ite, Missa Est. "Go! Mass is finished." The dismissal anthem in the Mass.

Jack, an upright piece of wood standing on a key of the harpsichord, bearing on its upper end a transverse piece of crow-quill to twang the string in passing, when the key is pressed by the finger. In the piano the Jack is the upright lever of the action, communicating the motion from the key to the hammer.

Jackson, William, an English violinist, organist and composer. Born at Exeter 1730. Died 1803. Author of several operas and dramatical works, and writings about music.

Jackson, William, an organist and chorus master, whose earliest business was that of a tallow-chandler, and who educated himself, was born at Masham 1816. Was the author of an oratorio "The deliverance of Israel from Babylon," 1845, and several cantatas. Died 1866.

Jackson, Samuel, an organist, composer and arranger of music, and teacher, in New York.

Jadassohn, Saloman, a many-sided composer of the present time, was born at Breslau in 1831, and studied with Hesse, Liistner, Brosig, and at Leipsic. In 1852 became resident in Leipsic and conductor of the "Euterpe" society. J. is a teacher of harmony, composition and piano in the Conservatorium, and a fruitful composer of piano pieces, songs, symphonies, etc.

Jadin, Louis Emmanuel, a French composer, of Belgian origin, conductor and teacher, who wrote very many patriotic songs, much chamber music, and several operas. Born 1768 at Versailles. Died in Paris 1853.

Jaehns, Friedrich Wilhelm, (written *Jähns*, yäns), royal music director at Perlin, was born 1809. He has composed and arranged much for the piano, and is author of an exhaustive thematic catalogue of the works of Carl Maria von Weber.

Jaell. Alfred (yäl), a distinguished piano-forte virtuoso, was born at Trieste, Ma.. 5, 1832, studied the violin and piano at an early age, and made his first public appearances as pianist at the age of 11. From this time forward his success as a virtuoso was very great. In 1843 he settled in Paris, but left at the time of the revolution in 1847, and soon afterwards came to America. In 1851 and 1852 he played with great success in Boston and New York. Since 1854 he has divided his time between England and the Continent. Jaell is an elegant pianist, with great fluency and neatness of technic, but not much depth. He married a pianist, Miss Trautmann, in 1866.

Jaffe, Moritz (yäf-fä), A good violinist and composer, living at Berlin. Born 1835. Author of two operas, a string quartette, etc., and a superior leader of a quartette.

Jahn, Otto (yän), the biographer of Mozart, and a distinguished philologist, archæologist and writer on art and music. Born June 16, 1813, at Kiel. Studied there and at Berlin and Leipsic; took his degree in 1831. Lived at Bonn 1855 to 1869. Died that year at Göttingen. His great work of musical interest is his "W. A. Mozart," 1856-59.

Jahrbuecher fur Musikalische Wissenschaft, "Yearbooks of Musical Science." Published in 1863 and 1867, containing many valuable papers. (Breitkopf & Härtel, Leipsic.)

Jaleo de Xeres (Spa. hä'-lä-ō dä hā-rĕs). A Spanish national dance, of a quick, light character. Frequently introduced in operas.

Jannota, ――― (yän-nōt'-tä), the leading Italian teacher of singing in Cincinnati.

Jean de Paris, "John of Paris," comic opera in 2 acts by Boieldieu. 1812.

Jenny Bell, comic opera in 3 acts by Auber, 1855. The scene is laid in England.

Jensen, Adolph (yĕn -sĕn), one of the most imaginative and pleasing composers of the present time. Born Jan. 12, 1837, at Königsberg. Was a pupil of Ehlert and Marpurg. He has published very many works, songs, piano pieces, etc., in a style somewhat resembling Schumann, but more pleasing and not so deep. His studies for piano, op. 32, are worthy of particular mention as affording an agreeable introduction to Schumann. Died at Baden-Baden, 1879.

Jephthah, Handel's last oratorio. His blindness came on during its composition. 1751. This subject was also set by Bartholomon at Florence in 1776, and Reinthaler about 1855.

Jerusalem, grand opera in 4 acts by Verdi, being a French adaptation of "I Lombardi." Also an oratorio in 3 parts by H. H. Pierson, 1852.

Jessonda, a grand German opera in 3 acts by Spohr 1823.

Jeune Henri, Le, opera-comique in 2 acts by Méhul. 1797.

Jeu (Fr. zhüh), play. The style of playing an instrument. Also a register in an organ.

Jeux (Fr. zhüh, plural of the preceding). Stops.

Jeux d' Anches (Fr. zhüh d'änsh). Reed stops.

Jeu Grande (Fr. zhüh grän'-dĕ). The full organ.

Joachim, Joseph (yō-äkh'-eem), the greatest of living violin players, was born at Kittsee, June 28, 1831. He began to play the violin at 5 years of age. In 1843, a boy of 12, already an accomplished player, he went to Leipsic, where his remarkable talent was recognized by all, and he remained with David, and at the same time made thorough studies in literature and musical composition, until 1850, when his career as virtuoso began, and has continued ever since with the greatest distinction and honor. In 1868 he became head of the "High School for Musical Execution" in Berlin, where he has since resided and labored, with the most beneficent results Joachim is noted for the breadth, grace, tenderness and deep feeling of his playing, as well as for his unapproachable technique, in which respect he is not surpassed by any. He is also a composer of exceptional ability. His greatest work is his "Hungarian Concerto," op. 11.

Joan of Arc, opera in 3 acts, by Balfe, 1837.

Joconde, ou Les Coureurs d'Aventure, comic opera in 3 acts, by Isouard, 1814.

John the Baptist, an oratorio in two parts, by Dr. G. A. Macfarren. Produced at the Bristol Festival in 1873.

Jodeln (Ger. yō'-d'ln). A style of singing peculiar to the Tyrolese peasants, the natural voice and the falsetto being used alternately.

Joie (Fr. zhwä). Joy, gladness.

Jommelli, Niccolò, (yōm-mĕl'-lee). A distinguished Neapolitan opera composer. Born at Aversa 1714, and thoroughly educated in music, at first at home, and afterwards in Naples. Jommelli made his first appearance as an opera composer in 1737, with great success. The following twenty years were passed at Venice, Vienna, Rome, and again at Naples, where for the most of the time his operas had distinguished success. Died 1774.

ă *ale*, ă *add*, ä *arm*, ā *eve*, ŏ *end*, ī *ice*, I *ill*, ō *old*, ŏ *odd*, ō *dove*, oo *moon*, ū *lute*, ŭ *but*, ü Fr. *sound*

35

Jones, Sir Wm., the learned orientalist, was author of a treatise on "The Musical Modes of the Hindus," 1784. Born 1746 at London. Died at Calcutta 1794.

Jongleurs (Fr. zhŏnh-glŭr). An old term for the itinerant musicians of the 10th and following centuries.

Joseph and his Brethren, the 8th of Handel's oratorios, 1743.

Joseph, opera comic in 3 acts, by Méhul, 1807. 2. Oratorio in two parts by Dr. G. A. Macfarren. Produced at the Leeds Festival, 1877.

Joshua, the 14th of Handel's oratorios, 1747.

Josquin, Després (yŏs-keen' dā-prā). One of the greatest masters of the Netherlands school, and the immediate predecessor in musical history of Lassus and Palestrina, was born about the middle of the 15th century, near St. Quentin. He was a prolific composer, and left 19 masses, about 50 secular pieces, 150 motets with sacred words, etc. His works sound somewhat meagre now, but he had genuine melody.

Jota (Spa. hō'-tā). A Spanish national dance in waltz time. Specimens may be seen in "Sarasate's Spanish Dances."

Jubel-Floete (Ger. yoo'-bĕl flō'-tĕ). An organ stop of the flute species.

Jubilate Deo (Lat. joo-bĭ-lā'-tĕ dee'-ō). "O be joyful in the Lord." The first words of the 100th Psalm; is used as a canticle in the order of Morning Prayer.

Jubilee Overture, The, a celebrated overture in E, op. 59, composed by C. M. von Weber for the festival at Dresden in 1818. It winds up with "God save the King."

Jubilee, The Peace. Two monster festivals by this name were held in Boston 1869 and 1871, under the inspiration and general direction of Mr. P. S. Gilmore. At the last there was an orchestra of 900, a large organ, a chorus of 14,000, and the audience room held about 40,000.

Judas Maccabeus, the 12th of Handel's Oratorios. Begun July 9, ended Aug. 11, 1746.

Judith. 1. An oratorio by Defesch, 1733. 2. An oratorio by Dr. Arne, 1764. 3. A "Biblical Cantata," by H. Leslie, 1858.

Juive, La (zhū-eev'). "The Jewess," opera in 5 acts, by Halévy, 1835.

Jullien, Louis Antoine, the famous bandmaster, and the first to bring a large orchestra to America, was born at Sisterton, April 23, 1812. In 1838 he began his career as a conductor in London, with an orchestra of 90 and a chorus of 80. From time to time he enlarged his resources, employed the greatest solo artists, started a store, leased a theater, and so made much money and rode on the highest wave of popularity, only to be overtaken finally by financial misfortunes. He came to America in 1853, and remained here until 1854. On his return to England he again lost heavily, removed to Paris, and finally died in a lunatic asylum near Paris in 1860. To this enterprising, if somewhat charlatanish, conductor, the English and American public owe important education in the taste for classical music and finished style of performance.

Jungste Gericht. Das, Spohr's first oratorio, 1812. Not the same as his "The Last Judgment."

Jupiter Symphony. The. Mozart's 49th and last symphony, in C (Köchel 551) 1788. The name was applied, perhaps, by J. B. Cramer.

Just, a term applied to all consonant intervals, and to the strings and pipes that give them with exactness.

Justo (Ital. yoos-tō). Exactness, precision.

Jungmann, Albert (yoong'-mŭn). A good pianist, and an elegant composer of piano pieces. Born 1824 at Langensalza. Lives in Vienna.

Kafka, Johann Nepomuk, pianist and salon composer, was born May 17, 1819, in Bohemia. Studied in Vienna, and since 1840 has produced a constant succession of pleasing compositions for the piano.

Kalkbrenner, Friedrich W. M., was in his day a great virtuoso pianist and a prolific composer. He was born near Berlin in 1788. Studied in Paris at the Conservatoire, where he carried off the honors for his piano playing. He at first settled in London, where he had fine success as a teacher and player, but in 1824 he returned to Paris, where he was received as a partner in the house of Pleyel & Co., piano-makers, and eventually amassed a fortune. His compositions for a time were held in the highest repute, and were so when Chopin went to Paris in 1831, but they are now forgotten. K. was an elegant pianist, but without a large tone or much depth of expression. D. 1849.

Kalliwoda, Johann Wenzelslaus, a violin player and popular composer, was born at Prague in 1800. He died at Carlsruhe in 1866. Was the author of 7 symphonies, besides a large number of concertos, quartettes, etc., which were melodious and well written, but not of permanent value.

Kammer (Ger. kăm'-mer), chamber. *Kammer Musik,* chamber music.

Kanne, Fr. A., a talented German composer and poet, born 1778 in Saxony, who left a number of operas and dramas. Died in Vienna, 1833.

Kapelle (Ger. kăp-pĕl'-lĕ), chapel. A musical establishment, usually orchestral. Formerly applied to the private band of a prince or magnate, but now applied to any orchestra. Thus, at Berlin, the Kaiserliche Königliche Kapelle (97 musicians called Kammermusiker) forms the regular orchestra of the Grand Opera, with two Kapellmeisters (conductors), a Concertmeister (leader, or 1st violin), and a Balletdirigent (ballet-master). [*Grove.*]

Kapellmeister (Ger. kăp-pĕl-mīs'-tĕr). Conductor of an orchestra. See above.

Keiser, Reinhard (rīn'-hārd kīz-ĕr), an eminent German opera composer of the olden time, born 1673. For 40 years from 1694 he remained at Hamburg, a favorite composer. In one year he wrote 8 operas. He composed his last opera, "Circe," in 1734, and died in 1739.

Keler-Bela (whose real name is Albert von Kéler) was born in Hungary in 1820. In 1845 he began study in Vienna, and in 1854 took command of Gungl's orchestra in Berlin. Presently he returned to Berlin and succeeded to the Leadership of Lanner's orchestra. Has composed many overtures, waltzes, marches, etc., characterized by brilliant style, and showy instrumentation.

Kellogg, Clara Louise, the favorite American soprano, was born in Sumterville, N. C., in 1842. She made her debut as Gilda in Rigoletto in 1861, since which she has been constantly before the public. She is a conscientious artist, has a voice of great compass and purity, and is highly esteemed in England and this country.

Kelly, Michael, an Irish composer of theatrical music. 1764-1826.

Kent Bugle, an improved form of the key bugle. It had a complete chromatic scale from $B\flat$ below the treble staff to C above. Superseded by sax-horns and cornets.

Keolanthe, Or the Unearthly Bride, opera in 2 acts by Balfe, 1841.

Keraulophon (kĕr-aw′-lŏ-phŏn), an organ stop of string tone and 8 ft. pitch.

Kettle Drums are copper or brass basins with a head of skin that can be tuned to a true musical note. Used by cavalry and in orchestras, always in pairs (tonic and dominant).

Key, a mechanical contrivance through which the finger produces or modifies a sound in instruments.

Key, a relationship of tones. All authentic modern music rests upon the normal key, or tonal system from which all our harmony is drawn. Taking any tone as tonic the remaining seven tones of the octave stand in the following relations to it: 9-8, 5-4, 4-3, 3-2, 5-3, 15-8, 2-1. These are the ratios of the major scale. The same tones may be used in the minor mode without alteration, but generally the *fifth* of the major is sharped so as to make a major seventh in the minor. Thus the tones C D E F G A B C make the key of C. If G sharp be taken instead of G, the key becomes A minor. The subject of tonality has been thoroughly investigated by Helmholtz, to whose "Tone Sensations" reference is made.

Key Note, the tone of a key from which all the others are determined. That tone of a scale which makes the best point of closing.

Kiel, Friedrich (keel), a German violinist, and distinguished master of counterpoint and fugue in the Berlin Hochschule for music. Is composer of a Requiem, a Missa Solemnis, and in 1874 an oratorio, Christus. Born 1821 at Puderbach.

King, Matthew Peter, an English composer of operas. 1773-1823.

King Charles the Second, opera in 2 acts, by G. A. Macfarren, 1849.

Kirche (keerk -hĕ), church.

Kirche-Cantaten, church cantatas, of which Bach left a large number.

Kirchner, Theodor (keerk -nĕr), one of the most talented of the disciples of Schumann, a composer of *genre* pieces for the piano-forte. Born 1874 at Newkirchen. Lives at Leipsic.

Kirnberger, Johann Phillip (keern-bār-gĕr). Composer and theorist (most of the latter being false), was born 1721. Lived at Berlin as Kapellmeister to the Princess Amelia. Died 1783.

Kit, a small violin.

Kittel, Johann Christian, a distinguished organ virtuoso and composer, one of the last pupils of J. S. Bach. Born at Erfurt 1732. Died 1809. His published works are not very important. His best pupil was Ch. Rink, of Darmstadt.

Klavier, see Clavier.

Klang (Ger. kling). Sound.

Klang-farbe (Ger, kling - fär - bĕ). Tone-color.

Klingemann, Carl (klĭng′-gĕ-män), a German literary man and poet, author of many of the songs which Mendelssohn set to music. Born at Limmer 1798. Died in London, 1862, as Secretary of Legation.

Klein (Ger. klīn). Little, small.

Klindworth, Carl, one of the best living musicians and pianists, most distinguished as editor of the famous "Jurgenson" edition of Chopin. Born at Hanover 1830. In 1850 he went to Weimar to study with Liszt, where he was the associate of Raff, Bülow, Prückner, Wm. Mason, etc., being especially intimate with the latter. From 1854 he lived 14 years in London. Since 1868 he has been professor of piano-forte in the Conservatory at Moscow. K. has distinguished himself, also, by his arrangement of the piano score of Wagner's "Der Ring des Nibelungen."

Kloss, Karl Johann Chr., a noted organ virtuoso, born 1792 at Mohrungen, and served as organist and director in various places. Died 1853 at Riga. Left many songs, big and little piano pieces, organ pieces, etc.

Klughardt, August, a talented German composer and director. Born in 1847 at Köthen, educated at Dresden, and in 1873 became Hofkapellmeister in Naustrelitz. Is composer of songs, piano pieces, overtures, etc., which show decided originality.

Knecht, Justin Heinrich (knĕkt), a noted organ, piano, and violin player, theorist, and composer of psalms, motets, cantatas, sonatas, etc., etc., and instruction books. Born 1752, died 1817.

Knee Stop, an organ stop worked by the knee.

Knell, a stroke of the bell, made at intervals, during funerals.

Knight, Joseph Phillip, an English writer of over 200 songs, best known of which is his "Rocked in the Cradle of the Deep." He is a good organist. Born at Stratford-on-Avon, 1812. Was at one time a clergyman.

Knorr, Julius, a German pianist, teacher, and writer about music, was born 1807 at Leipsic, and appeared in the Gewandhaus concerts with success, in the first Chopin piece ever played there. He was concerned with Schumann and Schunke in establishing the "New Journal of Music." Died June 1861.

Koch, Henrich Christoph (kōk), was a laborious theorist and musical lexicographer. Born at Rudolstadt, 1749. Died 1816.

ā *ale*, ă *add*, ä *arm*, ö *eve*, ĕ *end*, ī *ice*, ĭ *ill*, ō *old*, ŏ *odd*, ȯ *dove*, oo *moon*, ū *lute*, ŭ *but*, ü *Fr. sound*

Kœchel, Dr. Ludwig Ritter von (kü'kĕl). A learned musician and naturalist, the author of a thematic catalogue of all of Mozart's works. (Breitkopf and Hartel, Leipsic 1802.) Born 1800 at Stein. Died at Berlin 1877.

Koehler, Louis, a many-sided German musician, especially a pianist, musical writer and teacher, is known in all countries by his Etudes for piano. Born at Brunswick 1820, was educated under Sechter, Seyfried and Bocklet. Since 1846 he has lived at Königsberg, Prussia, as musical director, etc.

Körner, Gothilf Wilhelm (kŭr'-nĕr). A prolific German writer of musical text-books, particularly for the organ. Born 1809. Died at Erfurt 1865.

Kolbe, Oscar (kōl'-bĕ). A theorist and composer. Born in Berlin 1836.

Kollmann, A., a musician, born at Hanover in 1756, settled in England as organist at the German chapel in London. Was author of many text books in music. D. 1824.

Kontski, Antoine, a fine pianist and composer of many pleasing salon pieces. Born at Cracow, 1817. Lives in London.

Kotzwara, Franz, born at Prague, hanged himself in Ireland 1791, whether in remorse at having written his celebrated *morceau*, "The Battle of Prague," is not known.

Krakoviak (krä-kō'-vī-äk), called also *Cracovienne*, a Polish dance belonging to the neighborhood of Cracow. Is in 2-4 time, in 8 measure periods.

Krause, Anton (krow'-sĕ), a good pianist and capable director, born 1834 at Geithain in Saxony. Was educated at Leipsic, and in 1859 undertook the direction of the concerts, etc., in Barmen, as successor of Reinecke. Krause is author of 10 sonatas, 60 studies, etc., for the piano-forte, which are highly esteemed.

Krebs, J. L. K., a distinguished German organist and composer for organ, educated under Bach at Leipsic, and in 1737 organist at Zwickau. Born 1713. Died at Altenberg, 1780.

Krebs, Marie, the celebrated piano virtuoso, was born of a musical family in Dresden, 1851. In her 5th year she played B. F. Burgmüller's 25 studies, op. 100, with pleasure and the most satisfactory completeness. She pursued her studies with her father only. Her concert career commenced in 1862, since which she has played in all parts of Europe and in England and the United States, with the greatest success. Her playing is distinguished by splendid and complete technic, and genuine musical feeling, both in classical and brilliant music.

Kreisleriana (krīs'-lĕr-ī-ä'-nä), wreaths. Schumann's title of his op. 16, "eight fantasias for piano." 1838.

Krejci, Joseph, director of Prague Conservatorium of Music. Born 1822 at Milostin. An accomplished musician, a superior organist and skillful director, and a composer of church music (masses, etc.), as well as overtures, songs, etc.

Krenn, Franz, an excellent German organist, composer and director. Born 1816 at Dross, in Austria. Studied in Vienna with Seyfried. In 1844 he became organist, and in 1862 Kapellemeister in the Royal Cathedral of St. Michael. Is a composer of masses, vespers, a symphony, quartettes, etc.

Kretschmer, Ed, a fine organist and one of the foremost dramatic composers of the present time. Born 1830. Studied in Dresden, and in 1854 became organist there. Is Hoforganist and Director of the boys of the Royal Chapel. His "Geisterschlact" was sung with great success in 1865, and took the prize. His great 5-act opera, "Die Folkungers," was successful in 1874 and 1875.

Kreutzer, Konradin (kroit'-zĕr), a talented and favorite song and opera composer, born 1782 in Baden. Was well educated, and studied medicine. In 1805 he became pupil of Albrechsberger in Vienna, where he remained till 1811, and composed many operas. In 1817 he became Kapellmeister. Died in Riga 1840. K. was the author of very many successful operas, of which perhaps the best known is "Das Nachtlager in Granada."

Kreutzer, Rudolph, the same to whom Beethoven dedicated the famous " Kreutzer Sonata," was a violinist and composer, who was born at Versailles 1766. He was a fine musician, and especially a fine violinist, playing with great success throughout France and Germany. He was professor of the violin from the foundation of the Conservatoire, until in 1824 a broken arm compelled him to stop playing. Died 1831 at Geneva.

Kreutzer Sonata, a famous piece for piano and violin, Beethoven's op. 47, 1803.

Krieger, Adam (kreeg'-ĕr), a notable German organist and composer, 1634-1666.

Krueger, Wilhelm K. (kroig'-er), A noted pianist and composer of parlor pieces for the piano, born 1820 at Stuttgart. Was pupil of Lindpaintner. Is professor of piano in the Conservatorium.

Krug, Dietrich (kroog), a noted pianist, and author of a large instruction book for it, as well as many piano pieces. Born 1821 in Hamburg.

Krumhorn (crooked horn). An 8 ft. reed stop in the organ. Otherwise called "cremona," " clarionet," etc. The name is not now in use.

Kuecken, Friedrich Wilhelm, the melodious and distinguished song writer, was born at Blackede, Hanover, 1810. He studied counterpoint at Berlin, and with Sechter in Vienna, and orchestration with Halévy in Paris. K. was a prolific composer of operas, sonatas, etc., as well as the songs and duets on which his fame rests. Lives in Schwerin.

Kuhe, Wilhelm (koo'-ĕ), an elegant pianist and composer, was born in 1823 at Prague, and a pupil of Tomaschek, and later of Jul. Schulhoff at Cologne. Resides (probably) in London. Best known by his charming caprice "Feu Follet."

Kuhnau, Johann (koo'-nou). A very remarkable old musician, Cantor of Leipsic, and the greatest figure in German clavier music before Bach. He was the inventor of the sonata as a piece of several movements not dance tunes. Born 1667 at Geysing. Made cantor at Leipsic 1684. Died 1722.

Kullak, Adolph, a deep thinker in music and a teacher. Born 1823. Died 1862 in Berlin, Author of "Das Musikalischschön," 1858. and "Die Aesthetik des Clavierspiels," 1861.

ā *ale*, ă *add*, ä *arm*, ē *eve*, ĕ *end*, ī *ice*, ĭ *ill*, ō *old*, ŏ *odd*, ȯ *dove*, oo *moon*, ū *tute*, ŭ *but*, ü *Fr. sound*

Kullak, Theodor, the celebrated teacher, pianist, and composer, was born 1818 at Krotschins. He was a pupil of Czerny, and in 1846 was made Hofpianist to the King of Prussia. In conjunction with Stern and Marx in 1851 he founded a Conservatory of Music at Berlin. His own school of which he is still the head, the "Neue Akademie der Tonkunst," he founded in 1855, Is the author of many pieces, a great octave school, and one of the first piano-teachers in Europe.

Kummer, Friedrich August, a great violoncellist and composer for his instrument. Born 1797. Lived in Dresden, and died there 1879.

Kunkel, Jacob, a pianist, composer, and music dealer (Kunkel Bros.) was born Oct. 22, 1846, in Kleiniedesheim. Studied with his father and brother, L. M. Gottschalk, and afterwards with Tausig. Located in St. Louis in 1868, where he still resides.

Kunkel, Charles, pianist, composer and music dealer, was born at Sippersfeld, in the Rhine Phalz, July 22, 1840. Came to America at the age of 9, studied with his father who was a good musician. and with Thalberg and Gottschalk, removed to St. Louis in 1868, where he since resides.

Kunst (Ger. koonst, from *konnen*, to be able). Art.

Kunst der Fugue, "The art of Fugue." A remarkable work of Bach's, one of his very latest. A series of 24 *fugues on the same subject*, designed to illustrate the manifold powers of Fugue.

Kurz (Ger. koorts). Short, detached, staccato.

Kuertzen (Ger. kürt'-zĕn). To abridge.

Kyrie Elieson (Greek), "O Lord, have mercy upon us!" The opening anthem in the mass.

L, left hand.

La, a syllable applied to the sixth sound of the major scale. Also used in France as the name of the pitch A.

La (Ital. and Fr. lä), the feminine form of article.

La bemol (Fr. lä bā-mōl), the note A flat.

Labial, organ pipes with *lips*, called also *flue* pipes.

Labitzky, Josef (yō'-zŏf lä-beetz'-kĭ), the well-known dance-composer, born 1802 at Schonfeld. Began the world as 1st violin in 1820, and in 1821 removed to Carlsbad, where he still resides. He formed his orchestra in 1835. His dances are full of spirit, but not so poetical as those of Strauss.

Lablache, Luigi (lä-bllish'), the great basso, was born at Naples 1794. He was very musical, and as a boy a fine contralto, and as such sang the solos in Mozart's Requiem on the death of Haydn in 1809. He had talent for the 'cello. At the age of 20 he had a splendid bass voice of two octaves, Eb to Eb. From his debut in 1817 to his death in Paris 1858, Lablache was the foremost basso in Europe, and an actor and artist of the most sterling character. He was immensely large, about 6 ft. 4 in., and in his later years weighed nearly 400 pounds.

Lac de Fees, Le, opera in 5 acts, by Auber, 1839. The overture only has survived.

Lachmann, Karl, a many-sided German philologist, who has published a number of works on "The Chorus of the Greek Tragedy," the Niebelungenlied, etc., 1793-1851.

Lachner, Franz (läkh'-nĕr). One of the greatest masters in music at the present day, was born April 2, 1804, and from 1836 to 1 52 when he retired on a pension, he was h f-kapellmeister at Munich. L. is a prolific composer in the classical style, of songs, 4 operas, 8 symphonies, cantatas, etc., and is very highly esteemed in Germany.

Lachner, Ignaz, brother of the preceding. was born 1807. Assisted his brother at Vienna, etc., and in 1861 settled at Frankfort, where he fills many musical positions. He is also a prolific composer of operas, symphonies, piano-forte works, etc.

Lacrimando (Ital. lä-krē-män'-dō). Mournfully.

Lacrimoso (Ital. lä-krē-mō'-zō). In a mournful, pathetic style.

La diese (Fr. lä dī-äs'). The pitch ; A sharp.

Lady Henriette, a ballet pantomime in 3 acts, music by Flotow, Burgmüller and Deldevez. 1844. The libretto was afterwards expanded, and Flotow set it as "Martha."

Lady of the Lake, The. Cantata in 2 parts, music by Prof. G. A. Macfarren. 1877.

Laendler (Ger. länd'-ler). A country dance or air in a rustic and pleasing style in 3-4 time. Popular in Austria, Bavaria, Bohemia, and Styria. It is danced more slowly than the waltz.

La Grange. M'me Anna (lä gräng), one of the most distinguished and favorite coloratur singers of the present time, was born in 1825, at Paris. Studied singing with Bordogni. Made her debut in 1842, and had great success in all parts of Europe. She visited America in 1855, and again in 1869. Lives in Paris, where she is a prominent teacher of singing. M'lle Litta is one of the most distinguished of her pupils. She has a soprano voice of great compass, very finished execution, a lovely trill, and sang with true artistic conception and taste.

Lagrimoso (Ital. lä-grē-mō'-zō), and *Lagrimando*, weeping, tearful. In a sad and mournful style.

Lajeunesse, the family name of the distinguished prima donna, Miss Marie Emma Albani, (äl-bä'-nee). She was born in 1851 of French Canadian parents, near Montreal. In 1864 the family removed to Albany, whence she derived her pseudonym when she went upon the stage. Her finishing studies were made with Lamperti, at Milan, and her debut was in 1870, when the beauty of her voice, her pleasing method, and the intelligence of her singing speedily raised her to the commanding position she now holds. She was married to Mr. Ernest Gye in 1878.

Lallah Rookh. Moore's poem. 1. Opera by C. E. Horn, 1820. 2. Opera by Felicien David, 1862. 3. Opera in 2 acts, by Rubinstein, 1863. 4. Paradise and the Peri, by Schumann. 5. Paradise and the Peri, concertoverture, by Wm. Sterndale Bennett.

ā *ate*, ă *add*, ä *arm*, ē *eve*, ĕ *end*, ī *ice*, Ĭ *ill*, ō *old*, ŏ *odd*, ô *dove*, oo *moon*, ū *lute*, ŭ *but*, ü *Fr. sound*

Lambillotte, Pater Louis (läm.beel-yŏt-tĕ) a celebrated and popular church composer, was born 1797 at Charleroi, and at the age of 25 was kapellmeister in the Jesuit College in St. Scheul. In 1825 he joined the Order. L. has produced a great quantity of music for the church, which is showy, brilliant, and effective, but has little substance. Was also author of several works about music. Died in 1855.

Lament, an old name for harp tunes of the pathetic kind.

Lamentabile (Ital. lä-mĕn-tä-bē-lĕ). Lamentable, mournful.

Lamentations, the funeral music of the ancient Jews was called by this name. See also *Tenebrae*.

Lamentevole (Ital. lä-mĕn-tĭ-vōlĕ). Lamentful, lamentable.

Lamentoso (Ital. lä-mĕn-tō-zō). Lamentable.

La mineur (Fr. lä-mĭn-ŭr). The key of A minor.

Lamperti, Francesco (läm-pär-tee). The distinguished teacher of singing in Milan, was born at Savona, in 1813, studied at Milan, and in 1850 was appointed professor of singing in the Conservatory, from which he retired in 1875. L. teaches the old Italian method of Farinelli, etc. Mlle. Albani was his pupil.

Land lied (Ger. länd' leed). A rural or rustic song.

Lancer's Quadrille, a popular square dance for 8 or 16 couples.

Lang, B. J., the distinguished pianist, organist, conductor and teacher in Boston, was born in 1840. See Addenda.

Lange, Gustav (läng-ĕ), a pleasing pianist and favorite composer for his instrument, was born 1830 at Schwerstedt. Studied with his father, who was an organist, and later in Berlin with Gustav Schumann and Loeschhorn. Since 1860 has been very active as a composer, having published over 250 pieces.

Lange, S. de, the distinguished organist, pianist and composer, was born at Rotterdam, Feb. 22, 1840. He was taught by his father, who is yet organist in Rotterdam Cathedral. He studied composition under T. F. Dupont, Damcke, etc. From 1863 to 1874 he was located in Rotterdam as organist. He then spent a year in Basle, and one year in Paris, since which he has resided in Cologne as teacher of the organ and composition in the Conservatory. He is author of symphonies, string quartettes, overtures, and especially of interesting works for the organ.

Laughaus, Wilhelm (läng'-hous), a German violinist, composer and writer about music, born Hamburg, 1832. Studied at Leipsic, served as concertmeister and conductor at Düsseldorf, etc., and finally, in 1874, took up his residence in Berlin, where he is engaged in musico-literary labors, and teaches history in Kullak's Conservatory. Is author of string quartettes, etc.

Langsam (Ger. läng'-säm). Slowly. Equivalent to *largo*, or *adagio*, or *lento*.

Langsamer (Ger. läng'-säm-ĕr). Slower.

Languemente (Ital. län-gue-män'-tĕ). Languishingly.

Languendo (Ital. län-gwän'-dō), **Languente** (Ital. län-gwän-tĕ), **Languido** (Ital. län-gwē-dō). Languishing; feeble; with langor.

Lanner, Joseph, the celebrated conductor and composer of dance music, was born at Vienna in 1801. Became a conductor at a very early age, and died in 1843.

Large, the longest note formerly in use, equal to eight whole notes.

Largement (Fr. lärzh-mänh). Full, free in style.

Larghetto (Ital. lär-gät'-tō). A movement not quite so slow as *largo*.

Largo (Ital. lär'-gō), broad. A slow and solemn movement. This word is frequently modified by others, as *Largo assai*, very largo; *Largo un poco*, a little largo; *Largo ma non troppo*, largo, but not too much.

Larghissimo (Ital. lär-ghēs'-ē-mō), the superlative of *largo*. Extremely slow.

Larigot (Fr. lär'-ī-gō), shepherd's flute or pipe. An obsolete name for an organ stop tuned an octave above the 12th.

Larynx, the upper part of the *trachea*. It consists of five annular cartilages, placed above one another and united by elastic ligaments.

Last Shift, on a violin the shift to the 20th line, or E.

Last Judgment, The, the English version of Spohr's oratorio "Die letzten Dinge," 1830.

Lassen, Eduard, was born at Copenhagen 1830, but educated in Brussels, where he distinguished himself in composition, and finally, in 1851 received the great government prize. He went to Liszt at Weimar, who brought out at intervals three of his operas. On Liszt's resigning the directorship Lassen took his place, which he still holds. L. is a fine writer of the new school, having composed operas, songs, a symphony, overtures, etc.

Lassus, Orlando, or *Lasso*, a Netherlands composer of church music, born about 1530, who produced a great mass of church compositions, which influenced musical progress. D. 1594.

Latour, Jean, a French pianist, and composer, born at Paris 1766, and settled in London as pianist to the Prince of Wales. L. was a prolific author of divertissments, variations, etc., which were very fashionable in their day. He died in Paris in 1840.

Laub, Ferdinand (loub), a great violinist, the peer of Joachim and Wilhelmj. Born at Prague in 1832. After the usual European experience of virtuosi, he settled in Berlin in 1856 as teacher of violin in Stern's Conservatory. His tone was extremely pure, full and artistic. D. 1875.

Lauda Sion, the name of a sequence sung at High Mass on the feast of Corpus Christi, written by St. Thomas Aquinas, about 1261.

Lauds, a religious service held at daybreak.

Laurens, Alberto (real name Albert Lawrence), an English baritone singer. Born about 1835. At present a teacher of Italian singing in New York.

Laute (Ger. lou'-tĕ). The lute.

Lauterbach, Johann Cristoph, one of the first of living violinists, was born July 24, 1832, at Culmbach, studied with De Beriot, and made many concert tours since 1853. Resides in Dresden.

Lay, a tune or song.

Le, or before a vowel *L'* (Fr, lŭ), the.

Leader, the first or principal violin in an orchestra, the director of a choir.

Leading Motive, the principal motive of a musical period or piece. A motive becomes *principal* by being repeated more times than any other in principal key of the piece. This term is also used to denote the leading motives, or "catch" motives of Wagner, and many later composers. These are striking motives, each of which is introduced in connection with some one principal character. See also Wagner in Chapter LI.

Leading Note, the major seventh of any scale, so-called on account of its strong tendency towards the tonic.

Lebhaft (Ger. lāb′-hüft). Lively, vivacious, quick.

Lebrun, Francesca, a celebrated operatic soprano, born 1756. Died 1791. Had a voice of great compass and purity. She also composed sonatas, etc.

Le Carpentier, Adolphe Clair, a French piano composer and music teacher, born in 1809 at Paris. Died 1869.

Le Clair, Jean Marie, a celebrated violinist and composer for his instrument, born at Lyons 1697. Died 1764. Two of his sonatas were edited by Ferd. David, and are highly esteemed.

Lecocq, Charles, the popular composer of comic operas, operettas, etc., was born in Paris in 1832, entered the Conservatoire in 1849, and distinguished himself. His first successful opera was "Le Docteur Miracle," in 1857. Among his most popular pieces are "La Fille de M'me Angot," 1873, which ran for 500 nights consecutively. His works are distinguished for life, *brio*, and easy gayety.

Lecon (Fr. lā-sŏnh) lesson, an exercise.

Le Couppey, Félicien, a French piano composer, born in Paris 1814, educated at the Conservatoire, and in 1843 appointed professor of harmony there, and teacher of piano in the ladies classes. Is the author of many elementary and instructive compositions.

Lecureux, Théodore Marie, a French pianist, organist, and composer, was born at Brest 1829, educated in Paris, and in 1848 returned to Brest as organist and teacher of music. Is the author of many elegant and pleasing salon pieces.

Ledger Lines (perhaps a corruption of *leger*) short lines added to the staff above or below to extend its compass.

Leeds Musical Festival, was founded 1858. They are triennial 1874, 1877,1880.

Lefebure-Wely, Louis James (lŭ-fā′-br wā′-lē), a distinguished organ virtuoso and improvisatore, was born 1817 in Paris, became his father's assistant as organist at the early age of eight. At 15 was appointed his father's successor at St. Koch. Entered the Conservatoire in 1832. Was organist of the Madeline from 1847 to 1858, after which he went to St. Sulpice. Died 1869. Was a prolific composer of organ music, chamber music, symphonies, masses, a comic opera, etc.

Legare (Ital. lē-gä′-rō). To slur, or bind.

Legato (Ital. lē-gä′-tō). Slurred; connected. On the violin *legato* notes are performed with a single drawing of the bow. In singing, *legato* notes are delivered with one continuous tone. On the piano, *legato* requires every key to be held down until the next is struck. The legato is indicated by a curved line, drawn over or under the notes to be thus played.

Legatissimo (Ital. lē-gä-tees′-sō-mō, superlative of the preceding). As *legato* as possible.

Legende (Ger. lāg-ěn′-dě). A legend, or ballad.

Leger (Fr. lā-zhā). Light, nimble.

Legerement (Fr. lā-zhār-mänh). Lightly; nimbly; gaily.

Leggierissimo (Ital. lěd-jěr-ees′-sō-mō). Very lightly (superlative of Leggiero.)

Leggiero (Ital. lěd-jē-ā′-rō). Light, swift, delicate.

Leggieramente (Ital. led-jē-ěr-män′-tě), Lightly, swiftly.

Leidenschaft (Ger. lid′-ěn-shäft). Passion, feeling.

Leidenschaftlich (Ger. lid′-ěn-shäft-līkh). Passionately.

Leier (Ger. li′-ěr). A lyre, a hurdy-gurdy.

Leise (Ger. li′-zě). Low, soft, gentle.

Leiter (Ger. li′-těr). Leader, also the scale.

Leitmotive (Ger lit-mō-tēv). A leading motive.

Lemmens, Nicolas Jacques (lěm′-měn). A distinguished Netherland organist and composer for the organ, was born Jan. 23, 1823, at Zoerle-Parwys in Belgium. He studied the organ at the Conservatory in Brussels, and afterwards with Hesse at Breslau. In 1849 he became professor of the organ in the Conservatory in Brussels. L. has published many brilliant pieces for the organ in a school somewhat between the gravity of the German and the levity of the French; also an important organ school.

Lemmens-Sherrington, Mdme., wife of the preceding, is a prominent English soprano, who was educated at Brussels.

Lemoine, Jean Baptiste, was a French opera composer, born 1751. Died at Paris 1796.

Lemoine, Gabriel L., son of the preceding, was a prolific composer of piano and chamber music. 1772-1815

Leno (Ital. lā-nō). Weak, feeble, faint.

Lent (Fr, lānh). Slow.

Lentamente (Ital. lěn-tā-män′-tě). Slowly.

Lentando (Ital. lěn-tän′-dō). Going slowly. Synonymous with *rallentando*.

Lento (Ital. län′-tō). Slow. Frequently modified by other words, as *lento assai*, very lento; *lento di molto*, very much lento.

Lenz, Wilhelm von, Russian councilor at St. Petersburg, and author of "Beethoven and His Three Styles" (2 vols., 1852), "Beethoven: An Art-Study" (6 vols., 1855-1860), and an interesting little book on Piano-forte Virtuosi. Lenz is an inaccurate but entertaining writer.

ŭ *ate*, ă *at*, ä *arm*, ō *ore*, ĕ *en*, ī *ice*, ĭ *ill*, ō *old*, ŏ *odd*, o *dove*, oo *moon*, ū *lute*, ŭ *but*, ü *Fr. sound*

41

Leo, Leonardo (lā'-ō), one of the most celebrated Neapolitan composers, was born 1694, and died 1746. He wrote several operas and a large number of pieces for the church.

Leonhard, Hubert, a favorite Belgian violin virtuoso, composer and teacher for his instrument. Born 1819 at Bellaire. After the usual career of a virtuoso, he settled down in 1849 as professor of the violin in the Conservatory at Brussels.

Leonhard, Julius Emil, a notable German pianist, composer and teacher, born 1810, died 1831 in Leipsic.

Leonore ou l'Amour Conjugal. An opera-comique in 2 acts, words by Bouilly, music by Gaveaux. 1798. Translated into Italian, the book was composed by Paer in 1804. Translated into German, it was composed by Beethoven as "Fidelio." It was B.'s wish to call the opera Leonore, but he was overruled by the management of the theatre. His four overtures to it are: No. 1 in C, op. 138, composed in 1807; No. 2 in C, 1805, and played at the three performances of the opera; No. 3, C, 1806; Fidelio, in E, for the second and final revision of the opera. 1814.

Leschetitzky, Theodor (lĕs'-chĕt-ĭlt'-skī), a distinguished pianist, for some time professor of piano at St. Petersburg, but now living in Vienna. Is the author of many pleasing pieces for the piano. Born 1831. M'me Annette Essipoff was his pupil and wife.

Leslie, Henry David, was born in London, June 18, 1822. He became conductor of the choir which bears his name in 1855, through which he has established his fame as a refined and highly accomplished conductor of vocal music. Is the author of a symphony in F, 1847; "Immanuel," an oratorio, 1853; "Judith," oratorio, 1858; "Holyrood," cantata, 1860; "Ida," opera, 1864, etc., etc.

Lestocq, opera in 4 acts, by Auber, 1834.

Lesueur, Jean François, a French composer of operas, and teacher, born 1763, and in 1792-1706 appeared as the author of several operas. In 1813 L. succeeded Grétry at the Institut, and in 1818 became professor of composition at the Conservatoire. Died 1837.

Levezza (Ital. lĕ-vāt'-tsä). Lightness.

Liaison (Fr. lē-ā-zŏnh). Smoothness of connection, also a bind or tie.

Liberamente (Ital. lē-bĕ-rä-män'-tĕ). Freely, easily.

Libitum (Lat.). Pleasure; *ad libitum*, at pleasure.

Libretto (Ital. lē-brāt'-tō). A little book. In other words, the text of an opera or other dramatic piece of music.

License, an arbitrary deviation from the established rules. Justifiable only by some good effect thereby attained.

Lie (Fr. lē-ā'). Smoothly, the same as *legato*.

Liebeslied (Ger. lee'-bĕs-leed). A love song.

Liebig, Karl (lee'-bĭg). The successful founder of classical popular concerts in Berlin, was born at Schwerdt in 1808, and was for some time clarinettist in a regimental band. He established his orchestra in Berlin in 1850. Died in 1872.

Lieblich Gedacht (Ger. leeb-likh gĕ-däkht). The German name for the "stopped diapason," an 8 ft. flute stop in the organ.

Liebling, Emil (leeb-ling). Concert pianist and teacher, was born at Berlin in 1851, studied with Kullak, and came to Chicago in 1872, where he has since held high rank.

Lied (Ger. leed). A song.

Liedchen (Ger. leed'-kh'n). A short song, or melody.

Liedform (Ger.) A song-form.

Lieder-Spiel (Ger. lee-dĕr-speel). "A Song-play," an operetta.

Liederkreis (Ger. leed'-ĕr-krīs). A cycle of songs.

Lieder ohne Worte (Ger. leed-ŏr ō-nĕ vŏr'-tĕ). Songs without words. A title made famous by Mendelssohn.

Ligatur (Ital. lē-gä-toor'). See *ligature*.

Ligature, an old name for the *tie* or *bind*.

Light, a general name applied to any bright but unimportant composition.

Light of the World, The, an oratorio in two parts, by Arthur S. Sullivan, 1873.

Lilliburlero, a celebrated old Irish doggerel song and tune, the latter by Purcel.

Lilt (Scotch). To sing or pipe. Also the name of a quick tune.

Lily of Killarney, a grand opera in 3 acts, by Jules Benedict. 1862.

Lind, Jenny, the great soprano, was born at Stockholm, in 1820. Studied singing there and afterwards with Manuel Garcia in Paris. Her debut took place in 1842, but her reputation was not fully established until 1847. Her American tour under Barnum's management was in 1850 and 1851. In 1852 she married Mr. Otto Goldsmith, the pianist. She still lives in London.

Lindblad, Adolph Frederick, Swedish composer, mainly of vocal music, born at Stockholm in 1804. He was a teacher of singing, Jenny Lind being one of his pupils. Died 1878.

Lindpaintner, Peter Joseph von, a successful and industrious German composer, and a superior conductor, born at Coblenz, 1791. In 1819 he was appointed Kapellmeister at Stuttgart, and held that place until his death in 1856. He wrote 28 operas, 3 ballets, 5 melodramas and oratorios, 6 masses, and above 50 songs with piano accompaniment.

Linke (Ger. lĭn'-kĕ), left. The left hand.

Linley, an English musical family. Thomas, 1725-1795, was a composer of dramatic pieces, and takes high rank. Three of his daughters were successful singers. William, his youngest son, devoted himself to literature and music. 1767-1835.

Lipinski, Karl Joseph, an eminent violinist of the modern school, was born in Poland in 1790. After many concert tours, in which he was to some extent a rival of Paganini, L. became Kapellmeister at Dresden, where he died in 1861. His numerous compositions are now nearly all forgotten.

Lisbeth. The French title to Mendelssohn's "Son and Stranger." 1865.

Liscio (Ital. lē'-shē-ō). Simple, unadorned, smooth.

ŭ *ate*, ŭ *add*, ŭ *arm*, ē *eve*, ĕ *end*, ī *ice*, ĭ *ill*, ō *old*, ŏ *odd*, o *dove*, oo *moon*, ū *lute*, ŭ *but*, ü *Fr. sound*

42

Listemann, Bernhard Ferd., the distinguished violinist, was born about 1838. He graduated at Leipsic in 1856. In 1868 he came to Boston, where he has since resided, as teacher, first violin in quartette and symphony organizations, and at last in 1879 as conductor of his own orchestra.

L'Istesso tempo (Ital. lĭs-stäs'-sō tăm pō) The same time, in the same speed.

Liszt, Franz, the king of the piano-forte, and one of the most remarkably gifted men of the present century was born in 1811. See Chapter 50.

Litany, a solemn form of prayer.

Litolff, Henry Charles, the brilliant pianist and composer of salon pieces for piano, was born in London 1818, was a pupil of Moscheles, and made a successful public appearance, as early as the age of twelve. He removed to Brunswick as music publisher in 1851, and in 1861 to Paris, where he has since resided. He is also a composer of symphonies, overtures, etc.

Liturgy, the ritual for public worship in churches using printed forms.

Lobe, J. C., the distinguished teacher of composition and music at Leipsic, was born 1797 at Weimar, and appeared as solo flutist in the Gewandhaus orchestra in Leipsic in 1811. In 1842 he removed to Leipsic as editor of a musical periodical. He composed five operas, besides overtures, etc., but is best known by his letters on music, and his remarkably interesting *Kompositionslehre* (4 vols. 8vo., 1851 to 1867).

Lobegesang, eine Symphonie Cantata, the German title of Mendelssohn's "Hymn of Praise," op. 52, 1840.

Lock, Matthew, an English musician born 1653, died 1677. Best known by his music to "Macbeth," and "Tempest."

Loco (Ital. lō'-kō), place. Denotes that a passage is to be played as written, and not an octave higher or lower.

Lodoiska, comedy in 3 acts. Music by Cherubini. 1791. Also the same story set to music by Kreutzer. 1791.

Loeschhorn, A., an excellent pianist and musician, was born in Berlin 1819. He was a pupil of Berger. L. is a fine pianist, the author of many valuable studies and other pieces, and professor of piano since 1858 at Berlin.

Loewe, Karl, an industrious composer, born 1796 at Loebejuen, and died 1869. Loewe wrote 5 operas, many ballads and small pieces, and several instruction-books.

Logier, Johann Bernard (lō-jeer'), was born in 1780 at Kaiserlantern, and came to London at the age of 10. He made a great success and a fortune in England by a patent system of instruction on the piano and in harmony, which was for a time all the rage. He died near Dublin in 1846. He is said to have been the inventor of the keyed bugle.

Lohengrin (lō'-hĕn-grēn). A romantic drama in 3 acts, by Richard Wagner. 1847. First produced at Weimar by Liszt in 1850. See Chapter LI.

Lombardi, I (ō lŏm-bär'-dee). Italian opera in 4 acts, by Verdi. 1843.

Longa, a note equal to four whole notes. Not now in use.

Long Appoggiatura, a grace note, with out a stroke through the stem, which in old music occupies half or two-thirds the time of the following note.

Long Meter, Iambic tetrameter, a form of English verse, consisting of eight syllables to the line: ⌣ —│⌣ —│⌣ —│⌣ —│.

Long Pause, abbreviated L. P., implies a very long pause at a certain note or rest.

Lord of the Isles, The. Dramatic cantata by Henry Gadsby. 1879.

Lortzing, Gustav Albert, an opera composer born at Berlin, 1803. Died at Berlin, 1852. Although Lortzing was composer of very many light operas, of which the "Czar and Carpenter" is the best known, he died in neglect. His writing is pleasing and musicianly.

Loreley, Die, "The Loreley." An opera upon which Mendelssohn was engaged at the time of his death in 1847. 2. Also an opera by Max Bruch, 1864.

Lotti, Antonio, a celebrated Italian composer of operas, oratorios and church music, 1667-1740. One song of his, "*Pur Dicesti*," is still current and admired.

Loure (Fr. loor), a dance of slow time and dignified character, resembling the Gavotte.

Love's Triumph, opera in 3 acts, by Wm. Vincent Wallace, 1862.

Lowe, Edward, an English composer of church music, and professor at Oxford. Born about 1615. Died 1682.

Lucca, Pauline, (look-kä), the brilliant and pleasing operatic singer, was born in Vienna in 1842, made her debut in Berlin in 1861. She was in America in 1873.

Lucia di Lammermoor (loo'-tsē-ä dō läm'-měr-moor). Opera in 3 acts, by Donizetti, 1835.

Lucio Silla, a *Dramma per musica* in 3 acts, by Mozart, 1772.

Lucrezia Borgia (loo-krād'-zī-ä bŏr'-jū). Opera in 3 acts, by Donizetti, 1834.

Luestner, Ignaz Peter, a noted violinist and teacher, born 1792 at Pois-chwitz, lived mainly at Breslau, where he founded a school in violin playing, and died in 1873. His sons were all musical, and occupy prominent positions in different parts of Europe.

Luehrs, Carl (leers). A talented composer of symphonies, songs, etc. Born at Schwerin, 1824.

Luisa Miller, opera in 4 acts, by Verdi, 1849.

Lulli, Jean Baptiste, was one of the old masters in the time before Bach. He was a French composer of popular operas and sacred music. Born 1633 near Florence. Died 1687. L. was musical director to Louis XIV.

Lumbye, Hans Christian, a Danish composer of dances, born at Copenhagen 1808, was the leader of an orchestra, like Strauss's, Lanner's, Gilmore's, etc. Died 1874. His son George succeeded to his father's popularity and leadership.

Lurline (loor-leen). Grand opera in 3 acts, by Wm. Vincent Wallace, 1860.

Lusingando (Ital. loo-zēn-gän'-dō). Flatteringly, coaxingly. Whence, "in a soft and tender manner."

Lustigen Weiber von Windsor. "Merry Wives of Windsor," opera in 3 acts, by Otto Nicolai, 1849.

Luttuoso (Ital. loot-too-ō'-zō). Sorrowful, mournful.

Lute, a large and beautiful stringed instrument, with a long neck and fretted fingerboard, with from six to nine strings. The body was pear-shaped. Now obsolete.

Lux, Friedrich (loox), a distinguished organ virtuoso and composer, born Nov. 24, 1820, at Ruhla. Educated in organ and piano playing by his father, who was Cantor, and in 1851 music-director in Dessau. Is the author of a symphony and many considerable works.

Lwoff, Alexis, a Russian violinist, composer and writer, born 1799. Died 1870.

Lydian Mode. The church mode having the tones F G A B C D E F.

Lyre, an ancient stringed instrument. The modern lyre has its representative in the hurdy-gurdy.

Lyric, song-like.

Lysberg. Charles, properly Bovy, hence Bovy-Lysberg, a brilliant pianist and composer of salon pieces, was born in Geneva 1821. He studied the piano with Chopin in Paris, and published his first pieces, under the pseudonym of Lysberg, in 1836 or 1838. He resided in Geneva, and died in 1873.

M is used as abbreviation of *mezzo*, *metronome*, *mano*, etc. See "Abbreviations."

Ma (Ital. mä). But.

Maas, Louis, virtuoso pianist and teacher at Leipsic. Born about 1850.

Macfarren, George A., Mus. Doc., the English composer and President of the Royal Academy of Music, was born March 2, 1813, and educated in the institution of which he is now president. Dr. Macfarren had defective vision in his youth, and about 1865 he became entirely blind. In spite of this he has been a productive composer, being the author of several cantatas, operas, oratorios, part-songs, of which "St. John, the Baptist," is one of the best.

Macfarren, Mrs. Natalia, wife of the preceding, is a contralto singer and translator of opera libretti.

Macfarren, Walter, brother of G. A., is also a professor of the piano in the same institution, and a composer.

Macbeth, opera in 4 acts by Verdi, 1847. 2. Overture for orchestra in B minor, Spohr. 3. Also music to Shakespeare's tragedy, by Matthew Locke. 1673.

Madrigal (mäd'-rē-gäl). A composition for three or more voices in strict style, on secular words, popular in the 16th and 17th centuries. Madrigals were full of imitations and fugues, and sung without accompaniment. They were the predecessors of the modern glee.

Maestoso (Ital. mä-es-tō-zō). Majestic, stately, dignified.

Maestri, plural of *maestro*.

Maestro (Ital. mä-äs-trō). Master, composer, a skilful artist.

Maessig (Ger. mäs'-sīg). Moderate, moderately.

Maggiore (Ital. mäd-jē-ō'-rē). Greater, major, the major key.

Magnificat (Lat. mäg-nŏf-ĭ-kät). "My soul doth magnify the Lord," a part of the vesper service.

Maid of Artois, opera in 3 acts, by Balfe 1836.

Main (Fr. mänh). The hand, as *main droit*, right hand; *main gauche*, left hand.

Maistre, Mattheus le (otherwise known as Matthias Lemaitre), a distinguished Netherland composer. Born about 1510. Died 1577. From 1554 he was kapellmeister in Dresden.

Maitre (Fr. mätr), a master, director.

Majeur (Fr. mü-zhŭr). Major, major key.

Majesta (Ital. mä-yĕs-tä). Majesty, dignity.

Majeste (Fr. mü-zhĕs-tä). Same as the preceding.

Major, greater, as *major fourth*, greater fourth, etc.

Major Semitone, a diatonic semitone, as E F, B C, F sharp, G, etc.

Malan, Rev. César, a Swiss theologian, who composed church music. 1787-1864.*

Malenconico (Ital. mä-lĕn-kŏ'-nē-kō). Melancholy, sadness.

Malibran, Maria, one of the most distinguished and fascinating sopranos the world has ever seen, was the daughter of Manuel Garcia. Born 1808 at Paris. Made her debut in 1825, and immediately achieved success. She was married to De Beriot, the violinist, in 1836, the year of her death.

Mallinger, Matilde, a celebrated soprano in the Berlin opera. Born 1847. Made her debut in 1866.

Mancando (Ital. män-kän'-dō). Falling, decreasing, dying away.

Mandolin, a small and very elegant instrument of the lute kind, having frets like a guitar, and four or five pairs of strings, set in vibration by a plectrum. The lowest string is of gut "spun over," the next of steel spun, and the others of steel not spun.

Maniera (Ital. mä-nē-ā'-rä). Manner, style.

Maniere (Fr. mäu-ē-ar). Manner.

Mannerism, adherence to the same manner or peculiarities of style. The constant recurrence of the same chord or phrase.

Manns, August, the eminent conductor of the Crystal Palace concerts in Sydenham, was born at Stolzenburg, 1825. He became member of a military band, from which he was transferred to Gung'l's orchestra in 1848, and at length came to London in 1854, as sub-conductor, and in 1855 as full conductor in his present position, in which he has been of the greatest service to English musical taste by introducing the best German works in a superior manner.

Mano (Ital. mä'-nō). Hand.

Manual, pertaining to hands. The key-board for the hands, as distinguished from the *pedale*, the key-board for the feet.

Manual Coupler. A coupler connecting the keys of two organ manuals.

Mara, Gertrude Elizabeth, one of the greatest singers of the past century, born at Cassel 1749, died in 1833.

Marcia (Ital. mär'-tshō-ä). A march.

March, a quick, or at least decided rhythm, suitable for marching.

Marcello, Benedetto (mär-tshěl-lō), an eminent Venetian composer of cantatas, psalms, and church music. Born 1686. Died 1739.

Marchand, Louis, a French organist of distinction, 1669-1732.

Marchesi, Luigi (mär-kä'-zē), a fine operatic singer. Born at Milan 1755. Died 1829.

Marchesi, Mathildi de Castrone, the distinguished teacher of singing at Vienna, was born at Frankfort-on-the-Maine, 1826, and made her debut in opera in 1847. Since 1854 she has lived in Vienna. Her greatest recent pupil was Etelka Gerster.

Marchesi, Salvatore, husband of the preceding, is also a vocal teacher, and composer of songs, vocal exercises, etc. Born 1822.

Marchetti, F., one of the most distinguished opera composers at present in Italy, was born in 1833.

Marked, accented.

Markirt (Ger. mär'-kērt). Marked, accented.

Maretzek, Max (mär-ět-zěk), the well-known conductor, composer, and impressario, was born in 1821 at Brünn, and was educated at Vienna and Paris. His opera, "Hamlet," was written in 1843. He came to New York in 1847, where he has since resided.

Marinelli, Galtano, a prolific opera composer. Born 1760 at Naples. Died about 1811. Wrote 16 operas.

Maria di Rohan, opera in 3 acts, by Donizetti, 1843.

Marino Faliero, opera in 2 acts, by Donizetti, 1835.

Mario, Conte di Candia, one of the greatest operatic tenors, was born of a noble family at Genoa in 1812. His debut was made in 1838, after which he ruled king of operatic tenors until 1867, when he retired from the stage. He was married to Mdme. Grisi about 1846.

Maritana, opera in 3 acts, by Wm. Vincent Wallace, 1845.

Marpurg, Friedrich Wilhelm, eminent writer on music and its theory, born 1718. Died in 1795 at Berlin.

Marsellaise, La. A French revolutionary hymn, words and music composed by Rouget de Lisle in 1792.

Martellato (Ital. mär-těl-lä'-tō), hammered. Strongly marked. (From *martellare*, to hammer, also *martellando*, hammering.)

Martha, opera in 3 acts by Flotow, 1847.

Martini, Giovanni Baptista (mär-tee'-nee). Commonly called *Padre* Martini, one of the most scientific musicians of the 18th century, was born at Bologna 1706. He was ordained in the Franciscan order in 1722. Died 1784. Author of a history of music and a work on counterpoint; also of many church and secular pieces.

Marschner, Heinrich, one of the most talented German composers of recent times, was born at Zittau, 1795, and in 1830 was kapellmeister to the King of Saxony. He composed very many popular operas, and died full of years and honors, in Hanover 1861.

Martiri, I, "The Martyrs," opera in 4 acts, by Donizetti, 1840.

Marx, Adolph Bernhard, an elegant and fluent critic and theoretical writer upon music, was born at Halle, 1799, and, although educated for the law, became in 1824 the first editor of the Berlin *Musik Zeitung*, then just founded. He became professor in the University in 1830. Died in 1866. Was composer of two oratorios and other music.

Marziale (Ital. märd-zēǎ'-lē). Martial.

Masse, Victor, a pleasing French opera composer, was born 1822 in Lorient, studied with distinction in Paris, and has composed about 16 operas. Is a member of the Academy, and teacher of composition in the Conservatoire.

Masaniello (mäs-sä-nō'-äl-lō). Otherwise known as "La Muette di Portici," opera in 5 acts, by Auber, 1828.

Masnadieri, I, "The Brigands," opera in 4 acts, by Verdi, 1847.

Mason, Lowell, Mus. Doc., was born at Medfield, Mass., 1792, and died at Orange, N. J., 1872. He was a self-taught musician. His first book of psalmody was published in 1822, and was a step towards better music in New England. Dr. Mason was peculiarly an educator, and as such exerted an extremely important influence, which is still very perceptible. Owing to his early privations, he was not a musician in the learned sense of the term. But he had a fine sense for harmony, and the gift of writing simple four-part music agreeably and purely for voices. He was studious in his tastes, and collected a fine library, which was left to Yale College. He was a man of generous and noble character, as well as great ability, and would have distinguished himself in any walk of life.

Mason, William, Mus. Doc., son of the preceding, is a pianist and composer, born at Boston in 1829. Learned the piano young, and in 1851 studied with Moscheles and Hauptmann at Leipsic, and afterwards with Dreyschock at Prague, and Liszt at Weimar, where he was classmate of Bülow, Prückner, Klindworth and Raff. Mason is a fine harmonist, a good melodist, and a composer of remarkably elegant pieces for the piano. Since 1856 he has resided in Orange, N. J., and occupies leading rank in New York as teacher of the piano. He is also author of a new and very important system of piano-forte Technics.

Mass, the music for use during the service of the Mass.

Mathilde di Shabran, opera buffe in 3 acts, by Rossini, 1821.

Matilda of Hungary, dramatic opera in 3 acts, by Wm. Vincent Wallace, in 1847.

Matins, the first division of the canonical hours.

Matinee (Fr. mä-tǐ-nā). An entertainment given early in the day.

Mathews, W. S. B., was born at Loudon, N. H., May 8, 1837. Began the study of music at an early age, and became teacher at the age of 15. Began to write for "Dwight's Journal of Music" in 1859. Resides near Chicago as teacher of piano-forte, organ, and musical writer.

Mattei, Tito (tee -tō māt-tā'-ē), a popular composer of songs and piano pieces in London.

Mayer, Charles (mī'-ĕr), a favorite German piano virtuoso, composer and teacher, born at Königsberg 1799. Appeared early as a pianist. Lived much in St. Petersburg, and died in Dresden 1862. As a player he belonged to the school of Field.

May Queen, The. A pastoral cantata, by Sir Wm. Sterndale Bennett. 1855.

Mazurka, a rather slow Polish dance in triple time.

Measure, the grouping of pulsations in music. Measure is two-part, three-part, or four-part. There are also *compound* measures of these various grades, in which each unit consists of a triplet. Measure includes two elements, both of which are essential to the intelligibility of music; a steady movement through the piece, and a clear accent at the beginning of each measure. The longer measures take also secondary accents, at the beginning of their aliquot parts.

Measure-note, the note which represents a unit of time. It is always indicated by the lower figure of the time-signature, 4 for quarter-note, 8 for eighth, etc.

Medee, opera in 3 acts by Cherubini, 1797.

Mediant, the third note of the scale, the medial between tonic and dominant.

Medial Cadence, a passing or imperfect cadence.

Meeresstille and Glueckliche Fahrt, " Calm sea and Prosperous Voyage," poem by Goethe. Music by Beethoven in 1815. Also by Mendelssohn for orchestra only, 1828. Also by Rubinstein.

Mehlig, Anna, a distinguished pianist, born at Stuttgart 1846, educated there, and afterwards with Liszt, made her debut in England 1866. Was in America in 1873 and 1874. Resides in Stuttgart. Has great technic, a refined style, but somewhat cold.

Mehul, Etienne Henri, a celebrated French composer. Born 1763 at Givet. Went to Paris in 1781, and came out as a composer in his fourth opera in 1790. He wrote 24 operas, and many other works. Died 1817.

Meistersinger von Nuernberg, "The Master Singers of Nuremburg," opera, by R. Wagner, 1846.

Melange (Fr. mā-länzh'). A mixture.

Melancolia (Ital. měl-än-kō'-lïä). Melancholy.

Melodeon, a reed instrument having a keyboard like the piano-forte.

Melodie, of or pertaining to melody.

Melody, a tune; a symmetrically organized and completed period.

Melodia (Ital. mā-lō'-dïä). A melody.

Melodia, an organ stop of the flute tone, 8 ft. pitch. Commonly in the choir organ.

Melodie (Ger.) A melody.

Melodioso (Ital. mā-lō-dē-ō'-zō). Melodiously.

Melodrama, a drama illustrated by music interspersed, or frequently as accompaniment to the spoken dialogue.

Melusine, overture by Mendelssohn, 1833. Also set as choral work by Hoffman.

Meme (Fr. mām). The same.

Mendel, Hermann, editor of Mendel's *Musikalisches Conversations-Lexicon* (Musical Encyclopedia), was born at Hallé, 1834. He undertook his lexicon in 1870, and died in 1876, just as the work had reached the letter M. It has since been completed in 11 volumes, and is the most complete work of the kind.

Mendelssohn, Felix, was born at Hamburg, 1809, and died 1847. See Chapter XLVII.

Meno (Ital. mā-nō), less; *meno mosso*, less movement, slower.

Mensur, a measure.

Menuet (Fr. mü-noo-ě). A minuet.

Menuetto (Ital. mā-noo-ĕt'-tō). A minuet.

Mercadante, Xav., a well-known opera composer. Born at Altamura in 1798. In 1840 he became director of the Conservatorium of Naples. Died 1870.

Messa di Voce (Ital. mäs-sä dē vō'-tsheě). The gradual swelling and diminishing of the voice.

Messe (Ger. měs'-sě). A mass.

Mesto (Ital. mäs'-tō). Sad, mournful.

Mestoso (Ital. mäs-tō'-zō). Sadly, mournfully.

Messiah, The, an oratorio, by Handel, 1741.

Met, abbreviation of *Metronome*.

Metal, organ, a composition of tin and lead in varying proportions. Tin should be at least one-third.

Metronome (mĕt'-rō-nōm). A measure of time. A chronometer invented by Maelzel, consisting essentially of clock-work and escape wheel, and a pendulum swinging on a pivot in the middle of its length. It can be made to go slower by sliding a ball up towards the top of the pendulum. The rate is indicated by the letters M.M. for the metronome, a figure showing the place of the ball on the graduated scale of the instrument, and a note which is to occupy the time of a single tick.

Meter, the plan of verse according to its feet and length of lines.

Meyer, Leopold de (mī'-ĕr), An eccentric pianist, born 1816, a pupil of Czerny, visited America in 1845 and 1868, and lives in Paris and London.

Meyerbeer, Giacomo (gïä-kō'-mō mī'-ĕr-bār), whose real name was Jacob Meyer Beer, the celebrated opera composer, was born at Berlin of a wealthy Jewish family, 1791. His debut as composer was made in 1811. His best known operas were "Il Crociato," 1824, "Robert der Teufel," in 1831, and "Les Huguenotte," 1836, the "Prophete," 1849. Died 1864. All these operas are showy, and extravagant, rather than inspired.

Mezza, feminine of *mezzo*.

Mezzo (Ital. mät-tsō). Half, or medium.

Mezzo Soprano, a voice of soprano quality, but not so high as a pure soprano.

Mi (Ital. mō). The third tone of the scale in solmization.

Microphone (mī'-krō-fōn). An instrument for observing feeble sounds; a microscope for sounds.

Middle Voices, the inner voices in choral writing, the alto and tenor.

ă *ale,* ă *add,* ä *arm,* ē *eve,* ĕ *end,* ī *ice,* ĭ *ill,* ō *old,* ŏ *odd,* ů *dove,* oo *moon,* ü *lute,* ŭ *but,* ü *Fr. sound*

Mignon, opera in 4 acts, by Ambroise Thomas.

Mills, S. B., virtuoso pianist, composer and teacher, was born at Leicester, England, March 13, 1839. Studied at Leipsic, and came to New York about 1858, where he has since held a distinguished position.

Military Band, a brass band, or brass and wood (horns, trombones, cornets, tubas, clarinets, oboes, flutes, piccolo kettle-drum, snare-drum, and cymbal).

Minor, smaller.

Minor second, a diatonic semitone.

Minor third, a third equal to three semitones.

Minor triad, a triad with a minor third.

Minore (Ital. mē-nō´-rē), minor.

Minor Scale, the scale beginning with the syllable *La*, or the 6th of the major. See Mason's "Piano Technics," for a discussion of the M.S.

Minnesingers, minstrels of the 12th and 13th centuries, who wandered from place to place singing a great variety of songs.

Minstrels, wandering singers.

Minuet, an ancient, slow and stately dance in 3-4 time, usually in two strains.

Miserere (Lat. mē-sē-rā´-rē), "Have mercy," a psalm of supplication.

Missa, a mass. *Missal*, a mass-book.

Misterioso (Ital. mĭs-tā-rĭ-ō´-zō). Mysteriously.

Misurato (Ital. mē-soo-rā´-tō). Measured, in exact time.

Mixture, an organ stop composed of several ranks of pipes, designed to strengthen the harmonic over-tones in the klang. "Two rank" mixtures sound the 12th and 15th of the note struck. Three rank the 15th, 19th, and 22d. Modern mixtures do not contain the third of the chord (or any of its octaves, the 10th, 17th, 24th), but only octaves and fifth, and are voiced in flute quality. They impart a clear and ringing quality to the tone of the full organ.

Moderato (Ital. mŏd-ā-rä´-tō). Moderately.

Mode, a scale or key, "Major mode," major key.

Modesto (Ital. mō-dās´-tō). Modestly.

Modulation, a harmonic progression out of one key into another, by means of ambiguous chords. "Modulation of voice" means control of the voice.

Modus (Latin). A mode.

Moins (Fr. mwä). Less.

Molique, Bernhard (mō-leek´). An excellent violinist. Born at Nuremburg, 1802. Died 1869. Wrote concertos for violin, trios for piano, violin and 'cello, and an oratorio, "Abraham," 1860.

Moll (Ger. mōl). Soft, *i.e.*, minor.

Molto (Ital. mōl´-tō). Much, very much, a great deal.

Monochord, an instrument composed of a single string stretched over a sounding-board, along a graduated scale, for measuring musical intervals.

Monody, a composition on one subject, generally of a sad character.

Monteverde, Claudio, one of the greatest masters in his time. Born 1568 in Cremona. Died 1651. He wrote operas, and deserves particular honor for developing recitative.

Montre (Fr. mōnh-trä ´). "mounted," in front. Hence frequently applied to the diapason stop in an organ, because its pipes are often displayed in front.

Morceau (Fr. mōr-sō). A piece, a choice piece.

Mordent (Ital. mōr-dān-tē). A transient shake or beat, formed by the principal note and the next above. See supplement.

Moresca (Ital. mō-rĕs-kā), Moorish. A morris-dance, in which bells are jingled and swords clashed.

Morlacchi, Francesco (mōr-läk´-kee), a successful and meritorious opera composer, born 1784, died 1841.

Mornington, Earl of, father of the Duke of Wellington, was a composer of glees and church pieces. Born 1742 in Ireland.

Mortier de Fontaine, born 1818 at Warsaw, the first who played Beethoven's gigantic sonata, op. 106, in public.

Moore, Thomas, an English poet and song-writer, born in Dublin 1779. Published his *Irish Melodies* in 1823. Died 1852.

Morgan, George Washbourne, the distinguished organist, living in New York, was born in England about 1827, and came to New York about twenty years ago, where for a long time h was organist of Grace Church.

Moscheles, Ignatz, the distinguished piano virtuoso and teacher, was born at Prague in 1794. Studied with Zadraklia, and later with Dionys Weber and Clementi. He made his debut in 1815, and had famous success all over Europe. He resided in London as teacher, conductor and pianist, for some years, and joined Mendelssohn as professor of piano at the Leipsic Conservatory, in 1846, where he died in 1870.

Moses in Egypt, an opera, or oratorio, by Rossini, 1827.

Mosso (Ital. mōs´-sō). Movement, motion.

Moszkowski, Moritz (mōz-kō´-skĭ), one of the most gifted of the younger composers, was born about 1853, and resides in Berlin, where he was pupil of Kullak, and is a clever pianist. His compositions are mainly for the piano, and are fresh, musical and melodious.

Motette (mō-tĕt´). A motet; a vocal composition, with sacred words. The line between motet and anthem is not clearly drawn.

Motive, a musical figure or germ employed as a text. See Chaps. I. and X.

Motion, mode of progression. *Rhythmic* M. is progression in notes of uniform value, or in a particular rhythmic figure, through several measures or periods. See Chaps. VII., VIII. and IX. *Voice* M. is similar, parallel, contrary, or oblique. *Contrapuntal* M. is "two against one," "three against one," "four against one."

Mouthpiece, that part of a trumpet or brass instrument which is applied to the lips.

Mozart, Leopold, born 1719 in Augsberg. Died 1787. He was an excellent musician, and a tasteful and talented composer, and vice-kapellmeister to the Archbishop of Salzburg.

ă *ale*, ŭ *add*, ä *arm*, ē *eve*, ē *end*, ī *ice*, ĭ *ill*, ō *old*, ŏ *odd*, ò *dove*, oo *moon*, ū *lute*, ŭ *but*, ü *Fr. sound*

Mozart, Wolfgang Amadeus, son of the preceding, was born Jan. 27, 1756, at Salzburg, and died 1791. See Chap XLV.

Muette di Portici, ll, otherwise known as "Masaniello," opera in 5 acts, by Auber, 1828.

Mueller, A. E., organist of the St. Thomas Church at Leipsic, was composer, for the piano-forte, organ, orchestra, and voices. 1767-1817.

Mueller, C. E. R., an organist, pianist, and composer. Born in Chicago about 1347, educated at Stuttgart, and at present residing in Chicago, Is translator of Lebert and Stark's piano method.

Murska, Ilma di, the brilliant singer, was born about 1843, in Croatia, studied singing with Marchesi, in Vienna, and made her debut in 1862. Her voice is a soprano of about three octaves compass and great execution.

Murray, James R., composer of school and S. S. music, born at Andover, Mass., 1841.

Musette (Fr. moo-sĕt'), An instrument of the bag-pipe family. Also an air in 2-4, 3-4, or 6-8 of moderate tempo and smooth and simple character.

Music of the Future, a term ironically applied some years ago to the music of Wagner. The name was derived from his essay under the same title.

Musical History. The best accounts of, are Brendel's "*Geschichte der Musik,*" and Reissmann's, Ritter's two small volumes, and Hullah's "Lectures on Musical History," are to be recommended.

Musical Libraries. The best in this country are those of the Harvard Musical Association, the Boston Public Library, and that in Yale College.

Music Printing, from movable types, was invented more than a hundred years ago, but only within the present century has it become able to represent instrumental music neatly.

Musikalisches Opfer. "Musical Offering." A name given by Seb. Bach to a six-part fugue for strings, on a subject given him by Frederick the Great. 1747. This is arranged for the organ by Haupt, and played by Mr. Eddy and other virtuosi.

Muta (Ital. moo'-tä). Change. Directs the horn-player to change his mouth-piece.

Mutation Stops, organ stops not sounding the 8ft. pitch. Applied especially to mixtures, quints and twelfths.

Mute (Ital. *sordino,* Ger. *dämpfer*), a contrivance for deadening the sound of stringed instruments, by pinching the bridge and so restricting vibration.

Naaman, oratorio by Costa, 1864.

Nabuco, or **Nabucodonosor,** "Nebuchadnezzar," opera in 3 acts by Verdi, 1842.

Nachamung (Ger. näkh'-moong). Imitation.

Nachbauer, Franz (näkh'-bowr), a noted German tenor, born 1835 at Schloss Giessen.

Nachdruck (Ger. näkh'-drook). Emphasis, accent.

Nachdrucksvoll (Ger. näkh'-drooks-fōl). Energetic, emphatic.

Nachsatz (Ger. näkh'-sătz). The second half of a period.

Nachschlag (Ger. näkh'-schläg). A passing tone ; or, if one might say so, an appoggiatura *after* a note, instead of before it.

Nachspiel (Ger. näkh'-speel). After-piece ; concluding organ voluntary in the church service.

Nachtstuecke (Ger. näkht'-steek-ĕ). Night pieces ; *i. e.,* "nocturnes." A name given to Schumann's op. 23.

Naegeli, J. G., an eminent Swiss educator, composer and music publisher, born at Zurich 1768. Died 1836.

Nirinia, a cantata by Goetz.

Nagelclavier, a keyed instrument of 5 octaves, made about 1791.

Naked Fifths. Open consecutive fifths.

Nanini, Giovanni, a celebrated Italian composer, the first who wrote church music with organ accompaniment. Died about 1620.

Naples, School of. The chief masters of this class were Scarlatti, Durante, Leo, Cotumacce, Cafaro, etc. The Conservatories in Naples were founded 1535, 1576, 1589, and 1584.

Napoleon, Arthur, a promising pianist, born in Lisbon, 1847.

Naprownik, Eduard, composer and chief director of the Russian Theatre, in St. Petersburg, was born in 1839. Studied at Prague, distinguished himself in composition, and became director in St. Petersburg in 1861.

Nares, James, Mus. Doc., an English conductor, composer and organist of York Minster, born 1715. Died 1783. Author of harpsichord lessons, collections of glees, catches, twenty anthems, etc. Had little imagination.

Nasal, the reedy, unpleasant quality of the voice when it issues in too great a degree through the nostrils. The nasal quality is characterized by too much prominence of the 12th in the overtones.

Nasat, and **Nazard,** old names for the organ stop, now called the "Twelfth."

Nasolini, Sebastiano (nä-zō-lē'-nē), Italian opera composer, born in Piacenza, 1768, and at the age of twenty appeared with his first opera. "Separate scenes in his operas had talent," says Reissmann, and there were 18 in all. Died 1799 or 1810.

Natural, a character used to annul a sharp or flat.

Natural Key, a name improperly applied to the key of C, because in this all pitches are represented by staff-degrees in the "natural" condition.

Natural Trumpet, a trumpet without valves.

Natural Scale, the scale of C. See Natural Key.

Naumann, J. G. (now -män), a well known composer in his day, born 1741 near Dresden. Studied in Italy, where he produced his first operas. Was kapellmeister at Dresden, and died there 1801. He left 11 oratorios and 21 masses, and 12 operas.

Naumann, Emil, grandson of the preceding, also a composer of merit, was born at Berlin, in 1827, and resides chiefly in Dresden. In 1880 he succeeded W. Rust as organist of St. Thomas' at Leipsic.

Nava. Gaetano (nä-vä), a distinguished Italian teacher of singing, and composer of vocal exercises. Born 1802 at Milan. Died 1875. Among his pupils was Santley, the baritone.

Necessario (Ital. nä-tshes-sä'-rī-ō), necessary. Indicating that the passage must not be omitted.

Neapolitan Sixth, a chord consisting of a minor third and minor sixth to a given bass.

Neck, that part of a violin, or other similar instrument, extending from the head to the body, and carrying the finger-board.

Neefe, C. G., a musician of some distinction in his day, who was Beethoven's instructor. He was organist at Bonn. Born 1748. Died 1798.

Neige La, ou le Nouvel Eginhard, opera in 4 acts by Auber, 1823.

Negligenza (Ital näg-lē-jän'-tsä). Negligence, carelessness.

Neithardt, August Heinrich (nīt'-härdt), founder of the Berlin Dom-Choir, was born at Schleiz, 1793. Served in the army about twenty-five years, and in 1839 was made royal music director. Died 1861. Published a compilation of the best church music, in 8 vols.

Nel (Ital. nūl), also *Nella*, *Nelle*, *Nello* and *Nell'*. In the ; at the ; as *Nel stesso tempo*, in the same time.

Net (Fr. nä), also **Nett** (Ger. nĕt). Neatly, clearly, plainly.

Neron, opera in 4 acts, by A. Rubinstein, 1879

Neruda, a celebrated German family of violinists, of which M'me WILHELMINE NORMANN-NERUDA is the most distinguished living member. She was born at Brünn, 1840. Married a Swedish musician named Ludwig Normann. Plays much in England, and is a great favorite as leader of quartettes in the Popular Concerts.

Netherlands School. The, embraced such composers as Dufay, 1432, Ochenheim, 1513, Josquin de Prés, 1521. This school developed musical science, especially counterpoint, earlier than any other in Europe.

Neukomm, Sigismund Chevalier (noi'-kōm), was born at Salzsburg, 1778. Studied with Michael and Joseph Haydn, and appeared as a composer in 1808. He led a wandering life, always, however, having good appointments, and spent the last twenty years of his life between Paris and London. Died in Paris, 1858. His two oratorios, "Mount Sinai" and "David," and his symphony in E flat, were played several times in England. Was an industrious but uninspired composer.

Nexus, an old term for a phrase or sequence.

Nicht (Ger. nīkht). Not.

Nicht zu geschwind (Ger. nīkht zoo gĕ-schvīnd'). Not too quick.

Niebelungen ("*Der Ring des Niebelungen*"), "The Ring of the Niblung." A sequence of four operas or music-dramas, by Richard Wagner. First performed 1876. The four operas in the series are : *Das Rheingold* 1854, *Die Walküre* 1855, *Siegfried* 1857-1859, *Die Götterdämmerung* 1871.

Niccolini, Joseph, a prolific composer of Italian operas, born 1771, died 1843 at Piacenza. Author of 9 operas, 5 oratorios, 30 masses, 2 requiems, 100 psalms, etc.

Nicolai, Otto .(nīk'-ō-lī), composer of the popular opera, "The Merry Wives of Windsor," was born ir Königsburg, 1810, and after serving some years in Berlin as organist, appeared at Vienna as conductor in 1837. Was appointed kapellmeister at Berlin in 1848, and died in 1849, just after completing his most popular opera.

Nicolai, Wilhelm F. G., was born in 1829 at Leyden. Studied at Leipsic, and then with Schneider in Dresden, and returned to Leyden as an organ virtuoso. Is professor of the organ and conductor at the Hague.

Niedermeyer, Louis (nē'-dĕr-mī'-ĕr), a composer of operas, motettes, masses, and teacher of piano, born at Nyon, on Geneva Lake, in 1802. Studied with Moscheles and Förster. Resided mainly at Paris, where he died in 1861.

Niemann, Albert, the famous German tenor, was born 1831 at Magdeburg. Is "kammersänger" at Berlin, and played the part of Siegmund in "Die Walküre" at Bayreuth in 1876.

Night-Horn, a name sometimes applied to a 4 ft. flute in organs.

Night Dancers, opera in 2 acts by Loder, 1846.

Nielson-Rounseville, M'me Christine, the successful piano-teacher in Chicago, was born at Christiansand, Norway, Aug. 10, 1845. Was a pupil of Haberbier, at that time professor in Leipsic, and in 1871 came to America, where she has since resided. Was married to Dr. Rounseville in 1875.

Nilsson, Christine, the celebrated prima-donna, was born in Sweden, 1843, and early manifested her remarkable talent for music. She played the violin and sang from house to house. Her voice attracted attention, and she was sent to Stockholm, and afterwards to Paris, where she was pupil of Wartel. She made her debut in 1864 as Violetta. In 1871 she was in America. Her voice is of moderate volume, great sweetness and carrying power.

Nocturne (Fr. nŏk-tŭrn), also *Notturno*, a nocturne. A song-like composition of a soft and tender character, as if suitable for the hours of night. See Lesson XXXII.

Node, that point of a chord at which it divides itself when it vibrates by aliquot parts, and produces the harmonic overtones. Any overtone can be prevented by striking the string at its own node.

Noel (Fr. nō-ĕl). A Christmas carol or hymn.

Nohl, Ludwig (nōll), a well known writer on music and musical subjects. ("Mozart's Letters," "Beethoven's Letters," etc.) Was born in Westphalia, 1831. He was educated at Bonn and Heidelburg, and there since 1872 he resides as professor of musical history and aesthetics.

Nohr, Chr. Friedrich (nōr), a violin virtuoso and conductor at Saxen-Meiningen. B rn 1800. Wrote operas, a symphony, etc. Died 1875.

Non, not ; no ; as *non molto*, not much ; *non tanto*, not so great ; *non troppo*, not too much.

None (Ger. nō-nĕ). The ninth. Also the the last of the lesser hours in the Breviary.

Nonet, a composition for nine voices, or in nine voice-parts.

ä *ale*, ä *a.ld*, ä *arm*, ē *eve*, ĕ *end*, ī *ice*, ĭ *ill*, ō *old*, ŏ *odd*, ū *dove*, oo *moon*, ū *lute*, ŭ *but*, ü *Fr. sound*

4   49

Non nobis Domino, "Not unto us, O Lord." A celebrated canon sung as a grace after meat, at public dinners in England.

Non Plus Ultra, "Nothing more beyond." The bumptious title of a piano sonata by Woelfl, op. 41, in 1807.

Nonne Sanglante, La, opera in 5 acts by Gounod. 1854.

Norma, opera in 2 acts, by Bellini. 1832.

Normal, right ; natural ; proper.

Normal-ton (Ger. nŏr-mäl'-tōn). The tone A, to which orchestral instruments are tuned.

Normal Scale, the natural scale.

Normal School, a school for teachers.

North, James O., a teacher of singing in St. Louis. Born about 1830.

Notation, the signs by means of which music is represented. See Appendix.

Note, a sign of musical utterance. The *pitch* is indicated by the staff degree on which the note is played ; the *length* by the form of the note.

Note Printing. The earliest printing from movable types was by Ottaviano dei Petruccio, in 1466.

Note-Head, the oval part of the note, which occupies the pitch-place.

Note-Stem, the line running from the head.

Nottebohm, Martin Gustav, composer, teacher and writer on music, was born near Lüdenschied in 1817. Studied in Berlin with Berger and Dehn, and afterwards with Sechter. He was one of the chief editors of the critical editions of Bach, Handel, Beethoven, Mendelssohn and Mozart. His compositions include clavier trios and quartettes, solos for piano, etc.

Nourrit, Adolph, a highly gifted tenor singer in Paris, born 1802. Died 1839. Was professor of dramatic declamation in the Conservatory.

Novelletten, "Novellettes," the title of a series of 8 piano pieces by Schumann, op. 21, 1838.

Novello, Vincent, an English composer, editor and organist, was born in London, 1781. Was organist in several important churches, author and compiler of much church music, and died at Nice, 1861.

Novello, Clara, the celebrated soprano, daughter of the preceding, made her debut in 1833, and was the leading oratorio and operatic soprano in England for many years.

Novello, Joseph Alfred, eldest son of Vincent, was a bass singer, and the founder of Novello's "Sacred Music Warehouse," the first depot of music at a low price, and the beginning of the present firm, " Novello, Ewer & Co." Born 1810. Lives at Genoa.

Nozze di Figaro, Le, "The Marriage of Figaro," opera buffa by Mozart *(Figaro's Hochzeit),* 1776.

Nuances (Fr. nü-ähn-s). Lights and shades of expression.

Nuit Blanches. "Restless Nights." The title of a set of 18 lyric piano pieces by Stephen Heller, op. 82.

Number. The several pieces or sections of an opera or oratorio, are numbered for convenience of reference, etc. The overture is never counted.

Nunc Dimittis, "Now dismiss us." The canticle of Simeon, St. Luke, ii : 29, etc. A vesper song.

Nut, a slip of ebony or ivory glued to the neck of the violin, at the upper end of the fingerboard.

2. Of the bow, a piece of ebony or ivory over which the hairs pass.

O (Ital. ō), or.

Od (Ital. before a vowel ŏd), or, as, either.

Oakeley, Sir Herbert Stanley, Mus. Doc., was born at Ealing, July 22, 1830, and educated at Oxford. Studied music with Dr. Elvey and Schneider, of Dresden, and completed at Leipsic. In 1865 was appointed professor of music in Edinburg University. Composer of songs, anthems, etc. Is a good organist.

Obbligato (Ital. ōb-blē-gä'-tō). Necessary, obligatory, must not be omitted.

Oberon, romantic opera in 3 acts, by von Weber, 1826.

Oberthuer. Chas., a distinguished performer on, and composer for the harp, was born March 4th, 1819, at Munich. Resides in London, and has composed an opera, mass, and many compositions for harp.

Oberwerk (Ger. ō-bĕr-vŭrk). The upper manual on a two manual organ.

Obligat (Ger. ōb - lī - gät') Indispensable, necessary.

Oblique Piano, an English term for the diagonal arrangement of strings, usual in upright pianos.

Oboe (Ger. ō-bō-ĕ). A wooden reed-instrument of two foot tone. It is played with a double reed. It consists of a wooden tube about two feet long, with sound holes on the sides, like a flute. Has a somewhat plaintive and wailing tone.

Oboe d' Amour, an oboe exactly like the usual one, but tuned in A, a minor third lower.

Oboe di Caccio, an old name for an oboe standing in E♭ or F.

Oboe Stop, an organ stop consisting of impinging reeds and conical pipes of a small scale, usually in the swell organ. Owing to the reed and block being of metal, it has a harsher tone than the orchestral oboe.

Oca del Cairo, "The Goose of Cairo," opera buffa in two acts, by Mozart, 1783.

Ocurina (ō-kŭ-rē'-nä). Terra-cotta instrument somewhat resembling the flageolet.

O'Carolan, or **Carolan,** Turlogh, one of the last and most famous of the bards of Ireland. Born 1670. Died 1738, and was famous for his improvisations.

Octachord, an instrument or system comprising eight sounds, or seven degrees.

Octave, the eighth tone, in the diatonic scale, above or below any other. The octave is the most perfect consonance in music except the unison. Its ratio is 2 : 1. Octaves are equivalent in harmony.

Octave, an organ stop of diapason quality and 4 ft. tone, standing an octave above the diapason.

Octave Flute, a small flute an octave higher than the German flute.

Octave Successions, or "consecutive octaves," the parallel motion of two voices at the interval of an octave, are forbidden in four-part harmony, because they temporarily reduce the number of parts to three.

Octette, a composition for eight voices or instruments.

Ode, an air or song; a hymn of praise.

Oesten, Theodore, the famous arranger of teaching pieces for the piano, was born at Berlin, Dec. 31, 1813. Learned various instruments, and was in great demand as a teacher of piano-forte. Died 1870.

Oeuvre (Fr. ūvr), work; composition; piece. A term used in numbering a composer's productions in the order of their composition or publication.

Offenbach, Jacques, the famous composer of opera buffo, was born at Cologne, 1819, of Jewish parents. Studied music, became orchestral conductor, and appeared as composer in 1853. O. composed 69 pieces and 143 acts within 25 years. D. 1880.

Offertorium (Lat. ŏf-fĕr-tō'-rĭ ŭm). A hymn, prayer, anthem or instrumental piece played during the offertory.

Ohne (Ger. ō'-nŏ), without. *Ohne begleitung,* without accompaniment; *ohne pedals,* without pedals (in organ music); *ohne dampfer,* without dampers (with the pedal pressed down).

Old Hundredth, The, a tune long associated with the 100th Psalm. Supposed to have been written as early as 1551.

Ondeggiante (Ital. ōn-dăd-jō-ăn'-tŏ). Waving, undulating, trembling.

Onglour (Fr. ŏnh-glŭr). An old term for a performer on the lyre or harp.

Olimpiade, libretto by Metastasio, composed over 31 times, by Caldara, Leo, Pergolese, Hasse, etc.

Olympie, lyric tragedy in 3 acts by Spontini, 1819.

Open Diapason (dī-ă-pā'-sŏn). The most important stop in an organ. It consists of metal pipes, of large scale and free and solid tone, and forms the foundation of the tone of the full organ.

Open Harmony, or *Open Position,* a position of chords in which the three upper tones of the chord do not fall within the compass of an octave.

Open Pipe, an organ pipe open at the upper end.

Open Note, a tone produced by an open string, a free, uncramped tone.

Open String, a string vibrating through its whole length. Open notes on the violin have more resonance than those produced by "stopping."

Opera, a drama set to music for solo singers, chorus, orchestra, scenery, and dramatic action. The words of an opera are called the "Book," or "Libretto." Opera dates back to the 15th century. The principal schools of opera are the *Italian*, in which the singing is the chief thing, the *French*, in which the dramatic action is chief; the *German*, which aims at the complete union of action, singing, and musical description, and opera *buffa* in which the absurd and laughable is aimed at.

Opera Buffa, comic or buffo opera.

Opera, Italian. The greatest composers of this school were Donizetti, Bellini, Rossini, Verdi.

Opera, German. The greatest composers of this school were Gluck, Mozart, von Weber, and Wagner.

Opera, English, opera in English, by English composers. The principal masters of this school are Balfe and Wallace.

Opera, French. The principal composers are Halévy, Hérold, A. Thomas, and Meyerbeer, although the latter is also partly German.

Opera Seria, a serious or tragic opera.

Opera, Grand, opera in which the dialogue is carried on by means of recitatives.

Operetta, a little opera.

Ophicleide (ŏf-ĭ-klīd). A large bass brass instrument, of deep and powerful tone. It has a compass of three octaves from double B flat.

Opus (Lat. ō'-pŭs, abbreviated *op.*) Work. Used by composers in numbering their works in the order of their composition or publication, as op. 1, op. 2, op. 3, etc.

Opus Posthumus, a work published after the death of its author.

Orage (Fr. ō-räzh'), a storm. An organ stop intended to imitate the noise of a storm.

Oratorio, a species of musical drama consisting of arias, recitatives, choruses, orchestral accompaniment, etc., performed without dramatic action or scenery. O. was originally performed as a religious service. See Chapter XLI.

Orchestra, a full combination of stringed and wind instruments. A full orchestra should consist of not less than eighty to one hundred men, disposed as follows: 1st violins 20, 2d violins 18, violas 10, 'cellos 10, basses 10, oboes 2, clarinets 4, flutes 2, piccolo 1, bassoons 2, horns 8, trumpets 4, trombones 3, tuba 1, kettle-drums 2, snare drum, bass drum, triangle and cymbal. In reducing this the horns would be reduced to 4, and as a last resort to 2; the trumpets to 2, and the clarinets to 2. Other reductions would be made in the strings. The smallest number of strings compatible with blending is 5 1st violins, etc.

Orchestra, that part of a theatre occupied by the orchestra. The chairs adjacent to it.

Orchestrion, an instrument of the organ kind, arranged to be played by means of a tune-cylinder, or barrel, so as to imitate the sound of an orchestra. Large instruments of this class cost as high as $5,000.

Organ, a wind instrument the sounds of which are produced by pipes either flue or reed, and played by means of a key-board like the piano-forte. It was invented from A.D. 800 to 1400. The essential parts of an organ are a *bellows* to collect air and force it out through the pipes, *wind-ways*, a *sound-board* or *wind-chest* containing the valves and supporting the pipes, *keys* for opening the valves, and *pipes* for making the sound. Large organs contain one large bellows with several *feeders*, as many wind-chests as there are key-boards, and as many valves as there are keys. Concerning pipes see Organ Stop.

ă ale, ä add, ä arm, ō eve, ŏ end, ī ice, ĭ ill, ō old, ŏ odd, ō dove, oo moon, ū lute, ŭ but, ü Fr. *round*

Organ Music, music designed to be played upon the organ.

Organ Stop, or *Register* (German *Stimmung*, voice). A set of pipes voiced alike, one for every key in a key-board of an organ. Stops are classed as *diapason*, including the op. diapason, octave, and 15th ; *string*, viol di gamba, viol d'amour, salicional, keraulophon, dolce, and dulciana; *flute*, the flutes, nighthorn and stopped diapason ; *reed* the oboe, cornopeon, trumpet, clarinet, vox humana, vox angelica, musette, euphone, trombone, bombardon, etc.

Organ Stop, or *Draw Stop*, the knob at the side of the key-board, which moves the slides by means of which the pipes of a stop are shut off or admitted to communication with the valves.

Organ Builder, one who builds organs.

Organ Chamber, a small organ for use in a house.

Organo (Ital. ōr-gä'-no). An organ.

Organo Pleno (Lat. ōr-gä-nō plā'-nō). Full organ ; all the stops of the "great organ" drawn.

Organ Pieno (Ital. pē-ā'-nō). The full organ ; all the stops of the great organ.

Organ Touch, the proper method of touching the keys of an organ.

Organ Tone, a tone of uniform force from its beginning to end.

Organ Point (called also *Pedal point*), a bass tone prolonged for several measures while various coherently arranged harmonies are performed by the higher parts.

Organ Trio, a composition arranged for three single parts, employing two manuals and a pedale. There are six sonatas of Bach written in this form.

Organ Manual, the manual key-board of an organ. They are designated as great, swell, choir, and solo organs.

Organ Pedale, the pedale key-board.

Orgue Expressive (Fr. ōrg ĕgz-prä-sēf). The harmonium, or reed organ.

Orlandi, Ferdinand, a composer and professor of singing, born in Parma, 1777, appeared as opera composer in 1801. Appointed professor in the Mailand Conservatory 1800. Died 1840. Wrote 20 operas, masses, motettes, and over 100 different works.

Orthography, the art of correct spelling, in obedience to which one writes the chromatic tones according to their derivation and harmonic relation.

Osborne, G. A., a composer of pleasing pieces for the piano, was born at Limerick in 1806. Studied in Paris and came to London 1843, where he since resides.

Ossia (Ital. ōs-sē-ä). Or, otherwise, or else. Written above the staff in connection with an easier or different arrangement of the same passage.

Ossia piu facile (Ital. ōs-sē-ä pioo fä-tshŏ-lĕ), or else in this more easy manner.

Ostinato (Ital. ōs-tē-nä'-tō). Obstinate, continuous, unceasing, adhering to some peculiar melodic figure, or group of notes.

Ottava (Ital. ōt-tä'-vä). An octave or eighth.

Ottava alta (Ital. äl-tä), the octave above, or an octave higher. Marked 8va..........

Ottava bassa (Ital. bäs-sä). The octave below. Marked 8va bassa......, or 8va...... below the notes.

Otto, Ernst Julius, cantor in the Dresden *Kreuzschule* and teacher of theory, was a composer of many oratorios, 2 operas, masses, sonatas, trios, songs, etc. Born 1804. Died 1877.

Otto, Rudolph Karl Julius, a teacher of singing, and distinguished oratorio singer in Berlin. Born 1829 at Berlin.

Ou (Fr. oo), or.

Oulibicheff, Alexander (oo-lĕ-bǐ-chĕf). A Russian writer about music, best known by his "*Beethoven et ses trois styles*," was born in Dresden 1795, and died at Nischni-Novgorod in 1858.

Ouseley, Rev. Sir F. A. Gore (oos-lĕ), professor of music at Oxford, a writer on theory, and composer, was born in 1825.

Ouverture (Fr. oo-vär-tür). An overture.

Overture, an introductory instrumental piece to an opera or oratorio, or even for separate performance. Overtures are of two kinds, those in form of a sonata-piece, and *potpourri* overtures, composed chiefly of melodies occurring in the work following.

P., abbreviation of *piano* and *pedale*.

Pabst, August, born in Elberfelde, 1811, was made director of the Conservatory at Riga in 1857. Has composed four operas. His two sons, *Louis* and *Paul*, are talented pianists.

Pachelbel, Johann (päkh'-ĕl-bĕl), the immediate predecessor of Sebas. Bach, as composer, was born 1653 at Nürnburg, and occupied important positions as organist. Died 1706.

Pacher, Joseph A. (päkh'-ĕr), pianist and salon composer, was born 1816 at Daubrowitz. Came, at the age of 16, to Vienna, where he afterwards resided. Died 1871.

Pacini, Giovanni (pä-tshē'-nō), composer of Italian operas, born 1796, made his debut as composer at the age of 18, and lived at Venice, and afterwards at Milan. Died in 1867.

Pæon, a song of rejoicing ; a hymn to Apollo.

Paer, Ferdinand (pä'-ĕr), a composer of Italian operas, was born 1771 in Parma, where he made his first successes as a composer. Later he lived at Paris. P. wrote about 50 operas, and many other works. D, 1839.

Paganini, Nicolo (päg-än-ēn'-ē), the wonderful violinist, was born 1784 at Genoa. He grew up in poverty and cruelty, but perseve red in his study of the violin, in which he received assistance from many good masters, and in 1798 began his concert tours, in which he excited the astonishment and admiration of all Europe. He brought forth many compositions in new forms, which he called *Caprices*, which, with Bach's 6 sonatas, stand as the most original and remarkable works for the violin. Died May 27, 1840.

Paisiello, Giovanni (jō-vä-nē pä-ē-sēl-lō), a celebrated composer of Italian operas, was born 1741 in Taranto. Studied in Naples and appeared as composer at the age of 15. P. traveled over Europe, received with distinction everywhere, writing operas for Paris, London, St. Petersburg, etc. He wrote in all some 94 operas, and many other works, and died 1815 in Naples.

Paix, Jacob, a prominent musician and noted organist, born in Augsberg about 1550. He was organist in Lannigen, and made large and elaborate collections of motettes, songs, dances, etc., by the best composers before him.

Paladilha, Emil (pä-lä-dīl-ä), a French composer, was born 1844 in Montpelier, studying at home, and with Halévy, showing almost equal facility on several instruments, and made his appearance, as composer of a symphony in 1860. He has since produced a large number of compositions, including an opera, three masses, very many songs, with piano-forte accompaniment, as well as a second symphony, overtures, etc., for opera.

Palestrina, Giovanni Pierluigi de, (päl'-ēs-trē-nä), the father of Italian church music, was born about 1514 or 1524, studied at Rome with Claude Goudimel, and made his appearance as a composer in a volume of four and five-voice masses in 1554. P. instituted a reform in church music by composing it throughout for itself instead of from secular melodies as had been the previous custom. His music is deliciously pure and noble. He died 1594.

Pallavicini, Carlo (päl-lä-vē-tsē-nē), one of the finest opera composers of his time, was born in Brescia, and worked in Venice from 1666 to 1687. In 1672 he was kapellmeister in Dresden. He wrote many operas. Died 1688.

Pallet, a spring valve in the wind-chest of an organ, covering a channel leading to a pipe or pipes.

Palmer, H. R., Mus. Doc. Theorist, composer and conductor. Born 1834. Author of many popular works. His "Theory of Music" is extensively used. Received the degree of Doctor of Music in 1879. Resides in New York.

Pandean Pipes, one of the most ancient instruments of music, consisting of a number of reeds or tubes of different lengths, fastened together and tuned to each other, stopped at bottom and blown into by the mouth at top.

Panofka, Heinrich, violinist and professor of singing, was born at Preslau, 1807. Studied at Breslau and later at Leipsic. Entered upon his career as violinist, was a brilliant musical critic and correspondent of Schumann's paper, and settled in Paris about 1848, where he has published a number of works for vocal instruction.

Pantomime, an entertainment in which not a word is spoken or sung, but the sentiments are expressed by mimicry and instrumental music.

Panseron, Auguste Mathieu, teacher of singing and author of many works on it, was born in 1796 at Paris, educated there, and appointed professor in the Conservatoire in 1824. He was the author of several operas, and over 200 romances. Died 1859.

Panteleon, also *pantalon*, an old instrument of the dulcimer species, but larger. It was more than nine feet long, four feet wide, and had a hundred and eighty-six strings of gut, which were played on with small sticks like the dulcimer.

Papageno Harte (Ger. pä-pa-ghān-ō flōt-ē). Pan's pipes, a mouth organ.

Pape. Willie, a brilliant pianist and composer of several showy arrangements of favorite airs. An American, born about 1840, native of Mobile.

Papperitz, Benjamin Robert, was born in Pirna, 1826, and since 1851 teacher of piano at Leipsic.

Paradise and the Peri, a cantata, by Schumann, 1843.

Parallel Motion, progression of two voices in the same direction at the same distance apart.

Parallel Fifths, called also *Consecutive Fifths*, progression of two voices in the same direction at the interval of a fifth. Always forbidden.

Parallel Keys, the major and its relative minor.

Parepa Rosa, Euphrosyne, the great singer, was born in Edinburgh, 1839, made her debut in Malta at the age of 16. In 1867 she came to America, and awakened the most enthusiastic admiration. Died in London, 1875. She had a large, pure soprano voice, and sang with great fullness and steadiness of tone.

Parish-Alvars, Eli, a distinguished harpist and composer for his instrument, was born in London, 1808, and made his appearance as virtuoso at the age of 15. His tone was large and his execution elegant. He played Chopin's piano-forte sonata and Beethoven's and Hummel's piano-forte concertos, with the greatest ease. Died at Vienna 1847.

Parlando, (Ital. pär-län'-dō), accented, in a declamatory style.

Parody, music or words slightly altered and adapted to some new purpose.

Parry, John, an English musician, born 1776 in Denbight, and became very celebrated as a harp virtuoso and composer for his instrument.

Parsons, Albert R., a pianist, teacher and composer, the translator of Wagner's "Beethoven," born in Indianapolis about 1850, and educated at Berlin. Resides in New York.

Part, the music for each separate voice or instrument.

Parte (Ital. pär-tē). A part ; a rôle in an opera.

Parte Cantante (Ital. pär-tē kän-tän-tē). The singing, or vocal part.

Partimento (Ital. pär-tē-män-tō). An exercise, figured bass.

Partitur (Ger. pär-tī-toor'). A score ; full score. See Score.

Partita (Ital. pär-tī'-tä). An old term synonymous with variation.

Pas (Fr. pä). A step ; a dance.

ä *ale*, ă *add*, ä *arm*, ē *eve*, ĕ *end*, ī *ice*, Ĭ *ill*, ō *old*, ŏ *odd*, ô *dove*, oo *moon*, ū *lute*, ŭ *but*, ü *Fr. sound*

Pasdeloup, Jules (jool pä-dŏ-loo), the founder of popular classical concerts in France, was born in Paris in 1819. Educated at the Conservatory, where in 1833 he took the first prize for piano-playing. Appeared in 1851 as director of the *Society of Young Artists*, whose mission it was to introduce classical music, in which he has been very successful, and has gained the approval and favor of the public.

Pas Seul (Fr. pä-sŭl). A dance by one performer.

Passacaglio (Ital. päs-sä-käl'-yĕ-ō). A species of chacon, a slow dance in 3-4 time, the music consisting of divisions or variations on a ground bass, and always in a minor key.

Passacaille (Fr. päs-sä-käl). A passacaglio.

Passage, any phrase or short portion of an air, or other composition. Also used for *bravoura passages*, those parts of a piece which produce an *effect*, but do not belong to the melody of the piece.

Passagio (Ital. päs-säd-jē-ō), a passage.

Passamezzo (Ital. päs-sä-mät'-sō), an old, slow dance, little differing from the action of walking.

Passepied (Fr. päss-pē-ā'). A sort of jig, a lively old French dance in 3-4, 3-8, or 6-8 time; a kind of minuet.

Passing Notes, notes which do not belong to the harmony, but serve to connect those that are essential.

Passion Music, music composed for holy week.

Passions Musik, Bach wrote four passion oratorios, the best known of which is that according to St. Matthew, in 1729.

Passionato (Ital. päs-sē-ō-nä'-tō). Passionate, impassioned, with fervor.

Pasta, Guidetta (gwē-dĕt'-tä päs'-tä), a famous dramatic singer. Born at Como, 1798, made her debut at Verona in 1822, and sang with the greatest success throughout Europe. Her voice was of large compass, and very beautiful. Died 1865.

Pasticio (Ital. päs-tēt'-tshe-ō), a medley, an opera made up out of songs, etc., by various composers.

Pastoral, a musical drama on a rural subject. Also an instrumental composition in pastoral style.

Pastorale (Ital. päs-tō-rä'-lō). Pastoral.

Pastorelle (Fr. päs-tō-rĕl'). A pastoral.

Patetico (Ital. pä-tā'-tē-ko). Pathetic.

Patimento (Ital. pä-tē-män'-to). Affliction grief, suffering.

Patti. Adelina, and Carlotta, sisters, distinguished singers. *Carlotta* was born at Florence, 1840, and is noted for her delicate and brilliant execution. *Adelina*, born at Madrid, 1843, sang in concerts at an early age, and since 1859 has occupied the highest rank in Europe.

Pauer, Ernst (powr), pianist and composer, was born in Vienna, 1826, studied there with Dirzka and Sechter, and later with Mozart's second son. In 1851 he came to London, where he has since resided. Is a successful composer, but best known by his editions of Schumann's works, etc.

Pauke (Ger. poŭ-kĕ). A kettle drum.

Paul, Dr. Oscar (powl), professor of musical science in the University at Leipsic, was born 1836 at Freiwaldau, studied theology at the University of Leipsic, as well as music. In 1866 he was appointed to his present position, in which he has distinguished himsel.. Is teacher of the piano in the Conservatory.

Pause, a delay or sudden cessation of rhythmic movement by the prolongation of a tone or chord. The character ⌒ which requires this.

Pavana (Ital. pä-vä'-nä), a grave, stately dance, which took its name from *pavo*, a peacock. It was danced by princes in their mantles, and ladies in gowns with long trains, whose motions resembled those of a peacock's tail. It was in 3-4 time, and generally in three strains, each repeated.

Pavillon (Fr. pä-vē-yōnh). The bole of a horn or other wind instrument.

Pavillon Chinois (Fr. pä-vē-yōnh shēnwä). An instrument with numerous little bells, which impart brilliancy to lively pieces and pompous military marches.

Pax, Karl Edward, organist of the charity church in Berlin, was born at Glogau in 1802. A composer of men's songs, and instructive piano pieces. Died 1867.

Pedal, of or pertaining to the foot. Hence *damper pedal*, the lever by which the foot raises the dampers from contact with the strings; *soft pedal*, a lever operating mechanism for diminishing the tone; *swell pedal*, a lever for operating the blinds of the "swell organ;" *tone-sustaining pedal*, by means of which a tone is prolonged after the finger is removed from the key.

Pedal Piano, a piano-forte fitted with organ pedals for practice.

Pedal Point, see Organ Point.

Pedal Doppio, double the pedals, that is, play with both feet, a direction in organ playing.

Pedals, Combination, pedals for drawing stops in the organ.

Pellegrini, Angelo (pĕl-lĕ-grē'-nē). A dramatic composer, born in Como about 1805. His three operas are often given. *Etelinda* 1831, *La Vedova di Bengala* 1834, *Il disertore svizzero* 1841.

Pensoso (Ital. pĕn sō'-zō). Pensively, mournfully.

Pentachord, an instrument with five strings, a scale or system of five diatonic sounds.

Pentatonic Scale, a scale of five notes, sometimes called the Scotch scale, and similar to the modern diatonic major scale with fourth and seventh degrees omitted.

Pepusch, Johann Christoph, was born at Berlin 1667, where he lived 20 years, when he went to Holland, where his first compositions were published, and then to England, where he achieved great success as a composer. Died 1752.

Perdendo (Ital. pär-dän'-dō), **Perdendosi** (Ital. pär-dän-dō'-zō). Gradually decreasing the tone and the time; dying away; becoming extinct.

Period, a melodic or harmonic formation consisting of two or more sections, of which two must stand in the relation of antecedent and consequent. See Part Second.

Perkins, Henry S., a teacher and writer of choral music, was born at Stockbridge Vt., March 20, 1833. Studied music at Boston, and commenced his work as conductor of musical conventions in 1860. Is author of about twenty collections of singing-class and convention music.

Perkins, Jule E., brother of the preceding, a good pianist and composer, and a fine bass singer, was born at Stockbridge, Vt., 1845. Studied singing in Paris and Italy, and made his debut in opera there about 1868, with distinguished success. In 1873 he joined the Mapleson Opera Company in London. Died at Manchester, England, 1875.

Perkins, W. O., Mus. Doc., composer and teacher of music, brother of the preceding, was born at Stockbridge, Vt., about 1829. Studied in Boston, conducted conventions, etc., since 1860. Resides in Boston.

Perne, François Louis (pern), a learned French teacher of musical theory and composer. Born 1772 at Paris. Died 1832.

Persiani. Josefo (pär-sē-ä'-nē). An opera composer. Born in one of the States of the Church, 1805.

Perti, Giacomo Antonio (pär'-tē). A notable composer of the old school. Born 1661. His first mass was produced under his own direction in St. Peter's in 1680. Died 1756.

Percussion (Eng. pĕr-kŭsh'-ŏn). Striking, as applied to instruments, notes or chords; or the *touch* on the piano-forte.

Perfect, complete, satisfactory. The perfect consonances are unison, octave, fifth and fourth.

Perfect Cadence, a cadence consisting essentially of the chord of the dominant seventh, followed by the tonic, both chords uninverted, and the soprano and bass having the tonic in the last chord.

Perpetual Canon, a canon without an ending, like a round.

Pesante (Ital. pĕ-zän'-tĕ). Heavy, ponderous, with importance and weight, impressively.

Peschka-Leutner. Minna (pĕs-khä loit'-nĕr). A brilliant singer, long a favorite at Leipsic, and heard in this country in 1871. Born 1839 in Vienna.

Pestalozzi. Johann Heinrich (pĕs-tä-lŏt-zi), the celebrated teacher, was born in Zurich, 1746, and devoted himself to improving the method of teaching children by presenting to them " the thing before the sign."

Petrella, Enrico (än-rē-kō pā-trĕl-lū), an Italian composer of operas. Born in 1813, in Palermo, educated at Naples, and produced at the age of 15 his first opera. Was author of about twenty operas. Died 1877 in Genoa.

Peu (Fr. pŭh). Little, a little.

Pezze (Ital. pl. pāt-sĕ). Fragments, scraps, select, detached pieces.

Pfeife (Ger. pfī'-fĕ). Pipe, fife, flute.

Pfeiffer. Oscar, pianist, born at Vienna, 1828, made concert tours 1845-1867 in Europe. In 1864 went to Rio Janeiro, where also he had fine success. Composes for the piano.

Pflughaupt, Robert (pfloog howpt), a brilliant pianist. Born 1833 in Berlin. Studied with Liszt. Died 1867.

Phantasie (Ger. fän-tä-see). Fantasy, fancy, imagination.

Philidor, François André, a French opera composer. Born 1726. Died in London, 1795. P. was the inventor of French comic opera, of which he composed 22.

Philharmonic, lovers of harmony, a society devoted to the interests of music.

Philosophy of Art, the relation of art to the human mind. See Part Four.

Phone (Gr. fō -nē). The voice, a sound or tone.

Phonetik (Gr. fō-nĕt -Ik). System of singing, or of notation and harmony.

Phrase, a short musical sentence, a musical thought or idea which makes sense, but not complete sense.

Phrasing, the art of uniting tones into phrases, and separating phrases from each other, as well as the proper modulation of the sound so as to express the musical idea.

Phrygian, one of the ancient Greek modes.

Physharmonica (Gr. fīs-här-mōn -ĭ-kä). An instrument, the tone of which resembles that of the reed pipes in an organ, and is produced by the vibration of thin metal tongues, of a similar construction to those of the harmonium. The name is also applied to a stop in the organ with *free reeds*, and with tubes of half the usual length.

Piacere (Ital. pē-ä-tshā -rē). Pleasure, inclination, fancy; *a piacere*, at pleasure.

Piacevole (Ital. pē-ä-tshä-vō-lĕ). Pleasing, graceful, agreeable.

Piacimento (Ital. pē-ä-tshē-män -tō). See *piacere*.

Pianino (Ital. pē-ä-nē-nō). A small pianoforte.

Piano (Ital. pē-ä'-nō). Soft, gentle.

Piangendo (Ital. pē-ä-jän'-dō). Plaintively, sorrowfully.

Piano-forte. The distinguishing feature of the piano-forte is the use of an elastic hammer to strike the strings. Has been gradually evolved through countless modifications during the last two centuries. Steinway & Sons are the most brilliant and successful experimenters during the past twenty-five years.

Piano a queu (Fr. pē-ä -nō ä kŭh). A grand piano-forte.

Piano Score, a series of staves arranged for representing vocal music and its piano-forte accompaniment.

Piatti, Alfred, the celebrated 'cellist, was born in Bergamo, 1823, and appeared in public with great success at the age of 16. In 1846 he first came to London, where for the most part he has since resided. Is author of a number of pieces for 'cello and piano.

Pibroch (pē -brŏk). A wild, irregular species of music, peculiar to the Highlands of Scotland, performed on the bagpipe.

Picchiettato (Ital. pē-kē-ēt-tä -tō). Scattered, detached. In violin playing it means that sort of staccato indicated by dots under a slur.

Piccinni. Nicolas (pĭt-tshē'-nō), known under the name *Piccini*, a celebrated opera composer, the rival of Gluck, was born in 1728, near Naples. Educated at Naples. Appeared as composer in 1747, which was the beginning of a long and brilliant career as opera composer. P. lived chiefly at Naples. Died at Passy, 1802.

Piccinni. Louis, second son of the preceding, was born in 1766 at Naples, and was also a very good composer. D. 1827.

Piccolomini, Marie (pŏk'-kō-lō-mē'-nē), a pleasing singer, born at Siena, 1836. Made her debut at Turin in 1855. Came to America in 1855.

Piece (Fr. pē-ās). A composition or piece of music; an opera, or drama.

Pieno (Ital. pē-ā-nō). Full.

Pietoso (Ital. pē-ā-tō'-zō). Compassionately, tenderly. Implying, also, a rather slow and sustained movement.

Pifferari (Ital. pl. pĕf-fĕ-rā'-rō). Pipers.

Pilate. August (pī-lā'-tĕ), a composer. Born at Boucham, 1810, educated at Paris. Brought out his first opera about 1854.

Pince (Fr. pănh-sā). *Pinched.* See *pizzicato.*

Pipe, any tube formed of a reed, or of metal or wood, which being blown into at one end, produces a musical sound. The *pipe*, which was originally no more than a simple oaten straw, was one of the earliest instruments by which musical sounds were attempted.

Pipes of Pan. See Pandean Pipes.

Piesendel, Johann George, a distinguished German violinist. Born at Karlesburg, 1687. Played and conducted in all the principal cities in Europe, and died 1755.

Piston (Fr. pĭs-tōnh). A valve in a brass instrument. Hence *cornet à piston*, cornet with valves.

Pitch, means "point," the highness or lowness of sounds. That quality of tones which depends on the rapidity of the vibrations producing them. Pitches are named by letters, as A, A sharp, B, C, etc. The different octaves are distinguished as *large, small, once-marked,* etc., namely, Middle C and the six degrees above it belong to the "once-marked octave" and written ō, ū, etc., or c', d', e', etc.; the octave above this is the "twice-marked octave" c'', d'', e'', f'', etc. The octave below middle C is the "small octave," written c, d, e, etc., the octave below this the "large" octave, C, D, E, etc., below this the "double" octave, CC, DD, etc. Pitches are also distinguished as "8ft," "4ft," "2ft," or "16ft," according to the length of the pipes producing them. Organ stops are designated in this way according to the length of the pipe producing the tone for the finger-key two octaves below middle C. The standard pitch is 8ft. A stop of this pitch gives for every note sounds agreeing with the voice; 16ft. stops give sounds an octave lower; 4ft. stops an octave higher, 2ft. an octave higher still.

Pitch, Concert. French pitch is about 522 vibrations per second for middle C. Concert pitch is higher, about 540.

Piu (Ital. pē-oo). More. As *piu allegro*, more allegro; *piu forte*, more forte; *piu moto*, quicker, etc.

Pixis, Friedrich Wilhelm, an organist in Mannheim, 1770, a pupil of the Abbe Vogler. Author of a number of works for organ and piano.

Pizzicato (Ital. pĭt-sē-kā'-tō). *Pinched,* meaning that the strings of the violin, violoncello, etc., are not to be played with the bow, but pinched, or snapped with the fingers, producing a *staccato* effect.

Placidamente (Ital. plā-tshē'-dā-mŭn-tē). Calmly, placidly, quietly.

Plagal, ancient modes in which the melody was confined between the dominant and its octave.

Plagal Cadence, a cadence in which the final chord on the tonic is preceded by the harmony of the sub-dominant.

Plain Song, or **Plain Chant,** the name given to the old ecclesiastical chant when in its most simple state and without those harmonic appendages with which it has since been enriched. The ancient music for the psalms and liturgy.

Plaintif (Fr. plănh-tēf). Plaintive, doleful.

Plaque (Fr. plā-kā). *Struck at once*, without any arpeggio, or embellishment.

Plaquer (Fr. plā-kā'). To strike at once, speaking of chords.

Plectrum (Lat. plŏk'-trŭm). A quill, or piece of ivory or hard wood, used to twitch the strings of the *mandoline*, lyre, etc.

Plein Jeu (Fr. plănh zhŭ). Full organ. The term is also applied to a mixture stop of several ranks of pipes.

Pleno (Lat. plā'-nō). Full. See "Full Organ."

Pleyel, Ignaz (pli-ĕl), composer of a great number of instrumental works, was born the twenty-fourth son of his father, about 1757, near Vienna. Died 1831.

Pleyel, Camille, eldest son of the preceding, also a good composer, was born at Strassburg, 1792. Died in Paris, 1855.

Plica (Lat. plē'-kā), A kind of ligature used in the old music, as a sign of hesitation or pause.

Pneumatic Lever, a contrivance for diminishing the weight of touch on large organs, invented by Mr. Charles Barker, of London, and afterwards of Marseilles. It consists of a small bellows about 14 inches by 3, for every key. When the key is pressed it opens a valve into this bellows, which is immediately inflated and thereby opens the valves belonging to the key touched. The "pneumatic action" completely softens the touch, which on large organs amounts to several pounds per key, but it results in a loss of time. In order to diminish this as much as possible, the pneumatics are operated by a "heavy wind," of a pressure equal to a column of water 6 inches high, or thereabouts.

Pochette (Fr. pō-shĕt). A kit, a small violin used by dancing masters.

Poco (Ital. pō-kō). Little; as *poco a poco*, little by little; *un poco adagio*, a little adagio.

Pohl, Karl Ferdinand (pōl), the popular author of "Mozart and Haydn in London," Biography of Haydn, etc., is an organist, and was born 1823 at Berlin and studied in Vienna with Sechter.

Poi (Ital. pō'-ē). Then, after, afterward; *piano poi forte*, soft, then loud.

Polacca (Ital. pō-läk'-kä). A Polish national dance in 3-4 time; a dance tune in which an emphasis is placed on the first unaccented part of the measure.

Polka, a lively Bohemian or Polish dance in 2-4 time, the first three quavers in each bar being accented, and the fourth quaver unaccented.

Polonaise (pŏl-ō-nāz). A movement of three crotchets in a measure, the rhythmical pause coming on the last crotchet of the bar.

Polyphony, " many sounds." Applied to compositions consisting of three or more independently moving voices, as in fugue, etc. Distinguished from *Homophony*, in which there is but one melodious voice, the others being accompaniment, as in glees and American psalmody. See Chapter V.

Pomposo (Ital. pŏm-pō-zō). Pompous, stately, grand.

Poniatowski. Joseph, Prince, and kinsman of Stanilaus II, last king of Poland, was born at Rome, 1816. He was educated in music, and produced seven or eight operas.

Ponte, Lorenzo da, a famous writer of opera librettos, among them Mozart's "Figaro" and "Don Juan." Born 1749. Died 1838.

Popper, David, a distinguished 'cellist, born 1842. Lived since 1868 in Vienna.

Porpora, Nicolo (pŏr-pō-rä), the distinguished opera composer and rival of Handel, was born at Naples in 1686, educated there, appeared as composer in 1708, and after several years' wandering between Vienna, London, etc., in 1760 he returned to Naples, where he lived at the head of the Conservatory of San Onofrio. Died 1767. Wrote more than 50 operas, 6 oratorios, 4 masses, 29 other sacred works, 6 symphonies for chamber, etc.

Portamento (Ital. pŏr-tä-män'-tō). A term applied by the Italians to the manner or habit of sustaining and conducting the voice. A singer who is easy, and yet firm and steady in the execution of passages and phrases, is said to have a good *portamento*. It is also used to connect two notes separated by an interval, by gliding the voice from one to the other, and by this means anticipating the latter in regard to intonation.

Portando la voce (Ital. pŏr-tän'-dō lä vō'-tshĕ). Carrying the voice, holding it firmly on the notes.

Posaune (Ger. pō-zou-nĕ). A trumpet, a trombone, a sackbut, also an organ stop.

Potpourri (pōt-poor-rē). A medley, a *capriccio* or *fantasia*, in which favorite airs and fragments of musical pieces are strung together and contrasted.

Position, a shift on the violin, tenor, or violoncello; the arrangement or order of the several members of a chord.

Positive, an appellation formerly given to the little organ, placed in front of the full or great organ.

Possibile (Ital. pōs-sē'-bē-lĕ), possible; *il piu forte possibile*, as loud as possible.

Postludium (Ital. pōst-lū-dĭ-ŭm). After-piece, concluding voluntary.

Potter, Cypriani, pianist and composer. Born in London, 1792, where his father was a professor of music. Studied with Calcott, Crotch, and Woelfl. Was made professor in the Royal School of Music, and in 1825 president of the same. Died 1872. Wrote trios, duos, sonatas, and piano pieces.

Pral trill, the German name for the *mordente*, an embellishment consisting of two small notes preceding a principal one. See appendix.

Pratt, Silas G., pianist and composer, was born Aug. 12, 1847. Studied at first in Chicago, afterwards with Wüerst and Kullak, at Berlin, and still later with Liszt, at Weimar. Has written two operas, a symphony, many piano pieces, etc.

Precentor, the appellation given formerly to the master of the choir.

Prelude, a short, introductory composition, or extempore performance, to prepare the ear for the succeeding movements.

Precipitando (Ital. prä - tshē - pē - tän-dō). Hurrying.

Precipitato (Ital. prä-tshē-pē-tä'-tō). In a precipitate manner, hurriedly.

Precisione (Ital. prä-tshē-zō-ō-nĕ). Precision, exactness.

Preghiera (Ital. prä-ghē-ä'-rä). Prayer, supplication.

Preparation, that disposition of the harmony by which discords are lawfully introduced. A discord is said to be prepared when the discordant note is heard in the preceding chord, and in the same part, as a consonance.

Prestamente (Ital. prĕs-tä-män'-tĕ). Hurriedly, rapidly.

Prestezza (Ital. prĕs-tād'-sä). Quickness, rapidity.

Presto (Ital. prĕs'-tō). Quickly, rapidly.

Pressure tone, a sudden crescendo.

Prima (Ital. prē'-mä). First, chief, principal.

Prima Vista (Ital. prē-mä vē'-stä). At first sight.

Prima Volta (Ital. prē'-mä vōl'-tä). The first time.

Principal, the chief idea in a piece of music. See Chapter XIII.

Principal, an organ stop of diapason tone. In English organs the principal is the "octave," a 4ft. stop. In German it is the open diapason of 8ft. or 16ft.

Programme, an order of exercises for musical or other entertainments.

Programme Music, music designed to tell in tones a story derived from some poem, or legend. See Chap. XXI.

Progression, movement from one tone or chord to another.

Prosody, a term, partly grammatical and partly musical, relating to the accent and metrical quantity of syllables, in lyrical composition.

Prologue, Musical, the preface or introduction to a musical composition or performance; a prelude.

Professor of Music, the instructor or lecturer on music in a chartered college or school. An accomplished musician (English usage).

ă *ale*, ă *a ld*, ă *arm*, ĕ *eve*, ŏ *en t*, ī *ice*, ĭ *ill*, ō *old*, ŏ *odd*, ȯ *dove*, oo *moon*, ū *tute*, ŭ *but*, ü *Fr. sound*.

Pruckner, Dionys, a brilliant pianist, and a good teacher. Born about 1830. Studied with Liszt at Weimar, at the same time with Bülow, Mason, Klindworth, Raff, etc. Came to New York in 1874, but made only a short stay. Is now professor of Piano in the Conservatory at Stuttgart (1880).

Pruckner, Caroline, a distinguished German dramatic singer. Born at Vienna in 1832.

Prudent, Emil (prū-dänh), a brilliant pianist and composer of elegant fantasias and salon pieces, was born at Angoulême, 1817. Studied at the Conservatoire, and was much influenced by Thalberg. Died at Paris, 1863.

Prume, François, one of the most brilliant violinists of recent times, was born at Stavelot in 1816, appeared in public as violinist at an early age. Died 1849.

Prume, Jehin, nephew of the preceding, was also a fine violinist, and visited America in 1860. Born at Brussels, 1840.

Psalm, a sacred song or hymn.

Psalmody, the practice or art of singing psalms; a style or collection of music designed for church service.

Psalter, the book of Psalms.

Purcell, Henry, an English dramatic and church composer, was born in London, 1658, the son of a musician. His talent was such, that at the age of 18 he was organist of Westminster Abbey and the Royal Chapel. He composed music to many plays. Purcell had positive genius, and showed fresh and vigorous melodic invention. He had not the severe contrapuntal training of Bach or Handel, his contemporaries. Died at the age of 37 in 1695.

Quadrat (Ger. quäd-rät'). The mark called a natural. See Chromatic Signs in Appendix.

Quadrille (Fr. kä-drēl). A French dance, or set of five consecutive dance movements, called La Pantalon, La Poule, L'Ete, La Tenise (or La Pastourelle) and La Finale.

Quantz, Johann Joachim, 1697-1773. A distinguished musician in the employ of Frederick the Great, of Prussia, known especially as a flute virtuoso. His instruction book for that instrument marks an epoch in the development of the flute, and of flute-playing. Quantz was also an excellent violinist and oboist, was thoroughly acquainted with all the orchestral instruments in use in his time, and with the art and science of music. He left a large number of compositions, especially for the flute.

Quart (Fr.) A fourth.

Quarter-note, a black note, otherwise known as crotchet.

Quarter Rest, a rest equal to a quarter note.

Quarter-tone, a small interval of no precise dimension, because the "whole tone" itself varies.

Quasi (Ital. quä sē). As if, like.

Quartette (Ger. quär-tĕtt'). A composition for four voices or instruments.

Quart-Sex (Lat.) Fourth-sixth chord.

Quart - Septime (Lat.) Fourth-seventh chord.

Quatuor (Lat.) A composition for four voices.

Quaver, an eighth note.

Querflœte (Ger. kwär flō-tŭ). A German flute.

Querstand (Ger. kwär-ständ). A false relation in harmony.

Quieto (Ital. kwe-ā'-tō). Quietly, calm, serene.

Questa (Ital. quäs-tä). This, that.

Quick-step, a lively march, generally in 2-4 time.

Quintadena (kwĭn-tä-dē'-nä). An organ stop of soft, flute-like quality, which gives the twelfth quite plainly.

Quintaton (Ger. quĭn-tä-tōn'). A manual organ stop of 8ft. tone and stopped diapason quality, producing the 12th perceptibly. Also a pedal stop.

Quinten-folge (Ger.) Successions of fifths.

Quintette, a composition for five voices.

Quintole, a group of five notes.

Quint Gedackt (Ger. quĭnt ghe-däkkt). An organ stop of the stopped diapason species, sounding the fifth above.

Qui Tollis (Lat.) "Thou who takest away," part of the Gloria in Excelsis, usually set in music as a separate number.

Quoniam tu Solus (Lat.) "For thou alone art holy," part of the Gloria, usually set as a separate number.

R., right (hand).

Rackett, an old wooden wind-instrument, lower and deeper than the bassoon.

Raddoppiamento (räd-dŏp-pē-ä-män'-tō). Augmentation, reduplication; the doubling of an interval.

Radecke, Robert, a pianist, violinist and conductor, born at Dittmannsdorf in 1830. Studied with his father at Leipsic, where he distinguished himself, and in 1852 was made second director of the Leipsic Sing-Academie. Resides at Berlin. Has composed many songs, overtures for full orchestra, etc., and in many ways shown himself one of the first musicians of the present time.

Radical Bass, a bass exclusively composed of the roots of the chords.

Raff, Joachim (yō-äk-ĕm räf), one of the greatest composers now living, was born May 12, 1822, at Lachen in Switzerland. His first opera, "King Alfred," was composed in 1849. From this time on Raff has produced a long succession of works, all well written, although sometimes too carelessly, which have at length acquired currency throughout the world. They consist of 8 symphonies, 2 suites, 5 overtures, several concertos, very much chamber music, songs, piano pieces, etc., in all over 200 works. At present (1880) Raff is director of the Conservatory at Frankfort-on-the-Maine.

Rallentando (Ital. räl-lĕn-tan'-dō). The time gradually slower and the sound gradually softer.

Raimondi, Pietro, a highly esteemed composer and teacher of counterpoint in Rome, 1786-1853. Wrote more than 60 operas, 32 ballets, 150 psalms of the style of Marcello's, and very many other church pieces.

Rameau, Jean Philippe (rä-mō), a celebrated French composer and theorist, was born 1683 in Dijon. Educated at a Jesuit college. Appeared as writer of theoretical works in 1722, and ten years later as an opera composer. Died 1764.

Rans des Vaches (Fr. ränh dŏ väsh). Pastoral airs played by the Swiss herdsmen to assemble the cattle together for the return home.

Rapidamente (Ital. rä-pē-dä-mün'-tĕ). Rapidly.

Rapido (Ital. rä-pē-dō). Rapid.

Rappoldi, E. (räp-pōl'-dē), one of the best violinists of the present, was born in Vienna, Feb. 22, 1839. Is concertmeister of the Royal Opera at Berlin.

Rathberger, Valentine, a prolific old church composer, a Benedictine monk, born 1690.

Ratio, relation. The relation of the rate of vibrations in tones.

Rauzzini, Venanzio (roud-zē'-nē), an Italian singer and composer of operas, born at Rome 1747-1810.

Ravenscroft, Thomas, professor of music at Oxford, and one of the earliest English composers of psalmody, was born 1590. Died 1635.

Ravina, Jean Henri (rä-vē-nä), pianist and composer, was born at Bordeaux, May 20, 1818. Studied in the Conservatoire, and distinguished himself as a composer of salon pieces. Died 1862.

Re (Ital. rā). The second syllable in solmization. In French, the pitch D.

Rebec. A Moorish word signifying an instrument with two strings, played on with a bow. The Moors brought the Rebec into Spain, whence it passed into Italy, and after the addition of a third string obtained the name of *Rebecca*, whence the old English Rebec, or fiddle with three strings.

Rebel, François, a French opera composer, 1701-1775.

Recherche (Fr. rĕ-shĕr-shā). Rare, affected, formal.

Rechte Hande (Ger. rĕhktĕ händ'). Right hand.

Recitative (rĕc-I-tä-teev'). A musical declamation. See Chapter XXXVIII.

Redern, Count von Fr. Wilhelm, Prussian general intendant of the opera, and composer of occasional pieces, was born 1802 in Berlin.

Reduciren, to reduce, or arrange a full instrumental score for a smaller band, or for the piano-forte or organ.

Reed, a contrivance for procuring vibrations. The *free reed* consists of a socket and a thin vibrating slip of brass fastened to it at one end, the other end swinging completely through the opening in the socket at each vibration. Used in accordeons, concertinas, reed organs, harmoniums, and "free reed" stops in the organ. *Impinging* or *striking reeds*, consist of a steel socket with a triangular opening, and a vibrating brass tongue, which strikes against the socket in vibrating, and does not pass through, thus alternately opening and closing the pipe. Used in reed stops of the organ generally. The *reed of oboe* and *bassoon* consists of two thin slips of reed (woody fibre), closely approximated, which alternately close and open when blown through. The *clarinet* reed consists of a slip, or tongue of reed vibrating against the wooden socket, and is, therefore, an impinging reed. The harmonies of a reed are similar to those of a string, hence reed instruments take the place of strings in military bands.

Reed, Daniel, one of the old American psalmodists, published his first book, "The Columbian Harmony," in 1793. The music was illiterate.

Reeve, William, a successful English composer of musical dramatic pieces, and teacher of music, lived in London. Born 1757. Composed sixteen comic operas.

Reeves, Sims, the great tenor, was born at Woolwich, 1821, made his debut about 1840, after serious studies in London and Italy, and has since held highest rank among operatic and oratorio tenors. His son has in 1880 made a promising debut as tenor.

Recreation, a composition of attractive style, designed to relieve the tediousness of practice; an amusement.

Redowa (rĕd-ŏ-wä). A Bohemian dance in 2-4 and 3-4 time, alternately.

Refrain, the burden of a song, a ritornel; a repeat. See *Burden*.

Regel (Ger. rāg-ĕl). A rule.

Register, an organ stop.

Registration, the art of changing and combining stops so as to produce a musical effect in organ playing.

Regnard. Francis, Jacob, Paschalius and Carolo, four brothers, of Douay, in Flanders. They lived in the 16th century. Jacob and Francis left many compositions, especially the former, who was kapellmeister at Prague.

Rehearsal (rē-hĕr-säl). A trial, or practice, previous to a public performance.

Reicha, Joseph, 1746-1795. A distinguished violinist and composer of Prague. He left many compositions.

Reicha, Anton, 1770-1836, nephew of Joseph. A distinguished composer and theorist, also born in Prague. He lived for some years in Vienna, in the society of Haydn, Albrechtsberger, Salieri and Beethoven. The last twenty-eight years of his life he spent in Paris, where he was professor of counterpoint at the Conservatory. He wrote symphonies and overtures, and a great deal of chamber music. His first important publication dealing with the theory of music consisted in "36 fugues for the piano-forte, written on a new system." This new system consisted in answering the theme on every degree of the scale, instead of on the dominant. But as this principle is destructive of tonality, it failed to attain favor among musicians. He published works on melody, on harmony, and on composition, which were much used both in France and in Germany. He failed in his attempts at dramatic composition, but succeeded as an instrumental composer, and was universally respected as a learned and able musician, and a skillful teacher.

Reichardt, Johann Friedrich, 1752-1814. Kapellmeister in Berlin, and a prolific composer of operas and instrumental music, as well as a critic. In the latter field he lacked breadth of view and depth of insight, and here, as in his compositions, he failed to produce anything of lasting value. But he was of importance in the development of the German song, for he introduced a more energetic declamation, and hit upon a truer musical expression for some of Goethe's songs than had been found before. He is also the father of the German *Liederspiel* (Vaudeville), a play with popular songs introduced.

Rein (Ger. rīn). Pure, clear, perfect; *kurz und rein*, distinct and clear.

Rheinberger, Joseph (rīn'-bār-gĕr) one of the most talented composers of the present time, was born in Vaduz, 1839. Showed great talent for music, and was organist in church at the age of seven. He was educated at Munich, and resides there as teacher and conductor. Has written several operas, oratorios, organ pieces, piano works and chamber music.

Reinecke, Karl (rī'-nĕck-ẽ), composer, conductor, and piano virtuoso, was born June 23, 1824, in Altona. He was taught by his father, an excellent musician. At 18 years of age he made a successful concert tour to Copenhagen and Stockholm, engaged as conductor at Barmen in 1854. In 1859 he accepted a more important conductorship at Breslau. Since 1861 he has been the conductor of the world-renowned Gewandhaus concerts at Leipsic. He continues to be an excellent concert pianist, and has made many concert tours to London and elsewhere. He is also constantly engaged in composition, and has published more than 100 original works, among them symphonies, operas, masses, oratorios and overtures, and much chamber music.

Reinken, Johann Adam, a very celebrated organist, was born at Deventer, Province of Ober-yssel, in the Netherlands. His education was mainly obtained at Leipsic and and Hamburg, in the latter place studying with Scheidmann, whom he succeeded as organist at the St. Catherine Church. Bach made two journeys to Hamburg to hear him, the last time playing several hours for Reinken, who declared that the art of organ-playing, well-nigh extinct, had found a new exponent. He died at the advanced age of 99 years and 7 months, Nov. 24, 1722. He published but one work, entitled "Sonatro, concertanten, allemanden, couranten, sarabanden and chiquen for two violins and cembals."

Reinthaler, Carl Martin (rīn'-tä-lĕr), a German musician of some note as teacher of voice and director of various musical societies in Bremen, and also a school of vocal music, was born at Erfurt, Oct. 13, 1822. He is the author of an oratorio of note, "Gebtha."

Reissiger, Carl Gotlieb, a German musician of versatile talent as singer, pianist, and composer, was born Jan. 31, 1798, at Belzig. Became a pensioner in the Thomas school in Leipsic, where he studied composition and piano Later by the kindness of friends he received money to pursue his studies in Berlin, and later in Munich with Winter; after traveling through Italy, France and Holland he returned to Berlin and took a position as teacher in a church music institute. He was called in 1826 to Dresden to take the place of director of German opera, vacated by Marschner, and gave such evidence of his superior ability as a director that the King of Saxony appointed him as successor to the deceased von Weber. His compositions include operas, church music, masses, motettes, orchestral works, symphonies, and overtures, and also string and string and piano quintettes, quartettes, trio and duos, besides piano works, and songs. His songs, and especially piano and string trios were at one time very popular, but are almost unknown at the present time, D. 1859.

Reissiger, F. A., a brother of the above Born July 26, 1809. As composer, director and teacher he attained to some eminence in Norway, his adopted home.

Reissman, Dr. Phil. August, was born at Frankenstein, Nov. 14, 1825, where he also received his first musical instruction. In 1843 he went to Breslau, where he studied theory, composition, organ, piano, violin and 'cello, thus becoming practically acquainted with music in many departments. During a stay at Weimar he decided to follow literature, and to his literary works is due the greater part of his reputation. The following are his principal literary works, "From Bach to Wagner," "History of the German Song," "General History of Music," three books, "General Musical Instructor," "Manual of Composition," biographies of Schumann, Mendelssohn, and Schubert. The University of Leipsic conferred upon him the degree of Doctor of Philosophy in 1875. He resides in Berlin, and lectures on the history of music in the Conservatory.

Religiosamente (Ital, rĕ-lĭ-jē-ō-zä-mān'-tā). Religiously, solemnly, in a devout manner.

Rellstab, John Carl Frederick, was born Feb. 27, 1759, at Berlin. Died Aug. 13, 1813. He was the son of a printer, and made some improvements in that art. He organized in Berlin the first musical circulating library, and also was the first to write musical critiques for the public press. He did much for music in Berlin, by the introduction of artists in concerts. Among his literary works may be mentioned " An Examination into the Relation of Musical and Oratorical Declamation," and " An Introduction, for Piano-Players, to Bach's Method of Fingering, and his Embellishments and Manner of Execution."

Rellstab, Caroline, a daughter of the above, born April 18, 1794, at Berlin, died Feb. 17, 1814. She was rightly called one of the greatest singers of her time, possessing an organ of remarkable beauty and compass, from A♭ to F, coupled with great dramatic talent.

Rellstab, Henry Frederic Louis, a son of J. C., born April 13, 1799, died Nov. 28, 1860. A musical critic and writer of note. The following are among his works: A witty book entitled " Henriette " (Sontag), "or The Beautiful Singer : a History of our Day, by Freimund Zusehauer;" "Franz Liszt," "Ludwig Berger," biographies, and "The Condition of the Opera since Mozart's time."

Related, having much in common. Related scales, those differing in but one tone.

ā *ale*, ă *add*, ä *arm*, ē *eve*, ĕ *end*, ī *ice*, ĭ *ill*, ō *old*, ŏ *odd*, ô *dove*, oo *moon*, ū *lute*, ŭ *but*, ü *Fr. sound*

Relation, False, that connection which any two sounds have with one another when the interval which they form is either superfluous or diminished.

Religioso (Ital. rē-lē-jē-ō'-zō). Religiously, solemnly ; in a devout manner.

Reminiscence, reminiscence.

Remenyi, Eduard (rĕ-mān'-yē), a great violin virtuoso, born 1830, in Hewes, Hungary. From 1842-1845, studied in the Vienna Conservatory. At the breaking out of the Hungarian revolution he entered the army as an adjutant, and at its close came to America as an exile, and concerted through the country. In 1853 he went to Liszt at Weimar ; 1854 was appointed solo violinist to the queen of England, and later went back to his native land. Since early in 1879 he has been concerting in this country. His playing is characterized by great fire and dash.

Remote, far away. Remote keys are those having few tones in common, as C and F sharp, or F and C sharp.

Repeat, a character indicating that certain measures or passages are to be sung or played twice.

Repercussio (Lat. rĕp-ĕr-kŭs'-sĭ-ō). Repercussion ; the answer in a fugue.

Replica (Ital. rä'-plĭ-kä). Reply, repetition. See, also, *Repercussio.*

Reprise (Fr. rā-prēz). The burden of a song ; a repetition, or return, to some previous part ; in old music, when a strain was repeated, it it was called a *reprise.*

Requiem (Lat. rā-quĭ'-ĕm). A Mass, or musical service for the dead.

Resolution, the subsidence of a dissonance into the consonant tone it temporarily displaced.

Resonance, the reverberation or echo of sound.

Response, response or answer of the choir.

Rest, a mark signifying silence. Rests are of different forms, corresponding to note-lengths.

Retard, gradually, more slowly.

Retro (Lat. rä'-trō). Backward, the melody reversed, note for note.

Reuter. George (roi'-tĕr), a celebrated organist and composer of church and organ music. Born at Vienna, of 1666. *Karl* (called the younger), son of the above, born in Vienna, 1697, was also a noted organist. Died in 1770. *Romanus,* a Benedictine monk, born at Kallmilz, near Regensburg, 1755, and died 1806. A composer of note among his brotherhood in his time.

Reyer. Louis Etienne Ernst (rī'-ĕr), a French opera composer, born at Marseilles, Dec. 1, 1823.

Revoice, to restore the voice of a reed or organ pipe by removing the dust, and otherwise correcting the impairment of use.

Rhapsody (Eng. răp'-sō-dy). A *capriccio,* a fragmentary piece ; a wild, unconnected composition.

Rhythm (Eng. rĭthm). The division of musical ideas or sentences into regular metrical portions ; musical accent and cadence as applied to melody.

Rhythmic (rĭth-mĭk). Rhythmical.

Rhythmus, a rhythm.

Ribattuta (Ital. rē-bät-tōō'-tä). A beat, a passing note.

Ricci, Frederico (rĭ'-tshē), a dramatic composer born at Naples, 1809, and also a teacher of singing.

Ricci, Luigi, brother of the above, born at Naples, 1808, died Jan. 1, 1860. An opera composer of note.

Richardson, Nathan, a native of Gloucester, Mass., born about 1830. Studied music for several years with Dreyschock at Prague, and on his return to America in 1852, published his "Modern School for the Pianoforte," which was little else than a transcript of his lessons with Dreyschock. He established the firm of Russell & Richardson in Boston, and afterwards wrote R.'s "New Method for the Piano-forte," which has sold over 500,000 copies. Died 1858.

Richter, Ernst Friedrich Eduard (rĭkh'-tĕr), German composer and writer on theory, born Oct. 24, 1808, at Gross-Schönau. Received his education at Zittau and Leipsic. At the founding of the Leipsic Conservatory he was appointed teacher of harmony and composition. At the death of Hauptmann he was appointed cantor of the Thomas-Schule. As as composer he is known best by his church compositions, but his works on harmony, counterpoint and fugue, are what give him rank among musicians. He died in 1878.

Richter, Hans, one of the most distinguished orchestral conductors of the present time. Born about 1833.

Ries, Ferdinand, piano virtuoso and composer, was born at Bonn, Nov. 28, 1784, and died Jan. 13, 1838. R. was the favorite pupil of Beethoven for four years, and to his and Dr. F. G. Wegler's "Biographical Notes of Beethoven," we owe, in a large measure, our knowledge of Beethoven as man and artist. He was quite a prolific writer, but his works have in the main sunk into oblivion.

Riedel. Carl (rē'-dĕl), born Oct. 6, 1827, at Kronensberg. He was the founder and director of the now famous Reidelsche-verein, a choral society which has done much for the advancement of music in Germany, but especially in Leipsic, by bringing out the works of ancient and modern composers. He has made no great reputation as a composer, although many of his works have merit.

Rietz, Eduard (reetz), a noted German violinist and director, born in 1801 at Berlin, died 1832.

Rietz. Julius, brother of the above, born in Berlin, Dec. 28, 1812. A composer, director and teacher. Was director, in 1838, of the Gewandhaus Orchestra in Leipsic, where he also taught composition in the Conservatory. R. is the editor of many standard works in the Breitkopf & Härtel editions. Died Oct. 1, 1877.

Righini. Vincenzo (rĭg-ee'-nē), an Italian opera composer and director of great note in his time, was born at Bologna, Jan. 22, 1756. Although his operas were very popular at the time, they are never heard, and aside from an overture to "Tigranes," of great nobility, but few, if any, are heard at the present time. Died Aug. 19, 1812.

ă ale, ă add, ä arm, ĕ eve, ĕ end, ī ice, I ill, ō old, ŏ odd, ū dove, oo moon, ū lute, ŭ but, ü Fr. sour!.

Rimbault, Dr. Edward, a learned English writer about music, born at London June 13, 1816. Is author of many collections of music, a history of the organ, etc. D. 1876.

Rinforzando (Ital. rēn - fōr - tsän' - dō). Strengthened, reinforced; a repeated reinforcement of tone or expression; indicating that *several* notes are to be played with energy and emphasis.

Rinck, Christian Heinrich, a distinguished organist and composer for the organ, was born at Elgersburg in 1770, was a pupil of Kittel, a pupil of Bach's. In 1805 he became cantor Stadtorganist at Darmstadt, where he died in 1846.

Ripieno (Ital. rē-pē-ä'-nō). The *tutti*, or full parts which fill up and augment the effect of the full chorus of voices and instruments. In a large orchestra all the violins, violas and basses, except the principals, are sometimes called *Ripiéni.*

Ritardando (Ital. rē-tär-dän'-dō). Retarding, delaying the time gradually.

Ritenuto (Ital. rē-tĕ-noo'-tō), Detained, slower, kept back; the effect different from *Ritardándo,* by being done at once, while the other is effected by degrees.

Ritornell (Ital. rē-tōr-nāl'). The burden of a song; also, a short symphony or introduction to an air; and the symphony which follows an air. It is also applied to *tutti* parts, introductory to, and between, or after, the solo passages in a concerto.

Ritter. A. G., organ virtuoso and royal music director, was born at Erfurt, Aug. 11, 1811. Was pupil of Ludwig Berger, A. W. Bach, etc., and in 1847 became organist at the cathedral in Magdeburg. Is the author of many fine works for organ, and an instruction book.

Ritter, Theo, a pianist and composer, born about 1838 in Paris. He was a pupil of Liszt, and is a composer of merit. Was in this country in 1875, with Nillson.

Ritter, Freidrich Louis, Mus. Doc., a learned musician and professor of music in Vassar College, was born at Strassburg in 1837, and came to New York about 1864.

Ritter, Fanny Raymond, a brilliant soprano, teacher of singing, and fine writer about music, wife of the preceding, was born in Philadelphia about 1840, and shares her husband's labors at Vassar.

Ritual, an order of rites, hence the written order of public religious service.

Rive-King, M'me Julia, the distinguished piano-forte virtuoso and composer, was born at Cincinnati, O., in 1853. Early showed a talent for music, and played Thalberg's "Don Juan" fantasia in public at the age of eleven. Later she made some studies with Mills in New York, after which she went to Weimar, with Liszt. Returning to this country in 1875, she met everywhere the most distinguished success, and played highly important and artistic programmes in all parts of the country. She resides at present in New York, where she occupies a distinguished position.

Riverso (Ital. rē-vär'-sō). Reverse motion, the subject backward, in double counterpoint.

Rochlitz, Friedrich Johann, a writer about music, at Leipsic, born 1769, died 1842. Author of an elaborate collection of vocal music, etc.

Rode, Pierre, a favorite violinist, born at Bordeaux, 1774. He lived chiefly in Paris, and was distinguished for the elegance and grace of his play. Died 1830.

Roger, Gustave Hippolyte, 1815. A tenor singer of the Paris Opéra Comique, distinguished as well for his dramatic ability as for his singing. After he had passed his prime as an opera singer he became professor of singing in the Paris Conservatory. D. 1879.

Rohr (Ger. rōr). Reed, pipe.

Rohrfloete (Ger. rōr'-flŏ'-tĕ). Reed-flute, a stopped diapason in an organ.

Role (Fr. rōl). A part or character performed by an actor in a play or opera.

Romance (Fr.) See *Romanza.*

Romantic, strange, striking. See Part Sixth.

Romanza (Ital. rō-män'-tsä). Formerly the name given to the long lyric tales sung by the minstrels, now a term applied to an irregular though delicate and refined composition.

Romberg, Andreas, Dr., 1767-1821. A distinguished violin virtuoso, and a talented and skilful composer, most of whose artistic life was spent in Hamburg. He wrote six symphonies, eight overtures and much chamber music. His best known work is his setting of Schiller's "Lay of the Bell."

Romberg, Bernhard, 1767-1841. Cousin of Andreas, and associated with him in his concert tours for many years. He was a distinguished violoncello virtuoso, and a prolific composer for his instrument. He was also an accomplished musician, and was conductor four years in Berlin, and two years professor in the Paris Conservatory.

Ronconi, Dominico (rŏn-kō'-nē), 1772-1839. A renowned tenor singer with a wonderful voice, admirably trained. He was equally distinguished as a singing teacher. He taught in Milan, Venice and elsewhere in Italy, and also in Munich, Vienna and Paris, whither he was repeatedly called.

Ronconi, Felice, George and Sebastian, sons of Dominico, and all excellent singers. George was the best of the three.

Rondo, a round. See Chap. XIV.

Rondino (Ital. rŏn-dē'-nō), a little rondo.

Rondoletto (Ital. rŏn-dō-lăt'-tō). A short and easy rondo.

Root of a Chord. The greatest common measure of the system of vibrations producing the chord. The root is the *resultant-tone* of the chord, and remains unaffected by changes of position in the parts, or by inversion. Dissonant chords have properly no roots.

Rore, Cyprian de, 1516-1565. A very distinguished master, and one who contributed essentially to the development of music. He wrote many motettes and madrigals, in many of which he applied for the first time the results of his own experiments and those of his predecessors, Willaut and Zarlino, in chromatic tones and harmonies, thus increasing the means of musical expression.

Rosellen, Henri, 1811. An extremely popular piano teacher, of Paris, and the composer of a great number of popular parlor pieces. He was a pupil of Henri Herz in piano playing, and of Fétis and Halévy in composition.

Rosenhain, Jacob (rō-sĕn-hīne), 1813. An excellent pianist, teacher and composer of serious music; born in Mannheim, but settled for many years in Paris. He won the hearty praise of Mendelssohn and Schumann, and is respected by all who know him. He now lives in retirement in Baden-Baden.

Rosetti, Franz Anton (rŏ-sĕt'-tī), 1750-1792. A Bohemian musician and composer. He wrote oratorios, symphonies and chamber music.

Ross, John, 1764-1833. Organist of St. Paul's, at Aberdeen. He wrote six concertos for piano and orchestra, seven sonatas for pianoforte, songs, etc.

Rossi, Lemme (rōs'-sī), 1601-1673. Professor of philosophy and mathematics at the University of Pérouse, his native city. He wrote a work on the relations of the musical intervals.

Rossi, Luigi Felicio, 1805-1863. A respected professor of music and composer of church music in Turin.

Rossini, Gioachomo Antonio (rōs-sē'-nē), 1792-1868, was born in Peraro, of poor but musically gifted parents. His father was a trumpeter; he was also a devoted patriot, and his revolutionary enthusiasm caused him to be thrown into prison. While there, his wife was obliged to support the family, and being possessed of a fine voice and dramatic talent, went upon the stage as a prima donna. Young Gioachomo received musical instruction very early, though in a somewhat desultory and superficial way. Even after he entered the school of music at Bologna, in his 15th year, he was poorly taught in composition. But he diligently studied Haydn and Mozart, and soon felt the impulse to compose. After some eight or ten insignificant operas and other youthful works, which served to develop his talent and to give him skill in composition, he wrote "Tancred" in his 21st year. This work was so brilliant, so florid, so full of splendid, gorgeous effects, that it made a new epoch in Italian music, and retained its popularity all over Europe for many years. He had been poor, but his success with this and some other operas led to an engagement in Naples, where Barbaja, his theatre director, gave him valuable assistance, and made money for them both. He wrote here "The Barber of Seville," one of the best comic operas ever produced, and "Othello," in which he strove after dramatic characterization. This latter tendency he showed still more in his "Moses in Egypt," and especially in "William Tell," in which his work culminated. This was his last opera, and was written in 1830. He had now become a rich man, and lived in luxurious retirement the life of a cultivated and elegant gentleman and connoisseur until his death. His only important work after "William Tell" was his "Stabat Mater," a brilliant and imposing but not essentially religious work. He was twice married, both times happily, and his first marriage, especially, had an extremely favorable influence on the development of his genius. His was one of the great creative minds of our time. (F.)

Rouget de L' Isle, Claude Joseph (rō-jā dŭ leel), 1760-1836. The composer of the world-renowned Marseilles Hymn, perhaps the most inspiring battle song ever written. He wrote nothing else of importance.

Rousseau, Jean Jacques (roos-sō), 1712-1777. This distinguished philosopher and author was also possessed of decided musical talent. He lacked thorough technical training, but succeeded, nevertheless, in producing at least one opera which was decidedly successful. He also educated himself to be an authority in musical criticism, took an active part in the disputes between Sully and the Italians, and afterwards between the Gluckists and Piccinists, and contributed materially to the elevation and purification of French taste.

Rubato (Ital. roo-bā'-tō). Stolen; *i. e.* slackening or varying the time for the purpose of expression.

Rubini, Giovanni Battista (ru-bē'nē), 1795-1845. One of the most renowned singers who ever lived, and the best tenor in Europe in his day. His voice was extremely fine, and his execution astonishing. Among his best pupils was Mario.

Rubinstein, Anton Gregor (rū'-bĭn-stīn). The greatest piano virtuoso of our time, and also a noted composer, was born in Wallachia, in 1829. His life, except when he has been on concert tours in Europe and America, has been spent in Russia. He was for many years director of the Conservatory at St. Petersburg, and also of the Russian Musical Society at the same place. He has written songs, piano music, chamber music, oratorios, operas and symphonies, some of which are very important.

Rubinstein, Nicolaus, brother of Anton, director of the Conservatory of the Singing Society of the Russian Musical Society in Moscow.

Rudersdorf, Emilia, a renowned singer of our time. Born in Russia in 1822. Her father was a Dutch conductor, who went to Hamburg when she was a child. At her marriage with Professor Küchermeister she withdrew from the stage, but finally returned to it, then settled in London, and has now been for some years a teacher of singing in Boston.

Ruhe (roo'-ĕ). Rest, repose.

Rust, F. W. (roost), 1739-1796. Music director in Anhalt-Dessau. Pupil of Friedemann Bach, and C. P. E. Bach. He was a good, but not a prolific composer, his strength being devoted to the promotion of music and culture generally. He made the little principality an intellectual center of great importance.

Rust, W. K., youngest son of F. W. Rust, 1787-1855. He was an excellent pianist and teacher.

Rust, Wilhelm, grandson of F. W. Rust, organist of St. Luke's Church in Berlin, and since 1871, professor of counterpoint and composition in Stein's Conservatory in Berlin. Born in 1822. He is a distinguished composer, writer on musical topics, and editor of numerous works.

Sacchini, Antonio M. G., 1734-1786. A distinguished Neapolitan composer, pupil of Durante. He wrote many operas and much church music.

Sachs, Hans, 1494-1576. The most renowned of the so-called "master singers," and a prolific writer of verses. Lived in Nürnberg.

Sackbut, an old bass wind instrument resembling a trombone.

Sacred Music. Music composed for religious worship, or in a religious spirit.

Saengerfest (süng-ẽr-fest), a festival of German singers.

Saint-Saens, Chas. Carville, born 1835, one of the most noteworthy French composers. Has written symphonies, operas, and much else. Is best known in this country by his "Phaeton" and his "Danse Macabre." The former is a fine specimen of legitimate programme music; i. e., music which seeks to express a series of emotions, connected with a definite series of incidents. He is also an excellent organist and pianist.

Sainton-Dolby, Madame, an eminent English contralto and teacher of singing.

Sala, Nicolo, 1732-1800. A Neapolitan contrapuntist and opera composer.

Salicional (Fr. sä-lē-sĭ-ō-näl'). An organ stop of string quality and soft 8 ft. tone.

Salieri, Antonio, 1750-1825. Born in Venice. Lived mostly in Vienna. Prolific composer of operas, which had only a short-lived popularity. Was friend of Gluck, rival of Mozart, and teacher of Franz Schubert.

Saloman, Siegfried, born 1818. Danish composer and violinist. Has written operas and instrumental music; also lectures on the theory of music.

Saltarello, an Italian dance of the 15th century, in triple measure. Also a modern Roman folks-dance.

Salve regina (sāl-vē rä-gē'-nä), "Save, O Queen," a hymn to the Virgin.

San Martini, G. B. First half of 18th century in Milan. Talented composer. Wrote symphonies resembling the earlier ones of Haydn.

Sanftig (Ger. sänf'-tĭg). Soft, gentle.

Sangbar (Ger. säng-bär). Singable.

Sarabanda, or **Sarabande**, an old dance in 3-4 time, in slow and stately movement.

Sarasate, Pablo de, an extremely gifted young Spanish violinist of the present time. He already belongs in the first rank of virtuosi. Was a pupil of Alard, in Paris.

Sarti, Giuseppo, 1729-1802. Italian opera composer, pupil of Padre Martini. Was conductor and teacher in Milan, Venice, and at the court of Russia.

Satz (Ger. sätz). Piece. *Satz* is the German for piece, phrase, movement.

Saxhorn, a brass instrument of the trumpet kind, invented by M. Sax, in 1842; much used in brass bands.

Scale, the tones of a key arranged in regular order according to the pitch.

Scarlatti, Alessandro, 1649-1725. One of the greatest Italian composers, wrote operas, church and chamber music. Was made a knight, and was royal conductor in Naples.

Scarlatti, Domenico, son of A., 1683-1757. Wrote operas, church music, and much piano music, which is still prized. Was a superior pianist.

Scaria, Emil, Born 1838. One of the noblest bass singers of the present time. Pupil of Garcia.

Scena (Ital. shā'-nä), a scene, a distinct part of an opera or play.

Schad, Joseph. Born 1812. Pianist, teacher and composer. Professor at Conservatory of Geneva.

Schalmei (Ger. schäl-mī'), an 8 ft. reed stop in the organ.

Scharf, an acute "mixture" stop in the organ.

Scherek, Max. Born 1840. Violinist and composer in Pasen.

Scherzando (Ital. skĕrt-zän'-dō). Playfully.

Scherzo (Ital. skĕrt'-zō). Play, sport, jest.

Scherzoso (Ital. skĕrt-zō-sō). Merry, playful, jocose.

Schilling, Dr. Gustav, the musical literateur and writer about music, was born in Schwiegershausen, Hanover, in 1805, educated at Göttingen and Halle, and resided for some time in Stuttgart. Is author of a complete Encyclopedia of music (7 vols. 8 vo.), a theory of harmony, biographical notices, etc., etc. Came to America in 1857.

Schindler, Anton, the biographer of Beethoven, was born 1796 at Medl, studied the violin, and became opera conductor. In Vienna he became acquainted with Beethoven, and in 1840 published his book. Died in 1864.

Schira, Francesco Vincenzio, a dramatic composer, was born at Mailand, 1812, studied there in the Conservatory, and composed his first opera in 1833. Lived for several years in Lisbon as opera conductor, and died there of cholera.

Schisma, very minute interval equal to the ratio 32805 : 32768.

Schlag Instrumente (Ger.) Instruments of percussion; drums, cymbals, triangles, bones, etc., as well as all the dulcimer tribe, among which is the piano-forte.

Schmitt, Alois, a favorite clavier player of the old school, and composer for his instrument, was born in 1789 at Erlenbach. At the age of 14 he appeared as virtuoso, and studied composition with André, at Offenbach. Died 1866. Was composer of symphonies, quartettes, piano-pieces, etc.

Schmitt, Alois G., was born at Hanover in 1827, composed an opera at an early age, and appeared as pianist with success, especially in England. On his return to Germany he filled many positions as opera conductor, and composed much music, including several operas.

Schnabel, Joseph Ignaz, was a celebrated church composer of masses, etc. Born 1767 at Naumburg. Died 1831.

School, education, training.

Schneider, Friedrich Johann Chr., was born near Zittau in 1786. He was the son of an organist, and at the age of eight took his father's place at the organ. He began early as a composer, producing symphonies, piano and organ pieces, etc., and in 1812 was appointed organist of the St. Thomas Church at Leipsic, a place he left in 1821 for one at Dessau, where he died in 1853. He exerted great influence by the education of pupils, among whom were Baake, Gathy, Fritz Spindler, Robert Franz, Carl Anschütz, etc. He wrote 9 oratorios, 13 masses, 7 operas, 23 symphonies, 23 overtures, 60 sonatas, 7 concertos with orchestra, etc., etc.

ā *ale*, ă *add*, ä *arm*, ê *eve*, ĕ *end*, ī *ice*, ĭ *ill*, ō *old*, ŏ *odd*, ȯ *dove*, oo *moon*, ū *lute*, ŭ *but*, ü *Fr. sound*

64

Schneider, Johann Gottlob, brother of Friedrich, was also born at Altgersdorf, near Zittau, in 1789, and studied not only the organ but also the piano and all orchestral instruments, distinguishing himself particularly upon the 'cello. In 1811 he succeeded his brother as organist in the University church at Leipsic, and in 1812 became organist at Görlitz. During the 13 years in this position he studied organ building carefully, and effected various important reforms in it. In 1820 he came the second time to Dresden, and there resided until his death, April 13, 1864. Schneider's activity was great in three directions: as teacher, organ expert, and virtuoso performer.

Schneider, Johann Julius, royal music director, etc., was born at Berlin in 1805, the son of an organ builder. He showed great talent for music, and studied the piano, organ, singing, theory, violin, horn, etc., and presently occupied all sorts of prominent positions in Berlin as teacher, director, organist, and composer. He wrote operas, cantatas, 200 songs for male voices, a quintette for piano and wind instrument, organ pieces, 70 pedal exercises, 40 fugues, 80 choral preludes, etc. Has been the recipient of many honors.

Schoberlechner, Franz, composer and piano virtuoso, was born in 1797 at Vienna, a pupil of Hummel, began early as a composer, in 1824 received 10,000 rubles for an opera he brought out at St. Petersburg, and died 1843. Wrote 5 operas and various instrumental works.

Schoenfeld, Henry, was born in Milwaukee, Oct. 4, 1856. He is a pupil of the Leipsic Conservatory and Lassen, of Weimar. He is a composer of considerable merit. Among others, "The Easter Idyll," a cantata for solo, chorus and orchestra; several sonatas, pieces for piano, violin, chorus and songs, etc.

Schroeder-Devrient, Wilhelmine, a great dramatic singer. Born at Hamburg, 1804, the daughter of a celebrated tragedienne, made her debut in 1819, and in 1822 distinguished herself in Beethoven's "Fidelio." Died 1860.

Schubert, Franz Peter, the founder of the romantic school of composition, and the great master of song, was born Jan. 31, 1797, near Vienna. His father was a schoolmaster. At the age of eight he was choir-boy in the Lichtenthaler church, and began the study of music, and presently played the first violin with success. In 1810 he wrote his first fantasia for piano-forte for four hands, and from then until his death he produced a continual succession of compositions, in the form of songs (of which he left 600), sonatas, an opera, eight symphonies, masses and vocal works of all sorts, trios, duos, etc. Schubert is distinctly a melodist, yet as a harmonist and orchestral colorist he is also great. His songs are among the most beautiful works of this kind, and in the greatest ones, like "The Erl King," and "Gretchen at the Spinning Wheel," he extended the bounds of musical expression. In his longer works he is frequently diffuse. But his melodies are always fresh and spontaneous, in which respect he is like Mozart. See p. 190 for further observations on Schubert's relation to Chopin and Schumann. Schubert died 1828.

Schulhoff, Julius, piano virtuoso and salon composer, was born at Prague in 1825. Studied with Kisch and Tomascheck, and appeared in public successfully at the age of sixteen. In his 17th year he went to Paris, where he learned higher piano-playing from Chopin, Liszt, and Thalberg. Since 1854 he has lived in Dresden.

Schultze, Edward, violinist and leader of the famous Mendelssohn Quintet Club of Boston, was born in Germany about 1828, and came to this country with the Germania Musical Society, about 1852, and has resided since then in Boston.

Schulz, Johann Peter, a noted song composer, was born at Lüneburg, 1747, and became director of the theatre. Died 1800. Schulz exercised important influence on the development of the *Lied.*

Schumann, Gustav, called also "the Berlin Schumann," was born at Holdenstedt, March 15, 1815, and has lived most of his life in Berlin, where he is highly esteemed as composer and pianist.

Schumann, Robert, the greatest composer of the romantic school, was born at Zwickau, 1810. Died 1856. See Chapter XLIX.

Scharwenka, Philip. Born 1847. Teacher in Kullak's Academy of Music in Berlin, of which he was a pupil. Composer of symphonies and lesser works.

Scharwenka, Xaver, younger brother of Philip. Born 1850. Also a pupil of Kullak's Academy, and taught there for some time. Distinguished pianist and composer of pianoforte music, as well as chamber music.

Schweitzer, Anton, was a dramatic composer and kapellmeister at Gotha and Weimar. Born 1737, died 1787. Composed about 20 operas.

Scordato (Ital. skŏr-dä'-tō). Out of tune, false.

Score, all the voice-parts of a piece, arranged in parallel staves so as to show the entire instrumentation at a glance. *Orchestral score* contains all the orchestral parts; *vocal score,* all the voice parts; *piano score,* all the piano part, or the voice and piano parts.

Score-reading. The art or act of playing or thinking music from the orchestral score.

Seeling, Hans, a brilliant pianist and good composer, was born in 1828 at Prague, made a number of concert tours, and died at Prague in 1862.

Seligman, Hippolyte-Prosper, a violoncello virtuoso, born 1817 at Paris, and educated there. Is the composer of over 50 works, mostly operatic fantasies. Is the owner of one of the best of Nicola Amati's 'cellos.

Senfel, Ludwig, was one of the most noted German composers of church music in the 16th century.

Senza (Ital. sänd'-zä). Without; as *senza pedale,* without pedal; *senza ritard,* without retard.

Servo. Alex. Nikol (slä'-vō), a Russian opera composer and writer, a friend of Liszt and Wagner, was born 1820. Several of his operas were produced in St. Petersburg. Died 1871.

Servais. Adrien François (sĕr-vä), 1807-1866. One of the greatest violoncellists of his time. He wrote much for his instrument, and was professor of the violoncello at the Conservatory of Brussels.

Sextette, a composition for six voices or instruments.

Seyfried, Ignaz Xaver, Ritter von (sī'-freed), 1776-1841. Pupil of Mozart and Albrechtsberger. For 30 years conductor at the "Theater an der Wien," Vienna. Prolific composer of operas and church music.

Sforza (Ital. sfōr-tsä). Forced, with vigor.

Shake, a trill. See "Embellishments" in Appendix.

Sharp, a character indicating elevation. See "Pitch Notation" in Appendix.

Sherwood, William H., virtuoso pianist and composer, was born in Lyons, N. Y., 1854, the son of a music teacher. Studied the piano at an early age, and in 1871 went to Berlin, where he studied with Kullak, and afterwards with Liszt at Weimar. Since his return to America in 1875, Sherwood has appeared in all the leading cities with the greatest success in important and highly artistic programmes. Resides in Boston. Is one of the first pianists of our time.

Shield, William, 1754-1829. English composer of over 50 operas for Covent Garden Theatre.

Shift, position of the hand on the finger-board of the violin.

Si bemol (Fr. sē bĕ-mōl'). B flat.

Siciliano (Ital. sē-tshē-lĭ-ä'-nō). A dance of the Sicilian peasantry, in soft, slow movement, in 6-8 time.

Signature, sharps or flats placed at the beginning of a staff or movement to indicate the key. See "Chromatic Signs" in "Synoptical Chart of Musical Notation," Appendix.

Silbermann, Gottfried. Born 1683. One of the best organ builders of his time, and one of the original inventors of the piano-forte, substituting hammers for the quills of the old harpsichord.

Silvani, Giuseppo Antonio, first half of the 18th century organist in Bologna, and composer of much church music.

Simile (Ital. sē-mē-lĕ). Similarly, in like manner. Written after finger markings, indicates that the *fingering* is to be continued in the same manner. After *ped* means that the pedal is to be used in the same way thereafter.

Singer. Edmund. Born 1831 in Hungary. One of the greatest violin virtuosi of his time. Now professor in Stuttgart.

Singer, Otto. Born in 1833. Excellent pianist, composer and teacher. Now of the College of Music in Cincinnati.

Sin'al fine (Ital. sēn äl fēn'-ĕ). To the end, or to the word *fine*.

Singspiel (Ger. sĭng-spēl). A song-play, a play interspersed with songs, an opera.

Sinistra (Ital. sĭn'-ĭs-trä). The left hand.

Siren, an instrument for measuring the rapidity of vibrations producing given pitches. See Tyndal on sound.

Sivori, Ernst Camille. Born 1817. The greatest living Italian violin virtuoso. Also a thorough musician, and a composer for his instrument.

Skraup, Fr. 1301-:862. Bohemian opera composer. Also an excellent conductor and a composer of masses and of chamber music.

Slargando (Ital. slär-gän'-dō). Extending, widening, making the time gradually slower.

Slentando (Ital. slĕn-tän-dō). Becoming gradually slower.

Sloper, Lindsay. Born 1826. Pupil of Moscheles in piano playing. Studied also in Germany, became an excellent pianist, and is now a piano teacher in London. Has also composed piano-forte music and songs.

Slur, a curved line over two or more notes to show that they represent *legato* tones.

Smart, George. 1778-1867. Excellent conductor, and did much to promote the study of classical music in England. Founded the Philharmonic Society. Was a friend of Weber. Was also a good composer.

Smith, John Christopher, 1712-1795. Born in Germany, but lived in England in Handel's time. Was a pupil of Handel in composition. Wrote many operas. Was a good organist and a talented and accomplished musician.

Smith, Sydney, an English pianist and arranger of popular pieces. Born about 1840, and educated at Leipsic.

Smorzando (Ital. smōr-tsän'-dō). Extinguished, put out, gradually dying away.

Snare Drum, a small side-drum used in military music, deriving its name from two cords of gut stretched across one of the heads. These give it a hard metallic tone.

Soave (Ital. sō-ä'-vĕ). Softly, sweetly.

Soedermann, Aug. Johann, 1832-1876. Swedish composer of marked *originality*. Pupil of Richter and Hauptmann. Also an excellent conductor.

Sol (Ital. sōl). The fifth of the scale, the tone G in French.

Solfa. See Tonic Sol-Fa.

Solo, a piece for a single singer or player.

Somma (Ital. sŏm-mä). Extreme, great. *Somma espressione,* very great expression.

Sonata (Ital. sō-nä'-tä). An important form in instrumental music. See Chapter V.

Song, a short poem for singing. A short piece of music in lyric style.

Sonore (Ital. sō-nō'-rä). Sonorous, harmonious.

Sontag, Henrietta, 1805-1852. A renowned opera singer, distinguished for the beauty of her voice, the perfection of her method, and the astonishing facility of her execution. She commanded enormous prices. She married Count Rossi, of the Italian diplomatic service, and lived most happily with him until her death by cholera in Mexico.

Sopra (Ital. sō'-prä). Above.

Soprano (Ital. sō-prä'-nō). The highest female voice. The music for soprano voice.

Sordino (Ital. sōr-dē'-nō). A mute. A small instrument for obstructing vibration. In the *trumpet* it is a plug nearly closing the bell. On the *violin,* a small instrument for pinching the bridge.

Sospirevole (Ital. sōs-pē-rā'-vō-lĕ). Sighing, very subdued.

Sostenuto (Ital. sōs-tā-noo'-tō). Sustaining the tone.

Sotto voce (Ital. sōt'-tō vō'-tshĕ). Under the voice, that is, in a low voice, softly.

Speidel, Wilhelm, born 1826, in Vienna. An excellent pianist, and especially renowned as a Beethoven interpreter. Also an excellent composer and conductor, and one of the founders of the Stuttgart Conservatory.

Speidel, Ludwig, brother of Wilhelm, born in 1830. Distinguished critic, and one of the editors of the Vienna "New Free Press."

Spianato (Ital. spē-ä-nä'-tō). Smooth, even, *legato*.

Spiccato (Ital. spĭk-kä-tō). Pointed, detached. In *violin music*, "with the point of the bow."

Spindler, Fritz, born 1817. Fine musician, composer, and piano-forte teacher. Pupil of Fr. Schneider. Has written much piano-forte music, also chamber music and a symphony. Is a teacher in Dresden.

Spinet, an old instrument somewhat like the square piano.

Spiritoso (Ital. spē-rē-tō'-zō). In a spirited manner.

Spitz floete (Ger. spĭtz flö'-tĕ). An organ stop of a pointed flute-tone, generally of 8 ft.

Spohr, Louis, 1784-1859. Native of Brunswick. Distinguished composer and violin virtuoso. Also an excellent orchestral conductor. He wrote in all branches of composition, but especially operas and symphonies of high rank.

Spontini, Gasparo Luigi Pacificus, 1774-1851. One of the greatest Italian opera composers. He was a superior conductor, and was for more than twenty years director of the Royal Opera in Berlin, whither he was tempted from a conductor's post in Paris, by a large salary and great privileges. His greatest operas are "The Vestal Virgins" and "Ferdinand Cortez."

Sponholz, Adolph Heinrich, 1803-1851. Organist in Rostock, and composer of piano-forte music, songs, motettes and orchestral pieces.

Stabat Mater (stä-bät mä-ter). A cantata or oratorio by Rossini in 1832. The words are those of a very old hymn.

Staccato (Ital. stäk-kä-tō). Detached, distinct, separated. *Staccato* is of many grades, from the mild one made by the violin bow when reversed for each successive note, to the extreme *pizzicato* made by snapping the strings.

Staendchen (Ger. ständ'-khen). A serenade.

Stainer, Jacob, 1621-1683. The greatest violin builder of the Tyrol, and one of the greatest anywhere.

Stainer, Mark, born 1659. Brother of Jacob, also a violin maker.

Stainer, Dr. J., an English organist and composer, author of many arrangements for the organ, church music, etc.

Stamaty, Camille Maria, 1811-1870. Celebrated French teacher of the piano-forte, and composer of valuable studies for that instrument. He taught Camille Saint-Saens and L. M. Gottschalk.

Stark, Ludwig. Born 1831. One of the founders of the Stuttgart Conservatory, and one of the authors of Lebert and Stark's "School for the piano-forte." Lebert and Stark also wrote an "Elementary Instruction Book for Singing," and a "German Song School." Teacher of the piano-forte and of singing, also conductor and composer, especially of sacred and secular choruses.

Staudigl, Joseph (stow'-dIgl). 1804-1861. Austrian bass singer, renowned in opera, oratorio and songs. To his noble interpretations the songs of Franz Schubert owe a large part of their popularity. One of the greatest singers of this century.

Steffani Agastino, the Abbé. 1655-1730. One of the most distinguished composers and singers of his time. A Venetian. He composed operas, church music and chamber music.

Steibelt, Daniel, 1755-1823. Born in Berlin. Pianist and composer. As a player he was brilliant and effective, but lacked thorough training both in this and in composition. His works have no permanent value.

Steinway, the name of a family engaged in the manufacture of pianos in New York, under the name of Steinway & Sons. The founder of this firm, Henry Steinway, was born in Brunswick, 1797. It is now conducted by his two surviving sons, Theodore and William.

Stern, Julius. Born in Breslau in 1820. He is one of the ablest and best musicians of our time, excelling, as a conductor and teacher. His Conservatory of Music and Singing Society in Berlin are among the very best institutions of their kind.

Sterndale-Bennett, W. See Bennett.

Stesso mosso (Ital. stäs'-sō-mōs-sō). The same movement, *i.e.*, any given note, as an eighth or quarter, goes at the same speed in both movements.

Stockhausen, Julius. Born in Paris in 1826. He is a most distinguished singer of songs, and in opera and oratorio, and an excellent teacher and conductor. He is now director of the Stern Society in Berlin.

Stop, an organ register. See Register.

Stopped Pipes, organ pipes stopped at the upper end. In this case the sound wave is reflected back again to the mouth of the pipe, consequently stopped pipes are only half as long as open ones giving the same pitch.

St. Peter, an oratorio by John K. Paine, in 1873. Also by Sir Julius Benedict.

St. Paul, oratorio by Mendelssohn, in 1836.

Stradella, Alessandro, 1645-1670 (?). One of the best singers and composers of his time. He was born in Naples, and assassinated in Genoa.

Stradivari, Antonius, 1644-1737. The most renowned and best of all violin makers. He was born, lived and died at Cremona.

Stradivari, Francisco and Oruobone, sons of Antonius, and also good violin makers.

Strakosch, Maurice, born in Hungary in 1825. Pianist, composer and impressario. Lives in New York.

Strathspey, a lively Scotch dance, in common time.

ā *ate*, ă *add*, ä *arm*, ē *eve*, ĕ *end*, ī *ice*, ĭ *ill*, ō *old*, ŏ *odd*, ū *dove*, oo *moon*, ŭ *late*, ŭ *but*, ü *Fr. sound*

Strauss, Jos., 1793-1866. Conductor in the service of the Grand Duke of Baden. Violinist and composer of operas, overtures and chamber music.

Strauss, Johann, 1804-1849. Lived in Vienna, and is known the world over by his beautiful dance music. His sons, John, Joseph and Edward, are hardly less renowned for their productions in the same field. John, indeed, has also written comic operettas. His waltz, "On the Beautiful blue Danube," is the best known of his works.

Streng (Ger. strĕng). Strict, severe, rigid.

Strepitoso (Ital. strĕp-I-tō'-zō). Noisily, boisterously.

Stretto (Ital. străt'-tō). Pressed, close, contracted. That part of a fugue where all the subjects come together, or where the imitations take place more rapidly after each other. A quicker passage leading to a close.

Strict, severe, rigid.

Stringed Instruments. Instruments whose sounds are produced by *striking* strings (as in the piano-forte or dulcimer), *drawing* them (as in the harp or guitar), or the *friction of a bow* (as in the violin family).

Stringendo (Ital. strĕn-jăn'-dō). Pressing, hurrying, accelerating the time.

String Quartette, the violin family, consisting of violins, viola and cello. Music for these instruments, Also called "string band."

Strophe, a stanza.

Stueck (Ger. stük). Piece, air, tune.

Sub (Lat. sŭb). Under.

Sub-bass, the low bass. The violon. A pedal stop in the organ, 16 ft.

Subdominant, the fourth of the key.

Subject, the leading idea of a work.

Suite (Fr. swēt). A succession of pieces intended to be played in connection.

Sul (Ital. sool). On, upon the.

Sullivan, Arthur Seymour. Born 1842. He was a pupil of the Leipsic Conservatory, and is a talented and accomplished musician and composer. He has written works of considerable importance, including one or two oratorios, but is best known in this country by his comic operetta, "H. M. S. Pinafore," which had a most extraordinary run in 1879.

Supertonic, the tone above the tonic, the second of the scale.

Suppe, Franz von, was born in Dalmatia in 1820. He is a conductor in Vienna, and has composed operas, symphonies, quartettes, etc. He is best known by his comic operettas, of which "Fatinitza" and "The Beautiful Galatea" have been given in this country.

Suspension, a dissonant tone held over from a preceding chord where it was consonant, and finally *resolved* (generally downwards) into some proper tone of the chord into which it had intruded.

Svendsen, Johann Severin, was born in Christiana, Sweden, in 1840. He studied at the Leipsic Conservatory, and is a much admired and highly respected musician and composer. He has written admirable and original quartettes, symphonies and other works.

Swell Organ, that division of the organ whose pipes are enclosed in a box with movable *blinds*, operated by a "swell-pedal," thus making crescendo and diminuendo.

Symphony, the most important instrumental form, being, in fact, nothing but a large sonata for orchestra. See Chapters XV. and XVI.

Symphonic Poem, an orchestral composition in symphonic style, but not strictly so.

Syncopation, "a cutting into." a concealment of the measure accent, either by a false accent (accent on what would properly be an unaccented part of the measure), or by a prolongation of a tone out of a weak part of the measure past the moment when the accent should come.

Taborowski, Stanislaw. Born 1830. Violin virtuoso. Studied in Brussels. Lives in Russia.

Tacchinardi. Nicholas, 1776-1860. Distinguished tenor singer of Florence. Sang also in other Italian cities, and in Paris.

Tace (Ital, tä'-tshĕ). Be silent. Indicates that certain instruments are not to play. *Violini tacet*, violins be silent, etc.

Tact (Ger. täkt). Measure, time.

Tallis, Thomas, one of the greatest English contrapuntists of the 16th century. Was an excellent organist.

Tamberlik, Enrico, was born at Rome in 1820. One of the best tenor singers of our time. Taught singing in Madrid after 1867.

Tambourine, a small instrument of the drum family, consisting of a wooden hoop with holes in the sides, in which are jingling pieces of metal, and a sheepskin head stretched on it.

Tamburini, Anton, 1800-1876. A distinguished Italian bass singer. Sang in opera with Rubini, Lablache and others, and was their equal.

Tamtam, an Indian instrument of percussion.

Tansur, Wm. Born 1699. English contrapuntist and writer on music.

Tanto (Ital. tän'-tō). So much, so great. *Allegro ma non tanto*, allegro, but not too much.

Tantum Ergo (Lat. tăn'-tŭm är-gō). A Latin hymn sung at the benediction in the Roman Catholic service.

Tappert, Wm. Born 1830, in Silesia. Writer on music of great ability, and a strong Wagner partisan. Also teacher in Tausig's piano school in Berlin. Editor of "The Universal German Musical Journal" since 1878.

Tarantella (Ital. tär-răn-tăl'-lä). A swift, delirious sort of Italian dance in 6-8 time.

Tardando (Ital. tär-dăn'-dō). Lingering, retarding the time.

Tartini, Giuseppo, 1692-1770. One of the very greatest violinists of the 18th century. He was the founder of a new school of violin playing, and of a new system of harmony. He was the discoverer of the so-called "Combination tones." He was also a most distinguished teacher, sought by pupils from all countries. He was also an excellent composer, and wrote over 200 concert pieces for his instrument, the best known of which is the still renowned "Devil's sonata."

Tastatur (Ger. täs'-tä-toor). The keyboard of the organ or piano-forte.

Taste (Ger. täs'-tĕ). The touch of any instrument. Hence the key.

Tasto solo (Ital. täs'-tō sō'-lō). One key alone; in organ or piano music this means the parts in unison, without harmony.

Taubert, Ernst E., born 1838. Critic and composer in Berlin.

Taubert, Wm. C. G., born 1811. Pianist and conductor of the Royal Opera and orchestra in Berlin. Composer of no great significance.

Tausig, Carl, 1841-1871. Born in Warsaw. One of the very greatest of all pianists, with a technique so absolutely above all difficulties and so perfect as to defy criticism, and an innate fire and force hardly surpassed by the great Liszt himself, whose pupil he was. This fiery vigor was subdued and tempered by his intellectual tendencies and attainments, for Tausig was an earnest student of philosophy, and a lover of all higher intellectual pursuits. He was also an admirable teacher.

Technic, skill or ability in the mechanical part of any art. *Piano-forte technic*, the perfect use of the fingers; *pedal technic*, proper use of the feet; *vocal technic*, correct use of the voice.

Tedesco (Ital. tĕ-däs'-kō). In the German style.

Te deum laudamus (Lat. tā dā-ŭ n lawdā'-mŭs). "We praise Thee, O God," an old hymn of praise.

Telemann, George P., 1681-1767. Born in Magdeburg. Was 46 years conductor in Hamburg. Played organ, piano, violin and other instruments. Was a highly educated man, and a teacher and composer. Developed a great musical interest in Hamburg; wrote many operas there, and also much instrumental music.

Temperament, is a system of compromises by means of which twelve tones in an octave are made to do duty in place of about fortyeight which would be necessary to perfect intonation in all keys. Mathematically stated, temperament makes, for example, the major third equal to four-fifths divided by two octaves. That is, 3-2×1-2×3-2 <3-2×1-2×3-2 =81-64=5-4. Temperament is, therefore, a system of imperfect tuning peculiar to the piano and organ, in which all intervals except the unison and octave are more or less imperfect. Its advantages are the simplicity of the key-board of the twelve keys to an octave in place of forty-eight. Music itself is written without respect to temperament.

Tempestoso (Ital. tĕm-pĕs-tō'-zō). Tempestuous, stormy, boisterous.

Tempo (Ital. tăm'-pō). The time, the movement. The movement of music is approximately indicated by means of Italian terms, which refer generally to the unit of time, so that slow movements may yet have quick notes in them. Reissmann divides tempos into three classes: Slow, including *Largo, Grave, Adagio, Lento*, and *Larghetto*, which here stand in progressive order of speed, the slowest first. MEDIUM, "going," *Andante, Andantino, Moderato, Allegretto*. QUICK, *Allegro, Vivace, Vivacissimo, Presto*, and *Prestissimo*. Theorists are not agreed as to whether *Larghetto* is faster than *Largo*, or *Andantino* faster than *Andante*, but modern usage is as here indicated. For the meaning of the different terms look in the proper place.

Tenebrae (Lat. tăn'-ĕ-brā). Darkness, a Catholic service in holy week.

Teneramente (Ital. tĕn-ĕr-ă-măn-tĕ). Tenderly, delicately.

Tenerezza (Ital. tĕn-ĕ-rät-tsä). Tenderness, softness, delicacy.

Tenor, the highest male voice. Tenor *robusto* is a strong tenor.

Tenor C, the C next below middle C.

Tenuto (Ital. tĕ-noo'-tō). Held, sustained, held down its full time.

Ter (Lat. tĕr). Thrice, three times.

Terpander, a great Greek poet, composer and theorist, lived about the 7th century, B.C.

Terschak, Adolf, Born 1832. Flute virtuoso. Lives in Vienna.

Tertia (Lat. tĕr'-shĭ-ä). Third, tierce.

Terz (Ger. tărts). A third.

Terzetto (Ital. tăr-tsät'-tō). A short piece, or trio, for three voices.

Teschner, G. W. Born 1800. Teacher of singing in Berlin. Accomplished musician and indefatigable investigator, and collector of old music, of which he has published much, especially songs, and valuable vocal studies.

Testo (Ital. tăs'-tō). The text, theme or subject.

Tetrachord, a system or scale of four tones. An instrument producing four tones.

Text, the words of a song, or opera.

Thalberg, Sigismund, was born at Geneva in 1812, and died in Italy in 1871. He was a brilliant piano-forte virtuoso, and invented the peculiar style of playing which consists in carrying a melody supported by the pedal, while playing a rapid accompaniment in extended arpeggios. He was greatly admired as an executant in this peculiar style, but occupied himself very little with the works of masters, and was by no means a great interpretative or creative artist. His compositions are now little used.

Thema or **Theme** (Ger. tā'-mä). The principal melodic subject in a work. An air, which is afterwards varied.

Thematic Work, means literally, work on motives taken from the theme; it is now applied to any elaboration of motives, whether those of the principal theme of the piece or not. See Chapters I. and II.

Theory of Music, includes *Sound*, the science of musical tone; *Tonality*, the doctrine of scales and keys; *Harmony*, the doctrine of chords and chord-successions, *Counterpoint*, voice-relation; *Fugue*, the logical development of a subject; *Form*, the symmetrical arrangement of the parts of a work; *Orchestration*, the proper method of employing and combining instruments; *Technics*, the principles of correct performance, and perhaps *Æsthetics*, or the principles of the beautiful.

Thibaut, Anton, F. G., 1772-1840. Professor in Heidelburg University. Was a connoisseur in music, and wrote a valuable book on "Purity in Musical Art."

Third, an interval between any tone of the scale and the next but one above or below.

Thiele, Carl I., 1816-1848. Organist in Berlin, distinguished for superior technic and the imaginative quality of his playing. Left many important works for his instrument, which are the most difficult legitimate organ pieces yet produced.

Thomas, Ambroise, C. L., born 1811. Distinguished French opera composer, and director of the Paris Conservatory. His work best known in this country is "Mignon." He has also written instrumental music.

Thomas, Theodore, born in East Frisia in 1835. Has been a violinist and conductor in New New York since 1847. He developed and trained the finest orchestra yet seen in America, with which he made extended concert tours for many years. At the establishment of the Cincinnati College of Music in 1877, he was called to be its director, but resigned early in 1880 and returned to New York. He is a very superior conductor, possessing remarkable power of commanding his forces and making them realize his ideals, which are very high, his readings of great works possessing an unusually imaginative quality, and producing a remarkable effect on audiences.

Thomas, St., School in Leipsic. An old school for boys, where church music has been assiduously cultivated since the 13th century. It retains the endowments it had before the Reformation. Among its most distinguished Cantori, or directors and teachers of music were J. S. Bach, Moritz Hauptmann and E. F. Richter. Its choir of pupils, numbering 60, provides the music in the city churches, and sings motettes every Saturday P.M, in St. Thomas' church.

Tichatscheek, J. A. Born in Bohemia in 1807. A remarkable tenor singer. Held the first rank for many years in Vienna, Dresden and elsewhere. Retired from the stage in 1870.

Tiersch, Otto. Born 1838. Professor of Theory in Stein's Conservatory, Berlin. Has published works on harmony and other branches of theory, besides contributing many articles to musical newspapers, and to Mendel's Encyclopedia of Music.

Tietjens, Therese, 1831-1877. Born in Hamburg. Was a most distinguished prima donna of Her Majesty's Theatre, in London, and an artist of the highest rank.

Timbre (Fr. tähnbr), quality of tone.

Timpani (Ital. tŏm-pä'-nē). The kettledrums.

Timotheus, a distinguished Greek musician. Born 446 B.C. He was a reformer, and added five new strings to the seven-stringed lyre, adding also to the harmonic resources of his time by his experiments and discoveries. For this he was banished from Sparta, the sapient rulers of those parts fearing lest these innovations should corrupt the morals of their youth.

Tinctoris, Johann. Born about 1435, in West Flanders. Distinguished theorist, and author of the first Musical lexicon. Was also an excellent composer.

Toccata (Ital. tō-kä'-tü). An obsolete form of composition for the organ or piano-forte, requiring brilliant execution.

Todi, Maria F., 1748-1793. A distinguished Portuguese singer. Sang in the principal capitals of Europe in the important operas of her day.

Todt, J. A. W. Born 1833. One of the best living organists. Is organist and teacher in Stettin. Has composed much instrumental music, songs, psalms, a symphony, an oratorio, and a school of singing.

Toepfer, J. G., 1701-1870. Organist, theorist, and composer. Teacher in the Seminary at Weimar. Contributed much to the science of organ building, by placing it on a scientific foundation, to which end he devoted ten years to scientific study.

Tomascheek, J. W., 1774-1850. Bohemian composer, pianist and teacher of high reputation. Wrote a symphony, chamber music and smaller works.

Tomlins, Wm. I., vocal teacher and conductor, was born in England about 1844. Studied music in the Tonic Sol-Fa schools, and with G. A. Macfarren and Silas, came to New York in 1869, and resides in Chicago, where he holds leading rank as vocal conductor.

Tone, a musical sound. A sound of determinate pitch, and consequently of regular vibrations.

Tonart (Ger. tōn'-ärt). Key; as key of D, key of C.

Tonfarbe (Ger. tōn-fär'-bĕ). Tone-color, or *timbre*. The quality of tones. Timbre depends upon the number and relative intensity of over-tones present in the sound.

Tonic, the key-note. Speaking by ear, the *tonic* is that tone of a scale or key which makes the best ending or point of repose. Mathematically, it is the tone from which all the others in the key are determined, as shown in the article *Key*.

Tonic Sol-Fa. The name of a new and very simple English notation for vocal music, based on the fact that, in singing, pitches are determined by their relation in key, and not from melodic intervals or absolute pitch. Besides the notation, the system also includes a new and very much improved method of teaching music, by cultivating the musical perceptions more than is generally done. See *John Curwen*.

Tonkunst (Ger. tōn-koonst). The art of Music.

Tonleiter (Ger. tōn'-lī'-tĕr). Scale.

Tone-painting, representing scenes or emotions by means of tones.

Torelli, Guiseppe, one of the first violin virtuosi in Italy. A few years earlier than Corelli. Died 1708. Originated the violin concerto; wrote much chamber music.

Tottmann, Albert, born 1837. Violinist and musician. Lives in Leipsic. Is now writer on musical subjects, and teacher of theory and æsthetics.

ā *ale*, ă *add*, ä *arm*, ō *eve*, ŏ *end*, ī *ice*, ĭ *ill*, ō *old*, ŏ *odd*, ô *dove*, oo *moon*, ū *lute*, ŭ *but*, ü Fr. *sound*

Tourjee, Eben, Mus. Doc., the head of the New England Conservatory of Music at Boston, was born at Warwick, R. I., June 1, 1834. Studied music young, and early became a teacher, especially of choir singing. He founded the N. E. Conservatory in 1867, which has had a remarkable success. Dr. Tourjee has great ability as an organizer, and unlimited enthusiasm. It was under his efforts that the great Peace Jubilee choruses were formed, numbering no less than 10,371 members in actual attendance.

Traetta, Tomaso, 1727-1779. A renowned opera composer of the Neapolitan school.

Transition, a change; as of key, or style, or expression.

Transposing Instruments, those which play from notes higher or lower than the actual sound. All these instruments play from notes in the key of C. "B♭ instruments" play every thing a whole-step lower than written. Those "in D" play one degree higher. "In A," a minor third lower. "In E♭" a minor third higher. Bass instruments are usually written as they play. The transposing instruments are the clarinets, cornets, trumpets, trombones, and horns.

Traviata, La, (träv̈ē-ä´-tä), opera by Verdi.

Tremando (Ital. trä-män´-dō). Tremolo, or vibrating.

Tremolando (Ital. trä-mō-län´-dō). Vibrating. Chords marked *trem.* are played as shown in Appendix. (See "Abbreviations.")

Tremolo (Ital. trä´-mō-lō). A note or chord made to quiver, or shake.

Tremulant, a contrivance in the organ for producing tremolo.

Tretbar, Charles, was born in Brunswick in 1832. At present a prominent member of the house of Steinway & Sons, in New York, and the author of some very ingenious and instructive analytic programmes of classic symphonies and chamber music.

Triad, a chord of three tones, which are always a fundamental and its third and fifth.

Triangle, a small three-sided steel frame, which is played upon by being struck with a rod.

Trill, a rapid vibration between a chief note and its auxiliary above. See Embellishments in Appendix.

Trio (Ital. trē´-ō). A composition for three voices, instruments, or parts. A soft digression in simple binary forms. See Chap. XIII.

Triplet, three notes of equal duration performed in a unit of time, or an aliquot part thereof.

Triple time, triple measure. Measure consisting of three units or pulses, the first accented.

Tritone, a term in harmony signifying the augmented fourth, or the fourth and seventh of the key, which must not be heard together, except under certain limitations.

Tromba (Ital. trŏm´-bä). A trumpet, also a reed stop in the organ.

Trommel (Ger. trŏm´-měl). The military (or snare) drum.

Trombone, a very powerful instrument of the trumpet species, having a tube eight or ten feet long, with a sliding piece, by means of which it is lengthened or shortened, and thereby its fundamental is changed.

Trovatore, Il, opera by Verdi.

Troubadours, the bards and poet-musicians of Provence, about the tenth century.

Trumpet, a brass instrument of a brilliant tone. Compass about two octaves and a half. An 8ft. reed-stop in the organ.

Tschaikowsky, Peter. Born 1840. Russian composer of reputation; is teacher of composition in the Moscow Conservatory. Has written songs, piano-forte music, symphonies and operas, and a piano-forte concerto.

Tschirch, the family name of six brothers, the oldest of whom was born in 1808, all of whom were excellent German musicians.

Tuba (Lat. tū´-bä). A trumpet. The bass trumpet. An organ stop, of which the *tuba mirabilis* is the most powerful kind.

Tureu, alla tureu (Ital. toor-kä). In Turkish style.

Turkish music, is mostly of a wild and noisy character, based on keys not admitting of harmonic treatment according to our ideas.

Turn, a grupetto. See Embellishments in Appendix.

Turini, F., 1590-1656. Italian church composer and learned contrapuntist.

Tutta la forza (Ital. toot´-tä lä fōr-tsä). All the force, as loud as possible.

Tutte corde (Ital. toot´-tä kŏr-dä). All the strings. These words, or the abbreviation T. C. or expression *tre corde*, indicates the discontinuance of the soft pedal of the piano-forte.

Tutti (Ital. toot´-tē). All. Used in orchestral and vocal music after solo passages.

Tye, Chris., distinguished English Church composer of the first part of the 16th century.

Tympanum (Lat. tĭm´-pän-um). A timbrel, a drum.

Uebergang, transition.

Ugolino, Vincenzo, a distinguished Italian teacher and composer of church music, in the latter half of the 16th century. Died 1626.

Ulrich, Hugo, 1827-1872. One of the most gifted composers of the present time. Wrote symphonies and an opera, but succumbed to poverty and unfavorable circumstances, and failed to fulfil his early promise.

Umbreit. Carl Tho., 1763-1829. Distinguished German organist. Published valuable choral books.

Una corda (Ital. oon´-ä kŏr-dä). One string. This direction in piano music requires the use of the soft pedal. It ends at *tre corde*.

Unda Maris (Lat. ŭn -dä mä´-rĭs). Wave of the sea. An organ stop of a tremulous, wavy effect, a set of very slender pipes tuned slightly sharper than the others, thus producing waves or beat.

Unisono (Ital. oon-ĭ-sō-nō). A unison, in unison, two or more sounds having the same pitch.

Un pochellino, a very little.

Un, Una (Ital. oon, oon'-ä). One, a. *Un Poco*, a little.

Up Beat, the last beat in the measure.

Urban, F. J. Born 1838, in Berlin. Excellent musician and superior singing teacher. His instruction book on this subject is highly prized.

Ut (Fr. oot). The note C; the syllable originally applied by Guido to the note C, or *do*.

Ut bemol (Fr. oot bä-möl). The note C flat.

Ut diese (Fr. oot dï-äz). The note C sharp.

Ut supra (Lat. üt sü-prä). As above, as before.

Vaccai, Nicolo, 1791-1849. Italian composer of operas and church music.

Valotti, F. A., 1697-1780. Learned Italian musician and composer of church music.

Valse (Fr. väls). A waltz.

Valse de Salon (Fr. välse dŏ sä-lönh). A waltz for parlor playing, and not for dancing. See Lesson XX.

Van den Gheyn, M., 1721-1783. The most renowned organist and carillon player of the 18th century. Lived 40 years in Ghent.

Variations, repetitions of a theme or subject in new and varied aspects, the form or outline of the composition being preserved while the different passages are ornamented and amplified. See Lesson VI.

Vaudeville (Fr. vō-dŏ-vēl'). A country ballad or song, a roundelay; also a simple form of operetta; a comedy, or short drama, interspersed with songs.

Vecchi, Orazio, a distinguished Italian composer of the 16th century, and one who did much toward the development of dramatic music.

Velata (Ital, vä-lä'-tä). Veiled; a voice sounding as if it were covered with a veil.

Velocity, rapidity. For principles of velocity see Mason's Piano Technics.

Veloce (Ital. vŏ-lō'-tshě), **Velocemente** (vŏ-lō-tshŏ-män'-tĕ). Swiftly, quickly, in a rapid time.

Velocissimo (Ital. vŏ-lō-tshēs'-sö-mō). Very swiftly, with extreme rapidity.

Venetian School. Venice was an important musical center as early as 1400. Its greatest musical progress was made under the influence of the great Netherlander, Adrian Willaert, kapellmeister at St. Mark's Cathedral, who, with his pupils and successors, formed what is known in musical history as the Venetian School.

Veni sancti spiritus. "Come Holy Spirit," a hymn sung at the "Benediction" in the R. C. service.

Ventil (Ger. věn-tēl'). A valve. In organ building the name ventil is applied to large valves closing important wind-trunks, thus shutting off an entire department of the organ from its wind supply.

Veracini, F. M., 1685-1750. Italian violinist, next to Corelli, the best of his time.

Verdelot, Ph., end of the 15th and first part of the 16th centuries. Noted Belgian contrapuntist.

Verdi, Guiseppe, was born in Busseto, Italy, in 1813. He is a prolific composer of Italian operas, of which the best known, in his earlier style, is "Il Trovatore," a work popular on account of its pleasing and effective melodies, but poor in harmonic and contrapuntal treatment, and lacking in truth of dramatic characterization. In these points he has greatly improved in his later opera, "Aida," in which, as in his great Requiem Mass, he shows the influence of the modern German school.

Verhulst, J. J. H., born 1816. Lives in Amsterdam. Talented conductor and composer.

Vernier, J. A., born 1769, in Paris. Harp virtuoso, and composer for his instrument.

Verset (Fr. věr-sět). A little verse; a name applied to short lyric pieces for the organ.

Vervoitte, C. J. Born 1822. French musician and composer of church music. Able conductor of church music, and a learned antiquary.

Viardot-Garcia, Paulini Michelle Ferdinande, was born in Paris in 1821. She was one of the best singers of our time, and of all times. She was especially renowned as a dramatic singer. Lives in Paris as teacher of singing.

Vibrato (Ital. vē-brä'-tō). A strong, vibrating full quality of tone; resonant.

Victoria, T. L. Born in Spain about 1540. Lived in Italy. One of the greatest masters. Wrote much church music.

Vierling, George, was born in Frankenthal in 1820. He is a gifted and most accomplished musician, and the composer of numerous songs and choruses, besides instrumental music, including overtures and a symphony. One of his greatest works is "The Rape of the Sabines," written for chorus, solos and orchestra, which has contributed much to raise his reputation.

Villoteau, G. A., important writer on music. Accompanied Napoleon I. to Egypt in 1798, and investigated the origin and development of Egyptian and oriental music.

Vinae, V., 1835-1872. Bohemian composer, conductor and teacher. Wrote church and chamber music, and an opera.

Vinci, L. 1690-1734. Neapolitan opera composer and conductor of note.

Viola, a tenor violin, an instrument similar in tone and formation to the violin, but larger in size, and having a compass a fifth lower.

Viol da gamba (Ital. vē-ōl dŏ gäm'-bä). *Leg-viol*, an instrument formerly much used in Germany, but nearly obsolete. It was a little smaller than the violoncello, furnished with frets and five or six strings, and held between the legs in playing, hence its name.

Viola d'amore (Ital. vē-ō'-lä d'ä-mō'-rě). An instrument a little larger than the *viola*, furnished with frets and a greater number of strings, some above the fingerboard and some below. The name is also given to an organ stop of similar quality to the *gamba* or *salicional*.

ä *ale*, ä *add*, ü *arm*, ō *eve*, ŏ *end*, ī *ice*, ĭ *ill*, ō *old*, ŏ *odd*, ô *dove*, oo *moon*, ü *lute*, ŭ *but*, ü Fr. *sound*

72

Violin, a well known stringed instrument having four strings, and played with a bow. It is the most perfect musical instrument known, of brilliant tone and capable of every variety of expression. When, or by what nation this important instrument was first invented is not at present known.

Violoncello (Ital. vē-ō-lŏn-tshāl'-lō). The large or bass violin; the name is also applied to an organ stop of small scale and crisp tone.

Viola (Ital. vē-ō'-lä). A tenor or alto violin. Its four strings are c, g, d' and a'.

Violono (Ital. vē-ō-lō'-nō) or *Violon*, the double bass, the largest of the string family. The 'cello is the little violon. Violin is a feminine diminutive of viola.

Virginal, a small keyed instrument, much used about the time of Queen Elizabeth, and placed upon a table when played upon. It is supposed to have been the origin of the spinet, as the latter was of the harpsichord.

Virtuoso (Ital. vēr-too-ō'-zō). A skillful and masterly performer upon some instrument.

Vivier, E. Born 1821. French horn player and composer.

Vivo (Ital. vō'-vō). Animated, lively, brisk.

Vocalize (Ital. vō -kä-lēz). An exercise for the voice.

Vocalise, to practice vocal exercises, using vowels and the letter A sounded in the Italian manner (ä) for the purpose of developing the voice, and of acquiring skill and flexibility.

Voce (Ital. vō'-tshĕ). The voice.

Voce Flebile (Ital. vō-tshĕ flä'-bĕ-lĕ). A weeping voice.

Voce di Petto (Ital. vō'-tshĕ dē pāt'-tō). The chest voice, the lowest register of the voice.

Vogel. F. W. F., distinguished Norwegian organist and teacher. B. 1807.

Vogl. Heinrich. Born 1845. Bavarian tenor singer of high rank.

Vogl. Therese, wife of H. Born 1845. Also singer in Munich opera. Both she and her husband are admirable interpreters of the chief rôles in Wagner's operas.

Vieuxtemps, Henri, born in Belgium in 1820, is one of the most renowned violinists of the French school. He has composed much for his instrument, and is professor of the violin at the Brussels Conservatory.

Viotti, Giovanni Battista, 1753-1824. A renowned master of the violin and the founder of the modern school of violin playing. He wrote many concertos for the violin, and much chamber music.

Vittori. Loreto, a renowned Italian singer, composer and poet of the latter part of the 16th and the first part of the 17th centuries.

Vivaldi, Antonio, a distinguished Venetian violinist and composer of the latter half of the 17th century.

Vogl. J. M., 1794-1822. Distinguished opera singer in Vienna, who introduced many of Schubert's songs to the public.

Vogler, G. J. Abbé, 1749-1814. Theorist, composer and organist, much admired in his time, but of no great significance in his art.

Volante (Ital. vō-län'-tĕ). Flying; a light and rapid series of notes.

Volckmar, Wm., Dr., born 1812. Able pianist, organist, theorist and composer. His organ school has permanent value.

Volkmann, Robert, born 1815. One of the best living composers. Has written symphonies, chamber music, vocal and piano forte music.

Voss, Ch., born 1815. Piano teacher in Paris. Writer of popular pieces for piano-forte.

Vox (Lat. vŏx). Voice.

Vox humana (Lat. vŏx hū-mä'-nä). Human voice; an organ reed stop of 8 ft. tone, intended to imitate the human voice, which it sometimes does, though very imperfectly.

Vox Angelica (Lat. vŏx än-gĕl'-l-kä). An organ stop of 8 ft., usually a free reed.

Vuillaume. J. B., 1798-1875. The greatest of a large family of distinguished French violin makers.

Vulpius, M., 1560-1621. Cantor in Weimar, and composer of church music.

Von Weber, see Weber.

Volles Werk (Ger. fŏl'-lĕs värk). The full organ.

Voicing, the operation of improving the tone of reeds, pipes, or piano-hammers. In *reeds* this is done by bending the tongues in certain ways, so as to make the reed speak more quickly, and produce a better tone ; in *pipes*, by regulating the admission of the wind, the size of the mouth, etc. ; *pianos* are voiced by softening the hammers until harsh over-tones are suppressed. In all voicing the principal difficulty is to secure evenness or uniformity of quality.

Voix Celeste (Fr. vwä sä-lĕst'). An organ stop producing a wavy effect, on the same principal as the Unda Maris.

Volti Subito (Ital. vool'-tē soob'-ō-tō). Turn over quickly. In old music this or the initials V. S. frequently occur at the bottom of a page.

Vorspiel (Ger. fŏr'-spēl). A prelude, an introductory movement or overture.

Voluntary, an organ or choir piece introduced without announcement.

Wachtel, Theodore (väkh'-tĕl). Born 1824 in Hamburg. Was son of a coachman, and himself a coachman. Possesses an extraordinarily fine tenor voice, which he eventually trained and became one of the most admired opera singers in Europe.

Wagner, Johanna (Jachmann). Born 1828 niece of Richard Wagner. One of the finest dramatic singers of this century, distinguished equally as singer and actress.

Wagner. Richard, one of the greatest masters who has appeared in dramatic music. Born in 1813. See Chap. LI.

Wallace, Wm. Vincent, violinist, pianist and composer. Born in Ireland in 1814. His father was master of a military band, and the boy showed great aptitude for it, and at fifteen was successfully occupied in Dublin as a violinist. Then followed concert tours all over the world. His operas were "Maritana," composed in 1845, "Lurline" 1860, etc. He also composed a great number of piano pieces, many of which were popular in their day. Died 1865.

ă *ale*, ă *add*, ä *arm*, ē *eve*, ĕ *end*, ī *ice*, ĭ *ill*, ō *old*, ŏ *odd*, ô *dove*, oo *moon*, ū *lute*, ŭ *but*, ü *Fr. sound*

73

Walther von der Vogelweide, latter part of 12th century and first part of 13th. One of the greatest and most prolific of the Minnesingers.

Warren, George Wm., organist, composer, and teacher in New York, was born about 1830, is a popular composer of salon pieces for piano, songs, etc.

Wartel, Pierre F. (vär-těl). Born 1806. Distinguished French singing teacher. Has been also a fine tenor singer at the Grand Opera in Paris. Was master of Nillson, and many other prima donnas.

Wasielewsky, Joseph W. Born 1822. One of the first pupils to enter the Leipsic Conservatory. Pupil of Mendelssohn, Hauptmann and David. Excellent violinist. Best known in this country by his biography of Robert Schumann. Has written other equally valuable works.

Wauer, Karl (vowr), 1783-1857. Distinguished bass singer and actor at the Royal Opera in Berlin.

Webbe, Samuel, 1740-1824. Favorite English composer of glees and catches.

Weber, Carl Maria von (vä-bĕr), 1786-1826. One of the most important of the Romantic School of composers. His opera "Der Freischütz," opened a new epoch in that branch of composition. His instrumental compositions were also original, and many of them of very high rank. He was also a respected writer on musical subjects, a thorough musician, and an excellent pianist and conductor.

Weber, Constance, wife of Mozart and cousin of C. M. von Weber's father.

Weber, Dionys, 1771-1842, a highly respected Bohemian musician, teacher and composer, and one of the founders of the Prague Conservatory.

Weber, Gottfried, 1779-1839. A jurist of high rank, but still better known as a musician, teacher and composer, theorist and critic. His great work on musical composition has been translated into English.

Webster, J. P., an American melodist, and author of popular songs. Born about 1830, and died in Wisconsin in 1871.

Weckerlin, J. B. T. Born 1821. Praiseworthy French composer and music historian.

Weelkes, Thomas, distinguished English Madrigal composer of the latter part of the 16th century.

Wehle, Chas. Born 1825 in Prague. Piano virtuoso and composer. Lives in Paris, where he teaches and composes.

Weigl, Joseph, 1766-1846. Composer of operas and conductor in Vienna.

Weitzmann, Carl Friedrich, born 1808. Composer, teacher and theorist in Berlin. Best known by his theoretical and historical works. His "Manual of Musical Theory," translated by E. M. Bowman, is published in this country. D., 1880.

Wieck, Clara, see Clara Schumann.

Wieck, Marie, daughter of Fr. Wieck, and a distinguished pianist.

Wieck, Friedrich, 1785-1873. A most distinguished musician and teacher. Among his pupils were his daughter Clara, who became the wife of Robert Schumann, Schumann himself, Fritz Spindler, Anton Krause, Hans von Bülow, and other celebrated musicians. His two daughters, Clara and Marie, became celebrated pianists. His little book, "Piano and Song, how to teach, how to learn, and how to form a judgment of musical performances," should be in the hands of every teacher and student of music.

Wieprecht, W. F., 1802-1872. Prussian military bandmaster of great distinction, and an excellent composer of military music.

Wieniawsky, Henry, 1835-1880. A celebrated Polish violin virtuoso and composer. Not only were his technical attainments extraordinary, but his interpretative powers were of the first rank, and as he constantly strove to be a genuine artist rather than a mere executant, he commanded the highest respect.

Wieniawski, Joseph, brother of Henry, was born in 1837. He is a distinguished pianist, teacher and composer, and has rendered great service to his chosen art, especially in Moscow, where he taught for many years. He now lives in Warsaw.

Wilbye, John, was a distinguished English singing teacher and composer of madrigals at the end of the 16th and beginning of the 17th century.

Wilhelm, Carl, 1820-1873. A good German director of singing societies, and composer of much music, especially for male chorus. His most popular song is "The Watch on the Rhine."

Wilhem, Guillaume Louis Bocquillon, 1781-1842. A distinguished French singing teacher, composer, and writer of theoretical works. His instruction books are still prized.

Wilhelmj, August Emil Daniel Friedrich Victor, was born in Usingen, in 1845. He is the most popular violinist since Paganini. He is a virtuoso and artist of the highest rank, and is distinguished equally for his pure, broad, noble tone, the unsurpassable perfection of his execution, and his admirable interpretation of masters of all times and styles.

Willaert, Adrian, one of the most prominent musicians and composers of the 16th century. He was chapelmaster in St. Mark's Church in Venice, and was the founder of the Venetian school. He was a superior teacher and wrote a great amount of church music. His most celebrated pupils were Cyprian de Rore and Orlandus Lassus.

Willmers, Rudolph, was born in Berlin, in 1821. He was an excellent pianist, a pupil of Hummel. He was also a pupil of Fr. Schneider in theory, and became a thorough musician and a good composer. He died in 1878.

Winter, Peter von, 1754-1825. Bavarian conductor and opera composer of high reputation.

Wind-chest, that part of an organ which supports the pipes, and contains a windchamber and the valves and pallets, for supplying the pipes.

Wind-trunk, a large pipe for conveying wind from the bellows to a wind-chest.

Winterfeld, Carl G., 1784-1852. Distinguished jurist and a very prolific and reliable musical historian of Berlin.

Woelfl, Joseph, 1772-1814. Piano virtuoso and composer, known chiefly as a rival of Beethoven's in Vienna. His playing was much admired.

Wohlfahrt, Heinrich. Born 1797. Excellent teacher of the piano-forte, and author of numerous highly prized instruction and text books, which have had a wide circulation.

Wolf, a beat or dissonance in tuning, occasioned by the interference of imperfectly attuned vibrations. The sourness or dissonance of imperfectly attuned chords.

Wolff, Edward. Born 1816. Piano virtuoso and composer. Teacher in Paris.

Wolff, Heinrich. Born 1813. Violin virtuoso in Frankfort, and composer.

Wolff, Hermann. Born 1845. Composer and writer. Editor of the Berlin New Journal of Music.

Wolfram von Eschenbach, one of the greatest of the German Minne-singers. Died about 1220.

Wolfsohn, Carl, pianist, composer, conductor and indefatigable promoter of chamber music, was born in Germany in 1830. He came to this country about 1860, and settled in Philadelphia, where he gave chamber concerts for many years. In 1873 he came to Chicago and became the director of the Beethoven Society. Mr. Wolfsohn has three times played in public the entire series of Beethoven s 33 sonatas for piano-forte, and all the most important works of Chopin and Schumann.

Wollenhaupt, Herman A., a German pianist, and composer of popular salon pieces. Born at Skendlitz in 1827. Was a pupil of Hauptmann. Residing for several years in New York, where he died about 1865. Several of his pieces met with great success, the most famous of them being "The Whispering Winds," and "Valse Styrienne."

Work, Henry C., an American composer of popular songs, who, until 1861, was a journeyman printer. A lucky hit in a war-song led to the production of many more, which also were successful. Work is not a musician, and hence has not been able to develop his talent, as he otherwise might, and produce works of lasting value.

Zachau, Fr. W., 1663-1721. Excellent organist, composer and theorist. Was teacher of G. F. Händel, in Halle.

Zarlino, Giuseppe, 1517-1590. A renowned Venetian composer and theorist, chapel master at St. Mark's church. His theoretical works were of great importance, and mark the beginning of a new epoch.

Zart (Ger, tsärt). Tenderly, softly, delicately.

Zelenka, J. D., 1681-1745. Bohemian composer of church and instrumental music. Has a high reputation among connoisseurs.

Zellner, L. A. Born 1823. Theorist, composer and teacher, and Secretary of the Vienna Conservatory. A much honored musician.

Zelter, Carl F., 1758-1832. Professor in the Academy of Arts, and Director of the Singing Academie in Berlin. A composer of merit. Intimate friend of Goethe, and more or less acquainted with Schiller, Fichte, Hegel, Schleirmacher, Körner, Beethoven, Haydn, etc. The first teacher of Mendelssohn.

Ziegfeld, Florence, M. D., pianist and teacher, President of the Chicago Musical College,was born in Jever, in North Germany, in 1841, began his studies with Stiehl, and pursued them later at Leipsic, where he graduated in 1863. Came to Chicago in 1867, where he occupies a leading position.

Ziemlich (Ger. tsēm'-lĭkh). Tolerably, moderately.

Zingaresa (Ital. tsĕn-gä-rä'-zä). In the style of gypsy music.

Zithern, an instrument which may be called a compound of the harp and the guitar. The harmonies of the first named instrument are produced from it, and it possesses the sweetest notes pertaining to both, but not great compass.

Zwischen-spiel (Ger. tsvē-shĕn-spēl). Interlude played between the verses of a hymn.

ā ale, ă add, ä arm, ā eve, ĕ end, ī ice, ĭ ill, ō old, ŏ odd, ū dove, oo moon, û late, ŭ but, ü Fr. sound

NOTE. The thanks of the editor are due, and hereby tendered, to Prof. John C. Fillmore, of Milwaukee, for important assistance, amounting to the preparation of almost the entire biographical matter in the last twelve pages of this work.

ADDENDA.

A second edition of "How to Understand Music" being required much sooner than was expected, the opportunity is taken for remedying as far as possible the more noticeable omissions of the Dictionary. Several new biographical articles are added, and a large number of foreign words, principally German, which, although not generally recognized as strictly musical terms, are occasionally met with in the works of Beethoven, and very often in those of Schumann and the later German writers. As these terms are liable to embarrass students not familiar with German, it was thought advisable to include them here. In its present form, including the *addenda*, it is thought that this work includes all the terms and directions to be met with in the works of the classic and the principal modern writers. Many typographical errors of date in the biographical articles in the body of the work have also been corrected. The editor would take it as a favor if the reader will notify him by postal card of any errors he may happen to notice as he consults the work.

EVANSTON, ILL., Jan. 15, 1881.

Aber (Ger. ä -bĕr). But.

Accentuato (Ital. ät-tshän-too-ä -tō). Distinctly and strongly accented.

Accuratezza (Ital. äk-koo-rä-tät'-zä). Accuracy.

Aeussserst (Ger. ois´- sürst). Utmost, extreme.

Affetazione (Ital. äf-fĕt-tä-tsē-ō -nĕ). An artificial or affected style.

Afflitto (Ital. äf-flēt'-tō). Afflictedly, sorrowfully, with mournful expression.

Affrettando (Ital. äf-frĕt-tän'-dō). Hurrying, accelerating the time.

Africaine, L' (äf-rī-kān). Opera by Meyerbeer, 1849.

Agitirt (Ger. ä-gī-tĕrt). Agitated, hurried.

Aida (ää'-dä). Opera by Verdi, 1871.

Allargando (Ital. äl lär-gän -dō). Enlarging, broadening, *i. e.* more slowly and emphatically.

Allegramente (Ital. äl - lä - grä - män' - tĕ.) Gaily, joyfully, quickly.

Allegrissimo (Ital. äl-lä-grēs -sē-mō). Extremely quick and lively.

Alle (Ger. äl-lŏ). All.

Alternativo (Ital. äl-tĕr-nä-tē'-vō). Alternating one movement with another.

Amabilita (Ital. ä-mä-bē -lō-tä), Tenderness, amiability.

Ancora (Ital. än-kō -rä). Once more, repeat; also, yet, still.

Anfang (Ger. än' -fäng). Beginning.

Ankunft (Ger. än-koonft). Arrival, coming.

Ardamente (Ital. är-dä-män -tĕ). Ardently, with warmth.

Armonioso (Ital. är-mō-nē-ō -zō). Concordant, harmonious.

Arpa (Ital. är'-pä). The harp.

Arpeggiando (Ital. är-pād-jē-än'dō). Played in arpeggio, in imitation of the harp.

Aspiramente (Ital. äs-pē-rä-tä-män´-tĕ. From *aspirare*, to take breath audibly). With effort, with emotion.

Aufgeregt (Ger. ouf-gä-rēgt). Agitated.

Auflebend (Ger. ouf-lāb´-ĕnd). Reviving, returning to life; *a tempo*.

Aus (Ger. ous). From, out of.

Ausser (Ger. ous -sār). Out of, beside.

Ausdrucksvoll (Ger. ous -drooks-fōl). Expressive.

Ballmæssig ((Ger. bäl-mäs-sĭg). In dance movement.

Ballo (Ital. läl -lō). A dance or dance tune.

Battuta (Ital. bä-too -tä). A measure, in measured movement; *a battuta*, in correct time.

Belebt (Ger. bĕ-lābt'). Animated, sprightly.

Beschleunigen (Ger. bĕ-shlot -nō-ghĕn). To accelerate, to hasten.

Bestimmt (Ger. bĕs-tĭmt'). Distinct, determinate.

Bewegt (Ger. bĕ-vägt). Animated, rather fast.

Bewegung (Ger. bĕ - vä -goong). Motion, movement.

Bohemian Girl. Opera by Balfe, 1835.

Braham, John (brähm). A famous tenor singer, born in London, 1774. Studied with Leoni and Rauzzini, made his debut in 1796, In opera B, was for many years the composer of his own parts, which were universally popular. Had great versatility, and wrote many extremely successful songs. Died 1856.

Brioso (Ital. brē-ō -zō). Lively, vigorously.

Bull, Ole Bornemann, the Norwegian violinist, was born at Bergen, Feb. 5, 1810. He was designed for the church, but his love for music, and his success in a concert given during his career as a university student, determined his devoting himself entirely to music. From about 1830 his life was spent in concert tours throughout Europe, and after 1852 in most parts of the U. S. He had a home at

Cambridge, Mass., as well as at Madison, Wis., and Bergen, Norway, and lived by turns in all of them. He died greatly beloved by a large circle of friends, in 1880. As a violinist he was very eminent, and extremely popular with the common people.

Calmandosi (Ital. käl-män-dō -zē). Becoming gradually more calm.

Cantando (Ital. kän-tän -dō). In a melodious, singing style.

Capricciosamente (Ital. kä-prē-tshō-ō-zä-män'-tē). Capriciously.

Carmen. Opera by Bizet, 1875.

Cary. Annie Louise. This eminent and charming contralto was born in Maine in 1846. Her fine voice early obtained for her a local recognition, and she pursued serious vocal studies with Mr. John Dennett at Portland. After some years successful experience as a concert singer, she went abroad and studied in Paris and Italy. Miss Cary attained her earliest eminence as an oratorio singer. Since 1869 or 1870 she has been extremely successful in English and Italian opera. Her voice is of great purity and depth, and beautifully cultivated; and her phrasing is refined and satisfactory. She is one of the greatest singers of our time.

Chaque Mesure (Fr. chäk mā-zūr). Each measure; frequently used for the pedal in piano forte music.

Clarino (Ital. klä-rē'-nō), *Clarion.* A small, or octave trumpet; also a 4 ft. organ reed stop, tuned an octave above the trumpet stop. The term is also used to indicate the trumpet parts in a full score.

Coda (Ital. kō -dä). The *end;* a few measures added near the end of a piece of music, to make a more effective close.

Corrente (Ital. kōr-rän'-tē) or *Coranto.* An old dance tune in 3-2 or 3-4 time.

Crouch, F. Nicholls, a composer of many popular songs and ballads during the second quarter of the present century, of which the best known is " Kathleen Mavourneen." Came to America in 1845.

Damnation of Faust. Opera by Berlioz, 1846.

Damrosch, Leopold, a distinguished violinist and musical director, was born in Posen, in 1832, where his musical studies were begun. Was educated in medicine at Berlin, and in 1854 was a practicing physician in his native town. In 1855 and 1856 he appeared at Magdeburg and Berlin as solo violinist, with great success. He presently became conductor at the Stadt theater in Posen. In 1871 he came to New York as conductor of the "Arion" Society, and has since resided there. Is at present (1881) conductor of the Oratorio Society, of symphony concerts, etc. As a conductor D. is distinguished for energy and vigor of conception. Is a warm advocate of the Liszt-Wagner " music of the future," although a successful exponent of the classic. Is also a composer of violin and orchestral works.

Delicatissimamente (Ital. dēl-ē-kä-tē'-sē-mä-män'-tē). With extreme delicacy.

Deux (Fr. dü). Two.

Difficile (Ital. dē-fē'-tshē-lē). Difficult.

Distanza (Ital. dēz-tän-tsä). Distance, space between.

Distintamente (Ital. dēz-tēn tä-män -tē). Clearly, distinctly.

Divoto (Ital. dē-vō tō). Devoutly, solemnly.

Doch (Ger. dōkh). Yet.

Doctor of Alcantara. Opera by Eichberg, 1862.

Due (Ital. doo -ē). Two ; in two parts.

Durchaus (Ger. dūrkh'-ous). Throughout.

Eilend (Ger. il'-ēnd). Quick, speedy.

Einfach (Ger. in'-fäkh). Simple, plain, unornamented.

Einigen (Ger. in'-I-ghēn). Some, any.

Elegantemente (Ital. ēl-ē-gän-tē-män'-tē). Elegantly, gracefully.

Eli. Oratorio by Costa, 1855.

Energicamente (Ital. ēn ēr-jē-kä-män -tē). Energetically, forcibly.

Energisch (Ger. ēn-ār-ghīsh). Energetic, with emphasis.

Entschlossenheit (Ger. ent-shlōs -s'n-hīt) Resoluteness, firmness.

Ermattet (Ger. är-mät -tēt). Growing faint, weary.

Erstes (Ger. ērst'-ēs). First.

Erwachen (Ger. är-väkh -ēn). To awaken, to be aroused.

Espressione (Ital. ēs-prēs-sē-ō -nē). Expression, feeling.

Essipoff, Annette, virtuoso pianist, was born in Russia in 1853, studied principally with Mr. Leschetitzki, whom she afterwards married, and made her debut with distinguished success in 1870 or '71. She visited America in 1875, where she charmed all hearers by her playing no less than by her consummate virtuosity. M me Essipoff resides chiefly at Vienna, and plays in all the European capitals.

Estinto (Ital. ēs-tēn -tō). Becoming extinct, dying away.

Estremamente (Ital. ēs-trä-mä-män'-tē). Extremely.

Fatinitza (fä-tīn-ēt -zä). Opera by Suppé.

Ferne (Ger. fär-nē). Distance.

Festlich (Ger. fēst -līkh). Festive, solemn.

Feurig (Ger. foi -rīg). Fiery, ardent, passionate.

Fillmore, John C., a highly esteemed musician, piano teacher and critic, was born in Connecticut, 1843. Studied at Oberlin and Leipsic. Was for 9 years professor of music in Ripon College, Wis., and now resides in Milwaukee.

Folgen (Ger. fōl'-ghēn). To follow. The following, succeeding.

Fortsetzung (Ger. fört'-set-soong). A continuation.

Forza (Ital. fört'sä). Force, strength, power.

Frei (Ger. frī). Free.

Gebunden (Ger. ghē-boon -d'n). Connected, syncopated.

Gehender (Ger. gä -hēn-dēr). Going.

Gehalten (Ger. ghē-hält -ēn). Held, sustained.

ā *ale,* ä *add,* ä *arm,* ē *eve,* ō *end,* ĭ *ice,* ĭ *ill,* ō *old,* ŏ *odd,* ō *dove,* oo *moon,* ū *lute,* ŭ *but,* ü *Fr. sound*

77

Gemessener (Ger. gĕ-mĕs´-sĕn-ĕr). Measured, precise.

Gesang (Ger. ghĕ-säng). Singing ; the art of singing, a song, melody.

Gesangvoll (Ger. ghĕ-säng´-fōl). Songful; in a singing style. *Cantabile*.

Getragen (Ger. ghĕ-trä-g'n). Well-sustained, carried.

Giocondo (Ital. jō-kŏn´-dō). Cheerful, gay, merry.

Glissando (Ital, glēs-sän-dō). Sliding. A method of playing a run by sliding the finger rapidly along the keyboard of the pianoforte, or by sliding the finger along the violin string.

Gran (Ital. grän). Great, grand.

Granziosamente (Ital. grä-tsō-ō-zä-män-tĕ). Gracefully, smoothly.

Grosse (Ger. grōs-sĕ). Major, referring to intervals ; also, grand in style.

Gut (Ger. goot). Good, well, sufficiently.

Halten (Ger. häl-tĕn). To hold back, check.

Hastig (Ger. häs-tĭg). Hurrying, hastening.

Hastings, Dr. Thomas, one of the pioneers in American music, was born in Washington, Ct., 1784. In some way he discovered his talent for music, and began to teach in 1806. His first book, *Musica Sacra*, was published in 1817, and in 1822 his "Dissertation on Musical Taste." He was the sole or associate editor of some 16 books of church music. As a man he was studious, retiring and lovable. He was author of several hymns which are still in use.

Hauptsatz (Ger. houpt - sätz). Principal theme or subject; the motive or leading idea.

Heimlich (Ger. hīm´-līkh). Secretly, quietly, calmly.

Hoechst (hĕkst), Highest, utmost.

Huebsch (Ger. heebsh). Pretty, handsome.

Imperioso (Ital. ĕm-pā-rē-ō-zō). Imperious, pompous.

Improvisata (Ital. ĕm prō-vē-zä´-tä). Improvised ; in a fluent and off-hand style.

Inconsolabile (Ital. ĕn-kōn-sō-lä-bē-lĕ).

Innere (Ger. ĕn -nĕr-ĕ). Inner ; as the inner voices, or parts.

Innigkeit (Ger. ĕn -nĭg-kīt). Inwardness, feeling.

Innigsten (Ger. ĕn -nĭgs-tĕn). Most fervent, most devout.

Intimo (Ital. ĕn -tē-mō). Inward feeling

Introduzione (Ital. ĕn-trō-doo-tsē-ō -nĕ). An introduction.

Inversione (Ital. ĕn-vĕr-sē-ō -nĕ). Inversion.

Jagdlied (Ger. yägd´-leed). Hunting song.

Jeden (Ger, yä -dĕn). Each, every.

Joseffy, Raffaele (yō-sĕf -fi). Virtuoso pianist, was born at Miskolcs, Hungary, in 1852. He pursued his more advanced studies with Moscheles at Leipsic, and afterwards with Tausig. He made his debut in 1870, and at once attracted attention by the daintiness, uniform crispness, and brilliancy of his playing. His technique is superb, and his phrasing refined and musical He visited America in 1879.

where he has been very successful. He is rather a *genre* pianist, a wonderfully fine performer of small pieces, than an interpreter of broad and deep works.

Klagend (Ger. klä´-g'nd). Plaintive.

Kraft (Ger. kräft). Power, strength, energy.

Kraftig (Ger. kräf -tĭg). Powerful, vigorous, full of energy.

Kuerzung (Ger. kür´-tsoong). Abbreviation, shortening.

Laeva (Lat. lä´-vä). The left ; the left hand.

Lang, B. J., distinguished pianist, organist, conductor and teacher, was born at Salem, Mass., in 1840. Became organist in church at the age of 11. In 1858 became organist of the "Handel and Haydn" Society, of Boston, a position he still holds. Is also conductor of the "Cecilia" and "Apollo" Societies, and as such has brought out in Boston a brilliant list of master works, embracing the principal choral works of Schumann, Mendelssohn, Beethoven, etc., and in 1880 Berlioz's "Damnation of Faust," for the first time in America. Mr. Lang occupies a high social position in Boston, where he has so long held leading rank as concert pianist, piano teacher and musical educator.

Largamente (Ital. lär-gä-män -tĕ). Largely, fully ; in a full, free, broad style of performance.

Lebendig (Ger. lā´-bĕn-dĭg). Lively, quick.

Lebhaftigkeit (Ger. lāb-häf-tĭg-kīt). Liveliness, vivacity.

Leggendario (Ital. lĕd -jĕn -där´-Io). A legend.

Leggerezza (Ital. lĕd-jĕr-āt´-tsä). Lightness and agility.

Legno (Ital. län -yō). Wood ; *col legno*, with the bow stick.

Leicht (Ger. līkht). Light, easy, facile.

Ligato (Ital. lē-gä -tō). See Legato.

Linda di Chamouni (dō-tshä -moo-nē). Opera in 3 acts, by Donizetti, 1842.

Lungu (Ital. loon -gä). Long.

Lustig (Ger. loos -tĭg). Merrily, cheerfully, gaily.

Magic Flute, The (Ger. *Die Zauberflöte*, Ital. *Il Flauto Magico*). Opera in 4 acts by Mozart, 1791.

Mal (Ger. mäl). Times ; 20 *mal*, twenty times, etc.

Marcando (Ital mär-kän -dō). } Marked,
Marcato (Ital. mär-kä´-tō). } accented, well pronounced.

Marcatissimo (Ital. mär - kä - tēs - sē - mō). Very strongly marked.

Mayo, Oscar, was born in Germany in 1838. Studied music with Fesca, came to this country in 1860, and resides at Evanston, Ill. Is a piano teacher, a good musician, and a prolific composer of instructive and pleasing pieces

Mehr (Ger. mär) More.

Mehrere (Ger. mā´-rä-rĕ). More ; comparative of preceding.

Mephistopheles. Opera by Arrigo Boito, 1875

Merz, Karl, a prolific composer of piano music, songs, etc., and piano teacher. Was born in Germany in 1836, and since 1861 professor of music in Oxford Female College, Ohio. Is editor of Brainard's Musical World, and one of the most instructive and widely-respected writers upon music in this country.

Midsummer Nights' Dream. Music by Mendelssohn, consisting of Overture, 1826, Nocturne, and 11 other numbers, 1843.

Mirella. Opera by Gounod, 1864.

Mit (Ger. mĭt). With, by.

Möglich (Ger. mŏg'-lĭkh). Possible.

Monk, Wm. H., organist, and composer and arranger of church music, was born in London in 1823. In 1874 was made professor of vocal music in King's College, and occupies various educational relations. Was one of the editors of "Hymns, Ancient and Modern."

Moonlight Sonata. A name often, but foolishly, applied to Beethoven's sonata in C sharp, Op. 27, No. 2, composed in 1801.

Morendo (Ital. mō-rän -dō). Dying away, gradually diminishing in tone and time.

Mose in Egitto ("Moses in Egypt"). An oratorio or sacred opera by Rossini, 1818.

Moses. An oratorio by A. B. Marx, 1841.

Motiv (Fr. mō-tēv). Motive. See Chaps. i and x.

Moto (Ital. mō -tō). Motion, movement; *con moto*, with motion, rather quick.

Mountain Sylph. Opera by John F. Barnett.

Movement. Manner or rate of going. Hence employed as name for any piece of music, or part of a piece, so far as it continues in the same tempo. Thus a sonata has three or four movements. A "number" (as in opera or other dramatic work) frequently consists of several movements, which in performance are closely connected.

M. S. *Mano sinistra*, the left hand.

Munter (Ger. moon-tĕr). Lively; sprightly.

Nachlassend (Ger. năhk-lăs-sĕnd). Slackening.

Nachtlager in Granada. Das (Ger. näkht-lä-ghĕr in Grä-nä -dä). Opera by Kreutzer, 1834.

Nach-und-nach (Ger. näkh oond näkh). By little and little, by degrees.

Noch (Ger. nōkh). Yet, still, more.

Oberstimme (Ger. ō -bĕr-stĭm -mĕ). Treble, upper voice part.

Ombre, L' (Fr. lŏm'-br). Opera by Flotow, 1869.

Orphée aux Enfers. Opera in 2 acts, by Offenbach, 1858.

Orphée et Euridice. Opera in 3 acts, by Gluck, 1774.

Orpheus, or Orfeo. Opera by Monteverde, 1607. Also by Gluck, 1762.

Othello (Ital. *Otello*, ō-täl -lō). Opera by Rossini, 1816.

Overblowing is the production of a higher than the natural tone of a pipe, by forcing the wind. In the flute the upper octaves are legitimately so produced. In the organ it is apt to arise when too much wind is pumped into the bellows, to prevent which a safety-valve is provided.

Paine, John Knowles, organ virtuoso, composer, and professor of music in Harvard College, was born at Portland, Me., about 1840. Educated in Boston and with Haupt at Berlin, and since about 1869 professor at Harvard. Is author of an oratorio, "St. Peter," an elaborate and original work, performed by the Handel and Haydn Society in 1874, two symphonies, string quartettes, a mass, etc.

Parker, J. C. D., pianist, organist and composer, was born at Boston about 1836. Educated there and at Leipsic, and for fifteen years has occupied a leading position in the musical life of his native city. Is organist at Trinity Church, and author of a cantata or oratorio, "Redemption Hymn," part-songs, etc.

Passione (Ital. päs-sē-ō -nĕ). Passion, feeling.

Pausa (Ital. (pou-zä). A pause.

Pedale (Ital. pā-dă -lō). Pedal. The pedal keyboard of an organ. The abbreviation "ped." requires the use of the pedal.

Per (Ital. pār). For, by, through, in.

Petersilen, Carlyle, pianist and head of a school of music in Boston, was born in Boston in 1838, learned the piano with his father, who was a good teacher, and afterwards studied abroad. P. has rarely appeared in public, but since about 1870 has been prominently engaged as a piano teacher in Boston.

Phantastisch (Ger. fän-täs -tĭsh). Fantastic, fantastically.

Pianissimo (Ital. pē-än-ēs'-sē-mō). Extremely soft.

Piccolo (Ital. pē -kō-lō). Small, little. A small flute. Also a 2 ft. organ stop, of wood pipes.

Piu-e-Piu (Ital. pē-oo ā pē-oo). More and more.

Plaidy, Louis (plī -dy) celebrated teacher of the pianoforte and author of a book of "Technics," was born in 1810 at Wemsdorf. He was for many years a professor in the Leipsic Conservatory, retiring about 1871. He died in Grimma, 1874.

Pochetto (Ital. pō-kă t-tō). A little.

Pochissimo (Ital. pō-kēs s-sē-mō). A very little, as little as possible.

Poet and Peasant. Opera by Suppé.

Poi-a-poi (Ital. pō-ē ä pō-ē.) By degrees.

Popolare (Ital. pō-pō-lă -rē). Popular.

Postillon de Lonjumeau, Le. Opera by Adam, 1836.

Precis (Ger. prä-sēs). Precise, precisely.

Precedente (Ital. prä-tshē-dän -tē). Preceding.

Preciosa (prä-tshē-ō -zä). Music to drama, by Weber, 1820.

Precipitandosi (Ital. prä-tshē-pē-tän-dō -zē).

Precipitoso (Ital. prä-tshē-pē-tō -zō). Hurrying, precipitate.

Preciso (Ital prä-tshē -zō). Precise, exact.

Prestissimo (Ital. präs-tēs -sē-mō). Very quickly, as fast as possible.

ă *ale*, ă *add*, ä *arm*, ō *eve*, ĕ *end*, ĭ *ice*, ĭ *ill*, ō *old*, ŏ *odd*, ō *dove*, oo *moon*, ū *lute*, ŭ *but*, ü *Fr. sound*

Principio Ital. prēn-tshē -pĭ-ō). The principal, the leading idea or part.

Prophete, Le (prō-fāt). Opera by Meyerbeer; libretto by Scribé, 1849.

Puritani, I (ē poo-rē-tä'-nē). Opera by Bellini, 1835.

Quatre (Fr. kätr). Four.

Rasch (Ger. räsh). Swift, spirited.

Rauschend (Ger. roush'-ĕnd). Rushing, roaring.

Repetizione (Ital. rā-pĕ-tē-tsē-ō'-nĕ). Repetition.

Rice, Fenelon B., Mus. Doc., director of the Oberlin Conservatory of Music, President of American Music Teachers' Association, was born at Green, Ohio, in 1841, educated at Hillsdale College, Mich., graduated at Boston Music School in 1863, entered Leipsic Conservatory in 1867, was appointed Professor of Music in Oberlin College and Director of the Conservatory in 1871, where he has succeeded in building up a fine school, and exercises a commanding influence in favor of good music and sound musical education.

Rienzi (rē-änt'-sē). Opera by Wagner, 1840.

Rigoletto (rē-gō-lāt'-tō). Opera by Verdi, 1851.

Rigore (Ital. rē-gō'-rĕ). Rigor, strictness, firmness.

Rilasciando (Ital. rē-lä-shō-än -dō). Relaxing the time.

Risoluto (Ital. rē-zō-loo -tō). Resolute, bold.

Risvegliato (Ital. rēs-vēl-yō-ä -tō). Awakened, re-animated.

Ritardare (Ital. rē-tär-dä -rĕ). To retard, or slacken the time.

Ritenente (Ital. rē-tē-nān-tē). Detaining, holding back the time.

Ritmo (Ital. rēt - mo). Rhythm, cadence, measure.

Robert le Diable. Opera by Meyerbeer, libretto by Scribé, 1831.

Romeo and Juliet. Opera by Bellini, 1829. Also a symphony by Berlioz, 1840.

Root, George Frederick, Mus. Doc., one of the most distinguished and popular of American song writers, was born in Sheffield, Mass., Aug. 30, 1820. At an early age he became a pupil of Dr. Lowell Mason and Mr. Geo. Jas. Webb. In 1845 he became teacher of singing in Rutger's and the Spingler Female Schools in New York, and organist of Mercer St. Church, where he remained for ten years. His first popular song was "Hazel Dell," which was sung and whistled the country through. This was followed by "Rosalie, the Prairie Flower," etc. In 1860 he became head of the music firm of Root & Cady in Chicago, where he still resides. During the war the publications of this house were universally current. Mr. Root wrote many battle songs, elementary singing books, cantatas, etc.

Root, Frederic W., son of the preceding, was born 1846, in Boston. Is a prominent teacher of singing, composer and writer about music, in Chicago.

Saiten (Ger. sī'-t'n). Timbrel, strings of a violin.

Sanft (Ger. sänft). Soft, mild, smooth.

Santley, an eminent English baritone singer, born in 1838.

Schalkhaft (Ger. shälk -häft). Waggishly, playfully, capriciously.

Schlummerlied (Ger. shloom - mĕr - leed). Slumber song.

Schluss (Ger. shloos). The end, conclusion.

Schnell (Ger. shnĕll). Quickly, rapidly.

Schneller (Ger. shnĕl'-lĕr). Quicker, faster.

Schwacher (Ger. shvä -kĕr). Fainter, softer.

Schwangesange (Ger. shvän -gĕ-säng-ĕ). "Swan Songs;" title of a set of songs by Schubert.

Schumann, Clara (Clara Wieck), the greatest lady pianist who has yet appeared, was born Sep. 13, 1819, at Leipsic, and learned piano playing from her father. She made her first public appearance as pianist at the age of 9, and three years later made an extended and highly successful concert tour. In 1840 she was married to Robert Schumann, the composer. M'me Schumann has resided mainly at Düsseldorf, and as late as the end of the year 1880 played in public in various parts of Europe with the greatest success. Her technique is remarkable, and the artistic quality of her playing unapproachable; in spite of her age, she still plays with great fire and feeling.

Sciolto (Ital. shō-ōl -tō). Free, light.

Scioltamente (Ital. shē - ōl - tä - mān'- tē). With freedom, agility; easily, the notes being rather detached than legato.

Secco (Ital. sāk'-kō). Dry, unornamented, chord without arpeggio.

Secondo (Ital. sā-kōn'-dō). Second, a second.

Segno (Ital. sān'-yō). A sign: *al segno,* return to the sign; *dal segno,* repeat from the sign.

Segue (Ital. sā-gwĕ). Now follows, as follows; also, go on, in a similar manner.

Seguente (Ital. sĕ-gwän -tē). Following, next.

Sehr (Ger. sār). Very, much, extremely.

Sehnsuchtsvoll (Ger. sān'-sookht-fōl).

Seite (Ger. sī'-tĕ). Side, page, line.

Selon (Fr. sĕ-lōn). According to.

Semiramide (sā-mē-rä-mī -dē). Opera by Gluck, 1748; Meyerbeer, 1819; Rossini, 1823.

Semplice (Ital. säm-plē -tshĕ). Simple, pure, plain.

Sempre (Ital. säm -prĕ). Always, continually.

Sentimento (Ital. sĕn-tē-mān'-tō). Feeling, sentiment, delicate expression.

Sforzando (Ital. sfōr-tsān - dō). }
Sforzato (Ital. sfōr-tsä -tō). } Forced, one particular note or chord to be emphasized.

Sincerità (Ital. sēn-sā - rē - tä). Sincerity, simplicity.

Singbar (Ger. sīng-bār). That may be sung.

Singend (Ger. sīng -ĕnd). In singing style.

Sino (Ital. sē -nō). To, as far as, until.

Slentare (Ital. slĕn-tä -rĕ). To slacken.

Sonnambula, La. Opera by Bellini, 1831.

Spielend (Ger. speel -ĕnd). Playing.

Spieler (Ger. speel -ĕr). Player.

Staccatissimo (Ital. stäk-kä-tēs'-sē-mō). Very much detached, as staccato as possible.
Stark (Ger. stärk). Strong, loud, vigorous.
Staerke (Ger. stär'-kĕ). Vigor, force, energy.
Steigenden (Ger. stī-ghĕnd-ĕn). Ascending.
Stimme (Ger. stĭm'-mĕ). The voice, sound; also, the sound-post in a violin, etc.; also, a part in vocal or instrumental music; also, an organ stop.
Straff (Ger. sträff). Extended, full.
String Band. A band of stringed instruments only.
Subito (Ital. soo'-bē-tō). Quickly, immediately, at once.
Sussurando (Ital. soos-soo-rän'-dō). Whispering, murmuring.
Takt (Ger. täkt). Time, measure.
Tannhäuser (tän'-hois-ĕr). Opera in 5 acts, by Wagner.
Thayer, Eugene W., organist, composer and teacher, was born in Mendon, Mass., in 1838, studied in Boston and afterward in Berlin. Made a successful concert journey in Germany as virtuoso organist, and has since occupied various prominent positions in Boston, where he founded his Organ Studio in 1875. Is composer of a mass, many organ works, a large method, etc., etc.
Thorough Bass. The art of representing chord-successions by means of bass notes, and figures giving the accompanying intervals; the art of playing from such a bass. Hence, often used as equivalent to the word Harmony.
Tie. A curved line connecting two successive notes of the same pitch, to show that the second is a continuation of the first, and therefore is simply prolonged.
Ton (Ger. tōn). Tone, sound, voice melody; also, accent, stress; also, pitch of any note as to its acuteness or gravity; also, the key or mode.
Tornando (Ital. tŏr-nän'-dō).
Tosto (Ital. tōs'-tō). Quick, swift, rapid.
Tower of Babel. Sacred opera by Rubinstein, 1875.
Tranquillo (Ital. trän-kwēl'-lō). Tranquility, calmness, quietness.
Tre corde (Ital. trä kŏr'-dĕ). Three strings. Means that the soft pedal (one string) must no longer be held down.
Tristan and Isolde. Opera by Wagner, 1859.
Trois (Fr. trwä). Three.
Trompette (Fr. trōnh-pāt). A trumpet; also, a trumpeter; also, a reed stop in an organ.
Troppo (Ital. trōp'-pō). Too much.
Umkehrung (Ger. oom'-kä-roong). Inversion.
Umore (Ital. oo-mō'-rĕ). Humor, caprice, whim.
Und (Ger. oond). And.
Ungeduldig (Ger. oon-ghĕ-dool'-dĭgh). Impatiently.
Unit of Time. The time occupied by a single rhythmical pulsation; the primary element of the measure; a beat. See chap. vii.

Variazioni (Ital. vä-rē-ä-tsē-ō-nē). Variations.
Verlauf (Ger. fĕr-louf). The lapse, progression, what follows.
Verschiebung (Ger. fĕr-shē-boong). Delay, lingering, shifting. In German music, the soft pedal.
Viel (Ger. fēl). Much, a great deal.
Viertel (Ger. fēr-t'l). Quarter note.
Vigore (Ital. vē-gō-rĕ). Vigor.
Vigoroso (Ital. vē-gō-rō-zō). Vigorous, bold, energetic.
Vivace (Ital. vē-vä-tshĕ). Lively, quickly.
Vivacissimo (Ital. vē-vä-tshēs-sē-mō). Very lively, extremely vivacious.
Vivacita (Ital. vē-vä-tshē-tä). Vivacity, liveliness.
Vivente (Ital. vē-vän'-tĕ). Animated, lively.
Volkslied (Ger. fŏlks'-lēd). A people's song. A simple and natural melody.
Volkston (Ger. fŏlks'-tōn). People's song; a simple, natural melody.
Volta (Ital. vŏl'-tä). Time; also, an old air peculiar to an Italian dance of the same name.
Vorher (Ger. fŏr-hĕr). Before, formerly.
Vorigen (Ger. fŏr-ē-ghĕn). Former, preceding.
Vortrag (Ger. fŏr-träg'). Execution, delivery, the act of uttering.
Vorzutragen (Ger. fŏrt-zoo-trä ghĕn). To deliver, to utter.
Walkuere. Die (väl-keer'-ĕ). "The Valkyrie," opera by Wagner, 1855.
Warren, Samuel P., organ virtuoso and composer, was born in Montreal, in 1841, early showed unusual talent for the organ, his father being an organ builder. Held position as church organist at the age of 12. In 1861 he began his studies in Berlin with Haupt, Gustav Schumann, and Wieprecht. On his return to America, after one year in Montreal, he removed to New York in 1865 as organist of Grace Church, where he has since resided. W. is one of the greatest organists of our time, his playing being remarkable for refinement and musical quality no less than for ease and remarkable technique. His repertoire is very large. He is composer of many original compositions, as well as arrangements.
Webb, Geo. James, teacher of singing and organist, was born in Wiltshire, England, in 1803, studied music in childhood (although intended for the church), learning not only the pianoforte and organ, but also singing, harmony and the violin. In 1830 he came to America and settled in Boston, where he became colaborer with Dr. Lowell Mason in teaching and the production of musical works, many of which were very useful and successful in their day. The Boston Academy of Music was founded in 1836, with Messrs. Mason and Webb at its head. W. was one of the earliest conductors of symphony and oratorio performances in Boston, and for many years he held the highest rank there as teacher of the piano and singing. In 1870 he removed to Orange, N. J., and commenced his teaching in New York. He now resides (1881) in New York, and is still active.

Weich (Ger. vĭkh). Minor, in respect to keys and mode.

Weiter (Ger. vī -tĕr). More distant, broader.

Wenig (Ger. vān'-ĭg). Little.

Whiting, George E., organist and composer, was born at Holliston, Mass., in 1837, studied abroad in 1862 and 1874, between which times he held good positions as organist in Boston. In 1878 was appointed organist of the Cincinnati Music Hall, a position he still holds. Has composed important works for organ, as well as for chorus and orchestra. The best of these, "The Tale of the Viking," competed for the $1,000 prize in 1880, and missed it by one vote. W. is an original and versatile musician.

Whitney, Myron W., the distinguished basso, was born in Mass., in 1833. His magnificent voice attracted attention as early as 1855. He studied in Boston and afterward spent some time abroad, returning to this country in 1868, where he has ever since held the highest rank as an interpreter of the bass roles in oratorio. W. is in every way a great singer, and an artist of the highest rank.

Wie (Ger. vē). How, as.

Wieder (Ger. vē -dĕr). Again, anew, a second time.

Wiegenlied (Ger. vē'-ghĕn-leed). Cradle song.

Wind Band. A band of wind instruments—flutes, oboes, clarinets, bassoons and the brass.

Wood. The "wood," in English musical speech, includes all wind instruments except the brass.

Zampa. Opera by Herold, 1831.

Zeffroso (Ital. zĕf-fĕ-rō'-zō).

Zeichen (Ger. tsī -k'n). A musical sign, note, or character.

Zeitmass (Ger. tsīt'-mäss). Time, measure.

Zerrahn, Carl (tzĕr-rähn), the distinguished conductor, was born in Mecklenburg-Schwerin, in 1826. Went in 1848 to London with orchestra, "The Germania Musical Society," gave concerts for three months, then they came to America and traveled about for six years, giving concerts all over the U. S. and Canada. Z settled in Boston in 1854, was elected conductor of the Handel and Haydn Society, which position he has he'd ever since. Is also conductor of Harvard Symphony Concerts since their beginning in 1864, teacher of voice, harmony and the art of conducting in the N. E. Conservatory, conducts the annual musical festival in Worcester, and various other musical organizations.

Zegernd (Ger. tsō'-ghĕrnd). A continual retarding of the time.

Zu (Ger. tsoo) At, by, in, to, unto.

Zurueckhaltung (Ger. tsoo-rük-häl'-toong) Retarding, keeping back.

Zuspielen (Ger. tsoo- spĕl'ĕn). To play.

Zweimal (Ger tsvī -mäl) Twice.

ā ale, ä add, ä arm, ō eve, ŏ end, ī ice, ĭ ill, ō old, ŏ odd, ō dove, oo moon, ū lute, ŭ but, ü Fr. sound

(APPENDIX.)

Synopsis of Pitch Notation.

(Prepared expressly for this work.)

SECTION FIRST. PITCH.

Pitch is represented by the lines and spaces of the staff. These are called degrees. There are as many lines and spaces used as there are diatonic degrees in the scale of the music represented. For ordinary use the staff consists of five lines and the spaces belonging to them, chosen from any convenient part of the so-called GREAT STAFF of eleven lines. Pitches above or below this compass are represented by means of short or *leger* lines, and when in the highest or lowest pitches these leger lines become too numerous to be easily recognized by the eye, the abbreviation 8va......, is employed, as shown below at (*B*.)

GREAT STAFF OF ELEVEN LINES.

Showing the relation and pitch of the various Clefs and Staves used in Pianoforte and Vocal Music, and in Orchestral Scores; together with the letters indicating absolute pitch.

CHROMATIC SIGNS.

The chromatic signs are the ♯, ✕, ♭, ♭♭ and ♮. The sharp ♯ indicates an elevation of a semitone; it is applied only to natural degrees (see *a* below.) The double-sharp ✕ or ✖ indicates an elevation equal to two semitones; applied to "sharp" degrees. (See *b* below.) The flat ♭ indicates a depression equal to a semitone; applied only to natural degrees. (See *c* below.) The double flat, ♭♭, indicates a depression equal to two semitones; applied only to flat degrees. (See *d* below.) The ♮, restores a staff-degree to its "natural" condition and cancels any of the previous signs. (See *e* below.) In restoring a single sharp or flat after a double one, it is necessary to use a natural to cancel the double sharp or flat, and a sharp or flat to restore the degree to its desired condition. (See *e*.)

SYNOPSIS OF PITCH NOTATION.

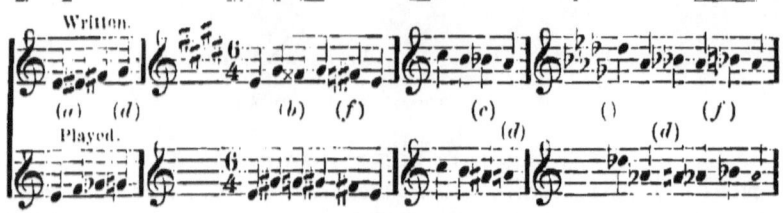

SIGNATURES.

Sharps or flats placed at the beginning to indicate the key, are called signatures. The sharps or flats so placed not only effect the degrees on which they are placed throughout the staff, but apply also to the octaves above and below on the same staff. In printed music the signature is repeated at the beginning of every line. In manuscript music the clefs and signatures are frequently omitted, except at the beginning of each piece or page. Example of staves with signatures and names of staff-degrees.

ACCIDENTALS.

1. An accidental affects all notes following it on the same staff degree in the same measure.
2. When the last note of one measure is affected by an accidental and the following measure begins with a note on the same degree, the accidental applies to that note also, but not to any that occur after a different tone has intervened in the same voice.

3. Accidentals are played as written. A single sharp or flat on a note already sharped or flatted in the signature, is not double-sharped or flatted by the single accidental, but only singly, the accidental having been introduced for precaution. See (*g*) below.

MARKS OF ABBREVIATION.

In order to save space, repetitions of groups of notes are sometimes indicated by marks of abbreviation, as at *k* above.

ARPEGGIO.

A tremolando effect in chords is indicated by bars running across the stems.

A waved line before chords indicates that the notes are to be played successively, beginning with the lowest note reached by the waved line, and not together. The Arpeggio begins at the time of the chord, and the tones follow each other very rapidly, and generally somewhat *crescendo* towards the last.

MELODIC EMBELLISHMENTS

TIME NOTATION.

A note indicates a musical utterance. The relative length or duration of several utterances in connection, is represented by the different note-forms which are named whole note, half, quarter, etc. Every note-form has a rest of corresponding value, which indicates a silence of the same length. A dot after a note or rest adds half to its value. A second dot adds half as much as the first, so that two dots increase the value of the note by three quarters.

NOTES AND RESTS.

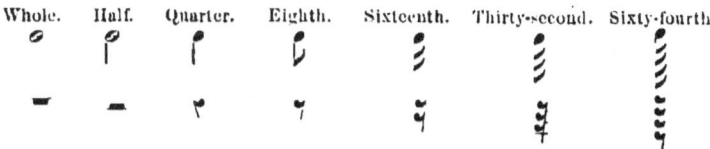

Whole. Half. Quarter. Eighth. Sixteenth. Thirty-second. Sixty-fourth.

EXPLANATION OF MELODIC EMBELLISHMENTS.

Prepared from the best authorities, expressly for this work.

1. THE LONG APPOGGIATURA.

This embellishment consists of a grace note which takes half (*a*), two-thirds (*b*), or ever the whole (*c*), of the time of its principal as shown in the examples following:

a. Long appoggiatura before a note which can be divided into two equal parts.   *b.* Before a note divisible by three, (a dotted note.)   *c.* Before a note to which another is tied.

The long appoggiatura is now usually written out in full in large notes.

2. THE SHORT APPOGGIATURA.

2. The short Appoggiatura is a grace note with a little stroke through its stem. It begins at the time of the principal note, and is played as quickly as possible—(*a, b, c.*)

Written.

a. Moderato.   *b. Presto.*   *c.* Before double notes.

Played.

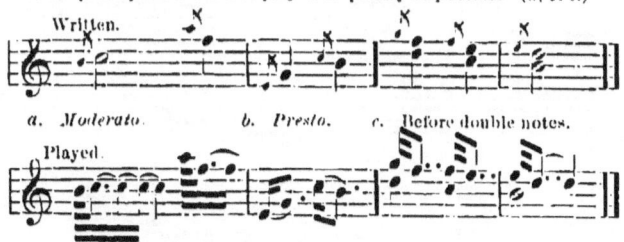

3. AFTER NOTES.

After notes consist of one or more grace notes introduced as passing or changing notes, in passing from one melody note to another. They are generally connected with their principal note by a slur, and never fall on an accent.

MELODIC EMBELLISHMENTS.

4. DOUBLE APPOGGIATURAS.

Double appoggiaturas consist of two grace notes preceeding a melody note. They begin at the proper time of the principal note (and therefore with the corresponding Base note), and are played as quickly as possible, the accent falling on the principal note.

5. THE TURN, OR GRUPETTO.

The turn consists of a principal note and two auxiliary notes, above and below respectively, which may be a whole step or a half step distant from the principal. Generally the upper auxiliary is the next tone above in the same key, and the lower a semitone below the principal. When the upper auxiliary is only a semitone above the principal, as in the case of turns on the 3rd and 7th degree of the scale, the lower auxiliary is played diatonic, and consequently a whole step below the principal, in order to avoid the misleading chromatic effect which would otherwise be produced. On the 5th degree of the minor scale, the lower auxiliary is played chromatic. The turn usually comes at the close of the principal note, as at *a, b* and *c* in the examples, where also is illustrated the use of accidentals in connection with the turn-sign. Sometimes, however, it comes at the beginning of a note, as at *d*, in which case the turn-sign stands directly over it. With dotted notes the turn comes between the note and the dot, as shown at *e* and *f*.

6. THE MORDENT, OR BOUNDING TRILL.

These two embellishments are precisely alike, except that one is made with the note below the principal, and the other with the note above. The first is distinguished by the vertical stroke through the sign, as at *a*, below. The other, also called Mordent by some, and *Pratt trill* or "Bounding Trill" by others, lacks the vertical stroke through the sign, and is made

MELODIC EMBELLISHMENTS.

with the note above. The same embellishment is sometimes written out in small notes as at *c*. According to Dr. Wm. Mason the *Pralltrill* should be accented on the *first* note as at *d*. In all cases the embellishment is to be played as rapidly as possible.

7. THE TRILL.

The trill consists of a rapid vibration or alternation of a principal note and the next above in the same key. A vocal trill should begin somewhat deliberately, but immediately become rapid, as shown at *a* below. It concludes with a turn, which, however, may sometimes be omitted in chain trills. On the pianoforte a long trill accompanied by a melody in the same hand, may omit the auxiliary note at the moment of sounding the melody, in order to facilitate the passage, as shown at *d*. It is of the greatest importance that the notes of the trill should be of equal power. At the start the auxiliary may be accented. Trills should vibrate at a uniform speed, after the motion is once established, and in some definite ratio to the time of the passage.

The trill begins with the principal note, and not with the auxiliary, although the contrary has been taught by eminent masters, and is sometimes required by a grace note as at *b* and *c* below.

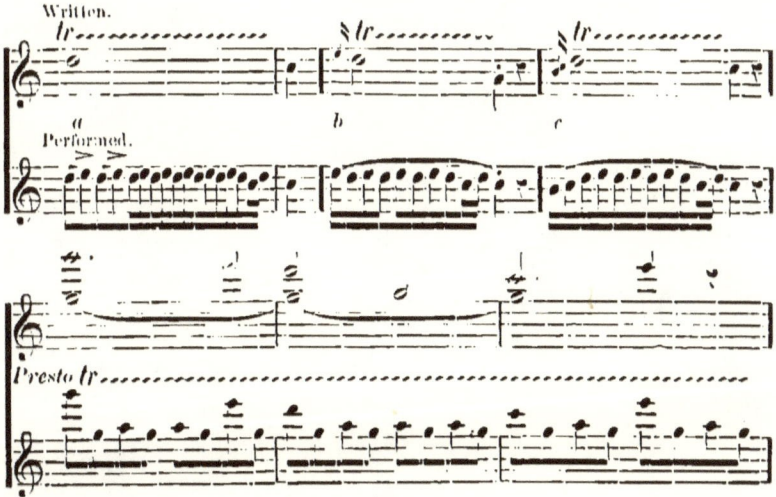

www.ingramcontent.com/pod-product-compliance
Lightning Source LLC
Chambersburg PA
CBHW022052230426
43672CB00008B/1148